The Cultural Industries in Canada

Problems, Policies and Prospects

Edited by Michael Dorland

James Lorimer & Company, Publishers
Toronto, 1996

James Lorimer & Company Ltd. acknowledges with thanks the support of the Canada Council and the Ontario Arts Council in the development of writing and publishing in Canada.

Permission has generously been given to use the following copyrighted material: Figure 3-1 (Newspaper Readership across Age Groups) is reproduced by permission of the Newspaper Marketing Bureau; Table 8-11 (Multiple-System Operators) and Figure 8-2 (Canadian Specialty Services Viewing Statistics) are used by permission of the Canadian Cable Television Association; Table 8-12 (Broadcasting and Cable) is used by permission of *Report on Business Magazine*; Figure 8-2 (Canadian Specialty Services Viewing Statistics), Table 8-6 (Viewing of Canadian Programs on English TV), and Table 8-7 (Viewing Time for Canadian and Foreign Programs) are used by permission of A.C. Nielsen; Figure 8-1 (Stations Tuned Per Week) and Table 8-14 (Net Advertising Volume for Canada) are used by permission of the Television Bureau of Canada.

Canadian Cataloguing in Publication Data

The cultural industries in Canada

Includes index.
ISBN 1-55028-494-0 (pbk.)
ISBN 1-55028-495-9 (bound)

1. Cultural industries — Canada.* 2. Publishers and publishing — Canada. 3. Communication and traffic — Canada. I. Dorland, Michael, 1948–

NX634.C84 1996   070'.0971   C96-950110-2

James Lorimer & Company Ltd., Publishers
35 Britain Street
Toronto, Ontario
M5A 1R7

Printed and bound in Canada

Contents

Tables and Figures

Tables

Figures

Acknowledgements

A number of persons and institutions are to be thanked for making the realization of this project possible. In the order of their appearance, they are: my School of Journalism and Communication colleague Paul Attallah, who first alerted me; Dennis Bockus of Colbourne Communications, Toronto, for his editorial advice and painstaking work on the initial manuscript; Carleton University deans John ApSimon (Faculty of Graduate Studies and Research) and G. Stuart Adam (Faculty of Arts) and Director of the School of Journalism and Communication Peter Johansen for their institutional support; my graduate student Carol Risebrough for her bibliographical assistance and for sharing some of my research obsessions; my undergraduate student Shawn W. Yerxa for sharing with me some of his obsessions; my graduate students in Comm. 27.531 over the past three years for responding with such enthusiasm to the elaboration of some of the ideas that frame this project; the contributors to this volume, each and every one, for not only making time for the project in their busy schedules and commitments, but also for sharing a sense of its importance; Eve Goldin, Research Librarian of the Cinémathèque Ontario, Loren Lerner and Percy Johnson, of Concordia University's Canadian Film and Video Research Project, for their assistance in tracking down obscure sources; Diane Young, Editor in Chief of James Lorimer & Company, for her patience and editorial thoroughness; and my Carleton colleague, best friend and life co-partner, Priscilla L. Walton, who shares it all.

Introduction

Michael Dorland

"You must talk with two tongues, if you do not wish to cause confusion."

— Marshall McLuhan

To understand Canada's cultural industries, it is necessary to grasp that the term refers simultaneously to industries that produce cultural commodities (films, books, TV programs and so on) as well as to a concept deployed in the discussion of specific Canadian policy problems. In other words, the term refers simultaneously to two orders of reality that intersect in paradoxical ways. One way to describe these two realities might be to say that one is economic and the other is cultural. But this only begs further questions, namely: what is the difference between the two? Where does the economy stop and culture begin? Are cultural industries more industrial than cultural, or is it, in fact, the other way around?

The discussion of such questions in the Canadian context has been particularly problematic, in part because of geographical and historical factors. It has been Canada's geographical fate to be located in the northerly half of North America, alongside the United States, whose history, economic and cultural development and rise to global pre-eminence have affected Canada in myriad and complex ways. In turn, much of the history of Canadian institutions has been profoundly preoccupied, often agonistically, with seeking the ways, strategies, symbols and indeed the language by which to demarcate Canadian activities from American ones and provide the space, ranging from the economic to the symbolic, in which such activities might be undertaken, continue and even flourish. As a result, the role played by the Canadian state in making such activities possible, in encouraging them and in framing the very language for their pursuit, has been fundamental, particularly in the sphere of culture.

"Culture," as the British critic Raymond Williams has famously noted, is "one of the two or three most complicated words in the English language" (1983: 87). While Williams does not say what the other equally complicated words might be, surely *economy* ranks as a likely candidate. In the Canadian context, the Odyssean task the state adopted as policy in the late 1920s was to attempt to navigate a Canadian course between the two trickiest words in the English language, the Scylla of culture and the Charybdis of economy, and in the process establish Canadian institutions of cultural production with a reasonable expectation that they would flourish. If it can be argued that the Canadian state in the late 1920s had, at best, the haziest notion of exactly what it was embarking upon, there seemed at the time to be good reasons to act. The 1920s was a period of heightened Canadian nationalism, although soon to be followed by the greatest economic collapse the modern industrialized world had ever experienced. It was also the decade in which new communications technologies — the movies, radio, and mass-produced magazines of an expanding American popular culture — were reaching across the globe, initially through the linguistic channels of the English-speaking world, where Canada offered the closest foreign market. The decade witnessed as well the growing confidence of the social sciences that they could provide a more scientific understanding of cultural phenomena, and, as a result, of culture's amenability to manipulations by state policy. For all these reasons, the Canadian state got involved in the field of cultural production, initially through the modest making of movies for government departments and by the mid-1930s with the creation of the Canadian Broadcasting Corporation in an ambitious, symbolically charged scheme to provide Canadian broadcasting to Canadians.

This is not to suggest that the hesitant advance of the Canadian state into the various fields of cultural production, from documentary film to radio broadcasting, from television news and televised drama to feature-film production — in short, the cultural industries — would turn out to be a big mistake. On the contrary, so began a wide range of interventions spanning most of the modern arts and producing a complex concatenation of state agencies and cultural industries, with significant ramifications for contemporary Canadian life and politics. So began as well the pursuit of economic success in which, from the most unprepossessing of beginnings, the Canadian film and television industry, or so its proponents claim, has grown to over a-billion-dollar-a-year business (Enchin, 1995: B2). Canada today, it is said, ranks second in the world after the United States in the production of film and television programming.

But it is also worth emphasizing that from the beginnings of the Canadian state's involvement in the policy fields of cultural production, there has been an enormous gap between the rhetorical ambitions established by the language of cultural nationalism and the means available for the creation of the cultural institutions that would materially embody the ambitions of Canadians to create their own national culture. In this gap between ambition and means, between the symbolically charged language of the 1930s and the poverty-stricken reality, arose the policy dilemmas to which the idea of the cultural industries in the Canadian context was to emerge as a solution. But understanding this would take some 50 years and require a great deal of experimentation (some successful; some not; all of it wrenching), whose history is sketched in the essays that make up this collection.

In that 50-year period, however, the organizing language of Canadian policy, reflected in a long and steady stream of Royal Commissions, white papers, public and parliamentary inquiries and legislative and regulatory modifications, effected a slow and difficult transition from the discourses of culture to the discourses of economy. And in that transition, Canada's cultural industries, in private broadcasting, in radio, film and television production, in magazine and book publishing, in recorded music production, in cable and satellite distribution did see the dawn of economic day. In some cases, such as private broadcasting, an industry emerged with considerable profitability; in others, such as book publishing or film production at certain times, attaining profitability would prove to be a far more precarious and longer-term endeavour. But in every case, state policy, whether in modifying the income tax act or postal rates, in establishing pools of public capital to subsidize film or television production, or in modifying the missions of public institutions to support rather than obstruct the growth of Canadian private production, proved decisive for the future direction of each cultural industry. The essays that comprise this collection trace out what the effect of state policy has been, evaluate its often ambiguous legacy, and examine the implications for the future in an increasingly competitive global environment, in which the once disparate components of the information economy are converging under the control of fewer, but larger, multimedia behemoths.

From the 1930s to the present, two distinct environments shaped the development of Canada's cultural industries. The first, and in certain respects perhaps the most complicated, is what could be termed *the symbolic environment*. The symbolic environment embodies the range of publicly owned crown corporations and agencies (e.g., the CBC, the National Film Board, the Canada Council, the Canadian Radio-Television and Telecommunications Commission, Telefilm Canada, and so on), the statutory legislation that defines their mandates (e.g., the Broadcasting Act), the parliamentary committees and ministries responsible for overseeing them, as well as the paper trail that has issued from these bodies over the years (e.g., CRTC public notices and decisions). These, along with the Royal Commissions since Aird (1928), have created and defined the symbolic and linguistic framework within which the economic development of Canada's cultural industries has taken place. Put simply, it has defined the rules, terms, conditions or turns of language by which players are authorized to enter and play the cultural industries "game" in the Canadian context. This crucial symbolic environment has been more often than not taken for granted, rather than carefully examined, to the detriment of academic and policy analysis. The present collection aims to rectify this absence and document in its stead the more complex reality of Canada's cultural industries.

The second environment could be termed *the industry environment*: understanding the economic circumstances that prevail in a particular cultural industry. One of the central problems that has historically dogged Canadian policy formation has been the sheer difficulty of developing accurate, reliable data with respect to each cultural industry. The reasons for this are numerous and complex, and broadly have to do with the confidentiality of income-tax returns, Statistics Canada's tendency to deal in sectoral aggregates, and the reluctance of economic actors to reveal publicly data essential to their own competitive survival. The upshot, however, has been approximative economic data, blurry industry portraits and contradictory policies. And this is, of course, compounded by changes in the symbolic environment (such as the belief in the determining effect of technological change or of new international trade rules as represented by the Canada-US Free Trade Agreement, NAFTA and the like). By drawing upon the most recent data available at the time of writing, the present collection offers an up-to-date snapshot of the contemporary situation of Canada's cultural industries.

More than has been the case with previous Canadian analyses, the essays that follow pay particular attention to these two dimensions of reality that Canada's cultural industries face — on the one hand, their insertion within the specificities of the Canadian policy environment and, on the other, their differential status as economic objects. As the essays that follow demonstrate, the English-Canadian cultural industries are distinguished by specific characteristics. Canada's cultural industries are enmeshed in a system of cultural production characterized by the not-always-conscious consistency of its fundamental goals, the longevity of its players, and the relative unanimity of their aims: deriving profit from the production and selling of made-in-Canada cultural goods and services.

Briefly stated, then, the central argument of this collection is that the way one approaches the cultural industries and the policies affecting them, as well as the language that one uses, is as important as the reality one imagines one is talking about, or making policy for. The Canadian discussion has historically been inflected in certain defining ways, which have been primarily defensive and introspective, with a restricted number of players huddling beneath the protection provided by the national state and calling this "culture." It is perhaps time that some alternative perspectives were allowed into what has been a confined and narrowly conceived symbolic arena. Paradoxically, it is precisely within this arena that Canada's cultural industries have learned to survive and expand; but that very paradox demands to be better understood. The Canadian experience, once considered a model of the negative consequences of cultural dependency that other nations had to avoid at their peril, has since become an example to other countries also faced with reconciling aspects of their cultural development with the rigours of an open economy. If the studies of Canada's cultural industries that follow help shed some light on what has been a far greater success story than it has been given credit for, then this book will have surely served its purpose.

References

Enchin, Harvey. 1995. "Film Industry Sweeter Than Maple Syrup." *The Globe and Mail*, August 18, B2.

McLuhan, Marshall. 1970. *From Cliché to Archetype*. New York: Pocket Books.

Williams, Raymond. 1983. *Keywords: A Vocabulary of Culture and Society*. London: Flamingo.

Part One

Print Industries

Book Publishing

Rowland Lorimer [1]

Background

In the late 1960s, as part of a general movement towards cultural self-assertion, Canada saw the establishment of many new book publishers. It also saw the establishment of policies directed at cultural industries in the book, magazine and film sectors. Ontario, the federal government and Quebec were quick to bring forward policies. Other provinces joined one by one, usually by extending cultural assistance programs provided to artists and writers. In the late 1980s and early 1990s, joint federal-provincial small business development programs were extended to the cultural industries.

Today, Canada has a vibrant but threatened book publishing industry that generates yearly sales of over $1.5 billion in publishers' receipts and $3 billion in retail sales. The industry is heterogeneous in size, location and genre orientation. It encourages new authors, in a range of genres, and responds to a wide range of political, cultural and social orientations, contributes to Canada's international presence and plays a key role in articulating Canadian ideas and realities.

The cultural achievement of the industry has been spectacular. Canadian creative genius and sensibility and Canadian commentary and analysis are recognized worldwide — just the opposite of 30 years ago. However, book publishing, particularly trade-book publishing, labours under marginal profitability and, as a result, the constant threat of collapse or inundation by imports.

Market Analysis

Books are produced for the Canadian market by Canadian-owned publishers and by foreign-owned publishers based in Canada and abroad. Canadian-based companies, both Canadian and foreign-

controlled, originate titles, often called own-titles. Origination requires publishers to cover all the development costs and risks: they
must become partners in the conceptualization of the project, gauge
the market, evaluate the ability of authors to produce marketable
manuscripts, assess and improve manuscripts when delivered, provide authors with advances against royalties when necessary, as well
as put forward all funds for production, marketing and distribution,
including editing, design and layout, printing, publicity, shipping and
so forth. Own-titles also include titles for which the publisher purchases the right to publish the title in the Canadian market. The
publisher may re-edit the manuscript and assess the market much as
described above. However, such a re-origination is considerably less
involving and, with marketing spillover from the U.S., considerably
less risky than origination itself.

The Canadian book market also contains books produced by foreign-based companies. Such books enter the Canadian market in
several ways. They may be purchased by the consumer directly and
brought into the country, bypassing Canadian publishers entirely.
They may be purchased by retailers and libraries from foreign or
Canadian-based wholesalers. They may be purchased through foreign-
based book clubs and mailed to the consumer. No current statistics
are available on the extent of these three activities. However, in 1985,
Statistics Canada estimated that value at $596 million, greater than
one-third of the overall market at the time. In subsequent reports, it
later acknowledged this figure to be an overestimate because it included such materials as catalogues.[2]

The more common way for foreign books to enter the market is
for Canadian-based companies to act as sole distributing agents for
titles. Acting as an agent for a title, the publisher's job is basically
importing and distributing. Usually operating under a general contract to sell the originating publisher's books in Canada, the publisher
purchases books, rather than the right to republish them, at deep
discounts (in the order of 60 per cent to 75 per cent), imports the
books, and makes some effort to represent or sell the book, through
promotion, publicity and distribution, to retailers, usually bookstores,
but also book clubs and other people who deal in books, or to
libraries.

Another dimension is important in understanding the Canadian
book market. It is language. The Canadian market is composed of
two distinct linguistic markets, English and French, both of which
are served by Canadian-owned and foreign-owned but Canadian-

based companies. With three significant exceptions — International Thomson, Torstar and, more recently, the Bronfmans — Canadian-controlled firms tend to be small trade or scholarly-oriented firms. (Larger firms do exist such as General-Stoddart, McClelland and Stewart and Douglas and McIntyre.) There are a smattering of Canadian-controlled firms in the educational market as well. The foreign-controlled firms are large, based in Ontario or Quebec, and are active throughout the entire range of publishing: trade, mass-market, educational, scholarly, reference and professional.

Production Statistics

Book production statistics are collected by Statistics Canada, a federal agency that surveys firms with annual sales exceeding $50,000. These collected data appear to take in 95 per cent of domestic sales but only about 50 per cent of titles. The remaining five per cent of sales are accounted for by the other 50 per cent of titles, a category that includes many government documents, self-published books and books published and given away by associations and other groups.[3] The reported statistics are consistently two years behind, are "more or less" accurate, report only some important market categories and are, year by year, deteriorating in comprehensiveness.

There are nine main variables to consider when attempting to understand book production statistics. They are:

1. number of titles published
2. sales (cited in terms of revenues to publishers or net sales)
3. sales in Canada and exports (or domestic and foreign sales)
4. language of publisher (which, most often, translates into the language of the book), English or French
5. market segment (i.e., trade books, mass-market paperbacks [sometimes included as part of trade], textbooks, professional and technical, scholarly)
6. ownership and control (foreign or Canadian)
7. own-titles and agency titles
8. new titles, reprints and titles in print
9. Canadian authorship of titles.

Title and sales data should be considered together. As Figure 1-1 indicates, title production has risen unevenly but steadily over the past 12 years. Over the past six years the total percentage increase in title production has been 32 per cent. As Figure 1-2 indicates, net

Figure 1-1
Total Titles Published, 1981–92

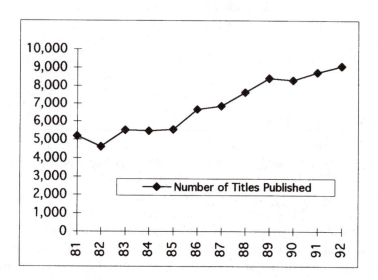

Source: Canada. Statistics Canada. 1989. Catalogue 87-001.

annual sales of book publishers and agents have reached $1.56 billion or about $3 billion in retail sales. In comparison with the six-year 32-per-cent increase in number of titles, there has been a 26 per cent increase in sales. However, after taking into account changes in the price of books, the increase in sales drops to approximately two per cent. Effectively, per-title sales have decreased over the past six years by 24 per cent, the same, as it happens, for own-title sales and agency-title sales. This is straining publishers and it is difficult to know how the industry is coping. It may be that profitable sectors have lower profits. It may be that there have been efficiency gains. It may also be that salaries have been stagnant. There are indications that each of these is playing a role, but the indications are not that firm.

Understanding exactly what is going on in the industry is difficult. Much commentary has been produced on Canada's book publishing industry, most of it devoted to the relatively small market share of domestic producers, i.e., those that are Canadian-owned and control-led; the importance of domestic ownership because Canadian-owned companies produce nearly 90 per cent of Canadian-authored books;

Figure 1-2
Total Net Sales ($000), 1981–92

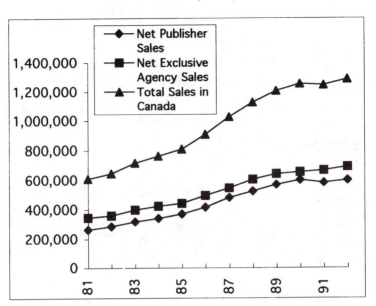

Source: Canada. Statistics Canada. 1989. Catalogue 87-001.

and the marginal profitability of Canadian book publishing. Often these discussions fail to distinguish between the trade-book market and other sectors. That is, arguments, and sometimes data, are used that combine all market segments, trade books, mass-market paperbacks, scholarly monographs, textbooks and professional and technical books. These market segments must be differentiated because, if the focus of the discussion is on culture, then the segment that should be examined is trade books and perhaps, and in a more limited fashion, mass-market paperbacks and textbooks. If the focus is on industrial development, then the data should be broader. The two linguistic markets also need to be separated because they have significantly different characteristics.

Figure 1-3 presents six years of title data (to 1992) in both languages, dividing it into two segments: trade books (not including mass-market paperbacks) and textbooks. It also shows Canadian authorship of all titles. The similarities in the total, trade book and Canadian-authored curves (the latter two are not additive) and the

Figure 1-3
Number of Titles, Trade Titles, Textbook Titles and
Canadian-Authored Trade Titles Published, 1987–92

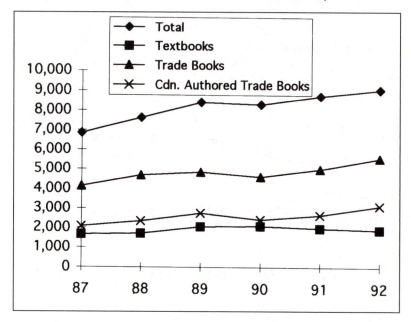

Source: Canada. Statistics Canada. 1993. Catalogue 87-210.

relatively flat output of textbooks, especially after 1989, mean that a substantial amount of the increase in overall industry title output is in the trade sector. In fact, the exact figures show that the trade-book title increase exceeded the overall title increase in percentage terms: 35 per cent (4125–5557 titles) as against 32 per cent (6847–9056 titles).[4] Canadian-authored trade titles published rose 52 per cent (2054–3120 titles), an indication of an increased concentration by publishers on Canadian authors, an increase that, if true, might be attributed to the apparent fact that Canadian authors, on average, sell 3.5 times more copies than do foreign authors for Canadian-controlled publishers and 8 times more copies for foreign-controlled firms (Lorimer, 1995).

Figure 1-4 presents trade-book sales data for the same six-year period, differentiating between own and agency titles. There are three points to notice. First is the high correspondence in the increases of agency-title sales and total trade-book sales. Second, this correspondence, in combination with the flat sales of own-titles, means that

Figure 1-4
Domestic Trade Book Sales ($000), 1987–92

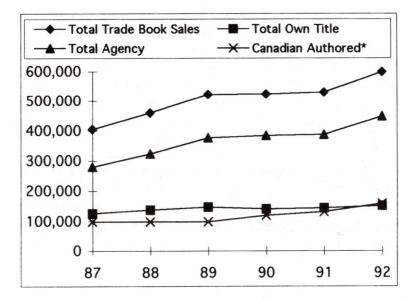

Source: Canada. Statistics Canada. 1993. Catalogue 87-210.

virtually all of the growth in trade-book sales is accounted for by
agency titles. To be precise, over six years the increase in overall
trade-book sales was 48 per cent ($404–$598 million), for own-titles
it was 20 per cent ($125–$150 million), for agency titles it was 60
per cent ($279–$448 million). When combined with the overall decline in per-title sales, these data suggest that the market is filling up
with low-selling books imported by both Canadian-owned and Canadian-based publishers. These imported books are certainly drag-
ging down average sales and may, through competition, be lowering
sales of publishers' own-titles. On the other hand, and this is the third
point, Canadian-authored books in all categories, including domestic
sales and exports increased by 62 per cent over the same six years
($97–158 million). This increase seems to reflect a relatively greater
resilience of such books in the trade market, increased exports by
Canadian-controlled companies, as well as increased use of Canadian
authors — or reporting of Canadian authorship — in other sectors
such as reference and textbooks.

This third point, the 62 per cent growth in sales of Canadian-authored titles, calculated on the basis of combined domestic and export sales (because Statistics Canada combines these components in its public reporting), is a highly significant finding from a cultural perspective. Basically, it means that Canadian book publishing is making a strong contribution to our ability to articulate our own priorities, realities, images and symbols. It is providing an effective vehicle for Canadian authors to reach the public. In fact, sales of Canadian-authored books are increasing slightly faster than the market as a whole. This is good news. However, these gains do not appear to be borne out in a 1991 reading study recently reanalyzed at the Canadian Centre for Studies in Publishing by Nancy Duxbury (1995). That study suggests Canadian authors have a market share of leisure reading of about 18 per cent, less than their share in 1978, when the last reading study was conducted (James Lorimer, 1983).

A comparison of trade-title production and sales to overall title production and sales shows that while trade-title production has increased from 60 per cent to 61 per cent of the overall book market, sales of trade titles have increased from 39 per cent in 1987 to 46 per cent in 1992. This percentage gain means that per-title sales of trade titles are decreasing less quickly than all titles combined. This may mean that the gap between high-selling segments such as mass-market paperbacks and educational and trade titles is decreasing and/or that sales of low-selling genres, i.e., reference and scholarly, are decreasing more rapidly than that of trade titles. Certainly, there are clear indications that reference and scholarly publishing sales-per-title are down.

Over the six years between 1987 and 1992, in both the title and sales data, foreign-controlled firms show a relative decline in market share: good news for the Canadian-owned sector and for government support policies aimed at this sector. A closer look at the data shows that while gains were made by the Canadian sector in own-titles, greater gains were made in agency titles than in own-titles. In other words, there is a change in who is importing. Across all categories of own-title books between 1987 and 1991, Canadian-controlled firms gained a two-per-cent share of the domestic market; agency titles gained a 10-per-cent share. In trade books, the respective gains were nine per cent for own and 13 per cent for agency titles. These gains by domestic producers are significant in terms both of dollars (about $10 million) and policy. However, from a cultural standpoint, agency titles contribute to increased competition for Canadian-

Figure 1-5
Book Export Sales ($000)

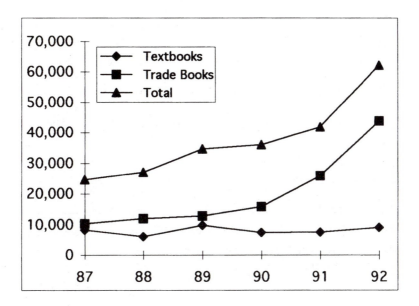

Source: Canada. Statistics Canada. 1993. Catalogue 87-210.

authored books in the marketplace, the majority of the Canadian-controlled sector's own-titles.

International trade is also of growing importance to the book industry. Exports take three forms: sales of books, sales of rights (the right to publish a title elsewhere or in a different format) and sales of services (e.g., providing publishing expertise). Statistics Canada reports exports in two categories, sales of books and "other exports." In 1992, total exports were $274.2 million. They accounted for 20 per cent of total sales for the year, far higher than their traditional level of about 10 per cent. (The U.S. exports less than 10 per cent of its books, while the U.K. exports around 30 per cent.) Compared to former years, they were up dramatically, by five per cent. In 1992, book exports themselves and trade-book exports grew by 49 per cent and 69 per cent respectively over 1991. Figure 1-5 presents these data. Both publishers and governments have invested heavily in gaining these sales. The Association for the Export of Canadian Books is the key agency here.

Table 1-1
Book Publishing General Statistics 1992–93

Size of Industry	$1,561	million
Sales in Canada of all titles	$1,286	million
Domestic sales of own-titles	$598	million
Domestic sales of own-titles by Canadian-owned firms	$374	million
Domestic sales of own and agency titles by Canadian-owned firms	$685	million
Export sales by Canadian-owned firms	$268	million
Titles published	9,056	
Canadian-authored titles published	6,466	
Canadian-authored English-language titles published	3,911	
Sales of Canadian-authored books by Canadian-owned publishers (in Canada)	$331	million
Exports	$62	million
Own-title sales	47%	of sales
Agency title sales	53%	of sales

Source: Canada. Statistics Canada. 1994. Catalogue 87-210.

Industry Structure

The preceding section has sketched some of the trends in the marketplace over a six- and a 12-year period. Data for the most recent
year (1992–93) fill out the picture of the industry.

Eighty-two per cent of the Canadian market is an English-
language market while the remaining 18 per cent is French-language.
That 82-per-cent market share can be represented as a 73-per-cent
share of all Canadian and export sales of own-titles (French-language
27 per cent) and a 92-per-cent share of agency-title sales (French-
language eight per cent). As can be seen, in agency and own-titles
the two markets have quite a different structure, with much less
agency publishing and much more own-title publishing in the
French-language market. In the English-language market, agency
sales of imported books exceed own-title sales (57 per cent as op-

Table 1-2
English-Language Firms: Profitability, Size and Grants

	% profitable	% receiving grants	Average grant as % of revenue
Small $50K-$200K	45	52	22
Medium $200K-$1M	67	75	23
Large $1M-$5M	73	67	7
Very Large* $5M-	53	26**	Not available

* Includes both French and English
** About 52% of very large companies are Canadian controlled
Source: Canada. Statistics Canada. Catalogue 87-210.

posed to 43 per cent). For textbooks Canadian-controlled publishers sell 51 per cent own-titles and 49 per cent agency titles. Within the English-language market, Statistics Canada reports that Canadian-authored titles hover around 70 per cent of all new own-titles, re-printed titles and in-print titles. (No comparable sales figure on Canadian-authored titles is available.) This 70 per cent is a healthy percentage, but it is made questionable because of the criteria used by publishers to report to Statistics Canada. To explain: in 1991 Statistics Canada reported that over 90 per cent of educational titles were Canadian authored (Statistics Canada, 87-210, 1993). They did not report on this variable for 1992. While 90 per cent is no doubt accurate — Canadian authors may indeed have participated in 90 per cent of new educational titles — it is doubtful that Canadian authors received anything near 10 per cent royalties (standard in the indus-try), for the resulting sales. In short, the 70 per cent figure probably overestimates the degree of participation of Canadian authors. It certainly is true that Canadian authors do not receive anywhere near 70 per cent of all royalties.

Canadian-controlled companies also have a 51 per cent market share of agency activity. Domestic trade-book sales account for 88 per cent of all trade-book sales. For books written by Canadian authors, 90 per cent of sales take place within Canada.

The financial position of English-language publishing companies after grants (both Canadian and foreign-controlled) is presented in Table 1-2.

As Table 1-2 indicates, there are a considerable number of unprofitable companies in all categories. Second, grants are a significant percentage of revenue for small and medium-sized companies. Third, in interpreting these figures, it must be borne in mind that profitability is merely an accounting device; to be a useful measure it must be considered along with the content of the balance sheet, volume of cash flow and salary expenditures.

In overview, English-language publishing is dominant by far over French-language publishing in Canada. It originates a significant number of titles, as well as importing and distributing a substantial number, especially in trade publishing. Generally, title production is increasing significantly more than sales, leading to lower per-title sales. In own-title production, the industry specializes in Canadian-authored titles, with limited activity in the purchase of rights and in the publication for the Canadian market of foreign authors. Such books tend to be imported and distributed as agency titles. It is also often the case that U.S. publishers are not interested in splitting off Canadian rights, either for titles they originate or for titles they may acquire the rights to publish. For these reasons also, Canadian publishers are not active rights traders. Finally, the industry is, overall, marginally profitable but only after grants.

Canadian-Controlled Publishing in French and English

In a counterproductive move, Statistics Canada decided, beginning in 1994, not to provide direct reporting for English-language, Canadian-controlled firms. The agency has also decided to present title data on some measures, and sales data on others, making useful comparisons impossible.

Based on publicly available data for 1992, the following summary statements about the industry and about Canadian-controlled firms, in contrast to foreign-controlled firms, can be made.

Canadian-controlled firms (both French and English-language) account for the following percentages of book sales:[5]

- 63 per cent market share of own-title sales ($374 million, T2) (This represents 29 per cent of the overall domestic market. Foreign-controlled firms have 17 per cent of the overall domestic market through sales of their own titles.)

- 61 per cent market share of all sales including exports ($953 million, T2)

- 53 per cent market share of sales in Canada ($685 million, T2)

- 85 per cent market share of own-title trade sales ($103 million, T9)

- 87 per cent market share of own-title trade and mass market paperback sales ($131 million, T9), and 51 per cent market share of agency-title trade sales ($133 million, T9).

Canadian-controlled firms account for the following in Canadian-authored sales:
- 96 per cent of domestic trade-book sales ($95 million, T13)

- 97 per cent of trade-book export sales ($49 million, T13)

- 91 per cent of all book export sales ($62 million, T2)

- 98 per cent of foreign sales ($268 million, T13).

Canadian-controlled firms also account for (in title production):
- 85 per cent of own-titles published (7724, T4)

- 88 per cent of own trade titles published (includes mass-market paperbacks) (4892, T4).

When all book publishing activity is aggregated, the data show the dominance (85 per cent) of Canadian-controlled publishers in title production, Canadian-authored trade-book title production and sales (96 per cent), and number of firms (299). They also show a diminished dominance (61 per cent) in overall sales and even less in domestic sales (53 per cent). If sales and title data are compared for trade books only (including mass-market paperbacks because Statistics Canada makes it impossible to exclude mass-market paperbacks even though they have the data) Canadian-controlled producers have an 87-per-cent market share and produce 88 per cent of titles, suggesting that they are only slightly underselling their competitors on a title-by-title basis in trade titles.[6] Together these figures mean that not only are Canadian-controlled publishers clearly dominant in the trade-book market, but also they are almost equally dominant in sales and title production. Moreover, they almost monopolize export sales in trade books (97 per cent) and in all segments combined (91 per cent), a result that questions the common wisdom that foreign-controlled publishers assist authors in gaining international recognition. A reasonable conclusion is that Canadian-controlled companies are effective publishers and marketers. Moreover, their major and increasingly predominant activity is in Canadian-authored titles, those titles which may have cultural significance. Canadian-authored trade and mass-market paperback own-titles published by both Canadian-controlled and foreign-controlled publishers (this aggregation is the finest Statistics Canada data allow) account for 88 per cent of domestic own-title trade-book and mass-market paperback sales, 97 per cent of export sales, and 91 per cent of combined domestic and export sales. Foreign-authored own-titles are a relatively insignificant category.

These figures confirm the perception that the focus of both the Canadian and foreign-controlled sectors of the industry is works written by Canadians. Moreover, Canadian-controlled firms are active exporters, gaining an extremely impressive 34 per cent of their sales in international markets: foreign-controlled firms achieve only 10 per cent in export sales.

Canadian-controlled companies have sometimes been portrayed as less efficient than foreign-controlled companies. The data show that Canadian-controlled companies publish almost three times as many new titles and reprints per employee as foreign-controlled firms. In addition, sales receipts per employee are 90 per cent of their foreign-controlled competitors. After taking into account differences in genre, there seems to be no evidence of less efficiency in the Canadian-controlled sector.

The Canadian-controlled industry has gone to significant lengths in trying to avoid industry concentration in market share and location. In general, there is a commitment to the notion that the industry can contribute the most to society, in the generation of ideas, information and development of authors, when numerous firms across the country are all seeking titles and authors. Heterogeneity of location is indicated by the spread of firms across the country depicted in Figure 1-6. Data are not provided by Statistics Canada for sales or title production by location. However, personnel expenditures across provinces show much the same pattern as that presented on firm location in Figure 1-6.

Figure 1-6
Location of Publishers by Province

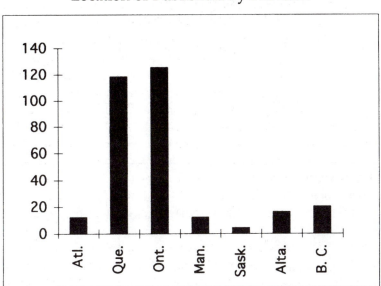

Source: Canada. Statistics Canada. 1993. Catalogue 87-210.

What Figure 1-6 does not reflect is the many small firms that do not report to Statistics Canada. There are about 80 book publishers in British Columbia (not 20 as Statistics Canada reports) and 14 in Saskatchewan (not 4) (Lorimer, 1989, 1993a). Table 1-3 adds to the picture of heterogeneity, reporting on firm size, titles published, grants received, and sales achieved.

Not to overestimate the situation, other data point to a limited heterogeneity. The Canadian English-language book publishing industry as a whole can be said to be dominated by about 50 Ontario-based firms, each with over $5 million in annual revenues, half of which have foreign owners. As Figure 1-6 indicates, in 1992, 125 Ontario firms accounted for 85 per cent of titles in Canada, excluding Quebec.

In spite of the concentration of ownership and activity indicated above, a policy of heterogeneity encourages a great deal of activity across the country, much of it invisible in Statistics Canada data, although the 27-per-cent title share (and five per cent of sales) for non-Ontario English-language firms hints at the nature and extent of this activity. The vibrancy of the Canadian writing community and

Table 1-3
Canadian-Controlled Publishers, Their Title,
Grant and Market Shares

Firm Size	Relative Number of Firms	Relative Title Share *	Grant Share**	Relative Market Share*
Small	28%	6%	6%	.007%
Medium	42%	21%	34%	5%
Large	13%	28%	36%	16%
Very Large	9%	45%	23%	78%

* Includes agents

** Does not include agents

Source: Canada. Statistics Canada. 1994. Catalogue 87-210.

its clear pan-Canadian focus is also a testimony to a policy of het-erogeneity. As a cultural policy, the encouragement of heterogeneity in the industry is a powerful device.

While profitability can equally mean social or cultural benefit, increasingly it is used to mean economic benefit. Like all cultural industries, the contribution of book publishing is important for what economists call its externalities (the benefit society or the individual gains over and above a direct benefit of consumption; e.g., through increased understanding). This kind of profitability is difficult to measure, however powerful it might be in the shaping of society. Financial profitability is easier to calculate and is important not only as a statistical measure, but also because it controls both the survival of firms and the nature and growth of the industry. Without financial profits, small firms cannot grow into large firms.

The Canadian-controlled sector accounts for $685 million in do-mestic sales, plus exports at $268 million. Government grants ac-count for $36 million or four per cent of overall income. This investment buys 6,002 full-time jobs and $220 million in salaries, with $28 million more going to part-timers (perhaps 650 full-time equivalent jobs at the industry average of $36,000 per year), and $69 million in author royalties. This represents a cost per job for granting sources of $5,414. For the federal government, after taking into account royalties at $36,000 per job, it is a cost per job of $2,584.[7]

Thus, independent of its cultural contribution, the sector can be seen to be a cost-effective job-creation program.[8]

Canada Council Data

The Canada Council provides grants for culturally significant books (and publishing programs), books that Canada Council juries think make a culturally significant contribution to Canadian writing. Support is available to offset net publication costs or deficits (Canada Council, 1994a). The eligible genres are children's books, drama, fiction, nonfiction, poetry and short stories. Gordon Platt, following work by Carol Martin, has prepared data on seven different variables based on data from clients of the Block Grant program. What we report here are highlights of Platt's analysis (Canada Council, 1994b).

The output of culturally significant titles, led by children's books, has grown between 1985 and 1993 by 55 per cent (1089–1688), while average number of copies sold in the first two years has apparently increased 37 per cent between 1985 and 1991. (These data run counter to Statistics Canada data and are questionable, not only because they show a countertrend to the overall aggregate as calculated by that agency, but also because informal industry information points to per-title sales decreases.) Average print runs for English-language paperbacks have increased substantially in children's books and fiction, nearly doubling, while they have remained steady for poetry and drama and declined in nonfiction. Average numbers of copies sold as a percentage of print run (within the first two years) have apparently remained steady at about 60 per cent. Average list prices increased slowly and steadily over the 1985–93 period (just slightly more than the Consumer Price Index) in every genre except children's books, where the increase was a very small $.43. French-language books are consistently higher-priced, 23 per cent higher than their English-language equivalents. Production costs as a percentage of price show a fairly slow but steady decline over the period from 37 per cent to 33 per cent. Only very small companies (less than $100,000 in sales per annum) showed a countertrend. Average per-title deficits also increased over the same period, 1985–1993, by 29 per cent. In spite of their higher sales, large companies stood out as having significantly higher deficits. (This may reflect accounting procedures more than it does material realities.)

What do these Canada Council data tell us? First, culturally significant titles usually show a deficit after two years. Second, the market for such titles is apparently expanding. Third, while prices are increasing at a rate slightly above inflation, production costs are diminishing as a percentage of price, leaving room for increased marketing, other spending or contributions to the bottom line. Diminishing production costs are apparently not resulting in lower per-title deficits.

Policy Structure

The history of book publishing policy in Canada dates back to before Confederation, to various iterations of British copyright law (e.g., the Imperial Copyright Act of 1842). Consistent with other British imperial legislation, this act favoured the development of British enterprise. It did so by protecting books published in London and Edinburgh. Canadian books were afforded no copyright protection at all. With the Americans pirating British copyrighted materials and shipping them into Canada, Canadian publishers and booksellers were doubly vulnerable. (See Parker [1985]; Gundy [1972]; and Lorimer and Duxbury [1992], for discussions of this early history.)

Canadian publishing thus began on an insecure footing, squeezed by two imperia. Canada passed its own law, the 1921 Copyright Act, which was proclaimed in 1924, and this act remained in force, with a number of minor revisions, until 1988. In the 1960s, book publishing policy began to develop beyond copyright law.

In the 1950s the Americans were putting the final touches on their takeover of English-Canadian publishing from the British. The Americans had seized on progressive education and were redesigning education and re-educating educators, American and Canadian alike. They also were being welcomed into Canada, not only into school and university classrooms, but also into bookstores, the minds of Canadians and the discourses of the country. Canadians woke up to the U.S. takeover of Canadian publishing with the sale of a venerable Canadian educational publisher, W. J. Gage and the similarly venerable, United Church-owned, trade-oriented Ryerson Press to Scott, Foresman, and McGraw-Hill, respectively. There was also a major incursion into the Quebec market by the French publishing giant, Hachette. As the leading edge of the baby boom came of age, Canadians woke up in an atmosphere of lies, deceit, extreme aggression in American policy towards Vietnam and the threatened sale of McClelland and Stewart, the single most important publisher of Canadian-authored literature.

This crisis atmosphere was the foundation of modern policy. It generated both investigations and interventions: in 1970 by the federal Department of Industry, Trade and Commerce; in 1971 by an Ontario royal commission; in 1972 by a Quebec law targeted at public agency purchases through accredited bookstores; and again in 1972 by the series of federal government initiatives that included:

> increased financial assistance to publishers in the form of block grants and translation grants through the Canada Council; a Book Purchase Program; export marketing assistance; and a co-publishing policy. This framework of support was expanded upon in 1975 with the announcement of the Promotion and Distribution Program of the Canada Council ... In 1977 Council programs were further enriched by the so-called "national unity" money, which provided new resources for the Book Purchase Program, translation assistance, a National Book Week and a special fund for children's literature (Department of Communications [DOC] News Release, June 18, 1986: 3).

These programs were cultural in their orientation and they followed the lead of industry, assisting publishers to follow their own direction in bringing cultural titles forward for Canadians to read. The industry labeled the assistance welfare-style grants because the grants served to keep the publishers in business from year to year but did nothing to make Canadian publishers more competitive against foreign firms.

In 1979, the Canadian Book Publishing Development Program (CBPDP) attempted to move beyond this type of grant with assistance targeted at the financial and economic base of the Canadian-controlled sector. While the bottom line was still cultural, the vehicle for addressing industry needs was to be industrial development assistance on top of assistance for cultural titles based on sales level and supported by the Canada Council. Actual fund disbursement, driven by a recession, caused a capital crisis and a hasty set of size and location-sensitive amendments to head off industry concentration through mergers and acquisitions undertaken by market-driven Canadian companies such as the repatriated Gage (DOC 1986 News Release: 4).

The 1974 Foreign Investment Review Act made possible a number of arrangements of net benefit to the growth of the Canadian-controlled sector. Included here was the distribution agreement reached by General Publishing with Simon & Schuster to distribute

Simon & Schuster books in Canada. This foreign investment control initiative spawned the ill-fated, observed-in-the-breach Baie Comeau Agreement, which existed within the Investment Canada Act, an act designed not to protect Canadian enterprise but to encourage foreign investment. Baie Comeau required foreign companies to divest themselves of Canadian-based book publishing companies should they purchase them as part of a larger corporate acquisition. (It also disallowed direct purchase of Canadian-based book publishers by foreign investors.) The intent was to patriate foreign-owned subsidiaries when their corporate parents changed ownership. This happened rarely and when it did, although 51-per-cent ownership rested with Canadians, control rested with the much bigger, much richer and much more powerful foreign owners. This was especially true when part of the ownership agreement included the right of either party to buy the other out at the highest price, as it did with Anna Porter and Bertelsmann in their joint venture with Seal Books (see Macskimming [1992]).

The lack of success of the 1979 CBPDP program, together with an emerging "cultural industries" development perspective, led Marcel Massé, the minister of communications at the time, to bring forward in 1986 a new program, the Book Publishing Industry Development Plan (BPIDP). As the government described the program, the approach was to focus on market mechanisms, industrial incentives (balanced with, but clearly separated from, increased cultural support) and the opening up of provincial textbook markets (DOC 1986 News Release: 14). In July 1990, Marcel Massé announced a complementary initiative, the Cultural Industries Development Fund, to provide greater access to capital for all cultural industries, including publishers. Moves were also made to discourage "buying around."

In 1993, with the renewal of the BPIDP program, control by government officials over grants to industry was strengthened with the establishment of four financial criteria, three of which had to be met by the applying publishers. They were: Minimum eligible sales that increased over the years of the program; sales-to-inventory ratios above a minimum level, established for each genre; sales of own-titles per employee above a minimum level, established for each genre; and minimum debt-to-equity ratios. In addition, export marketing assistance was made available and the postal subsidy program that allowed the industry to use the discounted "book rate" was replaced with quite generous subsidies for distribution and marketing costs, through the Publications Distribution Assistance Program (PDAP) (DOC, 1993).

What the 1986 program amounted to, and the 1993 changes confirmed, was a major departure. It appears that government officials felt they had enough information and could assemble sufficient expertise to forcemarch at least a certain sector of the industry to independence from grants. This amounted to policy leading industry, rather than industry goals and objectives leading policy. Moreover, the policy appeared to take little heed of the organizational requirements and scale of production necessary for such sectors as school textbook and mass-market paperback publishing. The industry did not strenuously object. There appear to be four reasons. The first is that the overall increase in funding appeared to be more than enough for everyone, especially when phrases such as "cultural and industrial balance" were used. Second, the program could be viewed as a response to industry entreaties for structural assistance. Third, the policies were developed in consultation with industry representatives. Fourth, the industry felt that it had little bargaining power with the Mulroney Tories. These middle two reasons would also be cited by government officials as justifications for their actions.

The industry, by contrast, seems to believe that if only sufficient support were provided to create a truly level playing field between domestic and foreign producers, then the Canadian publishing industry could become by far the dominant producer in all sectors and segments of the domestic market. Moreover, industry members seem to think this could be done by an expansion of all active firms across the board. They seem to see little need to restructure the industry, say through mergers and acquisitions of small firms to create a few large firms, or through aggressive expansion into new markets made possible by technological change. Such mergers and acquisitions, most would say, would weaken the rich and heterogeneous cultural foundations of the industry. Moving into such technologies as CD-ROM is appropriate only for a limited selection of titles and demands, at this point, considerable capital investment, and sales volumes far beyond what is feasible in the domestic Canadian (and export) market for the types of titles published by Canadian book publishers. The Department of Canadian Heritage (formerly the Department of Communications) appeared, at least until 1995, to favour large firms that seem to be market (as opposed to culturally) oriented, so that industry restructuring would lead to a rationalization of both the numbers and types of titles produced. In turn, this would lead to increased profitability and the chance to reduce grants, at least industrial support grants, to zero.

The dramatic reduction of industrial support to the industry that occurred in 1995, fully 55 per cent of funding, seems to have made the dispute moot.[9] It would appear that the federal government has signalled, through Paul Martin's first budget, its imminent departure from industrial support for the industry. Further cuts in March 1996, bringing the total to 61 per cent of funding, confirms this interpretation.

Provincial Policy

Like federal policy, provincial policy has two components, cultural and industrial. As provinces came on stream with assistance for book publishers, they usually did so with cultural assistance, by extending arts assistance programs. In Quebec, Ontario and Alberta a combined cultural and industrial orientation has prevailed more or less from the beginning. In the middle-eighties, however, the federal government began to lead the provinces into industrial support through a series of jointly funded economic regional development agreements (often called ERDAs). These agreements have included management evaluation, marketing and distribution assistance, professional development and technology.

Broadly, provincial programs are meant to pick up small and new publishers and some percentage of the support for cultural titles. With an increasing number of provinces embracing financial restraint measures in 1996 that are similar to those of the federal government, the industry is being forced to "consolidate and rationalize": title production is decreasing, firms are financially distressed and new firms are having to devise radically different formulae for survival, combining, among other things, technology and private subsidy. Certain provinces may see economic benefits in building cultural industries (e.g., Ontario, Quebec, B.C.) while others may cut their losses and depart the field. (An Ontario government report entitled *The Business of Culture* is an example of an aggressive plan for building cultural industries. It is extremely unlikely to be implemented by the Harris government.)

Technological and Cultural Issues

Perhaps the most interesting technological development in publishing is multimedia publishing: effectively, publishing on the Internet or on CD-ROM. Multimedia publishing represents a real opportunity for book publishers primarily because they own vast "content" libraries which, with added features, can be turned into saleable CDs. The preparation and mastering of CDs can be undertaken without a great deal more upfront investment than books require. The added advantage is that once that investment has been made, unit costs can come in at less than a dollar. The fly in the ointment for publishers who focus on the Canadian market is that CD-ROM publishing in particular, and multimedia publishing in general, benefit from extensive investment in dynamic integrations of sound, image and text that can only be recovered in a market much larger than Canada alone. Already a multitude of companies, including Disney, Microsoft and National Geographic, are producing inexpensive, high-end, mass-market materials that are both informative and engaging by adapting movie-production techniques. Interactive encyclopedias with hypermedia (markers that can be clicked on with a mouse to take the user into another layer of information) are common and include McClelland and Stewart's *Canadian Encyclopedia*. These multimedia productions set a level of consumer expectations that will make it difficult for Canadian titles with a smaller development budget to succeed.

In a Canadian context, it may be that CD-ROM publishing should take a magazine-based approach and include advertising as a way of subsidizing the cost of delivering the product to the audience.

A second technological issue comes from computerized distribution. US-based wholesalers, such as Baker & Taylor and Blackwells, have set themselves up to serve the entire North American market effectively and efficiently. However, by supplying books to Canadians, they circumvent the territoriality of copyright and/or distribution agreements in which a firm based in Canada is the "sole agent and distributor." This is "buying around," and the establishment of foreign megabookstores such as Borders and Barnes and Noble would increase its significance. Canadian publishers attempted to meet this challenge through an electronic ordering system called the Canadian Telebook Agency (CTA), now owned by Bowker, and by setting up regional wholesalers. Publishers have also lobbied for the inclusion of a distribution right: a law protecting their contracts, not uncommon in other countries, in the next revisions of the Copyright Act. However, over the long term, it is clearly in the interests of the U.S.-based chains to use their U.S. warehousing and distribution, if only because these functions have been part of their formula for success. They will be able to circumvent all but the strongest Canadian law, simply by persuading U.S. publishers to cease selling Canadian sole-distribution rights.

A third technological development combines printing and binding with ease of copyright clearance. Short runs are becoming so feasible that both bookstores and large publishers encourage professors and other educators to compile their own textbooks, a form of on-demand publishing. Current signs point to increased on-demand publishing and reprography revenue, with diminished book sales. This change has produced a hiatus in revenues that threatens the survival of some Canadian firms. Once revenues begin to flow from Cancopy, the Canadian copyright collective, it will be seen whether publishers and authors are worse or better off.

The cultural issues surrounding traditional book publishing centre on the economics of publishing for a small market. No knowledge-able person questions the fact that Canadian book publishing has been a cultural triumph over the past 20 to 30 years. Not only are Canadian letters alive and developing in Canada and around the world, bookstores are also filled with all kinds of Canadian-specific environmental, political, historical and sociological texts. There is also no doubt that this could never have happened without govern-ment support. Whether this can be maintained without continued government assistance is an open question.

However, the main rationale for government assistance — the development of the cultural industries — is as vulnerable in book publishing as in the other cultural industries. Assistance is under attack by those favouring fiscal restraint, by the powerful U.S. en-tertainment industry, increasingly joined by the British and other global producers, by Thatcherite social theorists who would uncou-ple cultural production and the activities of the state, by the increas-ing demands of all who feel themselves underrepresented and even from new young entrepreneurs who feel they would be able to estab-lish themselves, if only those who survive on grants were to leave the scene.

All is not well with Canadian book publishing.

Marketing and Distribution

Given these changing realities, there are two major marketing issues in book publishing. The first is whether increased marketing effort focused on fewer titles by Canadian-controlled firms could result in increased profitability. It is virtually impossible to answer that ques-tion. For it to work, the following would probably be necessary: a rethinking of the types of titles to be published, a reconsideration of the development and exploitation of intellectual property and a reorientation to initial investments in titles and authors. What we do know is that Canadian-controlled firms can compete on a title-by-title basis with foreign-controlled firms. We also know that the sum total of books published by Canadian-controlled firms receives about equal media support in Canada in commentary and reviews as do books published by foreign-controlled companies (CCSP, 1994).

The second marketing issue centres on economies of scale and brings in distribution. Imported books have always had and will likely always have a significant place in the Canadian marketplace. If such books are allowed in freely, they will continue to constrain both the production and profitability of Canadian-published titles. The formation of Chapters, out of a merger of Smithbooks and Coles, and the potential opening of other megabookstores in Canada, increases the already strong pressure for a North American distribution of books. For Canadian books to compete with imports requires a different publishing formula. So far that foundation has been Canadian authors and Canadian content. In the area of children's books it has been a different sensibility: good business practice coupled with an attempt to stimulate the child's imagination. The pressing question is: will such foundations be enough in the near and medium-term future? Book publishing will face difficult times if publisher-targeted grants are diminished along with other non-specific small business grants and if a distribution right allowing Canadian firms to invest the revenue they gain from selling foreign books in Canadian title production is not firmly established.

Current and Future Policy Issues

Current realities raise a number of policy issues in book publishing. Without federal and provincial grants, many firms will probably fold or change their orientation considerably. Many fewer titles of the types now available will be published, especially new fiction, poetry and books dealing with regional issues. Canadians will be less able to talk to one another through the medium of books. In the end, the imaginative and informational fabric of the country as a distinct national or binational, peaceful, tolerant, caring, outward-looking, multicultural community will weaken.

The delay in bringing forward the so-called Phase 2 revisions to the Copyright Act is working against the interests of publishers and in favour of readers as well as those who would wish for a continental book trade. Inclusion of a Canadian distribution right would assist Canadian-based publishers, both foreign and Canadian controlled. At best, it would assist in maintaining the current level of production of Canadian-authored titles. At worst, it would encourage greater agency activity and thus greater competition for Canadian authors.

Tax credits for investment in manuscript development, or even a better use of the tax system by publishers, could have a positive impact on part of the industry, probably mostly larger firms. It could encourage outside investment in manuscript development, bringing new venture capital to the industry. A continuing low dollar should help Canadian-published books compete with U.S. and other foreign imports.

The real competition for Canadian books are U.S.-inspired mass-market-oriented books, not just mass-market paperbacks, but books designed to appeal to everyone, on child-rearing, religion, humour, travel, world-figure biographies, and so on. As U.S. cultural hegemony wanes and Europe and Asia become increasingly important global economic and cultural players, the possibilities for Canadian publishers to increase their market share may increase. To do so, Canadian publishers would have to anticipate market changes and capture foreign rights from non-U.S., foreign publishers. This is no easy task because, once U.S. publishers increase their buying of rights, they will follow current practice and attempt to secure not just U.S. but North American rights. It is also possible that, as the average age of the population increases, mass-market books, i.e., books aimed at a general audience around the world, will lose market share. Certainly reading patterns suggest that older readers prefer locally and nationally oriented materials (Duxbury, 1995). On the other hand, with the World Trade Organization and the North American Free Trade Agreement pushing for ever-more liberal trade in cultural products, and with the so-called electronic highway placing people much more easily in touch with others all around the world (free trade in information), global products will receive yet another fillip to add to a spate of laws and regulations that favours global conglomerates (see Acheson and Maule [1994a], [1994b] for a discussion of copyright and international trade in cultural products and Lorimer and O'Donnell [1992] on the foundations of globalization).

Two paths, possibly three, appear to be dead ends. The first dead end is patriation of Canadian publishing through divestiture, as required by the Baie Comeau Agreement. So contrary to Canadian-style capitalism is forced divestiture and such anathema is it to the

U.S. that it is highly unlikely that any federal cabinet will support it. Similarly, widespread Canadian participation in the forest-eating mass-market paperback trade is virtually impossible. The economies of scale in production are insufficient to cover the losses created by unsold product that is pulped. In the third area, Canadian publishers have made little headway in the elementary–high school market. In spite of the fact that it is not, education in core areas such as language arts, math and science is still considered by educators to be an acultural, or at least a non-national activity; thus products produced for any child, anywhere, still reign supreme (Lorimer, 1984).

There does appear to be ground to be gained in two areas. The first is publishers' knowledge of their audiences. The knowledge of audiences acquired through creating books for and marketing them to readers is knowledge that has value for other cultural producers. While limited attempts have been mounted by Canadian-controlled book publishers to exploit this knowledge, for instance through teaming up with or acquiring a magazine, as Telemedia, Owl and Reader's Digest have done, much more is possible (see Driver and Gillespie [1992] for a discussion of knowledge of audiences). Canadian publishers also seem to have thought little and done less in the area of brand and trademark exploitation. This may hold some promise (see Lury [1993]).

In fighting U.S. dominance, Canada's cultural industries have not really attempted to use U.S. techniques to defeat U.S. producers at their own game. Primarily this is because Canadians have seen themselves engaged in cultural, not entertainment, production. José Marques de Melo (1995) provides an account of how managerial and production techniques for television were transferred from the U.S. to TV Globo in Brazil, thereby, in conjunction with favourable national legislation, providing a foundation for a Brazilian-based global television industry (which Rupert Murdoch has now purchased). Canada has a leg up, should it wish to enter global markets because it produces in English (see Collins [1994]) and it can understand the ugly elements of U.S. dominance and culture. Of course, an emphasis on world markets can lead to a dramatic shift in cultural contribution. As U.S. dominance of entertainment markets declines, as it inevitably will, Canadian producers may be well-placed to provide substitute products, especially if they can set up co-production arrangements with other countries, as has happened in the film industry. The equivalent to Alliance and Atlantis in the film and television industries is just beginning to emerge in book publishing.

Conclusion

These are uncertain times for Canadian book publishers, both Canadian and foreign owned. The environment in which they are operating is changing dramatically and quickly. They face megabookstores; publishers who are subsidiaries of vast entertainment and information conglomerates; technologies of production (digitization), together with the emergence of new products and the shift of some established products into CD-ROM and online formats; international trading regimes that favour dominant producers in gaining easier access to all markets; and fiscal cutbacks by all levels of government. Through tax laws, the federal government can make it possible for a wide spectrum of Canadians to lend support through investment to the blossoming of cultural production in the form of Canadian writing that book publishers can carry into the domestic and international marketplace. It remains to be seen whether the Chrétien Liberals will respond in this way. Canadians themselves, of course, hold a great deal of power. If we Canadians insist on purchasing only foreign authors and foreign titles and we allow our institutions — schools, universities and libraries — to do the same, then Canadian writing and publishing reflective of Canadian culture will shrink measurably. Publishers themselves have some control over their destiny. They must, of course, keep Canadian authors on their side by continuing to be competitive with foreign companies, based in Canada or not. They must do this especially with newly emerging authors who are writing for the world as well as for Canada.

There may be technological possibilities, e.g., CD-ROM anthologies combining text, voice and image. Why not a retrospective of a poet with audio and some video representations of her reading last year, 10 years ago and 20 years ago, complete with the poet's collected marginalia and commentary? Publishers could also seek out inexpensive production techniques that could be shared among industry members. After all, the creation of new products and new production methods are surely the foundation of capitalist enterprise. Canada's book publishers will also need to be aggressive with respect to exploitation of intellectual property. A not untypical attitude among authors and publishers is a spirit that respects authorial creativity and artistic integrity but neglects audience benefit. This modernist leftover need not be replaced with pandering to the baser side of human nature. Rather, if manuscripts are seen as illuminations of the human condition that, by virtue of their existence as owned intellectual property, can be exploited as a variety of cultural products, why not take them to the public in as many forms as can be profitably produced?

Notes

1. I wish to thank Nicole McGill for her research and chart-constructing assistance in preparing this paper.
2. Statistics Canada has not been able to find a method of replacing that figure and so, except for discussions in the industry of the problem of buying around (i.e., people and institutions buying books from foreign-based sources that Canadian-based agents or publishers have the sole right to distribute in Canada) direct imports are not estimated and therefore not discussed.
3. The National Library reports that in 1994, 11,896 new titles were placed on legal deposit. Unfortunately previous years' figures are not available. However, it is plain to see that legal deposits outnumber titles surveyed by Statistics Canada by more than a factor of two.
4. Statistics Canada reports data by industry sectors specifically defining them as trade book, textbook, reference, scholarly, and professional and technical. Further, within the trade–book category, three subcategories are defined: hardcover books, softcover books and mass-market paperbacks. Thus, unless otherwise noted, we will use the word "trade" to indicate hardcover and softcover but not mass-market paperback books, as reported to Statistics Canada. Coming at the category from another perspective, trade books can defined as books sold to the general public, most often through bookstores. We will also follow Statistics Canada's designation of own-titles, meaning titles originated by the firm either through purchase of rights or manuscript development. Note that we are focusing on publishing, not agency activity which is, essentially, importation and distribution. This latter category we will call, as Statistics Canada does, agency publishing.
5. The figure in parentheses is the absolute number on which the percentage figure quoted is based. The source is Statistics Canada's summary statistics on the book publishing industry, Catalogue 87-210. T= Table.
6. Traditional industry wisdom has been that the Canadian-controlled sector has always been unable to sell books as successfully as the foreign-owned sector. When the data are aggregated across all sectors, this appears to be so. But when trade-book data are examined and it is trade books in which the Canadian-controlled sector specializes (and it is really a shame that Statistics Canada has become so stingy with its data, making it necessary to include mass-market paperbacks with other trade books), the sales-per-title difference disappears. To provide a sense of sales differences between segments: in reference books, per-title sales are, on average, $147,219 while in scholarly publishing they are $15,362; in trade they are $53,965; in textbooks they are $120,031; in professional and technical $108,989.
7. This figure includes only direct grants to the publishing industry per se (see Lorimer [1995]).
8. Leisure-reading studies in general support the data presented in the body of this paper and add some further information. Over 17 years, there have been only

two general reading studies (James Lorimer, 1981 and Ekos, 1993 and Duxbury, 1995), both of which have methodological difficulties.

The 1978 reading study (James Lorimer) suggested that the leisure-book-reading public is a large group; in English Canada in 1978 it was some 9.5 million people and in 1991 (Duxbury) some 17.3 million. Book-reading ranks high as a major leisure-time activity (in terms of number of hours spent) not far behind television-viewing, visiting, radio-listening and relaxing. Women and young people seemed to read more than others in 1978 and fiction was read more often than nonfiction. High nonfiction categories include history, social science and biography.

The 1991 reading study confirmed book-reading as a major leisure-time activity in terms of hours and participation rate; 94 per cent of those surveyed spent an average of 7 hours per week reading, 4.4 reading books (Ekos). Reading books was ranked slightly ahead of newspaper and magazine reading. The 1991 data showed nonfiction reading ahead of fiction (70 per cent versus 64 per cent participation in the preceding week) with self-help books and manuals the leading genre category. Older people and women reported more reading. On average, questionnaire respondents reported that they had purchased six books over the last three months at an average price of about $12, a dramatic overestimation when compared with other estimates of the disposable income spending of families.

9. On February 28, 1995, Finance Minister Paul Martin announced budget cuts that included a 75 per cent cut to PDAP, the distribution assistance program, and 35 per cent cut to the BPIDP program for an overall cut of 55 per cent. Such cuts were far in excess of overall budget cuts. On March 1996, the minister announced a further six per cent in cuts.

References

Acheson, Keith and Christopher Maule. 1994a. "International regimes for trade, investment, and labour mobility in the cultural industries." *Canadian Journal of Communication.* 19, 149-169.

————. 1994b. "Copyright and related rights: The international dimension." *Canadian Journal of Communication.* 19, 171-194.

Aldana, Patricia. 1980. *Canadian Publishing: An Industrial Strategy for its Preservation and Development in the Eighties.* Toronto: Association of Canadian Publishers.

Barnet, Richard J. and John Cavanagh. 1994. *Global Dreams: Imperial Corporations and the New World Order.* New York: Simon and Schuster.

Canada. Department of Communications. 1986. *News Release June 18.* Ottawa: Department of Communications, Information Services.

————. 1993. *Book Publishing Industry Development Program and Publications Distribution Assistance Program. Applicant's Guide.* Ottawa: Department of Communications.

————. Statistics Canada. 1994. *Book Publishing 1992–93: Culture Statistics.* Catalogue 87-210. Annual. Ottawa: Minister of Supply and Services.

————. 1993. *Book Publishing 1991–92: Culture Statistics.* Catalogue 87-210 Annual. Ottawa: Minister of Supply and Services.

————— 1989. *Culture Communiqué.* Service Bulletin. Catalogue 87-001. 12 (4) 11. Ottawa: Minister of Supply and Services.

—————. 1985. Catalogue 87-525.

Canada Council. 1994a. *Project Grants to Publishers and Block Grants to Publishers.* Information Sheets. Ottawa: Canada Council.

—————. 1994b. *Canada Council Block Grant Program: Book Publishing Statistics to 1993.* (Draft) Ottawa: Canada Council.

Canadian Centre for Studies in Publishing (CCSP) 1994. *Canadian Books in Review.* Vancouver: CCSP.

Collins, Richard. 1994. "Trading in culture: the role of language." *Canadian Journal of Communication.* 19 (3, 4), 377-400.

Driver, Stephen and Andrew Gillespie. 1993. "Structural change in the cultural industries: British magazine publishing in the 1980s." *Media, Culture and Society.* 15 (2), 183-202.

Duxbury, Nancy. 1995. *The Reading and Purchasing Public: The Market for Trade Books in English Canada, 1991.* Toronto: Association of Canadian Publishers.

Ekos Research Associates. 1993. *Reading in Canada, 1991: Highlights.* Ottawa: Department of Communication.

Gundy, H. Pearson. 1972. "The Development of Trade Book Publishing in Canada." *Royal Commission on Book Publishing: Background Papers.* Toronto: Queen's Printer and Publisher.

Larsen, Peter (ed.). 1990. *Import/Export: International Flow of Television Fiction.* Paris: Unesco.

Lorimer, James and Susan Shaw. 1983. *Book Reading in Canada.* Toronto: Association of Canadian Publishers.

Lorimer, Rowland. 1995. "The future of English-language publishing." In Kenneth McRoberts (ed.). *Beyond Quebec: Taking Stock of Canada.* Montreal: McGill-Queen's University Press, 202-217.

—————. 1994. "What makes publishers publish, not always the market." *Logos.* 5(3), 118-123.

—————. 1993a. *A Harvest of Books: Book Publishing in Saskatchewan.* Vancouver: Canadian Centre for Studies in Publishing.

—————. 1993b. "The socio-economy of scholarly and cultural book publishing." *Media, Culture and Society.* 15 (2), 203-216.

—————. 1990. *Book Publishing in British Columbia, 1989.* Victoria, B.C.: Ministry of Municipal Affairs, Recreation and Culture.

—————. 1990. "Discourse and Reality: The Canadian Debate on Ownership in Communications." Paper given in Dublin at the annual meeting of the International Communications Association.

—————. 1984. *The Nation in the Schools: Wanted, a Canadian Education.* Toronto: OISE Press.

Lorimer, Rowland and Nancy Duxbury. 1994. "Of culture, the economy, cultural production and cultural producers." *Canadian Journal of Communication.* 19 (3,4), 7-37.

—————. 1992. "The struggle for Canadian publishing." In Helen Holmes and David Taras (eds.). *Seeing Ourselves: Media, Power and Policy in Canada.* Toronto: HBJ Holt. pp. 105-118.

Lorimer, Rowland and Eleanor O'Donnell. 1992. "Globalization and internationalization in publishing." *Canadian Journal of Communication.* 17(4), 493-510.

Lorimer, Rowland with Paddy Scannell. 1994. *Mass Communications: A Comparative Perspective.* Manchester: Manchester University Press.

Lury, Celia. 1993. *Cultural Rights: Technology, Legality and Personality.* London: Routledge.

Macskimming, Roy. 1992. "Baie Comeau gets sealed." *Quill and Quire.* October, 16.

———. 1993. "The precarious life of Canadian publishing." *Logos.* 4(1), 12-20.

Marques de Melo, José. 1995. "The development of the audio-visual industry in Brazil: From importer to exporter of television programming." *Canadian Journal of Communication.* 20 (3), 317-328.

McFadyen, Stuart, Colin Hoskins, Adam Finn and Rowland Lorimer (eds.). 1994. *Cultural Development in an Open Economy. Special Issue. Canadian Journal of Communication.* 19 (3, 4). Also available in monograph form: Waterloo, Ont. Wilfrid Laurier University Press.

Musa, Mohammed. 1990. "News agencies, transnationalization and the new order." *Media, Culture and Society.* 12 (3), 325-342.

Ontario. Ministry of Economic Development and Trade. 1994. *The Business of Culture: A Report of the Advisory Committee on a Cultural Industries Sectoral Strategy (ACCISS).* Toronto: Queen's Printer for Ontario.

Parker, George L. 1995. *The Beginnings of the Book Trade in Canada.* Toronto: University of Toronto Press.

Roach, Coleen. 1990. "The movement for a New World Information and Communication Order: a second wave?" *Media, Culture and Society.* 12(3), 283-308.

Sinclair, John. 1990. "Neither West nor Third World: the Mexican television industry within the NWICO debate." *Media, Culture and Society.* 12 (3), 343-360.

Tomlinson, John. 1991. *Cultural Imperialism.* Baltimore: Johns Hopkins University Press.

Young, David. 1990. "The Macmillan Company of Canada and the Canadian Book Publishing Industry during the 1930s." Paper given in Victoria at the annual meeting of the Canadian Communications Association, June.

2

Periodical Publishing

Lon Dubinsky[1]

Background

Periodical publishing in Canada is diverse, eclectic, invaluable culturally but fragile financially. It has been recognized as such throughout its history by editors, publishers, policy-makers and readers. Compared to other media industries, such as broadcasting, the industry is vastly smaller in size and revenue. However, many studies by the Canadian Magazine Publishers Association (CMPA) indicate that magazines reach over 70 per cent of the Canadian population. Like other cultural industries, periodical publishing has gone through significant economic and organizational changes during the 1980s and 1990s as a result of technological changes, the regulatory environment and shifting market conditions. The following recent development serves as a useful introduction to an account of the complex forces that have shaped the industry in English Canada.

In 1995, the federal government passed legislation that the magazine industry had been insisting on for some time. An excise tax of 80 per cent would be placed on the advertising revenues of "split-run" magazines. Split-runs are regional editions of foreign magazines that contain a minimal amount of local content but are capable of attracting large amounts of Canadian advertising dollars. These editions are one of the consequences of advances in printing technology. Pages from a home edition are transmitted electronically to a local printing plant, permitting publishers to target specific countries or regions, and gain access to local advertising markets, with minimal editorial changes and production costs.

It was the appearance of a "Canadian" edition of *Sports Illustrated* in 1993 that prompted the Conservative government to set up the Task Force on the Canadian Magazine Industry to examine the effect of split-runs. Bolstered by several studies and projections, the task force recommended placing an 80 per cent tax on the advertising revenues of split-runs on a per-issue basis, thus killing any incentive to produce them. The Liberal government of Jean Chrétien went beyond this recommendation in 1995. It exempted magazines that would otherwise be subject to the tax at the number of issues per year that were distributed in Canada prior to March, 1993 but did not include *Sports Illustrated*, which the task force was prepared to exempt if it did not publish more than seven issues per year.

The Canadian magazine industry was ecstatic and relieved, but its American counterparts immediately called the measure "discriminatory," claiming that it contravened NAFTA. Time Warner, the publisher of *Sports Illustrated*, and Mickey Kantor, President Clinton's chief trade negotiator at the time, were especially adamant. Canadian heritage minister Michel Dupuy, who announced the measure, seemed unfazed and cited legal advice that he had received. He insisted that the tax was not an act of protectionism but a survival measure for an industry that was economically fragile. Any future drain on advertising revenues would be the death knell for hundreds of magazines. The justification behind the tax and the minister's remarks was were affirmed by the task force. It repeatedly stressed that open trade should prevail, noting that no restrictions were being placed on the sale in Canada of foreign-produced magazines. Rather, the excise tax would restore balance and ensure competition for advertising revenue within Canada.

The proposed tax is not the first attempt by government to curb split-runs. In 1965, a custom tariff was imposed to stop foreign publishers from "dumping" magazines in Canada that contained minimal or no Canadian content and whose costs were almost totally recovered in their home markets. Electronic page transmission made circumventing the tariff possible because printed magazines no longer had to cross the border. Tariff 9958 became, not just ineffective, but obsolete. Split-runs demonstrate the complex forces at work in the world of periodical publishing. Technological change, market shifts and outdated government policy have converged to transform the magazine industry from 1981 to 1996.

Market Analysis

In *Canada's Cultural Industries*, Paul Audley begins the chapter on periodical publishing by noting that "magazines, unlike newspapers, are primarily a national rather than local medium" (1983: 54). The government's decision to impose an excise tax on split-run editions confirms the observation that policy aims to maintain the viability of a cultural industry across the country. Magazines that are synonymous with Canadian periodical publishing, such as *Maclean's* and *Saturday Night*, remain national in scope, as do long-standing small periodicals concerned with politics and the arts, such as *The Canadian Forum*. Each has maintained a dedicated audience that extends across Canada. However, during the past ten years, national policies and readership have also been affected by global and local realities that have altered many of the objectives and operations of all media industries, including magazine publishing. The split-run issue, for example, can be regarded in some respects as a contest over location. For American-owned media giants, such as Time Warner, Canada and other countries are new areas for profit in the form of advertising revenue.

Changing notions of place are also evident within Canadian magazine publishing. One of the more significant developments is the emergence of the city or regional periodical, such as *Toronto Life* and *Western Living*, which cater to a specific, localized readership that is for the most part upscale and affluent. However, there have also been failures, such as *Atlantic Insight*, which was intended to be Atlantic Canada's home-bred version of *Maclean's* and *Time*. Market segmentation is not always strictly geographical. Increasingly prominent are specialized magazines: sports periodicals, lifestyle magazines, art journals, health digests, business periodicals or computer magazines. These magazines, along with trade and industry publications, are a key source of revenue for the magazine divisions of large media interests such as Telemedia and Maclean Hunter, which recently became part of Rogers Communications. An audience apparently defined by specialization may sometimes cover a large geographical distance.

Statistics Canada's most recent *Periodical Publishing Survey* confirms this trend. (See Table 2-1.) It indicates that, on the whole, circulation, revenue and the number of periodicals have all declined during the past four years. Only magazines targeted at specific audiences have experienced growth. In 1993–94, their share of total circulation in Canada was 30.4 per cent, up from 18 per cent only four years earlier, which translated into a total circulation of 151.1 million copies.

The Canadian visual art periodical is instructive as an example. The readership is not large in mass-market terms; almost all of these magazines are nonprofit and most depend on annual grants from the periodical publishing program of the Canada Council. The more significant magazines include *Canadian Art, C, Parachute, Border Crossings* and *Vanguard*, until its demise in 1989. Readers of these periodicals, which are published in, respectively, Toronto (for the first two), Montreal, Winnipeg and Vancouver are found across the country.

It might be argued that art periodicals are a special case since they serve a small, select, if not exclusive, cultural community, but this is indeed the point. Magazines with mass-market dimensions, such as a sports periodical exclusively devoted to basketball, also have a specialized focus and readership. There are obviously more readers than players, but they nevertheless constitute a community of readers for which national boundaries are becoming insignificant. What is striking about periodical publishing in Canada is its diversity: according to Statistics Canada, there were 1,331 magazines in 1993–94. Indeed, Table 2-1 shows either stability or increases for special-interest periodicals and "other" magazines. These include business and trade periodicals.

Despite the number and types of Canadian magazines, many studies indicate that seven out of 10 are absent from Canadian newsstands. Most dealers and distributors sell primarily American fare. This is surely an economic barrier, but it has not altered the Canadian industry's diverse character. It remains eclectic and includes magazines as diverse as the drama journal *Theatrum*, the children magazines' *Owl* and *Chickadee*, the literary quarterly *Exile, Canadian Geographic*, the science magazine *Equinox*, specialty magazines such as *Healthsharing, Canadian Thoroughbred*, and appropriately enough *Masthead*, a periodical for magazine publishers.

Industry Structure

According to Statistics Canada, in 1990–91 the industry employed 4,657 full-time and 1,727 part-time paid workers as well as 3,993 unpaid volunteers, largely to be found at small and medium-size publications. These numbers do not include outside writers and other professionals who, in 1990–91, received approximately $24 million out of a total of $187 million paid in employee remuneration. The economic impact of the industry is considerable. A 1989 report commissioned by the Cultural Industries and Agencies Branch of the government of Ontario estimated that there were almost 16,000 full-

Table 2-1
Revenue, Circulation and Number of Periodicals

Category of Periodical	1989/90	1992/93	1993/94
General Consumer			
Revenue ($ millions)	418	356	316
Circulation (millions)	291	217	216
Number of periodicals	237	162	135
Special-interest			
Revenue ($ millions)	170	190	189
Circulation (millions)	94	149	151
Number of periodicals	443	389	386
Other			
Revenue ($ millions)	297	306	290
Circulation (millions)	137	138	129
Number of periodicals	813	849	810
Total			
Revenue ($ millions)	885	852	795
Circulation (millions)	522	504	496
Number of periodicals	1,493	1,400	1,331

Source: Statistics Canada. 1995. *The Periodical Publishing Survey.*

time jobs and a contribution to the gross domestic product of $715 million.

While labour is relatively unorganized, the industry itself is much more defined. Its principal players are large media companies with publishing divisions and small periodicals that, for the most part, are produced by single-magazine publishers. Medium-size magazines, like medium-sized businesses, are few. The recent Task Force on the Canadian Magazine Industry (1994) pointed out that there is a significant amount of corporate concentration: for example, the 12 largest publishers in Canada accounted for roughly 10 per cent of the magazines published in 1991. At the same time these publishers employed approximately 30 per cent of all full-time staff and received 51 per cent of all the revenue earned by the industry (1994: 19). Recent mergers affecting the industry have not resulted in the combining of publishing divisions or companies. In the 1995 takeover of Maclean-Hunter by Rogers Communications, a company with a large magazine division is now part of a media conglomerate with no other magazine interests. The issue therefore is whether Rogers will see fit to include magazine publishing in its expanding media empire, phase it out or sell off this part of Maclean-Hunter. If American trends are any indication, it is possible that magazine groups, such as trade publications, may become the subject of acquisitions or sell-offs by competing media conglomerates. Whether these developments will extend north of the border, as has been the case with book publishing, remains to be seen. If so, the government's competition watchdog and Investment Canada may play increasing roles in the organizational and economic future of magazine publishing in Canada. For now, magazine publishing is dominated by large Canadian interests or by multinational publishers. Table 2-2 shows the concentration of large publishers in the industry during the past five years.

As Table 2-2 indicates, the domination by large publishers extends only so far and has not gone much over the 50 per cent mark in either revenue, circulation or employment. What prevails is an eclectic industry, which also has hundreds of nonprofit periodicals, including the "little magazines," as they have been called historically. Thus, the media arena includes everything from consumer fare, such as *Canadian Living*, to literary magazines, such as *Rampike*. Each magazine operates with different economic expectations, turning a profit in the case of the former and the latter surviving primarily on government support, but both function within the confines of an industry that is subject to technological and economic factors, such as split-runs and declining postal subsidies.

These two radically different periodicals also demonstrate how periodicals contribute to a magazine culture in Canada and beyond. Magazines, as with any communications media, impart and distribute information and, in the process of transmission, also have the capacity to create a culture derived from their very use. Subscribing to a magazine, browsing magazine stands and making single-copy purchases amount to a form of membership, a kind of affiliation in which one becomes attached to and informed about a particular interest

Table 2-2
Concentration Ratio (Share of Industry Revenue, Circulation, Employment), 1989–90 to 1993–94

	1989–90	1990–91	1991–92	1992–93	1993–94
Total number of publishers	1,091	1,099	1,055	1,047	1,000
Largest 4 Publishers					
% share of revenue	40	38	37	39	39
% share of circulation	36	35	33	34	36
% share of salaries and wages	28	25	24	25	29
Largest 8 Publishers					
% share of revenue	50	48	46	47	48
% share of circulation	41	42	45	48	52
% share of salaries and wages	36	35	32	30	34
Largest 12 Publishers					
% share of revenue	54	52	51	52	52
% share of circulation	45	46	52	52	56
% share of salaries and wages	39	39	36	35	38

Source: Statistics Canada. 1995. *The Periodical Publishing Survey.*

through a specific cultural form. What distinguishes this magazine culture, especially in Canada once again, is diversity. The scope and contents of periodicals still seem unequalled when compared to the regular and specialty channels and sources in other media.

Policy Structure and Cultural Issues

A further resource in the creation and maintenance of a magazine industry and a magazine culture has been government and the publishers themselves. As for the latter, magazines as a cultural force and industry have been nurtured and promoted by the industry's advocacy organization, the Canadian Magazine Publishers Association (CMPA). Its close attention to policy issues, economic trends and technological changes never seems to abate: witness its constant lobbying against split-runs. However, the CMPA has been more than a watchdog: it relishes every opportunity to describe and emphasize the vitality and distinctiveness of the industry. This is more than a promotional or lobbying tactic. There is something both indispensable and unique about periodical publishing in Canada. As a source of knowledge magazines are prized more than newspapers, book publishing and broadcasting, all of which are much larger in size. The proof of the vitality of a magazine culture is nowhere more evident than in the membership of the CMPA, which reflects the industry's diversity. It consists of major players such as *Maclean's*, *Canadian Business* and the fashion magazine *Flare* as well as smaller periodicals, such as the literary quarterly *The Malahat Review*, the women's magazine *Herizons* and the aboriginal publication *Windspeaker*.

Government also contributes to a magazine culture. It may not always seem that way to the industry and to the CMPA in particular. While both were understandably pleased and relieved with the proposed excise tax on split-runs, conflict continues on several fronts. The CMPA repeatedly claims that the rapid and huge decrease in postal subsidies is threatening the life of magazine publishing. It also continues to call for the removal of the Goods and Services Tax (GST) on magazines. Historically, however, the federal government has been concerned with magazines and this can be measured in the number of commissions, task forces and studies that have addressed periodicals specifically or included them in a comprehensive review of culture and cultural policy. These include: the Massey-Levesque Commission on Arts, Letters and Sciences (1951), the Royal Commission on Publications (1960), the Davey Senate Committee on the Mass Media (1970), the Royal Commission on Newspapers (1981), the Federal Cultural Policy Review Committee (1982) and most recently the Task Force on the Canadian Magazine Industry (1994).

There have also been countless studies conducted or commissioned by the federal Department of Communications on magazine distribution and costs, such as the Woods Gordon report (1984). Several provinces have also undertaken reviews, such as the Ontario Cultural Industries and Agencies Branch (Ontario, 1989). All of these have stressed that Canadian magazines have an indispensable informational and cultural role. Cynics may consider such inquiries as regular lip service by the state, but policies have been enacted, in addition to the proposed tax on split-runs, that have contributed to the industry's economic viability and growth. What follows is a brief review of these actions.

Economic Background

By the late 1950s it was apparent that most consumer magazines read in Canada originated in the United States. It was debatable whether this amounted to the absence of a magazine industry in Canada or to one that was in constant crisis and jeopardy. The Diefenbaker government responded in 1960 by establishing the O'Leary Royal Commission on Publications which, among other things, reported that 80 per cent of the magazine industry was in foreign hands. In 1965, when the Liberals were in office, an amendment was introduced to the Income Tax Act that disallowed deductions for advertising directed at a Canadian market placed in a foreign-owned periodical, wherever printed. However, the Canadian editions of the two leading U.S. magazines, *Time* and *Reader's Digest*, were exempted from this provision. In 1965, the government also introduced Custom Tariff 9958, which prohibited the entry into Canada of split-run issues of foreign magazines. As noted earlier, this tariff ceased to be effective as a result of advances in printing technology and thus hastened the entry of new split-run editions into Canada.

The income tax change appeared to have no immediate effect on the growth of an indigenous Canadian magazine industry. By the time the Davey Senate Committee on the mass media convened in 1970, 70 per cent of all magazines still came from the United States. The total share of advertising for Canadian magazines had dropped further while *Time* and *Reader's Digest* had increased their share of Canadian advertising revenue from 43 per cent in 1958 to 56 per cent in 1969. The Davey Committee concluded that the decision to exempt these periodicals was a great error. In 1975, the liberal government introduced Bill C-58 to amend the Income Tax Act. It was aimed at diverting advertising revenue from *Time* and *Reader's Digest*, with the expectation that this action would increase the economic viability and growth of magazines owned and produced in Canada.[2]

The policy seems to have worked. Canadian periodicals now control a substantial percentage of the Canadian market. Since 1987, the total revenue from subscriptions, single-copy sales, advertising and other sources has been in excess of $750 million. The high point was

1989–90, when revenues topped $903 million. Declines followed; in 1990–91 and 1991–92, the totals were $883.9 million and $846.4 million respectively. Analysts attributed the decreases to the recession and the introduction of the GST. However, the most important indicator is the Canadian share of the domestic market which, based on the number of circulated copies per year, is now 67.6 per cent, according to the Task Force on the Canadian Magazine Industry (1994). The circulation for the top 20 and top 10 Canadian periodicals are much higher than those of their American counterparts. The CMPA (1993) shows the changes between 1983 and 1993, using data from the Audit Bureau of Circulation. (See Table 2-3).

Postal Subsidies, the GST and Grants

The magazine industry faces other economic constraints and challenges that are tied to government policies and programs. The most significant is the postal subsidy, which has been a crucial factor in the industry's viability. For over a hundred years, the intent of the postal subsidy was not to defray the mailing costs of publishers but to contain the cost of magazines for readers in a country as large as Canada. Today, mailing remains *the* form of distribution for magazines in Canada. The CMPA estimates that almost 50 per cent of all magazine copies in circulation reach their readers through the mail as paid subscriptions and a further 35 per cent are delivered as free, circulation-controlled copies. In 1986 the subsidy to Canada Post was $220 million (Keachie and Pittaway, 1994). The communications minister at the time, Flora MacDonald, announced that this level of support would continue for at least five years. However, in 1989 the government reduced the subsidy by half. It was, no doubt, an easy target for deficit reduction, compared to cutting social programs and other, more visible government initiatives. The following year, the government announced that it would begin phasing out all postal subsidies, except for those for paid-circulation magazines. Since then, the subsidy has been reduced to $72 million.

Canada Post continues to receive this subsidy but it has been very reluctant to accept magazines that qualify for support. As noted by Keachie and Pittaway (1994), it is in the interest of Canada Post to maximize the cost per copy while minimizing the number of magazines that qualify for the subsidized rate because this translates into more periodicals paying higher rates and therefore contributes to Canada Post's profit. However, under a new proposal being developed by the Department of Canadian Heritage, funding would no

Table 2-3
Highest Circulation Magazines, 1983 and 1993, Canadian Magazines & U.S. Spill Magazines in Canada (000's)

Who's gaining? The poor performance of U.S. magazines stands out in stark contrast to the performance of Canadian magazines. In 1983, combined per-issue circulation of the top 20 Canadian magazines outnumbered the equivalent U.S. magazines in the country by 3 to 1. In 1993, that competitive advantage has grown to a factor of nearly 5 to 1.

Not only have Canadian magazine circulation levels climbed, so too has the number of Canadian titles, giving advertisers more choices than ever before.

Year	Canada Top 20	US Top 20	Canada Top 10	US Top 10
1983	12,391	3,770	9,262	2,873
1993	14,944	3,128	10,630	2,148

Source: Canadian Circulations Audit Board, Audit Bureau of Circulation, PMB: Print Measurement Board

longer flow directly from the government to Canada Post. In its place an arms-length agency representing the industry and government would purchase distribution services from any number of sources, including, but not limited to, Canada Post. Keachie and Pittaway conclude "this would introduce competition into the distribution of magazines and promote the development of more economical delivery methods" (1994: 16).

Nevertheless, the industry is alarmed about the amount of money that will actually be available in 1996 when the subsidy to Canada Post is scheduled to end. There is understandable concern that the new agency will be unable to accomplish its objectives, especially if further cuts to the subsidy ensue. Thus far, Canada Post has absorbed the reductions. This may well be a signal to government that Canada Post is prepared to co-operate rather than lose its monopoly and its mandate to a new agency. Yet Canada Post's willingness did not stop the Liberal government of Jean Chrétien from proposing, in its first budget, additional cuts which, according to the CMPA, could mean a 20-per-cent increase in postal rates. It remains to be seen if the present government will maintain its commitment to have the agency in place with sufficient funds by 1996.

Two other economic factors continue to affect the development and viability of magazine publishing. One is the GST on magazines; the other is grants from the Canada Council and other government agencies.

Since the introduction of the GST in 1991, several studies have shown that it has had a deleterious economic impact on magazine circulation and costs. A 1993 CMPA study reported the following changes. In the first year of GST collection, the circulation of Canadian magazines dropped 5.7 per cent. Bad-pay rates (the percentage of subscribers who order a magazine but do not pay for it) increased by almost 50 per cent. The report estimated that, in 1991, the cost to its own members, based on this jump, was over $3 million. Equally significant was the 4.1 per cent of subscribers who short-paid on the GST amount on their orders — money that the magazines are required to pay whether the subscriber does or not. The renewal rates of many subscriptions declined and, in some areas of the industry, the decrease was as much as 45 per cent. The report also revealed that most magazines were forced to forgo or delay a price increase, even though production costs had risen, because the GST had already raised the cost seven per cent. As well, the report estimated that the GST contributed to reductions in spending on employment by the magazines, and to an overall 62.5 per cent decrease in profits during 1990–91.

Finally, there were calculations of the amount of GST collected in 1991 on the sale of magazines. For 1991 this included $17,009,300 from subscription revenue and single copies of Canadian magazines and $30,898,179 for sales and subscriptions to American magazines. However, the report discovered that an additional $15,832,633 was not collected on U.S. magazines. This is because it is impossible for Revenue Canada to get complete compliance. As the report emphasized, no other country with a value-added tax similar to the GST has managed to successfully collect a tax on foreign subscriptions. The CMPA, with some obvious justification, regards the GST as both unfair and unwarranted. First, by evading the tax, many American magazines are able to sell magazines at lower prices. Second, the CMPA points out that the tax appears to contradict the government's support of both culture and literacy since it is a financial disincentive to reading.

As one hand of government engages in a tax grab, the other continues to support magazine publishing through grant programs, albeit in reduced amounts relative to inflation. Since its inception in

1957, the Canada Council has funded a range of cultural publications. Initially only a handful of magazines were supported. In 1974 the Aid to Periodicals program was established within the council's writing and publishing section (Jutras, 1982 and 1986). Each year, this program funds on average 100 magazines in the visual, performing and literary arts. Its total annual budget has hovered around $2 million for the past four years, with grants varying from $5,000 for a small and select literary magazine to substantial funding for major art magazines, such as *Parachute,* which has received support averaging over $100,000 annually since 1982-83. These grants pale when compared to the amount expended by government on other media, not the least of which is the CBC. Many of these grants are a small price to pay for the survival of the recipients, given their quality, and international reputation.

Despite the adjudication process, many magazines have come to expect support on an annual basis, to the point that an attitude of entitlement has developed. This expectation may well create problems for the program if funding remains at the present level or further diminishes. It is especially difficult for new magazines to receive funding. For a new periodical to be eligible for grant consideration, it must publish at least three issues but once it meets this criterion it has to compete with existing publications that have received yearly support for considerable lengths of time and have developed substantial track records.

Meanwhile, the program makes do with less funding. On one recent occasion grant reductions and the mandates of three periodicals collided. In 1993, the Canada Council sent letters to three magazines, *The Canadian Forum, New Maritimes,* and *This Magazine,* and warned that if they did not increase their "artistic content," their funding would be reduced or terminated (CMPA, 1994). The move seemed to be an effort to cope with a decreased budget by stringently interpreting the program's mandate to support magazines whose primary purpose is covering the arts. Reaction from the magazine industry was swift and critical. It was pointed out that the three magazines covered cultural issues and that *The Canadian Forum* in particular had a tradition of regularly including articles about and reviews of the arts. It appears that the council has backed away from the warning. It has since appointed a committee, consisting of people with expertise in the arts and magazine publishing, to review its operations and policies.

The range of economic factors and realities indicates that policies and programs enacted by the federal government have contributed significantly to the industry's viability and growth. The income tax amendment and Tariff Item 9958 proved initially effective and the proposed excise tax on split-runs is expected to discourage any future editions. Government grants, in particular the Canada Council's Aid to Periodicals Program, have been and continue to be essential for many nonprofit cultural magazines which, in their own small way, have flourished. The GST, on the other hand, at least in the initial years of its collection, seems to have accounted for decreases in profit, subscriptions and productivity. However, some would argue that these declines were more attributable to the recession. On the economic front, and in governmental terms, perhaps the most ominous development is yet to come since the maintenance of a postal subsidy remains precarious.

As for earned revenue, advertising makes up approximately 65 per cent of the total for the industry. Subscriptions continue to be the dominant form of distribution for magazines in English Canada but combined with newsstand sales they still cannot match advertising's share of income. If any provisional conclusion can be offered at this juncture, it is that the industry remains fragile financially. Yet, in spite of economic uncertainty, it remains diverse and constantly exerts a will to survive. In many cases it flourishes.

Marketing Issues

Because only three out ten Canadian magazines are found on newsstands, circulation from this form of distribution is a tiny 6.7 per cent of the total. While the total number of copies sold is comforting, it does not translate into significant revenues as the sales price is not the major source of income. Advertising continues to be the lifeblood for most magazines, accounting for 65 per cent of total revenues. Even nonprofit periodicals that rely heavily on government grants seek advertising revenue. Table 2-4 shows revenues and expenses for all types of magazines during 1993–94. Advertising is *the* primary source of income, particularly for special interest and business and trade periodicals. Note as well that the profit after expenses and before taxes as a percentage of total revenue is also significantly higher for the magazines that rely more on advertising than on subscriptions sales as a source of income.

The crucial importance of advertising was also emphasized in the recent Task Force on the Magazine Industry report (1994). Noting that Canadian magazines are especially attractive to advertisers because they offer a greater choice and significantly higher readerships than other media, it concluded that split-runs would easily eat into this market. Using the availability of new ad pages as a quantitative indicator, a study (Cebryk, Jeness and McCracken, 1994) carried out for the task force offered the following predictions. For consumer periodicals, the study calculated that if split-runs were permitted, there would be approximately an additional 26,133 ad pages, or an increase of 37 per cent for those magazines that depend on advertising as a major source of revenue. For business and trade publications, the forecast was similar, about 39 per cent. Based on these projections, the study offered the following conclusion:

> With the increased supply of U.S. ad pages, the price of ads will decline. This will increase the total demand, but the decline in Canadian ad pages will be substantial, coupled with a lower ad price. Thus ad revenues for Canadian magazines are sure to shrink. Even magazines unaffected directly by loss of ad pages will be affected by the decline in ad prices (1994: 7).

The study also found the unit cost of producing a magazine is higher in Canada than in the United States.

> As a share of total revenue, U.S. publishing costs are significantly lower for editorial (by 3–6 per cent), production and printing (3–6 per cent) and administration and general expenses (1–4 per cent) These differences add up to give U.S. periodicals a much healthier before-tax profit (1994: 5).

The study pointed out that economies of scale account for these differences. Larger print runs reduce the unit costs of paper and technology as well as editorial and administrative costs. The study concluded that prospects for reducing costs in Canada are "relatively limited, given the smaller market" (1994: 5) thus making any loss in advertising revenue that much more detrimental.

A final indication of the indispensable role of advertising is the profitability level of Canadian magazines. The higher profit margins enjoyed by special interest and business or trade periodicals are a result of more advertising. Publishers that produce more than one magazine tend on average to be more profitable than single-magazine publishers. This finding led to the conclusion that a form of cross-

Table

Revenues and Expenses of Periodicals

	General Consumer Periodical	Special Interest Consumer Periodical
Revenues		
Advertising sales	158,476	113,020
Single-copy sales	40,807	12,980
Subscription rates	109,357	44,720
Back issues	412	598
Other revenues	6,480	17,856
Total revenue	315,532	189,174
Expenses		
Salaries, wages, fees	53,237	46,294
Non-salaries costs	251,887	133,503
Total expenses	305,124	179,797
Profit before taxes	10,408	9,377
Profit before taxes as a percentage of total revenue	3.3	5.0

Source: Statistics Canada. 1995. *The Periodical Publishing Survey.*

2-4

by Category of Periodical, 1993–94

Business or Trade Periodical	Farm Periodical	Religious Periodical	Scholarly Periodical	Total
177,227	19,614	2,504	14,408	485,250
1,172	7	459	215	53,639
16,978	5,652	15,836	6,843	199,385
270	10	18	776	2,083
14,961	751	5,605	7,407	53,060
210,608	26,034	24,461	29,649	795,419
56,632	8,684	8,243	8,468	181,558
131,798	15,860	16,594	19,037	568,680
188,430	24,544	24,837	27,505	750,237
22,178	1,490	-416	2,144	45,181
10.5	5.7	-1.7	7.2	5.7

subsidization occurs within multi-magazine publishers. They use their profits on successful ventures, which are derived primarily from advertising, to support other, usually small, publications.

Technological Changes and Distribution

The harsh economic realities affecting the magazine industry are not surprising, given government's preoccupation with deficit reduction and the competition for consumers from other media. By contrast, technological developments have been largely unanticipated and transformative. As noted at the outset, electronic page transmission rendered the custom tariff obsolete and could have been instrumental in taking away huge amounts of advertising revenue and readers. It is only one example of recent technological changes that affect every corner of Canadian periodical publishing and the magazine industry worldwide.

The first change came in the form of desktop publishing which, in the early 1980s, seemed to just happen overnight. One day most publishers, editors and designers were pasting up each issue manually; the next day computer technology and affordable software publishing programs were being acquired by even the smallest magazines. It is perhaps the periodicals with meagre resources, limited circulations and little or no profit margins that benefited most from the computer revolution. Generally, the result has been stabler production costs and increased operating efficiencies. In a 1994 issue of *Masthead*, a majority of respondents claimed that a desktop system pays for itself within two years (Kieran: 10). However, there is no let-up in new products. For the small and single-magazine publishers in particular, this development presents an opportunity to further streamline production and remain competitive. Yet continual investments in technology can translate into financial outlays that take longer to recover. The same issue of *Masthead* provided a glimpse of what is on the technological horizon. It includes, but is not limited to, such temptations as photo compact discs that will facilitate imaging and colour publishing as well as desktop scanners which are intended to further simplify layout and other prepress operations, supposedly at a reduced cost.

Today, the biggest technological challenges and opportunities for magazines are online services and other arteries of the so-called information highway. Hundreds of magazines are making their contents available electronically and in Canada these include *Saturday Night*, *Maclean's* and smaller publications, such as *Pathways*, a health magazine based in Oakville, Ontario (Ross, 1994). Others are available on CD-ROM, such as *Clik*, a Montreal arts "periodical" that began in late 1994, but like its cultural ancestor, the "little magazine," lasted only a few "issues." Much of the enthusiasm for electronic magazines centres on *Wired*, an American publication based in San Francisco whose subject, appropriately, is new forms of technology, such as virtual reality and CD-ROM. Not surprisingly, *Wired* was online electronically before it was available in hard copy. At Magazines 94, a magazine trade show held in Toronto, the founders of *Wired* and other media prophets were predicting the gradual death of the traditional magazine as a consequence of techno-economic developments. Yet, they admitted that much will depend on whether advertisers seize upon the opportunities for capturing consumers through electronic magazines. As Ross (1994) reports:

> *Wired* has carried stories on how advertisers will soon be able to buy the right to hitch their messages to specific stories or group of stories, and thereby reach minutely targeted groups of readers (1994: C3).

What are the consequences of these impending techno-economic changes for the Canadian magazine industry? Periodicals may have no choice but to make their contents available on the information highway. There is the possibility of increased revenue and readership, but the competition will be fierce and global as the market will be dominated by electronic newsstands, as they are already being called, that will invariably efface national boundaries. Coincident with the emergence of expanded markets and new carriers will be a contestation over the cost, ownership and distribution of information. It cannot be otherwise. A Canadian-produced magazine, like any information source, will have to pay for being available unless it chooses to restrict itself to a defined group of subscribers and, even in this scenario, cost is a factor. The owners of online services may also choose to limit what is available at the new newsstands, making distribution similar to the street and store venues that carry only three out of ten Canadian magazines.

An historical study by Marvin (1988) accounts for the complex relations and forces that surround the emergence of new technologies. Focusing on the development of electricity in the nineteenth century, Marvin makes the following claim.

The early history of electric media is less the evolution of technical efficiencies in communication than a series of arenas for negotiating issues crucial to the conduct of social life: among them, who is inside and outside, who may speak, who may not and who has the authority and may believed. Changes in the speed, capacity and performance of communications devices tell us little about these questions (1988: 4).

Rejecting an instrumental and technological explanation, Marvin "shifts to the drama in which existing groups perpetually negotiate power, authority, representation and knowledge with what resources are available" (1988: 5).

The same observation can be made about the impact of new technologies on magazines and other forms of print. It is not the speed, capacity and performance of the technology that is so much at issue as who will be participating in and controlling the flow of information and under what economic regime. These realities are already apparent in the magazine *Wired*, whose investors include the U.S. media power Newhouse Communications. Marvin argues that new technologies "intrude" on the contestation and control of re-sources by providing "new platforms on which groups confront each other." There may be changes, such as "the frequency and intensity of contact" but ultimately the so-called new developments are inex-tricably tied to old social relationships that are not so much displaced as reconstituted. Marvin concludes:

New practices do not so much flow from technologies that inspire them as they are improvised out of old practices that no longer work in new settings (1988: 4).

Marvin thus accounts for the social basis of technological change and in doing so confirms that matters of cost, ownership, distribution and ultimately power must be considered. Her observations assist in describing the emerging technological context for magazines and other established media forms but also call attention to the social and corporate basis of the information highway. More specifically, it is clear that much of the electronic space, Marvin's "platforms," will be increasingly occupied, if not controlled and owned, by communi-cations conglomerates. However, this does not mean there is no room for alternatives, nor can unanticipated consequences be excluded. As Raymond Williams insists:

No mode of production and therefore no dominant social order and therefore no dominant culture ever in reality includes or excludes all human practice, human energy and human intention (1977: 125).

As a result, two developments in the magazine industry bear watching. First, it is possible many consumers may retain a preference for the traditional magazine format just as they may for hardcover and paperback books and be prepared to pay the costs. Second, "instant magazines" may offer considerable potential. Using online services and communication networks, such as the Internet, these magazines could be compiled by groups who could put out a periodical, issue by issue with deadlines and limited contents, or produce a never-ending "magazine" about a particular and common interest. What is being described here is the assembling of information that will necessitate various kinds of searching and sharing. Matters of ownership, cost and distribution will have to be taken into account but production will also require traditional media practices, such as selection and editing, which, above all, are organizational in nature.

The Future of Periodical Publishing

When all economic, technological and organizational factors are taken into account the shape and substance of a *Canadian* cultural industry are evident. Unlike most other media, magazine publishing in Canada is distinguished by its indigenous content and local ownership. The CMPA reports, for example, that of the total editorial content of Canadian magazines 92.4 per cent was written in-house or by Canadian freelance writers while 93.4 per cent of illustration and photography was produced in-house or by Canadian freelancers. Some may dismiss this as an expression of parochialism while the economically minded might insist that magazine publishing remains Canadian because the size and earning potential of the market is small. Besides, since foreign publications, especially American ones, continue to dominate newsstand sales, it is unnecessary for them to own all the industry or control all the content. Yet, the split-run issue clearly showed that, when new revenue opportunities do emerge, the media giants may not be interested in buying Canadian magazines but are prepared to extend their own reach.

In the last analysis, perhaps a major reason why the federal government can and does continue to effectively regulate and support

Canadian magazine publishing is the size factor. In today's global economy, the creation of niches has become a consuming, if not a necessary, objective, whatever the product, service or medium. Magazine publishing, at least in Canada, may be a niche industry of its own making in the same way that many of its constituents have carved out a niche in a particular area or interest. The other factor that is perhaps responsible for the industry's survival and in many cases its flourishing is the magazine medium itself. Even in an age of technological wizardry and hundreds of television channels, magazines continue to be bought and valued. There is still something attractive in handling and perusing magazines, in browsing at the newsstand and the price for most seems inexpensive when compared to the cost of a book, CD, video, film or monthly cable fee.

Indeed, the future for magazines, and in particular magazine publishing in Canada, may not be so precarious and uncertain. What are the prospects for continued diversity and increased economic growth in a communications and cultural context that has become increasingly transnational, market-driven and subject to corporate megamergers? Single-magazine publishers have their work cut out for them but multi-magazine publishers will undoubtedly face more complex and fierce challenges, since most are divisions within media conglomerates. Greater profitability and growth will be the manifest objectives and as a result competition within companies will be as great as competition in the marketplace.

Another obvious concern is the effect of new technologies on magazines and the magazine industry. It will be a matter of constantly gauging the marketplace and deciding if interactive media and electronic distribution can maintain or increase revenues and readership. In this regard, some of the greatest scepticism comes from a most unlikely source, an influential media executive at the crossroads of the information highway. Addressing the 1994 American Magazine conference, Barry Diller, chairman of QVC, chastised magazine publishers for "rushing into the new media without first understanding it" and he insisted that "If you try to cram a magazine through a phone jack and call it interactive, you'll get nowhere (*Magazine World Update*, 1994: 4). Canadian publishers would be wise to heed Diller's advice: Canada is already an extensively wired nation and a quick embrace of new technologies must be carefully considered.

One cannot always anticipate the technological changes that lie ahead. Yet, there are transnational and market realities that are staring Canadian magazine publishing in the face. Online services, for example, may offer opportunities for distribution but first there is a need to know who and where the potential readers and subscribers are as well as how to bill them. Some American publishers saw these opportunities in split-runs. Canadian magazines would no doubt face similar barriers in many national markets and if they did not, the costs of electronic transmission and local printing and distribution would far outpace the revenue potential since the home market would not be large enough to cover the outlay. If Canadian magazines, large or small, intend to broaden their readerships and revenues, distribution and subscription may still necessitate traditional strategies. These include making contacts with specific bookstores, specialized newsstands, and trade and special-interest associations as well as using direct mail marketing.

Personal and local contacts are perhaps the most likely route for specialized magazines such as art periodicals, scholarly journals and other small special-interest magazines. Many editors and publishers can and do make use of these relationships in Canada and beyond. By contrast, it is the large specialized magazine with targeted audiences based on income and profession that is increasingly turning to direct marketing. Yet in both cases, we can expect greater use of the Internet and other electronic delivery systems.

Closing this chapter with an account of distribution strategies is in no way to reduce Canadian magazine publishing to some of its crass essentials. Rather, it is to emphasize that it is an industry clearly in transition. Some of the distribution and marketing strategies described are its old side and they remain substantially effective, even if considered in transnational terms. Periodical publishing's diversity, size, financial fragility and its continuing attractiveness as a medium of communication are its most persistent characteristics. Technological change, in combination with social and corporate influences, for better and for worse, will shape its future.

Notes

1. I wish to thank Brigitte Radecki and Ira Dubinsky for their assistance and comments in the preparation of this chapter. I also wish to acknowledge the Canadian Magazine Publishers Association for providing the necessary documentation and thank Catherine Keachie, its president, for her co-operation and timely analysis.
2. For a thorough review of government policies up to and including the introduction of Bill C-58, see: R.F. Swanson [1977] and I.A. Litvack and C. Maule [1981].

References

Audley, Paul. 1983. *Canada's Cultural Industries*. Toronto: James Lorimer and Company.

Canada. Federal Policy Review Committee (Applebaum-Hébert). 1982. *Report*. Ottawa: Minister of Supply and Services.

Canada. *A Question of Balance*. Report of the Task Force on the Canadian Magazine Industry. Ottawa: Minister of Supply and Services, 1994.

————. Royal Commission on Publications (O'Leary Commission). 1961. *Report*. Ottawa: Queen's Printer.

————. Royal Commission on National Developments in the Arts, Letters and Sciences (Massey Commission). 1951. *Report*. Ottawa: King's Printer.

————. Royal Commission on Newspapers (Kent Commission). 1981. *Report*. Ottawa: Minister of Supply and Services.

————. Senate Committee on Mass Media (Davey Committee). 1970. *Report*. Ottawa: Queen's Printer.

Canadian Magazine Publishers Association. 1994a. *Annual Report*. 1993–94. Toronto: Canadian Magazine Publishers Association.

————. 1994b. *Newsletter*, Issue 161. Toronto: Canadian Magazine Publishers Association.

————. 1994c. *Winning Readers in Canada from 1983 to 1993*. Toronto: Canadian Magazine Publishers Association.

————. 1993. *Effects of the Goods and Services Tax on the Canadian Consumer Magazine Industry*. Toronto: Canadian Magazine Publishers Association.

————. 1992a. *Split-Run Editions: The Danger to the Canadian Magazine Publishing Industry and Implications for Tariff Item 9958*. Toronto: Canadian Magazine Publishers Association.

————. 1992b. *Annual Report 1991–92*. Toronto: Canadian Magazine Association.

Cebryk, N., R.A. Jenness and M.C. McCracken. 1994. *The Canadian Periodical Publishing Industry: Executive Summary: A Study Prepared for the Task Force on the Canadian Magazine Industry*.

Jutras, L. 1986. "Report of the Canada Council's Programme of Aid for Promotion Campaign of Periodicals." *Canadian Periodical Publishers Association Newsletter*, 42, 1-8.

————. 1982. The Canada Council's Programme of Support to Periodicals. *Canadian Periodical Publishers Association Newsletter*, 7, 1-5.

Keachie, Catherine and Kim Pittaway. 1994. "Federal Policy and Canadian Magazines." *Policy Options*, January-February, 14-18.

Kieran, Michael. 1994. "Five Trends Worth Watching." *Masthead*, September, 8-11.

Litvack, I.A. and C. Maule. 1981. "Bill C-58 and the Regulation of Periodicals." *International Journal*, 36, 70-90.

"Magazine World Update," FIPP, International Federation of the Periodical Press, October 1994.

Marvin, C. 1988. *When Old Technologies Were New*. New York: Oxford University Press.

Ontario. 1989. *Report on the Cultural Industries and Agencies Branch*. Toronto: Department of Culture and Citizenship.

Ross, Val. 1994. "Is Writing on the Wall for Print?" *The Globe and Mail*, May 14, C3.

Statistics Canada. 1995. *The Periodical Publishing Survey*. Ottawa: Minister of Supply and Services.

Swanson, R.F. 1977. "Canadian Cultural Nationalism and the U.S. Public Interest." In *Canadian Cultural Nationalism*. Janice L. Murray (ed.). New York: New York University Press.

Taylor, Kate. 1994. "Turn-around Time for Canadian Art." *The Globe and Mail*, October 22, E7.

Williams, Raymond. 1977. *Marxism and Literature*. Oxford: Oxford University Press.

Woods, Gordon. 1984. *A Study of the Canadian Periodical Publishing Industry: A report prepared by Woods Gordon for the Department of Communications*. Ottawa: Department of Communications.

3

Newspaper Publishing

Christopher Dornan

Background

The newspaper industry is in many ways the perfect Canadian cultural industry, the model to which all the others aspire. Wholly Canadian-owned, it is generally profitable and entirely self-sufficient, and therefore neither requires nor requests public subsidy. Competition from the U.S. or other international interlopers is not a significant factor. Clearly vital to the politics, economics and culture of the nation, newspapers are purchased across all social classes. More people read newspapers regularly than attend Canadian films, read Canadian books, patronize the Canadian arts, purchase Canadian recordings or watch Canadian television drama and light entertainment. As a fact of this country's cultural life, newspapers are rivalled only by domestic sport and by news and current affairs programming on radio and television.

And yet, as a cultural industry, the newspaper business is comparatively ignored. It attracts little attention from the policy and academic communities and rarely features in the elaborate discourse of Canadian cultural policy. In part, this is because the industry itself does not court attention. In part, it is because the state has little excuse or opportunity to involve itself in the affairs of the press. In part, it is because the travails of the newspaper industry are often eclipsed by more pressing concerns, such as the threat to public broadcasting and the continued erosion of arts subsidies. At the same time, the familiar and seemingly unchanging pattern of the newspaper business has been overshadowed by dramatic developments elsewhere in the communication sector, such as the consolidation of the cable industry, the growth of specialty television franchises, and the increased pace of technological convergence.

Nonetheless, newspapers operate in the same economic environment that currently buffets the other cultural industries, and they are not immune to its effects. Indeed, their prominence as a cultural artifact has been steadily slipping. Competition for the time and attention of newspaper readers will only intensify. New means of delivering news, information and — crucially — advertising are already making themselves felt, even as the costs of producing and distributing newspapers continue to climb. Both within the industry and without, the suspicion grows that a confluence of circumstances and pressures is about to visit profound change on the newspaper as we know it. Predictions of its demise are doubtless premature, but it is altogether possible that the next two decades will see a revolution in the newspaper industry unmatched since the appearance of a truly mass circulation press in the late nineteenth century.

Industry Structure

Newspapers are like no other Canadian cultural industry. They are so distinct it is somehow odd to classify them as such. Other cultural industries exist in a state of suspended vulnerability. Given the nation's proximity to the United States, it is commonly assumed that market forces, left unmanaged, would wipe out everything from Canadian television networks to Canadian publishing houses, either killing them off or absorbing them into American multimedia conglomerates. Were that to happen, it would imperil Canada as a nation. It would mean the loss of crucial agencies of cultural expression and national debate; it would diminish if not obliterate an entire echelon of discourse (namely that provided by the public sector, whose mission is to provide what the private sector either cannot or will not); it would threaten cultural production as a sphere of domestic employment and investment. A country's culture — if it wishes to have a culture — cannot be administered by the branch plant operations of another country.

In the name of maintaining even minimal space for domestic cultural production, other sectors require robust regulatory intervention or sizeable public subsidy, and frequently both. They call upon a variety of state agencies for protection and promotion. They are in perpetual need of counsel, advocacy and revenue. They are, on the one hand, national strengths, and, on the other hand, political headaches. Consequently, they are the objects of full-blown administrative policies that are always in flux, as successive governments tackle the "problem" of the cultural industries via ever-shifting strategies, never managing to arrive at a satisfactory solution.

None of this applies to the newspaper industry. Like the domestic advertising industry on which they depend (and which is similarly often overlooked when cultural policy is discussed), newspapers are not licensed by the state nor do they solicit state support. Hence, the regulatory and policy apparatus that attends most cultural industries is pointedly absent. There is no CRTC for the newspaper industry, no equivalent of Telefilm or the Canada Council, no print version of the CBC or the NFB.

The industry's political shield is its historical legacy. The press in Western democracy has waged a 400-year struggle to liberate itself from church and state. This is what ostensibly guarantees a "free press" — one subject to no external authority save the rule of established law — and therefore privileges the news media to document and criticize the exercise of power. It is unlikely that Canadian newspapers would ever knowingly submit to Crown involvement in their affairs.

Pricing and market penetration are such that the industry makes money, rather than costs money; there is no drain on the public purse. Exclusively a private-sector enterprise, it nonetheless caters to a variety of tastes, from the high-toned and exclusive (*The Globe and Mail*, *The Financial Post*) through the omnibus (*The Toronto Star*, the Saskatoon *Star-Phoenix*) to the unapologetically populist (the *Sun* papers). Though it charts a range of tastes, the industry is still polite enough to draw the line at the type of tabloid excess practised in England, for example. As unregulated media go, the Canadian newspaper industry is generally dutiful and responsible.

As an industry, newspapers are an important employer, mostly of white-collar "knowledge workers." As a daily artifact, the newspaper is as indispensable to local advertising as is it to municipal and national political life. Far from being a comprador subsidiary of American interests, newspapers attract large amounts of controlling domestic capital and have spawned their own line of international press barons. Other people do not own our newspapers; we own other people's newspapers.

Domestic control over the newspaper industry was secured through tax legislation introduced in the Liberal government's budget of 1965. At the time, the only foreign-owned newspaper in the country was the Red Deer *Advocate*, owned by the proprietors of Britain's Liverpool *Post*. However, when *The Globe and Mail* was for sale in 1955, it had attracted offers from British newspaper baron Lord Rothermere and from the American William Loeb, publisher of the Manchester *Union Leader* in New Hampshire (Hayes, 1992: 63). Mark Farrell reports that in 1963, France's *Paris Match* organization expressed an interest in acquiring Montreal's *La Presse*. Such foreign incursions were effectively blocked by the Pearson government's adoption of the recommendations of the 1960–61 Royal Commission on Publications. The commission, under chairman Grattan O'Leary, had advocated that advertising placed in a foreign-owned publication should be disallowed as a tax deduction. This was the measure adopted in the 1965 budget, although because of fierce lobbying from the United States, exemptions were granted to *Time* and *Reader's Digest*, the two American-owned magazines operating in Canada at the time. It was not until 1976, under the Trudeau Liberals, that this exemption was revoked and the provisions were extended to advertising purchased on broadcasting outlets.

These measures had the effect of protecting Canadian newspapers from foreign poaching and competition. Since tax deductions were allowed only for advertising purchased from media outlets at least 75-per-cent indigenously owned, any foreign-controlled media corporation operating in Canada would be at a competitive disadvantage. The effect was to secure the national borders as a haven for domestic media corporations, which could then use their Canadian holdings as a base from which to launch international ventures. Thus Conrad Black's Hollinger Corp., for example, now controls *The Daily Telegraph* in London, *The Jerusalem Post*, the Chicago *Sun-Times* and the Fairfax chain in Australia, among other holdings. From the most modest beginnings, the Thomson corporation has grown in 60 years to an international colossus that — quite apart from its Canadian holdings — is the largest publisher of regional and local newspapers in Britain, owns more than 100 daily and weekly papers in the U.S., and has diversified into scores of financial, legal and academic publishing ventures and services.

Market Analysis

If Canadian newspapers are successful and self-supporting, why are they so rarely studied as a model for other cultural industries to emulate? There are two reasons. First, there is little incentive to examine newspapers in the policy, academic or financial communities, and little indication that their lessons might be usefully applied to industries such as sound recording or film. Second, no one believes the newspaper industry offers a model for the future in any case. When the future of the newspaper industry is considered, it is not spoken of in enthusiastic terms. "[Newspaper publishers] have been battening down the hatches for many years now," the investment analyst firm James Capel Canada Inc. told its clients in September 1995, "only to be faced with further challenges due to high newsprint costs, and limited pricing, circulation and linage growth" (1995). Of the various Canadian newspaper-based companies, Capel rated Thomson highest as an investment prospect "given its relatively smaller exposure to newspapers." In sum, the firm urged its clients to watch newsprint prices. If the cost of the raw material of newspapers declined, this would push up newspaper company stock prices. Investors were advised to then cash in and get out, since the longer-term prospects of the newspaper industry suggested a continued erosion in stock prices.

The most reliable indicator of newspapers' status as a cultural form is total circulation, which has been steadily slipping even as the nation's population grows. A 1993 Newspaper Marketing Bureau NADbank survey revealed that an average of 5,491,150 daily newspapers were sold in Canada on any given day, down from a peak of 5,824,736 in 1989. In 1995, the Canadian Daily Newspaper Association was obliged to report that in the year ending March 31, total circulation had dropped to 5.3 million copies, a loss of 3.3 per cent over 12 months, and that this drop was evenly spread across the industry. French-language papers fared slightly better than English-language papers, but they still lost 0.8 per cent circulation as opposed to a 3.8 per cent reduction in English Canada. (See Table 3-1.)

Two small papers closed over that time — *The Oshawa Times* and *The Evening Patriot* in Charlottetown — but the nature of the newspaper industry is such that these closures had a negligible impact on total circulation. Since few Canadians take more than one local newspaper, the readers of a newspaper that folds are forced to transfer their custom to another paper. When a newspaper fails, its competitors typically profit.

In the same period, The Barrie *Examiner* and *The Packet and Times* in Orillia, both in Ontario, ceased Sunday publication, which no doubt marginally depressed overall circulation, but by the same token, the *Sun* newspapers in Calgary and Edmonton added Saturday editions. Newspaper closings cannot account for the decline in circulation, although the decline in circulation is a factor in newspaper closings.

Table 3-1
Newspaper Circulation
Average Published Day Circulation of Top 20
Canadian Newspapers

Newspaper	1995	% change from 1994
Toronto Star	519,070	-3.2%
The Globe and Mail	314,972	-0.9
Le Journal de Montréal	287,986	0.0
Toronto Sun	250,695	-8.7
La Presse	212,527	-1.3
Vancouver Sun	210,964	-1.7
Ottawa Citizen	164,120	-4.8
The Gazette (Montreal)	159,108	-4.8
The Province (Vancouver)	158,687	-5.6
Edmonton Journal	157,873	-4.5
Winnipeg Free Press	145,214	-6.7
Hamilton Spectator	124,616	-3.3
Calgary Herald	121,690	-5.1
London Free Press	113,372	-1.3
Le Journal de Québec	103,047	-1.7
Le Soleil	102,920	+0.2
Financial Post	96,846	-4.9
Halifax Chronicle-Herald	96,744	-0.2
Edmonton Sun	82,145	-5.7
Windsor Star	84,206	-2.4

Source: Canadian Daily Newspaper Association circulation data, 1995 and 1994.

The industry blamed the bad news in 1995 on two presumably short-term developments, suggesting that the numbers were a temporary aberration. First, there were the baseball and hockey strikes. Without a steady supply of big-league sports coverage, readers who bought papers exclusively for sports news supposedly shunned the product. Second, the rise of the price of newsprint led to increases in the price of newspapers, and price jumps invariably temporarily depress circulation. Still, in the year before, total circulation dropped

Figure 3-1
Newspaper Readership across Age Groups

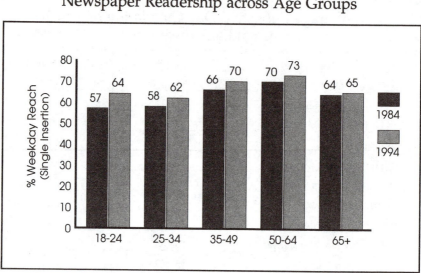

Source: NADbank+ '84–'94

0.8 per cent without the excuse of disruption in spectator sports. And for the foreseeable future, the political opposition to the forestry industry — if nothing else — will mean increased logging costs and therefore elevated newsprint costs.

However, although overall circulation figures are down, the industry steadfastly argues that overall readership is up. In September 1994, the Newspaper Marketing Bureau (NMB) announced that 67 per cent of adults surveyed said they had consulted a daily newspaper the day before, compared with 63 per cent in 1984. Ostensibly, this increase was not only true of all age groups, but most pronounced among younger readers aged 18 to 24. (See Figure 3-1.) The explanation for the discrepancy between these figures and circulation data is ingenious. Although tough economic times have meant fewer copies of newspapers sold, the NMB argues that people have been more inclined to pass along the papers they do purchase to friends, workmates or family members. In other words, fewer copies of newspapers in circulation has actually led to increased readership.

At the same time, the NMB survey underscored that newspapers were not only the preferred source of government, business and local news, but also for news of products and services as well as the most influential medium when it came to buying decisions. (See Table 3-2.)

Table 3-2
Adults' Preferred Sources of News

	Political news	Business news	News on products & services	Local news	Influence on buying decisions
Daily papers	40%	54%	27%	34.4%	27%
Television	36%	23%	20%	17%	17%
Radio	7%	6%	2%	5%	2%
Magazines	2%	3%	13%		9%
Flyers & Inserts			8%		11%
Weekly papers			4%	34%	4%

Source: NADbank '84–'94.

If these numbers are to be believed, there is nothing in the least amiss with the market base of Canadian newspapers. Certainly, the apparatus of the survey is impressive, since it involved 20,000 telephone interviews. The problem is that almost no one is convinced: not the financial analysts who pronounce on the long-term prospects of the industry, not the investors who determine the value of newspaper stocks, not the companies that have to decide where and how much to spend on advertising, and not, by its own conduct, the newspaper industry itself. It is not that the survey results are misleading, but merely that such figures are malleable. Nonetheless, it is imperative that the newspaper industry insist that its market base is secure. Since advertising rates are tied to circulation, any admission that newspapers are read by fewer and fewer people would harm revenue intake and undermine market confidence in newspaper stock. The NMB readership data are best read as a rhetorical gambit.

Compounding matters is the fact that the newspaper, like the other traditional media, faces the challenges posed by developments in new communication technologies and new alignments of media ownership. But while the new circumstances of the multimedia future present opportunities for expansion in many communication sectors, these same circumstances are widely viewed as threatening to the newspaper industry in its current form. More than anything, the growth of the new technologies fuels the suspicion that newspapers are poised on the brink of a monumental convulsion. The alternative is the present pattern of ever-escalating costs and ever-dwindling circulation — a trajectory that would seem to describe the eventual marginalization of a once-prominent cultural form.

Newspapers and Public Policy

The comparatively scant attention paid to newspapers by those who supposedly monitor the cultural industries is telling. The policy community largely ignores the press, unless corporate proprietors practically invite formal auditing by the state, as they did with the simultaneous closings that led to the Royal Commission on Newspapers (1981). Otherwise, the policy apparatus has no budget and no excuse to keep a steady eye on the newspaper business.

Banks, investment counsellors and brokerage houses pay some attention, but never with a view to the cultural or political life of newspapers. The financial community reduces everything to a rate of return. In the eyes of investors, developments that may be incontestably bad for the product — newsroom layoffs, or a reduced "newshole" (the amount of space in the paper devoted to editorial content rather than advertising) — will be seen as good, provided that they enhance profits. In any event, the action in media speculation has shifted to technology more advanced than daily doorstep delivery. Cable, satellite, telecom, computers, cyberspace — these are where capital is convinced the fortunes of the future are to be made.

The academic community, similarly, has overlooked the newspaper as an industrial artifact, and for many of the same reasons. The action has clearly shifted elsewhere. When the future is so visibly in flux, why bother with a medium whose history has already been written? For its part, as much as the newspaper industry spends on readership surveys and management think-ins, it has shown no inclination to underwrite academic studies of its affairs. Nor are university departments of media studies greatly interested. Newspapers are certainly objects of analysis, but usually this is limited to how their coverage of a specific issue was biased or "framed"; or how they shortchange their readers by catering to the bottom line and the lowest common denominator; or how they are ultimately ideological agents of an unjust social order, despite their claims to neutrality in news coverage and their political posture in defence of the public good. Half the time, they are only examined at all because they leave a permanent, cross-indexed record that is readily accessible via database and archive holdings, in a way that television does not.

As a cultural artifact, the newspaper is singularly uninteresting. At colloquiums and in seminar rooms, the talk is of the "postmodern" and the media's role therein. Hence, a book such as Steven Connor's *Postmodernist Culture* (1989) can cover the full media spectrum — architecture, the visual arts, literature, performance, TV, video, film, rock music and fashion — without once mentioning the newspaper. The postmodern condition is supposedly marked by epistemological scepticism and a weary awareness of the total theatricality of public life. Adrift in unanchored signification, the idiom of the moment is ostensibly the knowing wink, a playful awareness of established tropes, and at every turn a fondness for irony.

Is it any wonder the newspaper escapes the scrutiny of intellectuals? It is the last of the steadfastly un-ironic media. Its *raison d'être* is its deadpan credibility, which hinges on the authority of its voice. Newspaper journalism therefore cannot afford epistemological qualms. If, in the words of Armand and Michele Mattelart, there is a full-blown "crisis of models of rationality, of truth and norms, which affects the entire Western *logos*" (1992: 47), the newspaper industry is blithely and necessarily oblivious. For the most part, its reporting is formulaic and bureaucratized — a continual re-enactment of established tropes. For all that it trades in the novel and the shocking, the newspaper itself is a familiar package, rendered daily in the same rote format.

Irony, indeed. The newspaper was the first truly mass commercial medium, and therefore attuned from the start to the tastes of a vast buying public. It was not only a principal architect of modernity — rambunctious democratic discourse hitched to an insistent rationalism — but it remains the most eclectic of the popular media, the original compendium of the supposedly postmodern emblems of pastiche, bricolage and juxtaposition. Stories of catastrophe jam against happy headlines to warm the heart. The reader who routinely scans the stock listings may also turn habitually to the Marmaduke cartoon. Sports scores co-habitate with women's fashion layouts. Long before there was channel-surfing, there was the newspaper.

And yet the newspaper is a patently premodernist artifact, a medium whose idiom is unchanged from the nineteenth century. Quite apart from the comics and the opinionated commentary, the horoscopes and the telephone personals, the newspaper's point-of-purchase selling point has always been its front page; the front page has long been entirely given over to news coverage; and the news coverage is still rendered in the familiar objective voice, the hierarchical recitation of known facts. The medium is therefore one of the last popular redoubts of classical realism. Albeit increasingly marginalized, it is still a prominent, daily affirmation that the correct application of rules of inquiry and representation can yield trustworthy accounts of immediate events.

The intelligentsia therefore ignores the newspaper because, as a medium, the newspaper is not a participant in the roiling play of new modes of discourse. Although its stock in trade is currency and novelty, the newspaper works with yesterday's technology and the stale forms of address of a bygone era. In the eyes of academic observers of the media, the newspaper is a throwback. As a cultural artifact, its chief distinguishing feature is that it is, in a word, dull.

Though this has been true for decades, the two largest newspaper chains in the country have only recently admitted it openly. In 1993, the chief executive officer of Thomson Corp., Michael Brown, confessed that his company's newspapers were "cruddy" and that "Thomson Newspapers has a reputation well-deserved for very poor quality ..." (McNish, 1993). Similarly, in a speech to the 1995 convention of the Canadian Association of Journalists, Southam president Bill Ardell said of his company's papers: "We are not interesting, we are not accurate, we are not formatted properly and we do not reflect our community" (Cobb, 1995).

In large measure, the quandary of the omnibus daily can be traced to the difficulties it faces in competing for the time and attention of readers. With an ever-greater multiplicity of media offerings available, the newspaper simply pales in comparison. It has none of the high-energy interaction of Nintendo or the futuristic sheen of the Internet. While television splinters into narrowcast specialty channels for myriad tastes, the typical broadsheet still attempts to be all things to all people. Its longstanding advantage over television — that it could provide much more detail than the networks — has been lost, as CNN, Newsworld and CPAC now offer blanket coverage, live and in real time, of unfolding events as dramatic as the bombing in Oklahoma City and as dutiful as CRTC hearings. By comparison, it is the newspaper that now seems to offer only digests of events, delivered well after the fact. The increasing rapidity of electronic news coverage merely serves to accentuate the comparatively lethargic pace of newspaper production. By the time the morning paper arrives on the doorstep, its front page contents are little more than a confirmation of the previous evening's television news headlines.

The Concentration of Ownership

The dilemma of the newspaper is the end result of its past success, specifically in the drive toward universal circulation. The traditional history of the newspaper is told as a transformation from a partisan press supported by political patronage and subscription to a mass, commercial press dependent on advertising revenue tied to market penetration (see Kesterton [1967]; Rutherford [1978]; Schudson [1978]; Smith [1979]; Fetherling [1990]; Kesterton and Bird [1995]). This transformation led to the rise of chain ownership and the emergence of an ethos of objectivity in reporting, two developments that were intimately related.

Canada provided fertile ground for the formation of newspaper chains. The size of the country meant large distances between cities and towns, with the result that newspapers have been traditionally parochial in their base. Unlike England, where a small number of nationally distributed titles dominate the industry, in Canada each urban area has maintained its own newspapers. By 1911, Canada was home to 143 dailies. Chains composed of many titles came into being only because the country had numerous dailies, which were then available to be purchased by acquisitive press barons.

At the same time, the chains are themselves the result of economic incentive. Profits are increased by sharing the costs of newsgathering among member papers. The Southam empire began with one title, the Hamilton Spectator. By 1923 it also owned *The Ottawa Citizen, The Calgary Herald, The Edmonton Journal, The Winnipeg Tribune* and the Vancouver *Province*. The Thomson chain was begun by Roy Thomson in 1934, when he purchased the *Daily Press* in Timmins, Ont., establishing a pattern of acquiring small-circulation papers which are then run with a legendary stinginess. Although the Thomson Corp. has grown to multinational proportions — it once owned *The Times* of London and currently owns *The Globe and Mail* — it was built on the premise that while small-circulation papers may yield little profit individually, if one owns scores of them profit can be substantial indeed. Today, Southam and Thomson together control almost half of the newspaper circulation in anglophone Canada and both currently operate their own news services, so as to share copy throughout the respective chains and thus reduce editorial expenses. (Southam has also entered into a similar sharing arrangement with the independently owned *Toronto Star*.) As well, papers across the

Table 3-3
Number of Daily Papers by Province and Language

Province	Total	English	French	Chinese
B.C.	19	17		2
Yukon	1	1		
N.W.T.	0			
Alberta	9	9		
Saskatchewan	4	4		
Manitoba	6	6		
Ontario	45	43	1	1
Quebec	11	2	9	
New Brunswick	5	4	1	
Nova Scotia	7	7		
P.E.I.	2	2		
Newfoundland	2	2		
Total	111	97	11	3

Source: Matthew's Media Directory.

country contribute to and prevail upon Canadian Press, the news co-operative formed in the mid-1920s. (See Tables 3-3 and 3-4.)

Once newspapers began to share copy, and once wire services began to market news coverage to a variety of clients, it was inevitable that the various far-flung parochial papers would come to write in the same dependable voice. A mass press striving for ever-greater circulation cannot afford to alienate potential readers, so avowedly partisan coverage gives way to a political neutrality palatable to readers of various political stripes. At the same time, the ethos of objectivity inhibits corporate owners from skewing news coverage to their own advantage. Though more and more newspapers may be controlled by fewer and fewer companies, the rules of professional conduct in the newsroom supposedly protect the labour of journalists from the blandishments of unscrupulous proprietors.

But when circulation became the totem of profitability, the onus was toward universal circulation. This meant that the newspaper began to add functions and content so as to insinuate itself into the lives of almost everyone. The aim was to become not merely useful,

Table 3-4
Daily Papers by Ownership

Thomson Newspapers Co. Ltd.

Title	Location	Weekday circulation (1994)
The Globe and Mail	Toronto, Ont.	330,030
Winnipeg Free Press	Winnipeg, Man.	157,631
The Times-Colonist	Victoria, B.C.	71,328
Times News & Chronicle-Journal	Thunder Bay, Ont.	40,000
The Sudbury Star	Sudbury, Ont.	27,000
The Lethbridge Herald	Lethbridge, Alta.	25,048
The Observer	Sarnia, Ont.	23,833
Daily Courier	Kelowna, B.C.	21,543
Standard-Freeholder	Cornwall, Ont.	18,430
The Brandon Sun	Brandon, Ont.	17,748
Chatham Daily News	Chatham, Ont.	16,466
Daily Press	Timmins, Ont.	13,541
Daily Free Press	Nanaimo, B.C.	10,729
Penticton Herald	Penticton, B.C.	9,833
Lindsay Daily Post	Lindsay, Ont.	9,380
Daily News	Vernon, B.C.	8,413
Northern Daily News	Kirkland Lake, Ont.	5,800
Evening Telegram	St. John's, Nfld.	39,754

but indispensable. Thus, news coverage is today only a fraction of what the typical North American broadsheet offers. The paper is a daily almanac of classified and retail advertising; columns devoted to bird-watching, bridge-playing and stamp-collecting; movie listings, stock quotations, lottery results and TV schedules; supermarket inserts and automobile advertising supplements; sections devoted to real estate, fashion, women, youth, religion, home-cooking and child-rearing. For a pittance a day, it provides a handy and instantly disposable reference manual for living. As Anthony Smith points out:

Table 3-4 (cont.)
Daily Papers by Ownership

Southam Newspapers

Title	Location	Weekday circulation (1994)
The Vancouver Sun	Vancouver, B.C.	207,084
The Province	Vancouver, B.C.	173,155
The Ottawa Citizen	Ottawa, Ont.	166,639
The Edmonton Journal	Edmonton, Alta.	165,644
The Gazette	Montreal, Que.	156,968
The Calgary Herald	Calgary, Alta.	133,241
The Spectator	Hamilton, Ont.	123,288
The Windsor Star	Windsor, Ont.	85,723
Kitchener-Waterloo Record	Kitchener, Ont	81,702
The Standard-Freeholder	St. Catharines, Ont.	43,383
The Expositor	Brantford, Ont.	32,789
Kingston Whig-Standard	Kingston, Ont.	30,000
Sault Star	Sault Ste. Marie, Ont.	25,295
Sun Times	Owen Sound, Ont.	24,198
The Nugget	North Bay, Ont.	23,000
Prince George Citizen	Prince George, B.C.	23,000
The Burlington Spectator	Burlington, Ont.	22,834
Kamloops Daily News	Kamloops, B.C.	18,696
Medicine Hat News	Medicine Hat, Alta.	14,207
Daily Star	Cobourg, Ont.	5,196
Port Hope Evening Guide	Port Hope, Ont.	3,283

The newspaper sought to include the basic materials on which all the transactions of an individual life depend ... [B]y accumulating within the same pages an extremely heterogenous array of material, most newspapers in industrialized countries could by the second decade of the twentieth century command the attention of the entire consuming public. It was important

Table 3-4 (cont.)
Daily Papers by Ownership

Hollinger, Inc.

Title	Location	Weekday circulation (1994)
Le Soleil	Quebec City, Que.	95,798
The Leader-Post	Regina, Sask.	70,203
The Star-Phoenix	Saskatoon, Sask.	66,957
Le Droit	Ottawa, Ont.	37,285
Cambridge Reporter	Cambridge, Ont.	34,500
Le Quotidien du Saguenay-Lac-St. Jean	Chicoutimi, Que.	33,154
The Examiner	Peterborough, Ont.	28,045
Review	Niagara Falls, Ont.	23,000
The Intelligencer	Belleville, Ont.	19,087
The Guelph Mercury	Guelph, Ont.	18,048
The Examiner	Barrie, Ont.	12,000
The Packet and Times	Orillia, Ont.	10,887
Journal-Pioneer	Summerside, P.E.I.	10,630
Observer	Pembroke, Ont.	8,066
Alberni Valley Times	Port Alberni, B.C.	6,941
Trail Times	Trail, B.C.	5,867
Nelson Daily News	Nelson, B.C.	4,347
Daily Townsman	Cranbrook, B.C.	4,289
The Daily News	Prince Rupert, B.C.	3,500
Alaska Highway News	Fort St. John, B.C.	3,168
Peace River Block News	Dawson Creek, B.C.	2,368
Cape Breton Post	Sydney, N.S.	32,600
The Guardian	Charlottetown, P.E.I.	20,262
The Evening News	New Glasgow, N.S.	11,300
The Western Star	Corner Brook, Nfld.	11,240
The Daily Herald	Prince Albert, Sask.	10,041
Times Herald	Moose Jaw, Sask.	10,032
The Daily News	Truro, N.S.	9,507

Table 3-4 (cont.)
Daily Papers by Ownership
Toronto Sun Publishing Corp.
(Offered for Sale by Rogers, May 1996)

Title	Location	Weekday circulation (1994)
The Toronto Sun	Toronto, Ont.	254,258
The Financial Post	Toronto, Ont.	100,000
The Edmonton Sun	Edmonton, Alta.	85,761
The Calgary Sun	Calgary, Alta.	68,759
The Ottawa Sun	Ottawa, Ont.	51,035
Times-Journal	St. Thomas, Ont.	9,144
Daily Herald-Tribune	Grande Prairie, Alta.	8,248
Fort McMurray Today	Fort McMurray, Alta.	6,043
Daily Miner and News	Kenora, Ont.	4,900
Daily Graphic	Portage La Prairie, Man.	4,545

Groupe Québécor, Inc.

Title	Location	Weekday circulation (1994)
Le Journal de Montréal	Montreal, Que.	273,402
Le Journal de Québec	Quebec City, Que.	102,405
The Winnipeg Sun	Winnipeg, Man.	47,214
The Record	Sherbrooke, Que.	6,063

Les Publications J.T.C./Power

Title	Location	Weekday circulation (1994)
La Presse	Montreal, Que.	196,283
Le Nouvelliste	Trois-Rivieres, Que.	50,333
La Tribune	Sherbrooke, Que.	33,139
La Voix de l'Est	Granby, Que.	15,520

Table 3-4 (cont.)
Daily Papers by Ownership

Halifax Herald Ltd.

Title	Location	Weekday circulation (1994)
The Chronicle-Herald	Halifax, N.S.	95,563
The Mail-Star	Halifax, N.S.	50,901

Summit Publishing

Title	Location	Weekday circulation (1994)
The Times-Transcript	Moncton, N.B.	44,016
The Daily Gleaner	Fredericton, N.B.	30,874

NB Publishing Company Ltd.

Title	Location	Weekday circulation (1994)
Evening Times-Globe	Saint John, N.B.	33,700
Telegraph-Journal	Saint John, N.B.	28,292

Ming Pao Daily Newspapers Inc.

Title	Location	Weekday circulation (1994)
Ming Pao Daily News	Scarborough, Ont.	28,050
Ming Pao Daily News	Richmond, B.C.	19,500

East Kootenay Newspapers Ltd.

Title	Location	Weekday circulation (1994)
Daily Townsman	Cranbrook, B.C.	4,289
Daily Bulletin	Kimberly, B.C.	2,178

Table 3-4 (cont.)
Daily Papers by Ownership
Independent Titles

Title	Location	Weekday circulation (1994)
The Toronto Star	Toronto, Ont.	523,388
The London Free Press	London, Ont.	111,501
Le Devoir	Montreal, Que.	29,900
The Daily News	Halifax, N.S.	26,454
Red Deer Advocate	Red Deer, Alta.	23,310
L'Acadie-Nouvelle	Caraquet, N.B.	17,902
The Recorder and Times	Brockville, Ont.	16,711
The Beacon Herald	Stratford, Ont.	13,788
Daily News	Amherst, N.S.	4,300
The Reminder	Flin Flon, Man.	3,900
The Daily Bulletin	Fort Francis, Ont.	3,200
Whitehorse Star	Whitehorse, Yukon	2,900
Citizen	Thompson, Man.	2,770
Sing Tao Chinese Daily	Vancouver, B.C.	N/A

Source: *Matthew's Media Directory.*

that every reader be able to recognize in his daily paper all his roles — as citizen, voter, consumer, sports fan, moviegoer (1980: 13-14).

There were two immediate consequences of this tendency. The first was that, especially in North America, the daily paper became a physical monster of multiple sections. (Compare the weekday *Toronto Star*, for example, to a weekday edition of *The Times* of London.) The second, particularly pronounced in Canada over the course of the 1970s, was a rationalization of the industry in which a number of newspaper titles disappeared. Urban markets were just not large enough to sustain two or more of these behemoths competing head-to-head for the same limited pools of advertising and readers. Sometimes the casualties came as a result of a strike from which the paper could not recover (as in *The Montreal Star*) or simply because the title was worth more dead than alive (as in the closing of *The Toronto Telegram*, and the sale of its building and subscription list). Then, on August 27, 1980, *The Winnipeg Tribune*, owned by Southam, and *The Ottawa Journal*, owned by Thomson, closed their doors simultaneously. This left Southam's *Ottawa Citizen* with a monopoly market in the nation's capital and Thomson's *Free Press* with a monopoly market in Winnipeg. A side-deal gave Southam control of both Vancouver papers, the *Province* and the *Sun*.

Although new dailies have been added to the metropolitan markets, they have not been strictly replacements for these fallen titles. In Toronto, Edmonton, Calgary and Ottawa, the *Sun* chain has filled an available niche with its rowdy right-leaning tabloids, but these do not compete directly for the core readership of the omnibus dailies. Winnipeg has also seen the addition of a tabloid *Sun*, although one unaffiliated with the larger *Sun* chain. Thus far, attempts to launch a English-language tabloid in Montreal (as with Pierre Peladeau's short-lived *Daily News*) have met with failure. At the other end of the spectrum, *The Globe and Mail*'s satellite-printed national edition, established in 1980, is available in every urban market in the country. But the *Globe* merely skims an up-market readership rather than compete head-on with incumbent broadsheets. Without local TV listings, movie ads, sports coverage, municipal news or classifieds, outside Toronto *The Globe and Mail* is a paper one takes in addition to the local broadsheet, not instead of it.

The 1980 closings in Winnipeg and Ottawa raised sufficient concern about the concentration of ownership in the media to create the Kent Commission, which advocated strict policing of the corporate dealings of media companies in the name of market diversity. Among other recommendations, the royal commission argued that newspaper companies with multiple media holdings in local markets should be required to divest themselves of self-competing properties. This would have meant that the Thomson corporation, for example, would have had to sell *The Globe and Mail*, since as a national newspaper it penetrated markets in which the local paper was owned by Thomson.

None of these measures was ever enacted, but the commission nevertheless established a climate in which media companies could not behave with impunity in closing titles, purchasing competitors, or venturing into cross-media ownership. From 1980 to 1995, a period of relative stability descended on the newspaper industry. True, some titles changed hands (Maclean Hunter merged with the

Sun chain, while Southam purchased the independent Kingston *Whig-Standard*). Some titles shut down (Thomson closed the 123-year-old *Oshawa Times* and the 83-year-old weekly *Financial Times*). And Conrad Black's Hollinger corporation (through its subsidiaries Sterling and Unimedia) emerged as a new Canadian newspaper bloc. But for the most part, the action was in expansion, as the *Sun* entered Southam monopoly markets; the broadsheets spun off Sunday editions; *The Financial Post* turned from a weekly to a daily in direct competition with *The Globe and Mail*'s Report on Business section; Conrad Black and Paul Desmarais of Power Corp. each bought about 20 per cent of Southam's shares and became co-chairs of the Southam board; and the various chains either purchased or launched community weeklies serving growing bedroom communities.[1]

This stable but competitive environment yielded steady but unspectacular profits. Unfortunately, it also made for steady but unspectacular newspapers, and an ultimately disenchanted readership. The economic conditions that led to the perfect Canadian cultural industry have simultaneously crafted a product that is perpetually wanting, and even the traditional strengths of the omnibus daily are starting to look like liabilities. The newspaper has made itself into a daily, indispensable disappointment.

The Southam Corp. has long insisted that it is not so much a newspaper chain as a family, in which the member papers operate independently. And yet the pressures of joint ownership have led, most visibly in the case of Southam papers, to a bland homogeneity. When a newspaper is compelled to appeal to everyone, it must offend no one. Newspapers began as a medium of the streets, chronicling the variegated lives of the personalities who were actually its readers. They have since become civic stalwarts for whom it is more convenient to address a single, ideal reader: the vigilant taxpayer, the concerned citizen, the watchful parent, the home-team booster. In short: the mature, responsible community member and consumer.

The impulse is laudable, but the result is journalism that curiously does not seem to live among the people that it writes about, and therefore journalism without street credibility. The broadsheet's greatest triumph, its near-universal circulation, is therefore also its Achilles heel, because it dislocates the paper from the very community it covers. Familiarity breeds disenchantment, if not contempt, and the local rag begins to resemble the local cable company: just another infuriating monopoly.

Advertising

The typical Canadian newspaper is too local, and yet not local enough. Consider its advertising base. Classifieds are still its special preserve, but lucrative national campaigns — for breakfast cereals, gasoline, laundry detergent, headache remedies, and all the other humdrum purchases of the household — generally go elsewhere. Both television and magazines deliver more precisely targeted demographics, greater national reach and superior visual impact.

Meanwhile, truly local advertising slips through the broadsheet's grasp. For example, in every city there are scores of small pizza delivery operations, but few bother to advertise in the paper. Why? Because the paper blankets the city, while pizza parlours service pockets of limited circumference; because customers cannot find or remember a phone number from an ad buried somewhere in a multi-section newspaper; because periodically handing out flyers in invariably contested territory is more effective and less expensive than continually advertising in the local broadsheet.

The same applies to any restaurant in the delivery or take-out business, to dry cleaners and video stores, mechanics and doughnut shops. This leaves the newspaper to subsist on a thin stratum of retail advertising purchased by businesses exactly like itself — businesses whose trade is city-wide, but whose customers peter out just beyond the municipal boundaries: furniture outlets, supermarket chains, stereo stores, real estate agents, auto dealerships and franchise operations.

Even this traditional base of retail advertising revenue has been under pressure in recent years as a result of recession and slower economic growth. A report prepared by Kubas Consultants in April 1994 for the Canadian Daily Newspaper Association noted:

Virtually all of our important economic drivers have contracted during the early 1990s. Reduced economic vitality is the consequence of many factors. Lower housing demand and much lower house prices, publicized losses in employment (particularly in the blue collar or manufacturing sectors), rapidly shrinking (real) disposable income, much higher taxes, combined with unprecedented lack of consumer confidence and support of traditional values and institutions, have all conspired to restrain growth (1994a: 1.6).

Table 3-5
Average Annual Growth ($Real/Inflation-Adjusted)

% Change	1981–1986	1986–1991	1991–1995
Gross domestic product	+2.8	+1.9	+1.4
Personal disposable income	+1.7	+2.2	+1.9
Consumer expenditure	+3.0	+2.2	+1.9
Retail trade	+2.6	0.0	+1.6
Advertising revenues	+3.0	+2.1	+1.3

Source: Kubas Consultants, 1994a.

As economic growth faltered in the first half of the 1990s, advertising revenue declined. Since only some 20 per cent of newspaper revenues derive from newsstand sales and subscriptions, and 80 per cent from advertising, this had a deleterious effect. (See Table 3-5.)

More troubling for the newspaper industry was a shift in how businesses chose to advertise in papers. As the recession of the early 1990s made itself felt, many businesses shifted their advertising from what is called run-of-press (ROP) linage (ads printed on the pages of the newspaper itself) to insert linage, in which the advertising is packaged in special supplements inserted within the folds of the newspaper. Insert advertising merely piggy-backs on the newspaper's distribution and delivery system. Even as the economy slowly emerged from recession, many advertisers stayed with insert linage. Thus, in 1994, ROP linage fell 0.7 per cent, while insert linage grew 13 per cent. This is a significant adverse development for the newspaper industry for two reasons. First, insert advertising is dislocated from the actual content of the paper itself: one does not have to read the paper to be exposed to insert advertising. Second, insert advertising is less profitable to a newspaper than ROP linage.

Prospects for retail advertising offer little encouragement. In the wake of the U.S. retailing giant Wal-Mart's entry into the Canadian marketplace (via the purchase of 122 Woolco stores), other American "new-wave" retailers are poised to expand into Canada. However, this does not mean an influx of advertising dollars for Canadian newspapers. First, as Kubas Consultants notes, the increased sales of these U.S. firms in Canada will come at the expense of existing Canadian companies. For every retail sales dollar generated by American incursion, 70-80 cents will be siphoned from Canadian retailers, leading to bankruptcies and closures. Second, these U.S. retailers typically operate on a much lower advertising-to-sales ratio than their Canadian counterparts. Wal-Mart's ad-to-sales ratio is 0.3 per cent, compared with three to four per cent for Woolco. At the same time, as established Canadian retailers such as Eaton's move to what are called Every Day Low Pricing strategies, they have less call to trumpet occasional sales and specials. The result will be fewer advertising dollars spent by the retailing sector.

The long-term outlook for classified advertising is no better. Classifieds have always been the economic backbone of the parochial press. Nationally distributed print media cannot service small-scale or private local commerce such as used cars for sale, apartments for rent and help wanted personals. The broadcast media, despite the appearance of local cable real estate channels, cannot accommodate classified advertising. The new computer-based interactive communication technologies, however, are tailor-made for classified advertising.

A family in Toronto moving to Calgary will be able to browse the Calgary real estate listings at a distance, finding not merely descriptions of the homes on offer but images of them, both inside and out. Search functions will allow the buyer to restrict browsing to designated areas, or to homes of a particular age, or with select features, or within a certain price range — or any combination thereof. The specialty automotive customer will be able to connect with the specialty supplier. If one should need a fuel pump for a 1972 E-type Jaguar, a data-base search could presumably locate everyone in the city, the country or the continent with such an item to sell. The prospect of electronic advertising creates an entirely new marketing genre: classifieds that are simultaneously local and global in their reach.

There has already been movement in this direction. A Victoria-based company named JCI Technologies has created a national on-line employment service, listing more than 20,000 resumes and 4,000 jobs, which some 2,000 employers have used. Its plan is to offer auto and real estate advertising as well. For $3.6 million, *The Toronto Star* has purchased 27 per cent of JCI's subsidiary, Jobs Canada, with an option to buy another 12 per cent. The company is one of the first content providers on the Microsoft Network, the planned global online web, and it intends to establish itself on other online services.

As yet, online networks pose no appreciable threat to newspapers. But as the market penetration of cyberspace increases, the newspaper's high-end classified advertisers will almost certainly desert. And if the provision of classified advertising can be visibly severed from newsprint, its traditional medium of delivery, newspaper publishing will experience a seismic economic tremor.

Technological, Cultural and Other Issues

When information can be flashed electronically and instantaneously — perhaps more importantly, when the cost of doing so can be passed on to the consumer — the daily physical manufacture of newspapers seems mechanically unwieldy, insanely expensive, hideously wasteful and clearly obsolescent. Almost every newspaper has scrambled to assure its readers that its product includes recycled paper, but this assurance is a holding action at best. Because newspapers are made from wood pulp, they are in collusion with the forestry industry. And when chainsaws and waste are both political crimes, the newspaper is doubly guilty, because the multi-section embrace of the standard broadsheet means that everyone reads part of the paper, but no one reads it cover to cover. On recycling day, entire neighbourhoods lug their bundles of largely unread newsprint to the curb.

The environmental sins of newspaper publishing aside, the medium of newsprint means the industry is hostage to the suppliers of paper at a time when the cost of newsprint has been rising precipitously. From 1994 to 1995, the price of newspapers' raw material jumped 54 per cent, an increase cited as a major factor in the death of the 110-year-old Houston Post. Papers such as *The Ottawa Citizen* have trimmed the size of their pages so as to reduce the consumption of newsprint. The *Citizen* estimates it will save $1 million a year in this way, but there is something disconcerting about a newspaper whittling down its own physical incarnation out of economic necessity. The *reductio ad absurdum* is a newspaper that does away with newsprint entirely. Such a prospect is no longer so absurd. In the meantime, however, the newspaper industry is stuck with the present arrangement.

Readership among Young People

By the late 1980s and early 1990s, then, the mood within the newspaper industry was one of acute anxiety, if not outright panic. The schools of journalism at Carleton University and Ryerson both hosted conferences devoted specifically to the future of newspapers, and the topic was a recurring obsession whenever newspaper executives or editors were called upon to deliver speeches on the state of their industry. Although insiders uniformly insisted that newspapers would remain vibrant well into the multimedia future, the proclamations rang hollow, if only because they presented no clearly articulated vision for such a future, and the measures papers actually took to address their difficulties were stop gaps, uninspiring or outright failures.

For example, despite assurances by industry organizations such as the NMB that readership among young people was actually increasing, the industry itself clearly thought otherwise. It openly worried that young people were not only not reading papers, but might never acquire the newspaper habit. Traditional industry wisdom held that as young people grew older, launched careers, started families and assumed mortgages, they would turn to newspapers as an essential source of intelligence about the political and economic world. They would need to know how their tax money was being spent and how their investments were performing, and the newspaper would be there to serve that need. But by the late 1980s, the industry began to fret over the rise of aliteracy — the appearance of a generation that knew how to read but chose not to, that found its information and entertainment elsewhere.

Some studies seemed to confirm the industry's worst suspicions. Barnhurst and Wartella (1991), for example, surveyed 164 American undergraduates and found a pattern to young people's experience of the newspaper. Their earliest memories of the medium were not as a compendium of information, but as an implement used to swat the dog or as material used to line the bird cage or create papier maché. Inasmuch as the students remembered the newspaper in their childhood being read as a source of information, it was often an object of frustration. "From an early age students resented that their parents spent time with the newspaper, rather than paying attention to them" (1991: 199).

As the students entered school years, they were coerced by parents and teachers to pay attention to papers, often in the form of school assignments. Most were simply annoyed by the pressure. The only direct connections with the newspaper that truly registered were either when one's own name or picture appeared in its pages, or in the extra income that came from maintaining a paper route (a connection now increasingly lost as papers switch to adult carriers). By the time they had entered young adulthood, the students were generally aware that the world around them considered it important to read newspapers, and some had adopted the habit in a near-religious conversion, but many persisted in the belief that "the newspaper was not important to them or their current lives" (1991: 204).

This sort of testimony is important because it has had a direct influence on how newspapers have attempted to cater to a reluctant market. The competition with other media (in particular television), the complaints of readers that they do not have the time to devote to the voluminous contents of the paper, and the growing recognition that the readers of tomorrow may turn out to be a lost generation — all of these have combined to drive newspapers in an erratic course. On the one hand, there is the pressure to provide what television cannot, namely depth, context, analysis and sober second thought. This is a strategy that clearly works for an elite paper such as *The Globe and Mail*. In an omnibus paper, dense, lengthy articles may repel as many readers as they attract. On the other hand, as Barnhurst and Wartella point out:

> when newspaper executives have acknowledged that young adults seem uninterested in "hard" news and prefer comics and "soft" news, they have tended to use soft news in an effort to make the "hard" news more palatable ... [This] is a purely cosmetic solution. The pattern can be seen not only in the addition of soft features and children's "mini-pages" that are mostly fluff, but also in the move toward newspaper designs that are decorative and superficially attractive, mimicking television, which is a prime source of entertainment (1991: 208).

The embodiment of this trend is the American national newspaper *USA Today*, but many Canadian papers have tried a similar tack. The result has been a flurry of design and redesign in the Canadian newspaper industry, as titles tinker with their "look" in an effort to make the act of reading as undemanding as possible. Still, none of these initiatives has solved the problem. Young people greet the addition of pages or sections addressed specifically to them as groaningly patronizing. Traditional subscribers find a newspaper that has been dumbed down for younger or lazy readers irritating and insulting. And for all the effort expended on redesigning layout and format, the basic presentation of the newspaper has not changed in half a century. There is more colour and white space in today's newspapers, along with more graphic variety — and certainly, the product's aesthetic dimensions should not be overlooked — but most of the industry's design innovations have been at the level of fad and frippery. By 1995, in the same speech in which he vowed "to make newspapers more interesting," Southam president Bill Ardell conceded that "efforts to attract younger readers — in the 18 to mid-twenties range — had been a waste of time and had succeeded only in alienating the older (over 35) core of loyal readers" (Cobb, 1995).

Downsizing

Apart from hand-wringing over what the newspaper should contain and how it should be presented, over the past decade the industry's core strategy to maintain profitability has been to reduce expenditures. It has done so principally by shedding employees. First, it has invested in a range of new technologies, from computer pagination to digital cameras, which do away with the need for production personnel. Second, it has reduced the size of the editorial staff through steady attrition, early retirement incentives and outright layoffs. If there is a single characteristic that has marked the conduct of the newspaper industry behind the scenes over the past 10 years, it is this relentless downsizing.

It has not come easily or without consequence. The blue-collar employees are essential to the production of newspapers and therefore they have strong unions. At the 1993 conference of the Canadian Association of Journalists, Russ Mills, publisher of *The Ottawa Citizen* and a former vice-president of Southam, explained that "in the composing room of Pacific Press [the Southam subsidiary that publishes both the *Vancouver Sun* and the *Vancouver Province*] there are 170 people who have lifetime job guarantees ... The pressmen have manning agreements. The mailers have manning agreements. We can't touch those areas." The result has been a series of delicate industry-wide negotiations with unions to reduce newspapers' production expenses.

Editorial employees are less protected than their colleagues in production. At times it seems the only people not strictly essential to newspaper production are the journalists. If management has the support of the blue-collar infrastructure, a skeleton editorial crew with access to the wire services can keep a newspaper alive for months. Its basic commerce — movie listings, stock reports, sports scores, classified ads — is quite unaffected by the walkout or lockout of every reporter on the payroll. Hence, the editorial guilds have had little leverage with which to resist cuts in newsroom staff.

But however good for the ledger in the short run, this constant downsizing is ultimately harmful. First, fewer reporters means less robust local coverage when local coverage is key to a parochial press. Second, the combination of hiring freezes, layoffs, job insecurity and increased workloads has demoralized the newsrooms of the nation. In the 1970s, the complaint about the composition of newsroom staff was the lack of seasoned experience: those in their forties deserted the ranks of newspaper journalism for less stressful and more lucrative positions in public relations and elsewhere, leaving newspapers to be written by those in their twenties and edited by those in their thirties. By the mid-1990s, the complaint had been reversed: newsrooms were too old, not too young. Journalists lacked vitality, curiosity and enthusiasm for the job. In 1995, a conference of Canadian managing editors was told that fewer young journalists were even applying to work at newspapers, in part because their student-internship experiences had taught them that print newsrooms were unpleasant, dispirited places to work.

The Alternative Weeklies

This situation is all the more telling when one considers that across Canada the daily papers have been recently joined by a new, alternative genre of newsprint weekly that defines itself in opposition to the mainstream product by catering unselfconsciously to a younger demographic. As yet, these counter-publications — typically distributed free of charge — are no challenge to the big dailies, but they serve a niche market that the newspaper chains overlooked, and their flamboyance only serves to underscore the grey sobriety of the omnibus broadsheets.

They appeared first in the downtown cores of the bigger cities — Toronto, Vancouver and Montreal — where the resolutely vanilla personality of the big dailies was ill-suited to both bohemian and gentrified neighbourhoods alike. If nothing else unites yuppies and night owls, it is distaste for the homogeneity of franchise culture. Hence the success of Toronto's *NOW*. A weekly tabloid modelled on New York's *Village Voice*, it covers city politics with all the vigour of *The Toronto Star*, but with an unabashed political rambunction that no deadpan-objective omnibus paper would dare.

Its real preserve, however, is the local scene — bands, club life, repertory cinemas, theatre, novelists, poets, film-makers, media culture and weirdos. It not only gorges on ads for bars, concerts and performances, but it ensures that there *is* a local scene by publicizing it. It is also sufficiently anti-establishment to accept pages of advertising devoted to the sex trade. And while the broadsheets struggle unsuccessfully to reinvent the voice in which they write, *NOW* and its counterparts cheerfully explode the standard conventions of reportage with prose that is by turns glib, argumentative and idiosyncratic, writing not simply about gays, lesbians, computer geeks, the underclass and ethnic minorities, but *from the various points of view* of these disparate subcultural groups.

The big dailies ignored upstarts such as *NOW* until it became obvious they were raking in advertising revenue. In 1991, *The Toronto Star* tried to elbow its way into *NOW*'s territory with its own equivalent, *eye weekly*, but having surrendered the initial advantage, the *Star*'s offering is tainted as a knock-off of the genuine article. In any event, its target constituencies of honeycombed subcultures have little in common beyond disdain for the mainstream middle-class sensibilities of *eye weekly*'s corporate master.

A Regulated Future?

The newspaper industry is thus apparently boxed in by its circumstances. Its livelihood is founded on the dry objectivity of its reporting, but this objectivity only serves to make it a relatively colourless cultural form. It is seen as increasingly irrelevant by younger readers, but cannot alter its contents and format without alienating its older readers. It is necessarily packaged as a paper product, but this saddles it with hugely expensive production and distribution costs.

Inevitably, then, the newspaper companies are eyeing emerging interactive networked communication technologies as a new means of distributing their wares and services. In 1995, Rupert Murdoch of News Corp. announced that all the newspapers in his international stable would be published electronically within a couple of years (Reuters, 1995). The same month, as part of a move to reposition the company as a "marketing and communications" conglomerate, Thomson declared its intention to sell 21 of its smaller Canadian newspapers, 14 of them dailies (most of which were shortly purchased by Conrad Black). At the same time, citing fears that time was running out for newspaper companies to establish themselves in cyberspace, Thomson created a new media ventures group within its newspaper division to market electronic-based products (Mahood, 1995). Southam has been pursuing similar initiatives, including creating a multimedia research unit in Hamilton, Ont. Quebecor has also launched a subsidiary, Quebecor Multimedia. Every newspaper in

North America of any size and foresight has been scrambling to create an online version of itself.

However, the newspaper industry faces a number of difficulties in the transition to electronic publishing. First, in the immediate term, online interactive editions will merely establish an outpost in cyberspace; they will not replace the newsprint versions of newspapers. Second, it is not clear how advertising is to be conjoined to an electronic news service so that it can subsidize the considerable expense of a professional editorial operation. Third, the shift to online distribution may mean that newspaper companies will become vulnerable to corporate takeover by the multimedia conglomerates that actually own the distribution networks of cyberspace. The corporations that are building the information highway are the cable companies, the telecommunication companies and the computer giants. All of these are looking to link their infrastructural holdings with companies that can provide information and entertainment services to be marketed over the wires. The newspaper industry may therefore offer an attractive acquisition target. The question is whether in the multimedia future the newspaper companies will become players or pawns.

In effect, the Canadian newspaper industry has been hindered in its ability to position itself for the future by its actions in the past. When the Kent Commission sounded an alarm over concentration of ownership and ultimately recommended restrictions on newspaper chain expansion, the legacy was a climate in which newspaper companies were discouraged from vigorously pursuing cross-media ownership. So, in the early 1990s, when other media concerns were buying one another, merging and forming strategic alliances under the banner of "technological convergence," the newspaper industry sat on the sidelines. In 1994, it was a cable company that purchased a well-established newspaper group, not the reverse. When Ted Rogers acquired Maclean Hunter, he bought not simply a rival cable concern, but *The Financial Post*, *Maclean's* magazine and the *Sun* chain of newspapers.

This prompted an unusual response from the newspaper industry: an appeal to the state for competitive protection. In February 1995, the Canadian Daily Newspaper Association (CDNA) asked that cabinet and the CRTC overturn the decision to allow Rogers' takeover of Maclean Hunter. What the association really wanted, however, was a policing mechanism that would prevent Ted Rogers from favouring his own online services over his competitors'. The worry was that Rogers was in a position to use his ownership of the distribution networks to promote the electronic versions of his newspaper and magazine titles, at the expense of those being developed by Southam, Thomson and the other newspaper companies.

The intervention by the CDNA is understandable, but it marks a radical break with what has been a basic tenet of newspaper publishing in liberal democracies: that the state should have no authority to rule on the affairs of the press. It amounts to a plea for regulatory protection, and it points to a policy issue looming on the horizon. Once newspapers are available electronically, will they not have to submit to the regulatory authority of an agency such as the CRTC? If that happens, a fundamental change will have occurred and newspaper publishing may never be the same.

Notes

1. As this chapter goes to press, the newspaper industry has entered into a moment of volatility. The Thomson chain placed a number of titles on the market, some of which were purchased by Conrad Black's Hollinger, which has also agreed in principle to buy many of the others. Black also purchased the dailies in Regina and Saskatoon from the Sifton family. The cash-strapped Rogers corporation announced it was looking to sell the Sun chain of papers. And in late May 1996, Conrad Black purchased Paul Desmarais' shares in Southam, giving him 41 per cent of the company and making him the single largest shareholder. Together, these moves prompted a chorus of concern about concentration of media ownership, most of it directed at Conrad Black.

References

Barnhurst, Kevin G. and Ellen Wartella. 1991. "Newspapers and Citizenship: Young Adults' Subjective Experience of Newspapers." *Critical Studies in Mass Communication*, Vol. 8, No. 1.

Canada. Royal Commission on Newspapers. 1981. *Report*. Ottawa: Minister of Supply and Services.

Cobb, Chris. 1995. "Southam boss vows to make newspapers more interesting." *The Ottawa Citizen*, March 12.

Connor, Steven. 1989. *Postmodernist Culture: An Introduction to Theories of the Contemporary*. Oxford: Basil Blackwell.

Dornan, Christopher. 1993. "Citizen Black: A Field Manual." *Media Information Australia*, No. 68, May.

Farrell, Mark with Tim Creery. Forthcoming. *My Adventures in Print*. Ottawa: Carleton University Press.

Fetherling, Douglas. 1990. *The Rise of the Canadian Newspaper*. Toronto: Oxford University Press.

Goldenberg, Susan. 1984. *The Thomson Empire*. New York: Beaufort Books.

Hayes, David. 1992. *Power and Influence: The Globe and Mail and the News Revolution*. Toronto: Key Porter.

James Capel Canada Inc. 1995. *Notes to clients*. September 15.

Kesterton, Wilfred and Roger Bird. 1995. "The Press in Canada: A Historical Overview." In Benjamin D. Singer (ed.). *Communications in Canadian Society*. Third ed. Scarborough: Nelson Canada.

Kesterton, W.H. 1967. *A History of Journalism in Canada*. Toronto: The Carleton Library, McClelland and Stewart.

Kubas Consultants. 1994a. "Special Report on Newspaper Advertising and Marketing/Communication Trends: Newspapers in the '90s: Looking Ahead." April.

———. 1994b. "An Analysis of New Wave Retailers and their Potential Impact on the Canadian Marketplace." April.

Mahood, Casey. 1995. "Thomson zooming on to info highway." *The Globe and Mail*, Report on Business, May 20.

Mattelart, Armand and Michele Mattelart. 1992. *Rethinking Media Theory: Signposts and New Directions*. Minneapolis: University of Minnesota Press.

McNish, Jacquie. 1993. "Thomson CEO vows to mend newspapers." *The Globe and Mail*, Report on Business, May 12.

Miller, James. 1994. "Newspapers into Databases? A Critical Research Agenda for Newspapers of the Future." Paper presented to the Carleton University Media and Communication Research Centre.

Newspaper Marketing Bureau, Inc. 1995. *Canadian Daily Newspapers: Key Facts 1995*.

———. 1995. NADbank survey '84–'94.

Reuters. 1995. "Murdoch begs for paper." *The Globe and Mail*, Report on Business, May 20.

Rutherford, Paul. 1978. *The Making of the Canadian Media*. Toronto: McGraw-Hill Ryerson.

Schudson, Michael. 1978. *Discovering the News: A Social History of American Newspapers*. New York: Basic Books.

Smith, Anthony. 1980. *Goodbye Gutenberg: The Newspaper Revolution of the 1980s*. Oxford: Oxford University Press.

Smith, Anthony. 1979. *The Newspaper: An International History*. London: Thames and Hudson.

Vipond, Mary. 1992. *The Mass Media in Canada*. 2nd ed. Toronto: James Lorimer.

Part Two

Sound Industries

4

Sound Recording

Will Straw[1]

Introduction

In February 1994, the U.S.-based music trade magazine *Billboard* ran the front-page headline: "Oh Canada! One Nation Under a Groove" (*Billboard*, 1994a). The article that followed documented the international visibility and success of Canadian music within the global sound-recording industry. This success was evident at a number of levels: in the high international record sales registered by such Canadian performers as Snow, Céline Dion or the Crash Test Dummies; in the interest shown by multinational record firms in signing Canadian performers; and in the domestic success which the Canadian subsidiaries of multinational firms experienced with such recording artists as the Barenaked Ladies and Blue Rodeo. In September of the same year, a new album by the Tragically Hip sold an impressive (for a Canadian band) 200,000 copies in its first four days of release (*Billboard*, 1994f).

Over the next year, these signs of triumph would find confirmation in more convincing statistical form. In 1995, Statistics Canada reported that the market share held by recordings with Canadian content (as defined by the Canadian Radio-television and Telecommunications Commission) had risen from 8 per cent to 13 per cent of total industry sales over the previous five years. A more widely circulated statistic showed the dollar value of sales of Canadian-content recordings as having almost tripled over the same period, going from $36.7 million in 1989–90 to $92.7 million in 1993–94. This growth reflected a more general expansion of sales for the industry. Over the reporting year 1993–94, the dollar value of all sound recordings sold in Canada had grown at an annual rate of 16.5 per cent, reaching a 10-year high of $738 million (Statistics Canada, 1995).

This rosy economic news seemed to legitimize the more general good feeling that surrounded the international recording industry in the mid-1990s. Wandering through the cavernous space of the contemporary record superstore (a structure which scarcely existed a decade ago), one is struck by the abundance of materials from all periods and places, by the sense that the industry is much less reliant than in the past on a limited number of contemporary hits (Straw, 1994). Performers appear to reach the top of popularity charts without obvious signs of compromise or stylistic dilution. Pearl Jam, Nine Inch Nails, Green Day and Offspring have all emerged from relatively marginal audience bases to sell several million copies in North America. The top-ten lists in trade magazines contain fewer and fewer groups with a broad appeal, and the phrase "mainstream rock" now has little meaning. Rather, as one reads down a best-seller chart, one moves from one purist taste to another, from gangster rap to country music to industrial noise. None of these records sell like the blockbusters of a decade ago, but the spreading of sales across a much wider range of titles seems to indicate a welcome pluralism.

During this same period, however, two major Canadian record store chains — A&A and Discus — folded, victims of a new retail environment increasingly dominated by multinational and highly capitalized superstores. As tariffs on imported sound recordings moved towards the point of total elimination — an effect of the Free Trade Agreement with the U.S. — some worried that distribution would now follow north-south corridors reaching into the U.S., rather than the east-west pathways that had always assured a certain distinctiveness for the Canadian market (*Billboard*, 1985). Finally, since no musical style, apparently, was too marginal or underground for major multinational firms, the fate of small, Canadian-owned firms that had long nurtured those styles seemed uncertain. In 1993, musicians spoke excitedly of the major-label representatives who were combing the bars of Halifax in search of new alternative rock groups to sign. However, Canadian independent record companies complained they could no longer compete with the advances and worldwide release plans offered by the majors, and their own place within the Canadian industry had become even more fragile (see *Billboard*, [1994b]).

Amidst these contradictory tendencies, the sorts of things traditionally said about sound recording and music in Canada have lost much of their pertinence. Cultural nationalists who, for decades, called on large record companies to take an interest in Canadian music now find them actively doing so, with possibly devastating effects on the domestic recording industry. In 1991, for example, the Dream Warriors, Jane Siberry, the Jeff Healey Band, Kon Kan, Myles Goodwyn, the Tragically Hip, Maestro Fresh-Wes and k. d. lang all signed directly with the U.S. offices of major record companies, throwing the long-term usefulness of their Canadian subsidiaries into doubt (*Billboard*, [1991a]).

Market Analysis

Claims about the distinctiveness of Canadian musical tastes are often difficult to verify because of the prevalence of stereotypes of regional cultural identity. In 1959, *The Financial Post* reported the results of a survey showing that Maritimers have a greater per capita penchant for western music than any other Canadians, while British Columbians favour the classics (De Norber, 1959). More recently we were told that Francophone residents of Quebec buy disproportionate amounts of classical music and are among the world's most avid consumers of European-derived progressive rock (*Billboard*, 1975, 1977). In 1995, *La Presse* reported on the apparent lack of interest of Toronto-based record companies in rock groups working in Montreal and tied this to a general perception that Quebec musical culture is dominated by light pop (*La Presse*, 1995). Writing on Canadian music in the New York *Village Voice*, and referring to a tradition that runs from Joni Mitchell through Jane Siberry, Katherine Dieckman suggested that "moody girl singers grow on trees up there" (Dieckman, 1994).

Well-entrenched beliefs about the specificities of Canadian musical taste have long been used to justify the failure of record companies to sign (and radio stations to play) African-American musical forms, despite evidence that shifting population patterns have transformed the cartography of national tastes. Toronto, for example, has been ranked among the world's largest markets for reggae music; Montreal, during the 1970s, was considered the second-largest North American market for rhythm-and-blues-based disco music (*Billboard*, 1979). Specialty magazines in Britain and the U.S. have regularly commented on the liveliness of the hip-hop or Indo-American pop scenes in Canadian cities (see Fletcher [1991]). The invisibility of these forms and their audiences in studies or general perceptions of Canadian music has much to do with the small-scale,

Table 4-1
Revenue from the Sale of Recordings, by Origin of the Master Tape, 1988–89 to 1992–93 (in millions of $)

	1988–89	1989–90	1990–91	1991–92	1992–93
Produced by reporting organization	19.6	31.2	41.3	46.7	53.6
Leased from production company in Canada	65.3	47.2	51.2	55.3	65.0
Leased from production company in another country	307.5	369.8	406.5	408.8	518.7
Unspecified	8.4	8.2	9.8	12.8	4.7
Total	400.8	454.3	508.7	597.7	642.0

Source: Statistics Canada, 1994b.

parallel industrial circuits that sustain them. However, it also reflects the persistence of models which treat music as folk culture and privilege forms with long historical pedigrees.

It is clear, nevertheless, that sound recordings bought in Canada are overwhelmingly of non-Canadian origin. Table 4-1 shows the relationship between record sales and the country of origin of the master tapes from which recordings are actually made. This is more revealing than citing the country of origin of finished sound recordings since — for reasons to be explained later — the domination of the Canadian industry by non-Canadian repertory is achieved through subsidiary branches operating in Canada rather than through the import of finished commodities. In 1992–93, sound recordings pressed in Canada, but based on master tapes imported from elsewhere, accounted for 80.8 per cent of total industry revenues.

In Statistics Canada's breakdown of sales by musical genre, the broadly defined category of Top 40/rock disco accounted for more than half of the total revenues from sound recordings in Canada

Table 4-2
Revenue from the Sale of Recordings by Musical Category, 1992–93

	In Millions of Dollars	% of Sales
Adult-oriented popular music	114.9	17.89
Top 40/rock disco	344.5	53.66
Classical and related	64.9	10.1
Jazz	19.7	3.06
Country and Folk	44.6	6.94
Children's	17.9	2.78
Other (including "unspecified")	35.6	5.54
Total:	642.0	99.97

Source: Statistics Canada, 1994b; percentages calculated by the author (percentages total less than 100% due to rounding).

during the year 1992–93 (the last period for which breakdowns of this sort were made public) (Table 4-2).

A cursory examination of the number of new titles released within each category and of the degree to which these releases were considered Canadian content (Table 4-3) suggests some reasons for the strength of non-Canadian repertory in Canada. The percentage of titles with Canadian content classed as Top 40/rock disco is significantly less than the weight this category carries in overall record sales (26.75 per cent versus 53.66 per cent). Categories in which there are large numbers of titles with Canadian content (such as the amorphous Other) are relatively unimportant in terms of sales (23.77 per cent vs 2.78 per cent). Canadian production of sound recordings, we might conclude, is less oriented than non-Canadian production towards high-selling categories.

The introduction of the compact disc, in 1983, has had important effects on the markets for recorded sound. By contributing to the elimination of vinyl records, the CD divided the market into a high end (dominated by the CD) and low end (in which cassettes continue to dominate) (for one account of this division, see Frith [1988]). In

Table 4-3
New Releases by Genre as a Percentage of
Total New Releases

	% of New Releases with Canadian Content	% of New Releases without Canadian Content
Adult-oriented popular music	13.81	11.74
Top 40/rock disco	26.75	35.22
Classical and related	9.21	23.97
Jazz	4.90	5.7
Country and Folk	16.93	8.51
Children's	4.60	2.14
Other (including "unspecified")	23.77	12.70

Source: Statistics Canada, 1994b; percentages calculated by the author (percentages total less than 100% due to rounding).

1993, only 33 per cent of Canadian households had a CD player, while 74 per cent had an audio cassette player. Nevertheless, in 1992–93, compact discs accounted for 62 per cent of all revenues from recorded music in Canada, suggesting that a relatively small percentage of the population is spending a great deal of money on this format (Statistics Canada, 1994a).

Just as important, perhaps, the introduction of the CD into Canada hastened the virtual elimination of the single. As the production of vinyl singles came to an end, neither the cassette single nor the CD-single replaced it to the extent they had in other countries. In Canada, CD-singles were, until very recently, priced at $8 or $9 — a level perceived by consumers as excessively high — and record companies operating in Canada have generally failed to market the single as a legitimate recording format. (In 1994, PolyGram announced a line of CD-singles at a retail price of $3.99, a move intended to jump-start the flagging CD single [*Billboard*, 1994c]). Revenues from cassette and CD-singles in Canada totalled $5.9 million in 1992–1993, compared to $396.8 million for CD albums and

$236.9 million for full-length cassettes. Vinyl albums, during the same period, accounted for $2.2 million (Statistics Canada, 1994b).

The decline of singles, traditionally purchased by young adolescents, has gone hand in hand with a shift in buying patterns towards those musical forms associated with adult buyers, such as classical, jazz and what Statistics Canada conventionally calls "adult-oriented popular music." While sales of country music remained relatively stagnant between 1988 and 1993, and those of Top 40/rock disco increased 30 per cent, revenues from the sale of adult-oriented, classical and jazz recordings more than doubled over the same period (Statistics Canada, 1994b). The disappearance of singles has, however, strengthened one sector of the recording industry in which Canada has traditionally done well — the production and marketing of compilation albums, often through television advertisements. Declining production and distribution of dance-music singles in Canada has led such companies as Quality and Nu Musik to regularly collect recent dance-music tracks on compilation albums, serving a national market for dance music that is seen to be more responsive and more discriminating than that in the United States (*Billboard*, 1994e).

Industry Structure

Like most cultural industries, the sound-recording industry may be divided, provisionally, into three phases: the production, distribution and exhibition or retailing of commodities. The extent to which these activities have been controlled by single firms has varied historically. In the sound-recording industry, there are few cases of firms achieving — or even seeking — the total integration of all three. (Even the Virgin retail chain has cut all ties with the record label of the same name.) In Canada, differences among these phases reflect the extent to which each has been under Canadian control. Record retailing, marked until recently by small-scale specialty retail outlets and general merchandise stores, has historically shown higher levels of Canadian ownership than record distribution. In record production, there are, at any given moment, hundreds of Canadian-owned recording companies actively involved in signing performers and producing master tapes. Combined, however, Canadian-owned firms accounted for only 22.8 per cent of the newly released titles and 20.3 per cent of total industry revenues in 1992–1993 (Statistics Canada, 1994b).

It is as a result of changes in the nature and ownership of record distribution that the Canadian sound-recording industry has acquired its distinctive present-day structure. In the United States and Canada, the distribution of records was a relatively chaotic, regionally differentiated activity until the late 1960s, when consolidation was undertaken by so-called major, multinational record companies. The result was what has come to be known as the branch distribution system. Beginning in the United States, major recording firms set up distribution branches: fully owned operations that could deliver records to stores coast to coast. These structures were partly the effect of a wave of record company mergers in the 1960s, but the integration of distribution activities fuelled even more industry concentration. With branch distribution in place, large recording firms (e.g., Warner Brothers, Columbia Records) found their own output was not sufficient for steady and profitable operations. They sought affiliation agreements with smaller labels, whose product they would distribute, or bought up independent labels to ensure a steady stream of titles. Over time, to be a major record company meant having a national distribution system, even if the product came more and more from outside or subsidiary sources.

In Canada, beginning in the late 1960s, major multinational firms undertook the same consolidation of national distribution. The existence of Canadian subsidiaries of the major multinationals — of Warner Brothers, Columbia, RCA, PolyGram, MCA and Capitol — mirrors an international pattern; these firms have set up national branches and manufacturing plants in many countries. That they do so — rather than simply import records pressed elsewhere — has often been ascribed to a desire to keep a finger on the pulse of national markets, the better to gauge the distinctiveness of national tastes and sign emerging performers (Garofalo, 1993). In Canada, however, the existence of branch plants is more directly the result of tariffs on imported recordings — tariffs that have fluctuated from 10 to 15 per cent, but stood at 14 per cent in the mid-1980s, before the signing of the Free Trade Agreement with the U.S.

Tariffs at this level were sufficient to discourage the direct import of manufactured records from the United States and led, over several decades, to the establishment of Canadian subsidiaries for virtually all multinational firms. By the mid-1970s, most such firms had developed coast-to-coast distribution networks. Having done so, they possessed distribution facilities which few, if any, Canadian-owned companies could match

I have described elsewhere how the Canadian-owned sector of the sound-recording industry was transformed in the early 1970s (Straw, 1993). Before then, Canadian-owned record companies developed out of the distribution or manufacturing sectors of the industry and moved backwards from these activities into signing artists and producing master tapes. As multinational firms increased their control over distribution and, to a lesser extent, record manufacturing, most of the Canadian record companies that had begun in this way lost their primary sources of revenue. (Quality Records, which began as a record manufacturer in 1950 and expanded into distribution and record production, was one of the few to survive this restructuring, but was forced to redefine its role in order to do so.) By the mid-1970s, the more common pattern in Canada was one in which record companies were launched by talent managers and booking agencies, as entities engaged principally in the production of master tapes. Attic, Aquarius, True North and dozens of other firms came into existence. The principal assets of these firms were rosters of performers rather than pressing plants or distribution networks.

The industrial structure that took shape during this period persists today. In its functioning — and in its contradictions — one may see, condensed, the familiar thematic of Canadian history and cultural development. A coast-to-coast distribution system has served to construct a national musical culture even as the building of this structure has consolidated the hold of foreign-owned firms on the Canadian market. In the drive to maximize this structure's profit-making potential, nevertheless, multinational firms have turned to Canadian entrepreneurs for products to distribute, contributing to the growth of a Canadian-owned recording industry and the popularization of Canadian music. At a time when the Canadian subsidiaries of multinational firms showed little interest in Canadian performers, domestic independents sought out and signed these performers. The risks frequently led to a firm's demise, but they also led to occasional success and a certain prosperity. (In 1994, for example, Attic Records celebrated its twentieth anniversary, claiming that it had generated $110 million in revenues since its inception [*Billboard*, 1993]).

Over the last twenty years, multinational firms have signed many Canadian performers, but their involvement in Canadian music has more often been to distribute recordings and provide occasional capital funding for Canadian-owned recording companies. Over time, this structure adopted the contours of an informal but consistent division of labour, in which Canadian firms acted as artist-and-repertory operations — signing performers and producing master tapes — while multinational firms pressed records and distributed them to stores.

Changes in Industry Structure

This division of labour, however, has begun to wither in the 1990s. As foreign-controlled companies become more active seekers of Canadian talent, small Canadian-owned labels find that future uncertain. Some, as an executive of Intrepid Records suggested, might move from popular music into genres, such as classical music, where major-label interest in Canadian performers is weaker (*Billboard*, 1994b). As the markets for recorded music fragment, there are fewer and fewer niches left as the exclusive terrain of small independent firms. Indeed, major multinational firms have themselves come to rely on accumulating relatively small market segments in a number of territories rather than seeking to produce large-scale, blockbuster successes.

These changes have produced a curious mirroring in the international recording industry. As major firms construct global audiences from national niches, small independent firms that had hitherto dominated these niches in their own countries find their room to manoeuvre shrinking. To survive they, too, must move into international markets, licensing their own products in other territories, selling publishing and other rights on a country-by-country basis, and picking up the inventory of other small national labels for distribution. Canadian labels such as Attic and Stoney Plain devote increasing attention to developing affiliations with labels in such countries as South Korea or Norway to release Canadian repertory or catalogue materials.

The growth of so-called custom-service companies in the recording industry may further jeopardize the long-term health of that strata of Canadian-owned labels that has dominated the domestic industry over the last two decades. Custom-service companies act as brokers for performers or small production companies, arranging for the mastering, pressing and, in many instances, distribution of sound recordings. In Canada, these include RDR Promotions and Sunrise Audio Duplication (*Billboard*, 1994d). The rise of custom brokers of this sort is part of the broader tendency towards do-it-yourself record production, a tendency nourished by the aesthetic principles professed by alternative rock culture and enabled by digital technologies. More and more, new rock bands are signed directly by multinational labels on the basis of a self-produced demo tape or recording rather than after a stint on an independent label.

Policy Structure

State policy has shaped the development of the Canadian recording industry principally through tariff laws. These laws stimulated the development of a national industry — albeit one dominated by the subsidiaries of multinational firms — and resulted in an elaborate coast-to-coast system of record distribution. The effects of eliminating these tariffs, because of free trade agreements, are as yet barely perceptible. (The lowering of tariffs on cultural commodities is worth recalling, nonetheless, whenever it is claimed that culture was kept off the table in the FTA and NAFTA agreements.) It is clear, for example, that small-scale specialty distributors have increased their importation of foreign-produced records as a result of the reduced costs which have come with free trade (Kelly, 1991). At the same time, the multinational Thorne-EMI has announced the building of a compact-disc manufacturing plant in Canada, suggesting that the predicted transfer of manufacturing activity to the United States is not imminent.

The best known instance of public policy designed to stimulate sound-recording production in Canada involves radio. Throughout the 1960s, concerns about the fate of Canadian music led to pressure on the federal government to compel radio broadcasters to play more Canadian music. Walter Greely, publisher of the trade magazine *RPM*, was influential in mobilizing pressure for Canadian-content regulations for radio. These regulations were implemented in 1971, as a condition of licence for radio stations. They resolved the thorny question of defining Canadian content by instituting a point system whereby points were awarded for the involvement of Canadians in the composing, performing and production of musical selections.

These regulations are not the concern of this article. What needs to be acknowledged, however, is the widespread (and, indeed, international) perception that they have been successful, perhaps one of the most genuinely effective instances of activist cultural policy in Canadian history. At the same time, however, in their use of one industry to transform another, they are emblematic of the unequal relationship of different industries operating within Canada to public control and influence.

By the end of the 1970s, Canadian-content regulations were the source of regular tensions between the radio and recording industries. Radio stations complained increasingly that record companies were not releasing titles in sufficient quantity for them to meet the requirements and that too many titles did not meet international standards of sound quality or aesthetic achievement (*Billboard*, 1982). More generally, pressure was building for direct government support of the recording industry itself, following the model of programs initiated to support the film and television industries.

A federal program for the sound-recording industry came as the culmination of a series of events originating in one of the lesser-known regulations imposed by the CRTC on broadcasters. As a condition of licence, radio stations are required to demonstrate support for local musical talent, support that has historically been more gestural than genuine. In 1982, CHUM Limited, Moffat Communications, Rogers Broadcasting Limited, CIRPA (The Canadian Independent Record Producers Association) and CMPA (The Canadian Music Publishers Association) together created FACTOR, the Fund to Assist Canadian Talent on Record. (FACTOR's francophone equivalent is Musicaction.) FACTOR became a channel through which radio broadcasters could channel money to the Canadian music industry. A jury system was established to evaluate applications, and funding was given to produce demo tapes, organize promotional tours, make promotional video clips and a variety of other activities.

FACTOR has proven highly effective. In 1986, when the federal government began to direct funds to the sound-recording industry, it used FACTOR's disbursement structures rather than establishing its own. The Sound Recording Development Program began by contributing $5 million annually to FACTOR, maintained this over several years and reduced the amount only slightly in the 1995 federal budget. A legacy of the Tory government's emphasis on the cultural industries as agents of economic development, the SRDP remains a unique example of collaboration between the private and public sectors. It has been particularly successful in spurring the revival of French-language music within Quebec since the early 1980s. (Forty per cent of the funds available to FACTOR/Musicaction are given to French-language production.)

Technological and Cultural Issues

The sound recording industry in the mid-1990s has been shaped by the rise of the compact disc. In this process, one finds clear evidence for the claim that large firms in the cultural industries remain large, not through a comparative advantage in seeking out new talent or exploiting emergent trends, but in developing large back catalogues which, over time, stabilize revenues and reduce costs per title. One of the paradoxes of the sound-recording industry (and of the home video industry) is that its dependence on large inventories of physical commodities has grown just as predictions of the demise of the record as physical object have become more common. For a half-decade or more, players within the sound-recording and home video industries have considered and tested online delivery systems that would download titles onto blank carriers or home-based storage systems.

These systems have not yet moved beyond the experimental stage. As music files become available on the Internet, however, and as digital radio broadcasting moves towards implementation, there is a growing urgency to reform the legal regimes that govern the exploitation of artistic rights. Copyright reform, in Canada as elsewhere, is shaped by the growing perception, on the part of firms within the cultural industries, that their business is increasingly centered on the marketing of rights rather than tangible objects.

In the Canadian context, we may note several developments that testify to this shift in industry emphasis and strategy. The first is the negotiation of a new mechanical rate to determine payments to be made to composers for the sales of recordings. In 1988, in the first round of copyright reform in Canada for 64 years, the mechanical rate was raised from two cents per composition to a variable rate that rose with inflation, in regular increments, to reach 6.47 cents per composition in 1993. With the second phase of copyright reform seemingly imminent, attention has been focused on enshrining so-called neighbouring rights, which may include provisions for performers (and not composers exclusively) to be reimbursed for broadcasting and other uses of sound recordings. While the push for neighbouring rights is typically phrased in language that emphasizes artists' right to compensation, the principal effect of these rights would be to create revenue streams for record companies from airplay and other uses of their recordings. At present, record companies have access to these revenues only through their control of the publishing companies that share composer royalties. Digital radio, Internet-based delivery systems and the encoding of musical compositions in software and video games have all made copyright reform a major focus of record industry lobbying.

The North American Free Trade Agreement Implementation Act of 1994, which included amendments to Canada's Copyright Act, enshrined a so-called rental right, which granted the recording industry the ability to authorize or prohibit the rental of their products.

Acting on the industry's behalf, the Canadian Recording Industry Association (CRIA) and the Canadian Independent Record Production Association (CIRPA) decided not to authorize the rental of recordings from their member companies, a move which effectively put an end to the record rental business in Canada (Industry Canada, 1994). The principal impetus for the Canadian industry to bar record rentals has come from the U.S. recording industry, which, itself, has moved to block record rentals and pressured Canada to do so in the interests of harmonization.

Marketing and Distribution

Marketing

One of the distinctive features of the sound-recording industry is that it produces its own commodities and is the principal source of the content for another entertainment industry that uses these commodities, virtually free of charge. Since the postwar period, radio broadcasters have drawn on recorded music for their programming, initiating a relationship whose dynamic has helped to transform the culture of popular music. Inasmuch as they sell audiences, rather than sound recordings themselves, radio broadcasters often make use of music in ways that run counter to the objectives of record companies. In particular, radio stations have contributed to the fragmentation of musical markets and audiences by insisting on precise alignments of musical taste and demographic niche. More than other cultural industries, the record industry has relied on exposure through other media to stimulate sales of its products, rather than on direct advertising.

One effect of this interdependence is the vulnerability of record companies to shifts in the programming policies of radio stations. Since the late 1970s, as radio broadcasters have sought the older audiences deemed to be more attractive to advertisers, they have reduced the amount of music programming that is current. As a result, radio stations play a much-reduced role in the popularization of current record releases, recycling music whose familiarity was achieved years or decades earlier. (In many cases, this pursuit of older demographics has led radio broadcasters to cease playing music altogether; the development of all-news or talk radio has important implications for the marketing of music.)

Against this backdrop, the emergence of music video networks in the early 1980s assumes importance. When MuchMusic began operating in 1984, its effect on the marketing and consumption of music was immediately evident. MuchMusic offered a national outlet for new and current music in a country whose radio broadcasting has, for the most part, been local in scale. (The programming of the CBC, with some exceptions, has not been a significant force in influencing the sales of popular music recordings.) MuchMusic has lessened geographical differences in taste, both between regions of the country and between the city and small town. This has resulted in the dissemination of a relatively connoisseurist approach to music, of which the popularization of alternative rock in the 1990s is a striking example.

At the same time, MuchMusic has contributed to the embedding of music within complex layers of discourse *about* music, surrounding it with performer gossip, concert news and other information. These have played a clear role in the current success of Canadian performers. If the traditional weakness of English-Canadian music has much to do with its failure to develop the apparatus of celebrity (apparatus so evident in Francophone Quebec), music video networks have worked to remedy this. Their emergence runs contrary to the patterns of development of radio formats over the last decade, which have been based on the assumption that audiences will listen to music while having little interest in the culture which surrounds it.

Record Distribution

The structures by which sound recordings are distributed in Canada are an overlay of old and new forms of commerce. Distribution is dominated by the branch operations of major, multinational firms, whose strength rests on their ability to move product into specialty record stores coast to coast. In English Canada, at present, the principal distributors are all multinational majors, with ownership of diverse national origins, as Table 4-4 suggests.

Branch distribution coexists with other, older forms of record distribution. Rack-jobbers are firms that supply recordings to such non-specialty outlets as pharmacies or department stores, renting space for record racks, which the rack-jobber will monitor and replenish as required, in return for a portion of sales revenues. Rackjobbers have long been associated with distinct classes of product (such as deleted records, or country music cassettes sold in fuel stations), but much of their market share results from contracts with large department stores or general goods outlets. Their links to such outlets

Table 4-4
Ownership and Market Shares of Multinational Record Companies Operating in Canada, 1st Quarter 1995[2]

Sound Recording Distribution Companies (the "Majors")	Ownership	Market Share (1st quarter, 1995)
PolyGram	Philips (Holland)	19.9%
MCA	Seagram's (Canada)	19.1%
Warner Music	Time-Warner (US)	19.2%
EMI	Thorne-EMI (Great Britain)	12.4%
Sony Music	Sony (Japan)	11.8%
BMG/RCA	Bertelsmann (Germany)	8.2%

Source: *The Record*. 1995.

have contributed to a strong association between rackjobbing and those musical forms (such as easy-listening, instrumental music) directed at older buyers.

In Canada, the largest rackjobbing firm, Saturn Distributing, stocks the recording sections of the Zellers and Bay chains. In doing so, it reaches customers who may never visit a specialty record retail outlet and handles classes of product (such as budget classical or vocal music titles) often unavailable in record stores themselves. Another major rackjobber operating in Canada is the U.S.-based Handleman Company, whose Canadian division looks after the shelves of K-Mart, Sears, Eaton's and Canadian Tire, and whose historical link to the Wal-Mart chain has been perpetuated with the recent entry of that chain into the Canadian market.

An alternative form of distribution is supplied through one-stops, warehouse operations that make available a wide variety of titles from different companies to small retail stores. Cargo Records of Montreal, for example, offers a one-stop service to independent, alternative-rock-oriented outlets, importing small quantities of dozens of titles, which are frequently in formats (such as the seven-inch vinyl single) no longer handled by the Canadian subsidiaries of multinational firms. One-stops are likely to assume new importance as the international circulation of marginal musical forms and formats (such as the 12-inch vinyl dance single) nourishes distribution circuits and retail structures parallel to those of major multinational firms.

Record Retailing

The retailing of music in Canada at present shows evidence of several countervailing tendencies, each of them rife with lessons about the shifting social location of music and musical tastes. One of these is the resurgence of record clubs operating through the mails, of which BMG Music offers the best-known example. Designed to reach the older adult buyer, new or revamped record clubs signal a shift in emphasis — a shift which has much to do with the increased reliance of major firms on marketing their back catalogues. Like the television advertisements through which they are publicized, record clubs are founded on the assumption that the record buyer in the mid-1990s is much more casually involved in music than the typical buyer of a decade ago and that this buyer must be reached at home rather than in the space of the retail record store.

This space has itself changed over the last decade, as the architectural form of the superstore has superseded the small mall stores and mid-sized retail outlets that dominated record retailing in the 1970s and early 1980s. Record stores have grown in size to accommodate the wider range of titles now available, an expansion of choice that signals the reliance of record companies on reissues rather than current product alone. In a market increasingly organized around niche tastes, profitability at all levels of the sound-recording industry requires that firms service a wide range of markets. This, in turn, necessitates large and varied inventories, and the superstore has emerged to house this variety.

For the Canadian record retail industry, however, this has meant a major shake-up and a decline in domestic ownership. When the A&A and Discus chains, both of them longtime players in the Canadian retail sector, went bankrupt in the mid-1990s, it was a result of their inability to raise the capital required to construct large retail structures and maintain expanded, slow-moving inventories over lengthy periods of time (Brent, 1994). With the exception of the Sam's chain, which has adapted to these new conditions, the retail industry in Canada is increasingly dominated by multinational chains — in particular, HMV — which maintain superstores in most major cities of the world. Indeed, HMV's entry into the Canadian market in 1986 signalled the beginning of a new competitive rush to dominate the retail market, causing Sam's to expand the number and size of its stores and encouraging regional chains, such as the British Columbia-based A&B Sound, to move across the country. At the time of writing, the U.K.-based Virgin chain had announced plans to build megastores in Montreal and Vancouver.

As the sound-recording industry reaches new levels of profitability, competition within the retail sector will likely grow even more intense. Wal-Mart's entry into Canada and the movement of warehouse stores in the electronics or food industries into record-retailing have resulted in intense price wars. This has resulted in retail prices for CDs in Canada that are among the lowest in the world and in claims that profitability is being sharply reduced (*The Record*, 1994a.) Virtually all record retail chains have moved into selling video cassettes, software and video games, not simply because these industries have converged, but because the profit margins on these other items are seen as more attractive than those on sound recordings.

As the record retail industry within Canada has expanded, the Canadian-owned sector of the record-production industry has remained within quite circumscribed boundaries. Virtually every Canadian label of significant size has turned to music publishing and the marketing of rights as an important source of revenue, but few have made notable moves into other media. While Canadian-owned film and television production companies, such as Alliance or Atlantis, have evolved into multimedia conglomerates, domestic record companies have thus far limited their activities to the sector in which they began.

Conclusion

It has become commonplace in articles on the Canadian recording industry to begin by lamenting the underdeveloped state of research on the subject. In *Canada's Cultural Industries*, Paul Audley compared this apparent underdevelopment with the unending stream of reports and analyses on Canadian film and television. More than ten years later, there is still no book-length study of the Canadian record industry, though a decade of public policy has left a paper trail of consultants' documents and industry profiles.

What persists is a sense of the enormous difficulties that researchers confront in attempting to analyse — structurally or historically — the

Canadian recording industry. Fragile and undercapitalized, this industry nevertheless includes, at any given time, several hundred entities calling themselves record companies, whose activities vary widely in type and scale. The number of these companies testifies to the relative ease with which anyone can start a record label — it is cheaper to do so than to make a film or launch a radio station — but it is an effect, as well, of growing uncertainty over the term "record label" itself. As multinational firms begin more and more to license completed master tapes rather than produce them, the largest and best-known Canadian record companies frequently have little to do with the signing of groups and production of master recordings.

This has occurred against the backdrop of a declining role for traditional forms of promotion and, in particular, a decline in the role of radio airplay. In its place, audiences for performers have come to be built on what everyone in the industry now calls the grassroots level — through marketing independent cassettes, long-term touring, exposure on alternative rock video programs, the accumulation of airplay at the college radio level. In an earlier period, these would have ensured continued commercial marginality; now, they are seen as means of authenticating musical products for an audience that has broken down into relatively insular and highly suspicious taste-groups. It is only the diversity of these promotional channels that perpetuates the sense that they are grassroots and credible; together, in fact, they are as effective and grand in scale as any single channel that preceded them.

It is in this context that we may understand the interest of Canadian subsidiaries of multinational firms in searching the Halifax or Hamilton music scenes for possible signings. What they seek are signs that performers themselves have already successfully built a grassroots following that may be expanded through the intervention of a major firm. The labour of audience-building, which was once carried out by small, independent Canadian-owned firms like Attic, is now expected from performers themselves before they record or from the basement operations that constitute the new Canadian independent label sector. The lesson of the Barenaked Ladies, studied closely within the record industry, is that a group or a local scene left to flourish on its own will produce the indicators of potential success upon which high sales levels may then be built. The success of the Barenaked Ladies was built on the sale of thousands of home-duplicated cassettes; other bands are now encouraged to follow the same path in demonstrating the loyalty of their fan base to a potential corporate home.

It is easy, given this situation, to celebrate the apparently organic relationship between performers and their grassroots. Nevertheless, as I have argued elsewhere, an industry preoccupied with the authentication of music and performers has little interest in bringing about the crossover between audiences or encouraging the stylistic hybridity that were typical of an era dominated by Top-40 radio — these are now too readily seen as signs of compromise or complicity (Straw, 1994). One effect of this is that the racial and ethnic boundaries around musical forms seem stronger, more impermeable, than at any point in recent memory. Those same aesthetic premises and strategic considerations that emphasize grassroots followings and a loyal fan base have worked to strengthen what might be called the ethnicization of Canadian music — they circumscribe its audiences within relatively insular spaces of racial or ethnic identities. Indeed, the more people have attempted to define a Canadian sound, the more they have been drawn to using descriptive terms — whimsical, windy, quirky, wide-open, expansive — which offer almost a caricatural formula for musical whiteness.

The international success of certain Canadian performers is taking place against the backdrop of a number of significant developments within the music industries worldwide. Here, there are important contradictions to be noted. One can observe, obviously, the ongoing tendency towards corporate concentration — towards the domination by an oligopoly of multinational firms, particularly in distribution. At the same time, however, there is little of the homogenization and international uniformity that was expected from this concentration. Simon Frith suggested, a decade ago, that the function of multinational record companies was to pluck performers from national cultures and transform them into international stars. This happens in some prominent cases, such as Bjork from Iceland or Snap! from Germany. What is striking, however, is the extent to which multinational firms now operate in national markets with local performers whose chances of international success are quite limited.

Unexpectedly, there is a heightened autonomy of national music markets. Record industry personnel and the general discourse of the music industry press are in virtual agreement on this fact: this is a period in which the tastes and buying patterns of national music audiences have diverged considerably from each other. There is, for example, a broad split between European and North American tastes, of a sort not seen since before the British Invasion of the early 1960s. Apart from this broader split, a resurgence of national musical performers and styles in the individual countries of the European Community belies the notion of a common European cultural space. Germany, for example, has witnessed a resurgence of German-language pop music and high levels of domestic success for indigenous dance music. Meanwhile, the British music market, where teen idol performers reach No. 1 while remaining unknown outside the U.K., is increasingly insular as well. (In 1993–94, no new British band achieved a significant presence on the North American sales charts.)

In Canada, this tendency is not as evident. Tastes and preferences in Canada overlap with those of Europe in certain kinds of dance music and with those of the United States in alternative rock and its derivatives. Nevertheless, we may see a trend towards autonomization in the high levels of success achieved here by acts who have, for the most part, failed outside the country. The Tragically Hip, who are the most successful Canadian performers in recent Canadian history, sold more copies of their latest album in Canada in the first four days of its release than they sold of all their previous albums in the United States over the past five years. Sales of Barenaked Ladies recordings in Canada similarly have exceeded those in the U.S. by a factor of eight to one.

The difficulty we face in trying to gauge or predict the place of Canadian music within a global cultural economy is compounded by the more longstanding problem of determining its place within a national culture. As the cultural form that serves most publicly to mark differences of class, ethnicity or cultural background, music has been a persistent challenge to those attempting to define a unique Canadian aesthetic. This is amplified by the traditional methodological difficulty of isolating the content of music so as to decipher its connection to national cultural preoccupations. In 1995, as Canadian recording artists celebrated what *The Globe and Mail* called "their extraordinary starburst of artistic excellence," (1995) this success was often read through the prism of a cultural populism that saw it as proof that the days of nationalist complaining and reliance on public support for culture were at an end. Coming, as it did, after two decades of well-conceived and widely welcomed policies designed to build the infrastructures of a national recording industry, this success might, at the very least, receive another interpretation.

Notes

1. I would like to express my thanks to Vincent Doyle, Aurora Wallace, Chris Robinson and Gildas Illien who, at different points over the years, have helped with my research into the Canadian music industries. Thank you, as well, to Karyna Laroche and Jody Berland, who as collaborators in the past have taught me a great deal. Portions of the research on which this article is based were funded by grants from the Fonds pour la Formation de Chercheurs et l'Aide à la Recherche (Quebec), the Social Sciences Research Grant program at McGill University, and a research allowance from The Centre for Research on Canadian Cultural Industries and Institutions (which is itself supported by Heritage Canada and Alliance Communications Corporation.)

2. The market shares presented here are for album sales as calculated by the Canadian trade magazine *The Record*, April 17, 1995, p. 3. These are the market shares for companies of non-Canadian ownership. The two Canadian-owned firms achieving significant market shares are Quality, at 4.0 per cent and Cargo, at 2.3 per cent.

References

While the most useful ongoing source of information on the Canadian sound recording industry is the trade magazine *The Record*, published in Toronto, the U.S. trade magazine *Billboard* publishes very useful coverage of the Canadian industry (thanks in large measure to the knowledge and contacts of the magazine's Canadian correspondent, Larry LeBlanc). Statistics Canada's *Sound Recording* survey, an annual compendium of industry statistics, was discontinued in 1995, and its final issue covered the fiscal year 1992–93. (More limited information on the year 1993–94 was included in the Statistics Canada Daily for March 22, 1995.) Statistics Canada's quarterly publication, *Focus on Culture*, regularly carries information on sound recording and musical culture in Canada.

In the absence of an authoritative history of sound recording in Canada, the best source of information on the past is *The Encyclopedia of Music in Canada*, 2nd ed. (Toronto: University of Toronto Press, 1992.)

Berland, Jody and Will Straw. 1992. "The Music Industries in Canada." Entry in *The Encyclopedia of Music in Canada*, 2nd ed. Toronto: University of Toronto Press.

Billboard. 1994a. "Oh Canada! One Nation Under a Groove." February 5, 1.

———. 1994b. "Canada Majors Move into Indie Territory." February 12, 84.

———. 1994c. "CRIA Kicks Off Drive to Support CDs." March 26, 1994, 70.

———. 1994d. "Custom Service Firms Ride Indie Boom: Companies Offer Variety of Services at Low Cost." August 27, 52.

———. 1994e. "Club Scene Spurs Sales of Compilations: Dance Music Gaining a Strong Foothold at Retail." September 17, 1994, 61.

———. 1994f. "MCA Gets Hip with No. 1 Canadian Hit." October 15, 1, 100.

———. 1993. "Attic Records Tops Canada Indies: Keeps Competitive with Changing Focus." July 31, 40.

———. 1991a. "Many Canadian Acts Still Outside the Int'l Spotlight." March 23, 72.

————. 1991b. "High Ground for Plain: Label Marks 15th Year." April 20, 68.

————. 1985. "A&M Chief Lacoursiere: One Voice for Free Trade." December 14, 85.

————. 1982. "Top 40, AOR Acts Ready Fall Releases." September 11, 50.

————. 1979. "Montreal May Be Continent's 2nd Best City." March 17, 84.

————. 1977. "Gold Mine Market for Labels." January 29, Q-10.

————. 1975. "CHOM-FM Is Making Big Strides After Hurdling Obstacles." October 11, 70.

De Norber, Eugene. 1959. "Maritimers Go 'Western' But B.C. Likes Classics." *The Financial Post*, vol. 53, no. 15, January 24.

Brent, Paul. 1994. "Virgin Tunes into Canada." *The Financial Post*, November 10, 1.

Dieckman, Katherine. 1994. "Paperbacks: Northern Lights." *The Village Voice, Literary Supplement*, April, 32.

Fletcher, Tony. 1991. "The Sound of Toronto." *Jocks* [UK] 53, March, 38.

Frith, Simon. 1988. "Picking Up the Pieces: Video/Pop." In Simon Frith, (ed.). *Facing the Music*. New York: Pantheon Books, 88-130.

Garofalo, Reebee. 1993. "Whose World, What Beat: The Transnational Music Industry, Identity, and Cultural Imperialism." *The World of Music*, vol. 35 (2), 16-32.

The Globe and Mail. 1995. "Pop goes Canadian music." (Editorial). March 28, A20.

Industry Canada. 1994. *Study on New Media and Copyright: Final Report*. Prepared for Industry Canada, New Media, Information Technologies Industry Branch, June 30.

Kelly, Brendan. 1991. "Alternative Rockers Thrive Thanks to Free Trade, GST." *MTL*, April, 40-41.

Laroche, Karyna and Will Straw. 1989. "Radio and Sound Recording Policy in Canada." *Australian-Canadian Studies*, Vol. 7, Nos. 1-2, 163-166.

La Presse. 1995. "Si Toronto boude le rock québécois, deux groupes risquent de changer les choses ..." March 25, D3.

The Record. 1994a. "Price Wars Part of the New Era in Music Retailing." April 11, 1.

————. 1994b: Q&. May 16, 1994, 13.

Statistics Canada. 1994a. "Where Culture Meets the Bottom Line ... Change in format produces rapid growth in revenues in the record industry." *Focus on Culture*, vol. 6, no. 3 (Autumn), 1-3.

Statistics Canada. 1994b. *Sound Recording 1992–93*. Ottawa: Minister of Supply and Services.

————. 1995. *The Daily* (electronic). March 22, 1995.

Straw, Will and Edward Moogk. 1992. "The Canadian Recording Industry." Entry in *The Encyclopedia of Music in Canada*, 2nd ed. Toronto: University of Toronto Press.

Straw, Will. 1993. "The English-Canadian Recording Industry Since 1970." In Tony Bennett, Simon Frith, Larry Grossberg, John Shepherd and Graeme Turner (eds.). *Rock and Popular Music: Politics, Policies, Institutions*. London: Routledge, 52-65.

————. 1994. "Organized Disorder: The Changing Space of the Record Shop." *Fuse*, vol. xvii, nos. 5-6, 27-31.

5

Radio

Michel Filion[1]

Since it appeared three-quarters of a century ago, radio has encountered numerous challenges in the context of Canada's vast geography and low-density demography: it had to survive economic hardship, overcome competition from other media, such as television and, on the cultural front, distinguish itself from the powerful American broadcasting system. Moreover, this evolution was steered by politics that assigned ambitious objectives to Canadian radio as a potentially efficient nation-building instrument. The federal state's involvement in the radio industry resulted in a particular broadcasting structure in which private and public elements had to coexist. As the first electronic mass medium, radio played a central historical role in the development of the whole broadcasting system (both radio and television), which in turn has been and still is heavily influenced by the Canadian social, economic, political and cultural context.

At least three phases marked the structural evolution of Canadian radio broadcasting.

Historical Background

Towards Federal Involvement, 1905–1932

From the turn of the century until the Great Depression, Canada benefited from constant economic growth, due mostly to foreign investments. As British interests progressively gave way to American interests, the economic evolution of the country was largely in the control of outside forces. Long-term vulnerability to foreign domination brought about strong reactions from nationalist milieux. Like railroads during the second part of the nineteenth century, radio broadcasting was soon considered a potentially efficient nation-building tool. But from 1905 to 1932, radio was, above anything else, a commercial device.

The Radiotelegraph Act of 1913, which followed the Wireless Telegraphy Act of 1905, gave the Canadian state power to license the use of airwaves which were considered public property just like other natural resources. In 1919, the Canadian Marconi Company launched radio station XWA in Montreal (it became CFCF the next year). During the 1920s, stations popped up everywhere.

Even so, Canadian radio was facing foreign competition and integration into the American broadcasting system — in spite of a 1923 amendment to the Radiotelegraph Act that gave only British subjects the right to broadcasting licences. This measure, which failed in the long run, was a modest effort to prohibit the use of Canadian airwaves by American interests. Nevertheless, by the end of the 1920s, the largest Canadian stations were affiliated either to the CBS or NBC networks. Such partnership became inevitable since federal jurisdiction was limited to issuing licences and managing the radiowave spectrum allocated to Canada under international agreements. Radio program contents remained nearly free of constraint. This situation resulted in an abundant use of foreign (i.e., American) programs, mostly in English Canada (Filion, 1994: 54-58). Canadian content nevertheless became part of the debate over the future of Canadian broadcasting, while the commercial stations' insistence on freedom became a rite of nationalist contestation.

In 1929, the report of the Royal Commission on Radio Broadcasting, under the chairmanship of John Aird, highlighted several major problems: the urban concentration of Canadian radio stations, their commercialization, the general mediocrity of programs, regional isolation, and, last but not least, the overwhelming presence of American stations and programs. The Aird report supported the same centralizing movement which characterized the formation of the federal state: the federal government should take over private radio.[2]

In spite of representations by the Canadian Association of Broadcasters, created in 1926 to foster and protect the interests of existing radio stations, the public audiences of the House of Commons Special Committee on Radio Broadcasting were dominated in 1932 by the Canadian Radio League, an influential lobby skilfully lead by Graham Spry, the father of public broadcasting in Canada:

Because of the power of the American radio group, because of the failure of private enterprise, because of the inadequate advertising revenue available for Canadian Radio Broadcasting, because no scheme of broadcasting upon a national scale has been proposed that does not require a subsidy either direct or from the listener, because the fullest use of musical talent and educational resources cannot be made under commercial guidance and, above all no agency so powerful as broadcasting should be owned and operated by irresponsible agencies, the Canadian Radio League advocates the public ownership of radio broadcasting stations (Canada, 1932: 565).

Canadians were challenged by Spry to choose between the "State or the United States." Interestingly, this debate was held while the available North American radio frequencies were being allocated. Without a strong representation at the international level, Canada might very well have been outperformed by its southern neighbour (Vipond, 1992: 172-192).

The Broadcasting Act was passed in 1932. It created the Canadian Radio Broadcasting Commission (CRBC), which was empowered to decide upon the numbers and locations of radio stations in Canada. The CRBC was also mandated to establish a national radio service. National private radio networks were forbidden, but private regional chain-broadcasting was permitted (Vipond, 1994: 156). The act enabled the expropriation of commercial stations and, therefore, hinted at an eventual state monopoly. The CRBC intended not only Canadian ownership but, more precisely, *public* ownership of radio. The CRBC was to be financed by licence fees and public subsidies, which made it dependent on Parliament.

The Golden Age of Public Radio, 1932–58

Until its reformulation in 1958, the Broadcasting Act of 1932 ensured federal control over radio. In principle, radio was virtually entirely state controlled. But, nationalization began in an adverse economic and social conjuncture: the Great Depression of the 1930s heavily hit countries, such as Canada, that were dependent on exports, particularly of unprocessed natural resources. The Second World War put an end to the Depression but not to increasing Canadian dependence on American capital and the American market. In fact, the Canadian and American economies became even more integrated.

This was the context in which the Canadian broadcasting system took form, inspired but not bound by the Aird Commission's recommendations. Private radio stations escaped nationalization and the

CRBC, never properly funded, inevitably turned to commercial advertising. Thus, national radio, from its very beginning, was a compromise between nationalism and commerce.

The 1936 Broadcasting Act created the Canadian Broadcasting Corporation (CBC). Its mandate was to establish a national radio service and to control the broadcasting system as a whole. During the next two decades, the CBC was successful with the first assignment, but less so with the second: private stations developed technical expertise and became financially secure. Many of them found their affiliation with the national (CBC) network very profitable since the public broadcaster provided its affiliates with free programs, under the condition that time be reserved for chain broadcasting. Always facing potential conflicts of interest, the CBC — as the national broadcaster and the system regulator — imposed little regulation on its affiliates (or on private independent stations either).

This mixed system of public and private ownership was to cease the day the CBC was capable of assuming by itself the national service, but this was not easy. In order to expand broadcasting coverage, the corporation issued many licences to private interests, especially with the arrival of television in 1952. Before long, production costs exceeded the resources of the Canadian Broadcasting Corporation and, to a certain extent, the resources of Canadian society in general.

The main objectives of the Canadian system, although founded in legislation, were in fact hardly realizable. This was made evident in reports of two royal commissions. The Royal Commission on National Development in the Arts, Letters and Sciences, chaired by Vincent Massey, considered in its 1951 report that it would be perilous for Canada to recognize officially the existence of private stations. Nevertheless, in 1957, the Royal Commission on Broadcasting, chaired by Robert Fowler, recommended the complete integration of the private sector into the Canadian broadcasting system, in order to control commercial stations and to encourage them to participate more actively in achieving broad national objectives.

The Broadcasting Act of 1958 was a very liberal interpretation of the Fowler report, which placed the private sector — henceforth allowed to create its own networks — and the public sector on equal grounds. To manage this change in public policy, both sectors were to be refereed by an independent regulatory institution, the Board of Broadcast Governors. This demonstrates a substantial evolution of the Canadian broadcasting system: the 1932 Act foresaw the nationalization of private undertakings, the 1936 Act made them complementary to the national service, and the 1958 Act gave commercial stations enough autonomy to compete with the CBC. For the first time, legislation addressed Canadian ownership and recommended that only Canadian citizens or corporations incorporated under the laws of Canada or any province be licensed to broadcast.

Liberalism and Competition Since 1958

Until very recently, the broadcasting industry was characterized by expansion and growth. Demography, social effervescence and transnational culture are among many factors which contributed, and still do today, to the development of mass media. To satisfy popular demand, notably for television, it became almost inevitable to resort to private enterprises. The creation of commercial networks, allowed by the 1958 act, was definitely authorized by the 1968 Broadcasting Act. Its concept of a single broadcasting system was a paradox, as the system in reality consisted of two distinct components, with different objectives, in principle regulated by a single "independent" public authority, the Canadian Radio Television Commission (which became the Canadian Radio-television and Telecommunications Commission in 1976). The mandate of the CRTC is to implement the policy set out in the Broadcasting Act. Passed in 1991, the latest version of the act reconducts the CRTC and the CBC in their respective roles.

The Canadian Market

From the 1920s on, when radio sets were scarce (there were only 10,000 in 1923), broadcasting grew at a very rapid rate: by the end of the decade, more than a half-million sets were in use in Canada. Slowed down by the Great Depression, radio broadcasting nevertheless kept growing in numbers and coverage. By the end of the 1940s, radio broadcasting reached the great majority of the Canadian population even though urban areas were privileged. During the 1950s, very few Canadian households did not own at least one radio set (Filion, 1994: 172-173). As television expanded at a phenomenal rate, radio adapted: before long, it found its place in automobiles and greatly benefited from the miniaturization brought by the transistor. Since the 1970s, radio broadcasting quality has been augmented by the expanded use of the FM band, which became a direct competitor to the more traditional AM stations. This phenomenon occurred as

Table 5-1
Share of Hours, Listeners Aged 12 and Over

	Weekdays	Weekends
Home	56%	72%
Automobile	21%	18%
Work	21%	7%
Elsewhere	2%	3%

Source: Radio Marketing Bureau. 1993. *Radio Facts Book.*

the emergence of new musical genres made radio listening very popular.

According to the Radio Marketing Bureau (1993), radio reaches 95 per cent of all Canadians, who weekly spend an average of 22 hours listening to radio (24 hours are devoted to television), an increase of 10 per cent since the end of the 1980s. Radio listening far exceeds the time Canadians spend reading books, newspapers and periodicals (Ekos Research Associates, 1991). Almost every household in Canada owns at least one radio set and close to 50 per cent have three or more. Furthermore, nine motor vehicles out of ten are equipped with radio.

Threatened by the introduction of television in the 1950s, radio survived as a distinct medium (Crissell, 1986). Before long, radio drama largely vanished and was replaced by information and musical programs. Because evening prime time is almost entirely monopolized by television, radio is at its peak on mornings, when listeners are waking up and commuting to work. Between 7:00 and 9:00 A.M., a quarter of the population tunes in, but this figure declines shortly after noon; between noon and 4:00 P.M., radio and television reach approximately one-tenth of the population, but after 4:00 P.M., television increases its audience up to 40-per-cent during evening prime time (8:00–10:00 P.M.) while radio's listening level oscillates between seven and nine per cent (CRTC, 1988: 22).

Measuring radio audience behaviour remains an approximative exercise. Exact numbers of listeners tuning to a particular channel at a particular time varies among survey firms. Furthermore, gauging the audience's appreciation is virtually impossible. Although the Canadian Association of Broadcasters (CAB) recently recommended a rigorous upgrading of radio measurement (CAB 1989: 67), the radio (and survey) industry nevertheless relies on establishing a link between the share (volume of listeners) and appreciation of programs. Advertising rates are a function of numbers of listeners: in Canada, the private independent stations seem to capture over 83 per cent of listening time, compared to 10 per cent for the CBC and four per cent for U.S. stations (CRTC, 1991: 15). Since 1975, commercial advertising has almost completely vanished from CBC radio as a voluntary measure ratified by the CRTC in the renewal of CBC licences (CRTC, Decision 74-70). Competition for advertising is nonetheless fierce among private stations.

The Economics of Radio

For decades, radio expanded with some stability. At present, radio is suffering an unprecedented crisis. This crisis is related to the lasting economic recession of the 1990s, but the crisis also appears to be structural. As public funding is under close scrutiny, advertising revenues are declining or at least shifting to new poles. In the meantime, the radio industry is facing new technological challenges, such as digital radio.

To address the immediate economic crisis and the longer-term future of the radio industry, the minister of communications announced two working groups in March 1992, the Working Group on the Economic Recovery of Radio and the Working Group on the Future of Radio, both under the Radio Action Plan Consultative Group (RAPCG), whose membership included representatives from the Department of Communications, the CRTC, the CBC, the Canadian Association of Broadcasters, private networks, campus and community radio, and the recording industry. Such co-operation reveals an unusual state of anxiety. Both reports were amalgamated and published in a single report to which we will often refer in the following pages (RAPCG, 1992).

Structure

In Canada, public radio belongs to CBC; provincial governments are practically absent in this sector, unlike in public television. Canadian public radio is, in reality, state broadcasting (Raboy, 1990). Free from the constraints of commercial advertising, state broadcasting can present a more original (some would say a better-quality) program that does not have to compete with private-sector programs for large and popular audience shares, an otherwise vital pre-condition

Table 5-2
Number of Originating AM Radio Stations in Canada

Types of Stations	1994	1988	
CBC-owned and operated	29	73	-44
CBC-affiliated	11	18	-7
Private independent	301	307	-6
Campus	9	10	-1
Educational	-	1	-1
Community and native	5	5	-
Ethnic	6	6	-
Total	361	420	-59

Source: CRTC. 1988. *Annual Report*; CRTC. 1994. *Originating Stations.*

for generating revenues. Nevertheless, its relatively marginal situation with the Canadian audience (and taxpayers) renders the CBC vulnerable to budget cuts in an era of governmental downsizing. The CBC possesses and operates its own stations, but, to ensure total coverage, it also depends on private, independent stations, which, as affiliates, broadcast a mix of national and local programs.

Even more marginal than public radio, community radio is collective property and is mandated to serve a defined clientele: campus, native and ethnic stations are among this group. Nonprofit community radio is mainly financed by government subsidies.

Private radio is essentially a commercial undertaking to serve local markets. More flexible than the CBC, it is encouraged by the broadcasting legislation to participate in national objectives. The 1991 Broadcasting Act declared that "private networks and programming undertakings should, to an extent consistent with the financial and other resources available to them, contribute significantly to the creation and presentation of Canadian programming, and be responsive to the evolving demands of the public."

In raw numbers, as well as in financial terms, the private stations make up by far the most important group in the radio industry: 70 per cent of radio stations and 83 per cent of audience share in Canada. While no recent data are available on the level of concentration or

Table 5-3
Number of Originating FM Radio Stations in Canada

Types of Stations	1994	1988	
CBC-owned and operated	35	28	+7
CBC-affiliated	9	6	+3
Private independent	185	151	+34
Campus	26	23	+3
Educational	2	2	-
Community and native	176	81	+95
Ethnic	2	2	-
Total	432	296	+136

Source: CRTC. 1988. *Annual Report*; CRTC. 1994. *Originating Stations.*

cross-ownership, private radio appears to be fragmented and composed of small businesses which often operate in small communities:
among the 155 companies which operated radio stations in 1992, 66
per cent operated a single or two stations, only ten companies owned
ten or more stations, and no one broadcast group owned more than
five per cent of all radio stations in the country (RAPCG, 1992: 12).

Unlike American stations, which are actually lowering programming costs by networking, Canadian stations have made local programming commitments to the CRTC. Therefore, most private
stations remain independent even though some are owned by or
affiliated to groups such as Telemedia and Radiomutuel in Quebec,
where large-scale networking is more developed than elsewhere in
Canada (Raboy, 1992: 28). But in Quebec as well as in the rest of
the country, most stations are independent or part of small networks
and therefore play a definite local role.

The 14-per-cent decline of AM stations in the last five years is
due to technical and financial factors. Since the mid-1980s, the AM
band has been virtually saturated (Audley, 1983: 196-197) and does
not always provide good reception because of interference. AM
stereo transmission is technically possible but necessitates the adoption of improved standards by the transmitting stations and radio set
manufacturers (CAB, 1989: 71-73). Actually, it seems easier to move

stations from one band to the other. For example, in November 1989, the CRTC approved CBC's request to switch its two Ottawa radio stations, CBO and CBOF, to the FM band, essentially to improve urban reception, particularly at night. A distinction is then made between CBC radio (AM and FM mono) and CBC stereo (FM solely). One focuses on news and current affairs, local and regional services and popular music. The other is devoted to classical music and jazz, culture (literature and history) and radio creations.

Perceived as "talk-oriented," private AM radio stations are handicapped by their more traditional (i.e., general) program. FM stations offer less news, less talk and specialized music programming (easy listening, adult contemporary, hard rock, and so on). Audiences, such as young adult consumers, are therefore targeted with greater precision, an interesting prospect for advertisers.

At first sight restrictive, the musical program format provides each station category a relatively faithful audience for a very specific product and market. This has been taken in by the television industry, which is now competing with radio for morning information, as well as the news, weather and sports covered by specialty channels. Television competition is also developing in music, as more and more stations are offering stereo, particularly music channels such as *MuchMusic* and *Musique Plus*: with an FM-quality reception, video clips might very well appeal to many. The substantial increase of FM radio, one of the fastest-growing sectors of the broadcasting industry, might soon result in a serious decline of revenue for AM radio as the advertising market becomes more and more fragmented.

Revenue Trends

At its beginnings, the CBC drew revenues from transmission licences issued to broadcasters and annual private receiving-set licences, which were phased out in 1953, to be replaced by a sales tax on radio and television sets. Today, CBC radio depends almost exclusively on public subsidies: $324.8 million was allocated to CBC radio services in 1994, compared to $307.4 million in 1993 and $293.4 million in 1992 (CBC, 1994: 4).

Campus, community and native radio's sources of funding are mixed and include advertising revenue, donations, institutional funding as well as government subsidies. On the other hand, private stations are completely dependent on advertising revenues. The economic situation and the structure of the industry (shares of the advertising market) play an important direct and indirect role in the

Table 5-4
Profitability of Canadian Private Radio Stations
($ millions)

		1993	1992	1991	1990	1989
AM	Revenue	385.5	426.0	443.5	468.9	473.3
	Expenses	409.8	437.5	449.7	455.9	440.5
	PBIT (%)	-11.3	-7.4	-6.1	-1.5	2.8
FM	Revenue	353.9	342.4	311.9	310.3	296.0
	Expenses	299.4	286.6	260.9	252.7	240.5
	PBIT (%)	12.0	12.8	12.9	15.3	15.3
Total	Revenue	739.2	768.4	755.4	779.2	769.3
	Expenses	709.3	724.1	710.6	708.6	680.0
	PBIT (%)	-0.1	1.6	1.7	5.2	7.7

Note: PBIT = Profit Before Income Taxes

Source: CRTC. 1993. *Radio and Television Statistical and Financial Summary.*

financial wealth of the radio industry. In Canada, private stations operate in 288 different communities, among which 238 communities (83 per cent) have less than 50,000 inhabitants. In 1990, over half of the radio stations had revenues of under $1.1 million and only seven per cent generated profits over $800,000. In 1992, it was estimated that 60 per cent of private stations were in debt (RAPCG 1992: 12-14). This trend particularly affects AM stations, whose profit before income taxes (PBIT) is drastically declining (see Table 5-4).

For a long time, the radio broadcasting industry has been generally profitable. Paul Audley noted in 1983, that radio stations in Canada had had a steady 11-per-cent share of total media advertising expenditure since 1970 (1983: 202). However, 38 per cent of the commercial stations (mostly the smallest) were losing money (Audley, 1983: 203). Since the end of the 1980s, the radio industry has suffered from low profitability, a phenomenon most obvious in the AM sector. (See Table 5-5.)

Table 5-5
Profitability of English and French Radio Private Stations, 1992 ($ millions)

		English Stations	French Stations
AM	Revenue	362.3	62.0
	Expenses	360.3	75.2
	PBIT (%)	-4.3	-25.5
FM	Revenue	263.6	78.8
	Expenses	223.4	63.2
	PBIT (%)	11.8	16.3

Note: PBIT = Profit Before Income Taxes

Source: CRTC. 1993. *Radio and Television Statistical and Financial Summary.*

This structural problem began before the economic recession of the early 1990s. A long-term decline in radio's share of advertising and increasing competition among stations are the predominant factors here. In the mid-1980s, marketing expenditures, which made up 75 per cent of the total advertising revenue base for radio stations, shifted from media advertising to promotional activities for local markets, at the national level. U.S. advertising in Canada by emerging large retail stores, such as Price Club and Wal-Mart, made scant use of media advertising. At the same time, the net increase of new licences significantly reduced the advertising revenue per station (RAPCG, 1992: 16-19). This situation led the industry to rationalize and ultimately close stations. The recent merger of the two major networks in Quebec (Telemedia and Radiomutuel) into Radiomedia resulted in the closure of six AM stations. Some, such as CKCH-Hull, had been in operation for over 60 years. This merger might open the door for others in the near future. Concentration could eventually bring about centralization, retransmissions (to the regions) and greater content uniformity.

Among the proposed solutions to these financial problems are regulatory measures (such as relaxing licence fees) and a technological leap into digital radio. Traditionally, private stations have complained about the unfair competition generated by direct state involvement: but, unlike television, CBC radio has not impinged on the advertising market since the mid-seventies. As short-term relief to help private stations overcome their poor financial situation, it was suggested in 1992 that all stations be exempted from the payment of CRTC licence fees for three years. Licence fees generate $10.7 million (RAPCG, 1992: 35-36). This solution was not accepted since the CRTC relies on licence fees for its own operations. The commission is nevertheless preoccupied by the financial situation of radio stations, particularly AM radio: since 1986, they have been free to advertise as much as they wish. Before, AM stations were restricted to 250 minutes of commercial content per day and 1,500 minutes per week. Noting that such regulation had not increased advertisements to an unacceptable level, the CRTC in 1993 removed the 150-minute-a-day limit imposed on FM licensees (Grant et al., 1993: 880-1).

Economic Impact

Radio plays a significant economic role in Canada: 12,000 employees, close to $500 million in salary and benefits, and over $750 million dollars in advertising revenue (RAPCG, 1992: 7). Radio stations are producers as well as purchasers of programs: many performing organizations benefit from royalty payments. Expenses total over $700 million dollars per year (see Table 5-4), not counting CBC expenses.

Because of this substantial economic impact, and because of the precarious financial situation the radio industry finds itself in, there is no doubt that public policy authorities (i.e., CRTC, Parliament, et cetera) are sensitive to arguments for deregulation as forwarded by the Radio Action Plan Consultative Group (1992: 28). While regulation is regarded by the private sector as an additional burden (unless it protects the industry), economic viability is considered by the public authorities an essential condition for the Canadian broadcasting system.

Policy

Canadian nationalists have long been preoccupied by the country's political, economic and cultural sovereignty. Since the 1930s, the challenge has been presented as the protection of Canadian mass media against the powerful American system by means of a cultural boundary out of the "49th Paradox" (Gwyn, 1985). Historically, state intervention has aimed to create cultural identity as a means of national defence (Globerman, 1983: 40) and national unity. But, does the state alone have the power to shape the production of culture?

As the national broadcaster and regulatory body, the CBC was mandated to settle the fundamental problems of the commercialization and Americanization of Canadian broadcasting and to monitor the Canadian broadcasting system. Nevertheless, challenged by the establishment of a national network in both official languages and by two modes of broadcasting (radio and television) since the 1950s, the CBC could hardly escape from importing programs and financing its operation with commercial advertisements. Austin Weir, who was directly involved in this process, states:

> Commercials [programs] were important in the network schedules, not for the revenue alone but perhaps even more for the hours they filled with popular, audience-building programs. This relieved the Corporation of the obligation of filling a great deal of time with what, in many cases, due to the CBC's very limited budget, must inevitably have been mediocre productions. To fill sixteen hours daily with programs of the high standards expected from the Canadian Broadcasting Corporation was no small task (Weir, 1965: 225).

Commercial programs were financed by advertising while sustaining programs were generally offered by the CBC as a gratuity to its affiliated stations. In a context where the national broadcaster itself had to lean on imported programs and on advertisements generated by large American corporations such as General Foods, Procter & Gamble and Lever Brothers (Filion, 1990: 241-242), it would have been surprising to see rigorous regulation of the independent and affiliated stations by the very same CBC. To limit the use of foreign programs, the CBC forbade the broadcasting of recorded programs between 7:30 P.M. and 11:00 P.M. But a specific regulation for Canadian content on radio would only appear later.

Since 1958, control over broadcasting in Canada has been centralized in a single authority because radio and television in theory formed a single system. The CRTC exercises its power through the licensing process as the licence terms and conditions are, in principle, compulsory requirements assigned to each station or network. As an administrative tribunal, the commission must also regulate the whole radio industry according to the Broadcasting Act. Canadian content is undoubtedly the ultimate objective of the broadcasting system and has been regulated on television since 1959. Surprisingly, the first regulation imposing foreign import quotas on AM stations was not introduced until the 1970s. The situation was then critical. In 1968, Canadian musical selections accounted for between four and seven per cent of all music played (Audley, 1983: 193). The 1970 regulation imposed a 30-per-cent minimum of Canadian content. In 1986, new regulations were introduced covering both AM and FM radio although different requirements applied.

For the rising FM sector, requirements varied from 10 per cent for the "Easy listening" format to 30 per cent for "Country" stations. Subject to a daily limit of commercial advertising (150 minutes), FM radio benefited from an incentive to encourage Canadian content since the CRTC's radio regulation stated that commercial messages broadcast during Canadian feature segments would not be considered commercial messages. However, since 1991, every popular FM station must, like AM radio, play a minimum of 30-per-cent Canadian selections, scheduled in a reasonable manner throughout each broadcast day. The latest definition of Canadian musical content was introduced in 1993. Any musical selection that meets two of the following conditions is deemed to be Canadian: the music or lyrics are performed by a Canadian, the music is composed by a Canadian, the lyrics are written by a Canadian or the musical selection is a live performance recorded or broadcast in Canada.

This regulation aims to expose Canadian musical performers to Canadian audiences and to strengthen the Canadian music industry. Cultural and industrial objectives are closely interrelated. In addition, stations licensed to operate in French, either on the AM or FM band, must devote at least 65 per cent of their weekly vocal selections to French. This regulation aims to preserve language diversity, particularly in metropolitan markets such as Montreal, where English-language stations are overrepresented (Tremblay, 1990: 236). Furthermore, French-language popular music broadcasters are encouraged to strive for a Canadian content level of 50 per cent, which apparently is attained in many cases (Grant et al., 1993: 667). Conversely, English-language stations are invited to promote and financially assist Canadian talent (CRTC, 1990). But private stations actually find the Canadian talent development commitments (CTD), approximately $20 million in 1991, too costly (RAPCG, 1992: 21) (see Table 5-6).

These commitments are often made on a voluntary basis by broadcasters who wish to foster their application for a licence. As a condition of licence, the Canadian talent obligation nevertheless becomes compulsory. It is generally admitted that "the persistent shortage of high-quality Canadian music for private radio to play" is due to "the increasing cost of music production, promotion and distribution and the structure of the international music industry [which] make the Canadian music industry's existence a constant struggle" (CAB, 1989: 8). According to the CAB, FM radio typically needs 1,100 different selections a week and AM radio needs 500 to 600 (CAB, 1989: 48), which creates a Canadian content supply problem (30 per cent of the above figures) the recording industry cannot overcome. Radio plays a substantial role in the promotion of Canadian artists through CTD commitments and air-play, since more than half of broadcasting time is filled with recorded music: "Airplay, rather than live performance, is the most available form of promotion for most Canadian artists, especially newcomers" (Leblanc, 1990: 8-9). And this is only possible if broadcasters respect Canadian content regulation, not only by providing the expected quotas but also by scheduling Canadian selection in a "reasonable manner during the broadcast day."

Another good example of an important regulatory objective which then becomes a commercial burden is spoken-word regulation. A spoken-word program contains no music other than background music and musical themes. Starting in September 1991, FM commercial radio stations were required by policy to devote a minimum of 15 per cent of their broadcast week to oral content. A number of stations had to raise their level of spoken word from a previous average of 10-12 per cent and therefore had to increase their investment in original (i.e., Canadian) programs. According to the CAB, talk-oriented programs cost more to research and produce than music-oriented programs (CAB, 1989: 38). In June 1993, this requirement was revoked by the CRTC and replaced with a requirement that FM stations devote a third of their broadcast week to local programming (Grant et al., 1993: 707).

Technology

More and more, digital radio is presented as an essential tool for the radio industry to remain technologically competitive (RAPCG, 1992: 51-59). Digital radio surpasses services offered by conventional analog AM and FM radio and offers CD-quality transmission. Furthermore, it can also provide data transmission if properly developed. Introduced in Europe at the end of the 1980s, digital radio has been

Table 5-6
Canadian Talent Development Commitments
($ million)

	1991	1988	Growth
Cash contributions	9.96	5.88	69%
Indirect expenses	10.11	1.85	447%

Source: RAPCG, 1992: 44.

studied by the CBC and the CAB; both agree on its importance as a replacement technology for the AM and FM bands, which are, at the moment considered inadequate for efficient satellite transmission. At the World Administrative Radio Conference, held in Spain in 1992, Canada was allocated the range 1452 to 1492 MHz (L-Band) for terrestrial and satellite services and is, therefore, finally free of the constraints of the U.S. allotment plan (RAPCG, 1992: 54).

Experimental digital transmitters were tested in Toronto and Barrie in 1992. The transition to digital radio progressed in March 1994 when Digital Radio Research Incorporated (DRRI), a joint CBC-CAB initiative, opened the first permanent digital radio stations in Toronto and Montreal (CBC, 1994: 13-14, 61). According to the Task Force on the Implementation of Digital Radio, every AM and FM radio station will have been transferred onto the L-Band by 2010 (TFIDR, 1993: 28). It is believed that this will put the Canadian manufacturers in a leading and therefore highly competitive position on the world market. But, even in the best scenario, such a transition might be risky (digital transmission still has to be accepted as the new standard by the international community) and costly both in terms of the Canadian economy (the cost of massive digital radio implementation remains hypothetical) and Canadian culture. Historically, new technologies have been a force of "denationalization" by exposing Canadians to additional foreign cultural products (Seigel, 1983). So far, the discussion over digital audio services has led to controversy. For instance, in September 1993, the federal cabinet referred the CRTC back to its previous decision to issue licences for audio digital radio transmitted by satellite and distributed by cable to Cogeco (Montreal) and Shaw Cable (Edmonton). Cogeco was planning to offer 38 channels among which only seven were of

Canadian origin; Shaw proposed seven Canadian channels of a total of 37.

Culture

Throughout the history of Canadian radio, American "imperialism" has been considered a major threat. On the one hand, economic imperialism jeopardized the emerging Canadian radio system as major American networks could have easily overwhelmed stations north of the border before the Broadcasting Act of 1932 put an end to this movement. On the other hand, cultural imperialism — a more subtle form of influence — is probably as strong as ever today, notwithstanding Canadian-content regulations and incentives for Canadian talent development. Canadian nationalists have many good reasons to fear for the country's cultural sovereignty, especially in an era of free trade and market globalization. So far excluded from the free trade agreements, culture might very well be part of future negotiations. In 1985, the CRTC president declared: "Should broadcasting or structural elements of our cultural industries be included in free trade negotiations directly or indirectly, there could be substantial challenges to your industry and to Canadian cultural sovereignty. ... Let's not kid ourselves: our government will be pressured to make concessions if it wants to get significant benefits" (CRTC, 1986: xv).

Although difficult, protecting the industry might be a relatively clear task if measured in terms of production, employment figures, profits, and so on. Trying to define culture, however, is challenging nor does this always enhance democracy. Since the first Royal Commission on Broadcasting in 1929, not only has the American presence been a phobic object, but the fear has also extended to a flourishing popular culture. Interestingly, the Aird report was not opposed to American programs of good quality coming to Canada, though the quality of a program remained undefined. Reproduced by every subsequent public inquiry, a similar argument has also been made by many who took part in the national service: "If men conceive of radio as a powerful means for human communication, they are likely to advocate a different policy for its development and control than if they regard it as a vehicle for the lightest and most casual entertainment, something that makes few lasting impressions," wrote Frank Peers (1969: 14). Public criticism of radio originated primarily from a certain social elite which tended to foster its own cultural needs and political aspirations: Marc Raboy (1990) clearly demonstrated how broadcasting, in spite of its mandate to serve the Canadian public, became a political instrument, but until recently, very few scholars have addressed the dominant discourse on culture from a critical perspective:

> The debate over the future of Canadian radio during the 1930s has usually been characterized as a debate between those who wanted Canadian culture defended against American influences. Yet the radio debate did not revolve solely around the origins of Canadian broadcasting; indeed, many stations provided programs which addressed national, regional, and local concerns. Instead, what seems to have been at work here was an attempt on the part of cultural nationalists to distinguish sharply between high and low culture, and to delineate cultural uplift from mass entertainment (Nolan, 1989: 517).

Section 3(g) of the Broadcasting Act states that "the programming originating by broadcasting undertakings should be of high standard," but fails to provide any criteria. Historically, this section finds its origins in the public inquiries such as the Aird Commission or the Massey Commission who considered private stations' programs as regrettable, inexpressive and unimaginative. When culture is essentially seen as "cultivated education," the cultural industry becomes an undesirable phenomenon. Only the state can counterbalance large corporations' tendency to massify culture without indoctrinating the population by "manufacturing consent" (Chomsky and Hermann, 1988).

Today, it is the cultural industries that are represented by the state as the vital links of Canadian culture: "Culture is the very essence of our national identity. Nourishing that identity are the cultural industries, whose artists are more assured than ever but whose institutions face long odds against success" (Department of Communications, 1987). *Deregulation, self-regulation, profit* and *competition* are now key words in the management of the Canadian broadcasting system. The objective is to transform the cultural industries into profitable undertakings by conquering the domestic market and, ultimately, foreign markets. Yet many of the most successful Canadian artists are recognized as such only when they succeed in the American market. To do so, they must offer an "American-flavoured" product. In this context, is it possible for the radio industry, and conversely for other Canadian cultural sectors, to "encourage the development of Canadian expression by providing a wide range of programming that reflects Canadian attitudes, opinions, ideas, values and artistic creativity [and] by displaying Canadian talent in entertainment programming" as prescribed by the Broadcasting Act?

Has radio in fact succeeded in nurturing Canadian culture? One must understand that there are many forms of Canadian culture, though not all of them are officially recognized. Nor is American culture monolithic either. If the Canadianization of radio broadcasting has been a success in terms of ownership, since only Canadian citizens or corporations (in which at least four-fifths of owners or controlling persons are Canadians) are issued licences, it has been less so in terms of Canadian content. The 30-per-cent quota recently imposed hardly meets the spirit of the act. And yet public authorities are responsible for this situation. Although broadcasters are limited by the Canadian-content quotas only in a minimal fashion, very few broadcast more Canadian music than what is imposed. It should be stressed that CBC targets of 50-per-cent Canadian content for popular music and 20-per-cent for classical music were met in 1993–94 (CBC, 1994: 44). These outstanding results, which have been praised by the Juneau Report (1996), must be tempered by the CBC audience share, which includes only about 10 per cent of listener population. As most stations prefer to broadcast foreign selections, for many reasons such as the appeal of American popular culture and the relative scarcity of Canadian hits, broadcasting undertakings are also responsible for the semi-failure of the Canadian system.

Further, sub-section 3(s) of the Broadcasting Act remains ambiguous as it states that "private networks and programming undertakings should, to an extent consistent with the financial and other resources available to them, (i) contribute significantly to the creation and presentation of Canadian programming, and (ii) be responsive to the evolving demands of the public." Yet it still has to be demonstrated that Canadians prefer Canadian cultural products. The case of prime-time television is obvious enough to suggest that many Canadian consumers (or listeners) are not reluctant to buy or listen to foreign products (Collins, 1990). In so doing, listeners are equally responsible for the semi-failure of the broadcasting system to meet its initial objectives. As a system, radio involves several actors who share the responsibility at different levels (Grossberg, 1992, de la Garde et al., 1993).

At the same time, there is a general sense of satisfaction with radio in Canada since ownership is mostly Canadian and listening seems to be almost entirely devoted to Canadian stations. However, new technologies have the potential to change this situation. A fundamental question thus remains: do Canadians, in their daily cultural practices, oppose any resistance to foreign cultural production? Is the audience nothing more than a commodity produced by broadcasters and sold to advertisers (Smythe, 1981)? Or, are listeners, as part of the media production process, active and critical users? This issue has not been sufficiently addressed yet.

Conclusion

In Canadian radio's first phase, American airwave imperialism posed a serious threat to the Canadian radio industry. Since direct state involvement began in 1932, American influence has become more subtle. Canadian ownership as well as Canadian official representation at the international level were finally secured, although foreign cultural influence remained strong, in a context of economic growth and continental integration, and in spite of a national broadcasting system in theory controlled by a federal institution, the CBC. The third and last phase of evolution has seen the competition from private stations become official, while regulatory mechanisms are put in place to contain American influence and promote a Canadian cultural identity. This remains the ultimate objective of state intervention in broadcasting.

Audience shares for national radio are nevertheless minimal in comparison to private commercial stations, while Canadian radio is fragmented and experiencing considerable structural changes. Profits are declining, mostly on the AM band in French Canada, where mergers might predict further changes, while new technologies such as audio digital transmission might open a new era of prosperity or might equally lead the industry towards financial ruin. Radio still has a substantial economic impact in Canada. Public authorities, led by the CRTC, are sensitive to the industry's economic viability and, in spite of culturally aimed regulations such as Canadian content, are more and more deferring to deregulation. At the eve of the twenty-first century, it appears that cultural identity will surrender to financial considerations. As cultural industries are preoccupied by massive diffusion and large-scale profitability, the cultural uplift long defended by a nationalistic elite is hardly likely to find its place in the radio broadcasting system. The privatization of the CBC, although still theoretical, seems actually less heretical than it did only a few years ago.

For decades, the private stations have been blamed — in some cases unfairly — for their propensity to foster American popular culture. Consequently, public authorities have been blamed for their laxity concerning economic interest. Paul Audley rightly stated in 1983 that while Canadian ownership may be a necessary condition for achieving the goals of the Broadcasting Act, which are to safeguard and enrich the Canadian culture, it is not a sufficient condition (Audley, 1983: 191). Only very recently has the idea emerged that policies, commercial strategies and cultural practices have mutual influences. As a system (or market), radio is actually defined by the converging (and sometimes diverging) roles of economic actors (broadcasters and advertisers), political actors (public authorities) and cultural actors (listeners or users). The political intervention and economic situation are relatively well documented since the state and the broadcasters, private and public, have monopolized the debate over radio and other media. By contrast, the mass of cultural actors remains outside the debate as listeners are rarely given the opportunity to express their viewpoints other than by consuming or rejecting cultural products: doing so, more or less consciously and within the limit of what is offered to them, they nevertheless play a vital role in the cultural industry process. In this sense, their role in whether or not the creation of a distinct Canadian society remains an objective to be pursued is still far from over.

Notes

1. The author wishes to thank Candace Loewen and Jean-Stephen Piché for their patient editorial review of this chapter.
2. As for recommendations aiming to give provinces an active role in content supervision, a draft bill presented in December 1929 to the Radio Service of Marine Branch (responsible for the application of the Wireless Telegraphy Act under the Department of Marine and Fisheries) was decisively abandoned in 1932 when the Privy Council in London decided against the provinces in favour of the federal government (Filion 1994: 31). Henceforth, the jurisdiction over the airwaves would rest in the hands of Ottawa even though disputes (mostly with Québec) continue to this day.

References

Ang, I. 1991. *Desperately Seeking the Audience*. New York: Routledge.

Audley, P. 1983. *Canada's Cultural Industries: Broadcasting, Publishing, Records and Film*. Toronto: James Lorimer.

Canada. Mandate Review Committee — CBC, NFB, Telefilm (Juneau). 1996. *Report*. Ottawa: Department of Supply and Services.

————. Task Force on the Implementation of Digital Radio. 1993. *Digital Radio: The Sound of the Future*. Ottawa: Department of Supply and Services.

————. Department of Communications. 1987. *Vital Links, Canadian Cultural Industries*. Ottawa: Department of Supply and Services.

————. 1932. *Special Committee on Radio Broadcasting. Minutes of Proceedings and Evidence*. Ottawa: King's Printer.

Canadian Association of Broadcasters. 1989. *Radio Strategic Plan and Analysis*. Ottawa: CAB.

CBC. 1994. *Annual Report, 1993–94*. Ottawa: CBC.

Collins, R. 1990. *Culture, Communication and National Identity: The Case of Canadian Television*. Toronto: University of Toronto Press.

Crissell, A. 1986. *Understanding Radio*. London: Methuen.

CRTC. 1994. *Originating Radio Stations*. CRTC hand-out.

————. 1993. *Radio Market Report, 1989–93*. Ottawa: CRTC.

————. 1993. *Radio and Television Statistical and Financial Summaries, 1988–93*. Ottawa: CRTC.

————. 1992. *Radio Financial Summaries, Private Broadcasting, 1987–92*. Ottawa: CRTC.

————. 1991. *Annual Report, 1990–91*. Ottawa: CRTC.

————. 1990. *Annual Report, 1989–90*. Ottawa: CRTC.

————. 1988. *Annual Report, 1987–88*. Ottawa: CRTC.

————. 1986. *Annual Report, 1985–86*. Ottawa: CRTC.

————. 1974. *Canadian Ownership in Broadcasting. A Report on the Foreign Divestiture Process*. Ottawa: Information Canada.

De la Garde, R. et al. 1993. *Small Nations, Big Neighbour. Denmark and Québec/Canada Compare Notes on American Popular Culture*. London: John Libbey.

Ekos Research Associates. 1991. *Reading in Canada, 1991*. Ottawa: Department of Communications.

Ellis, D. 1979. *Evolution of the Canadian Broadcasting System: Objectives and Realities, 1928–68*. Ottawa: Department of Communications.

Filion, M. 1994. *Radiodiffusion et société distincte*. Montréal: Éditions du Méridien.

————. 1990. Pour mieux comprendre la publicité à la radio de Radio-Canada entre 1934 et 1958. *Communication*. Vol. 11, No 2, 231-249.

Globerman, S. 1983. *Cultural Regulation in Canada*. Montreal: Institute for Research on Public Policy.

Grant, P. et al. 1993. *Canadian Broadcast and Cable Regulatory Handbook*. Toronto: McCarthy Tétrault.

Grossberg, L. (ed.). 1992. *Cultural Studies*. New York: Routledge.

Gwyn, R. 1985. *The 49th Paradox. Canadian North America*. Toronto: McClelland and Stewart.

Hahn, R. 1981. *The Role of Radio in the Canadian Music Industry*. Toronto: Richard Hahn.

Herman, E.S. and N. Chomsky. 1988. *Manufacturing Consent. The Political Economy of the Mass Media*. New York: Pantheon.

Leblanc, L. 1990. *A Report on Canadian Recordings and Canadian Radio*. Ottawa: CRTC.

Nolan, M. 1989. An Infant Industry: Canadian Private Radio, 1919–36. *Canadian Historical Review.* Vol. 52, No 4, 496-518.

Paul McKnight Communications. 1993. *A Study of Canadian Talent Development Initiatives.* Vancouver: Paul McKnight Communications.

Peers, F. 1979. *The Public Eye: Television and the Politics of Canadian Broadcasting, 1952–68.* Toronto: University of Toronto Press.

———. 1969. *The Politics of Canadian Broadcasting, 1920–51.* Toronto: University of Toronto Press.

Raboy, M. 1992. *Les médias québécois: presse, radio, télévision, cablodistribution.* Boucherville: Gaëtan Morin.

———. 1990. *Missed Opportunities: The Story of Canada's Broadcasting Policy.* Kingston: McGill-Queen's University Press.

Radio Action Plan Consultative Group. 1992. *An Action Plan for Radio: "Today's Crisis in the Private Radio Industry" and "Tomorrow's Opportunities for Canadian Radio."* Report submitted to the Minister of Communications.

Radio Marketing Bureau. 1993. *Radio Facts Book.* Toronto: Radio Marketing Bureau.

Siegel, A. 1983. *Politics and the Media in Canada.* Toronto: McGraw-Hill Ryerson.

Smythe, D. 1981. *Dependency Road: Communications, Capitalism, Consciousness and Canada.* Norwood: Ablex Publishing.

Tremblay, G. (ed.). 1990. *Les industries de la culture et de la communication au Québec et au Canada.* Sillery: Presses de l'Université du Québec.

Vipond, M. 1994. "The Beginnings of Public Broadcasting in Canada: The CRBC, 1932–1936." *Canadian Journal of Communication,* Vol. 19, 151-171.

———. 1992. *Listening In. The First Decade of Canadian Broadcasting, 1922–1932.* Kingston: McGill-Queen's University Press.

Weir, A. 1965. *The Struggle for National Broadcasting in Canada.* Toronto: McClelland and Stewart.

Part Three

Image/Data Industries

6

Film and Video Production

Ted Magder

In 1951, the Massey report, the first full-scale review of Canada's cultural activities, came to this rather ominous conclusion in its chapter entitled "Films in Canada": "The cinema at present is not only the most potent but also the most alien of the influences shaping our Canadian life. Nearly all Canadians go to the movies; and most movies come from Hollywood ... Hollywood refashions us in its own image" (Canada, 1951: 50). From the earliest days of the cinema, Canada (more than any other country in the world) has been inundated by the movies of Hollywood. Canadian audiences soon became accustomed to the narratives and genres of Hollywood. Hollywood's stars were Canada's stars. Moreover, in the period before the arrival of television, Hollywood produced over 500 feature films about Canada, conservatively estimated to be ten times the number of feature films that Canadians made about themselves (Berton, 1965; Clandfield, 1987). Most of Hollywood's "Canadian" films were shot on the studio backlots or in the southern California countryside. Their depiction of Canadian life was stereotypical in the extreme. Canada was a wild and scenic outback, sparsely populated by prospectors, lumberjacks, fur traders, Indians and Mounties. And of course it was almost always snowing. By the late 1950s, Hollywood's films about Canada were the rule. Canadian films were the exception, "foreign films" in their own national space.

The Massey report did not dwell on the statistical evidence that underpinned its conclusions, nor did it provide a rigorous analysis of the structure of the film industry in Canada. Instead, the chapter on film, like the rest of the report, was an emotionally charged plea for a government-led strategy to promote Canadian culture in the interests of national survival. The issue had been put on the political agenda before, but after the publication of the Massey report the question of the state's role in cultural matters became an ongoing public concern. The question of culture was a question of identity. Film-making in Canada was saddled with a heavy responsibility: it was to counteract the pernicious and alien influences of Hollywood. Cultural issues were political issues of the highest order. The future of the nation was at stake.

Since the 1950s, the marketplace for film and video production in Canada (and elsewhere) has undergone a dramatic shift: from theatres to a widening array of television-based entertainment services located inside the home. From the 1950s to the early 1970s, television's success cut sharply into movie theatre attendance. In the last two decades, the proliferation of new television channels based upon cable and satellite delivery systems and the widespread use of video cassette recorders have turned the home into the principal site for the distribution of cultural products based upon "moving images." During this period, Hollywood retained its dominance over the global market for feature films and extended its corporate clout into the markets for home-based entertainment. In 1993, for example, the U.S. film industry generated a $4-billion surplus, second only to exports from the defence and aerospace industries in its contribution to U.S. balance of trade (*The Wall Street Journal,* 26 March 1993: R6). (Table 6-1 gives some indication of the extent to which Hollywood's products dominate the global marketplace and the growing importance of foreign markets to Hollywood's revenue stream.) In 1986, the major studios received 65 per cent of their revenues from the U.S. market. By 1991, the U.S. market accounted for 53.2 per cent of revenues and foreign markets accounted for 46.8 per cent. During this period, total revenues generated from foreign markets more than doubled, from $6.7 billion in 1986 to $13.4 billion in 1991 (Ibid.: R16).[1] These figures include revenues generated from film and video sales and ancillary activities, such as theme parks and licensed products. In the last forty years, the major Hollywood studios have diversified their activities to include virtually every facet of cultural production and distribution, from television programs and cable systems, to publishing and sound recording, to video games and toys, to clothing and children's furnishings. Despite early misgivings, Hollywood has learned to love television and the proliferation of entertainment and leisure products that typify consumer culture.

As Hollywood was beginning to adjust to the new markets for home-based entertainment, the Canadian film production industry

Table 6-1
1992 Market Share of Feature Films Distributed to Theatres, According to Country of Origin

	Market Share of American Films	Market Share of National Films	Market Share of Other Films
Canada (except Quebec)	96%	2%	2%
Quebec	83%	3%	14%
France	58%	35%	7%
Spain	77%	9%	14%
Great Britain	84%	14%	2%
Australia	76%	9%	15%

Source: Groupe Secor, 1994: 24.

also underwent something of a transformation. In the early 1960s, renegade film-makers at the National Film Board (NFB) tried their hand at feature film production, ultimately leaving the NFB to pursue its interest in the feature-length format in the private sector. In 1963, the Quebec-based Association professionnelle des cinéastes joined forces with the recently formed Directors' Guild of Canada to urge the federal government to provide support to the development of private-sector feature film production. Their plea was given added validity by Nat Taylor, one of the luminaries of Canada's private film industry. Taylor suggested that the Hollywood studios were more interested than ever in securing independent productions for their distribution businesses. According to Taylor, Canadian producers had an advantage over their European counterparts because they could produce films that were "practically indistinguishable" from American ones. As he put it: "We shall have a production industry in Canada, a good and thriving one, if our government ever gets around to extending a helping hand" (cited in Magder [1993: 106, 107]).

The helping hand came in the form of the Canadian Film Development Corporation (CFDC), established in 1968 with an initial budget of $10 million. The Canadian government has been involved in financing private-sector film production ever since. With the establishment of the Canadian Broadcast Program Fund in 1983, the CFDC was renamed Telefilm Canada and became a key player in the production of programming destined for the television market. Since the mid-1980s, most provincial governments have also established programs and agencies to assist film and television production. In 1992–93, total government expenditure in the film and video sector was roughly $340 million of which $254 million, or roughly 75 per cent, came from federal sources (Statistics Canada, 1994c: 15).

Despite the influx of public money and an array of policies designed to increase Canadian film and television production, the challenge posed by the Massey report is still on the public agenda. Though private-sector film and video production in Canada has grown exponentially since the 1960s, the Canadian film and video market is still inundated by Hollywood productions. This chapter focuses on the development of the private feature film industry in Canada and the subsequent emergence of independent film and video production for television.[2] It will underline the importance of government policy in this sector, particularly in terms of investment capital and loans. We shall also have occasion to trace the emergence of core companies that are increasingly integrated into the global marketplace for film and television production.

The Canadian Market

Theatrical Market

The theatrical market for movies has declined precipitously since the arrival of television in the 1950s. Theatrical attendance reached a peak in 1952, when Canadians went to the movies an average of eighteen times each that year. By 1980, Canadians went to the movies an average of four times a year. In 1991–92, attendance had dropped to a little more than two times a year (Audley, 1983: 222; Statistics Canada, 1994a: 36). Primarily because of increases in ticket prices and concession sales (which account for approximately 25 per cent of revenues), theatrical exhibition continues to be a profitable undertaking. In 1991–92, total theatrical revenue in Canada was roughly $500 million. The profit margin for theatres in Canada was 11.8 per cent in 1991–92, down from 13.2 per cent in 1987–88.

The Canadian theatrical market is dominated by two chains: Cineplex Odeon and Famous Players. Famous Players was formed in 1920 by a group of Canadian investors (see Pendakur [1990]; Magder [1993]). In 1930, U.S.-based Paramount Pictures took over control of Famous Players. In 1994, control of Famous Players was transferred to another U.S.-based entertainment firm, Viacom, after its successful takeover of Paramount Communications.

The Odeon chain of theatres was established by Canadian investors in 1941. In 1945–46, it was sold outright to the Rank Organization, then Britain's largest vertically integrated film company. In 1984, the Odeon chain was purchased by Cineplex, which had been started in 1977 by Garth Drabinsky and Nat Taylor. In 1987, MCA, a diversified U.S. entertainment company (and parent of Universal Pictures), purchased a 50-per-cent equity interest in Cineplex Odeon. Through fits and starts, Cineplex Odeon has grown to become one of the largest exhibitors in North America. In 1993, it controlled 1,630 screens in 365 locations across North America (567 screens in 133 locations in Canada), which account for approximately 8 per cent of total North American box office revenues (Cineplex Odeon, 1994).

The dominance of Famous Players and Cineplex Odeon is one of the distinguishing characteristics of the Canadian film market. Between them the two chains receive about two-thirds of annual theatrical revenues in Canada (Ellis, 1992: 98) and maintain ongoing supplier arrangements with the Hollywood majors. Famous Players has first-run rights in Canada to all MGM-United Artist, Paramount, and Warner Bros. films, while Cineplex Odeon has exclusive first-run rights to the films of Columbia and Universal Studios. The two chains share the distribution rights for films from other studios (Pendakur, 1990: 118). This arrangement helps to reduce business uncertainty for the major chains, and all but guarantees the best available screen time for the feature films distributed by the American majors. It also has the effect of marginalizing feature films distributed by the non-majors (which includes virtually all Canadian films), both in terms of access to most first-run, high-profile theatres and in terms of the most attractive play dates, such as the Christmas season.

Home Video and Television

Theatres no longer constitute the major market for feature films. According to the Motion Picture Association of America, 1988 was the first year that the home video market generated more worldwide revenue for U.S. movie distributors than feature films did, accounting for $3,811 million in revenue compared to $3,338 million from box offices. In 1991, on worldwide revenues of $13,418 million, home video accounted for $5,714 million or 42.6 per cent, to be followed by theatres for $4,629 million or 34.5 per cent, and television revenues of $3,075 million or 22.9 per cent (*The Wall Street Journal*, 26 March 1993: R16).

More than 70 per cent of Canadian households now own at least one video cassette recorder. The retail market for rental home videos in Canada was estimated in 1994 to be worth close to $1.4 billion a year, while home video sales were worth another $400 million; in total, the value of the home video market is more than four times greater than total receipts from box-office revenues (*Playback*, 9 August 1994: 4). For film and television productions, television itself is still the major market.[3]

Domestic and Foreign Share of Market

Throughout the 1980s and into the 1990s, the percentage of Canadian theatrical screen time devoted to foreign films has hovered around 97 per cent (Table 6-1). As a study by NGL Consulting (1992: 47) pointed out, "in any given year, the volume of foreign films in Canada outnumbers Canadian films by ten to one." Moreover, in English-Canada especially, Canadian films are typically given screen time only in the largest urban markets and even then are often confined to a single screen for a quick one- or two-week run at specialty theatres.

The box-office returns for Canadian feature films are very poor; Canadian feature films almost never recover their budgets from theatrical admissions. Between 1987 and 1990, only three of 48 Canadian films released in English Canada earned more than $500,000 in gross box-office receipts (*Black Robe, Dead Ringers* and *Jesus of Montreal*). Seventy-five per cent of the films released earned less than $100,000, and 60 per cent earned less than $50,000 (NGL, 1992: 114; see also Groupe Secor [1991: 45-78]). During the same period, the gross box-office receipts in Quebec for Canadian films were significantly higher; nine films earned over $500,000 and 46 per cent earned more than $100,000. In 1993, the top ten Canadian feature films grossed closed to $5 million in box-office receipts; the three top films (*La Florida, Shadow of the Wolf*, and *Matusalem*) accounted for close to 80 per cent of the total (*Playback*, 14 February 1994: 2). By comparison, the top grossing American films shown in Canada average more than $10 million; blockbusters gross closer to $20 million.

While information on the home video market is sketchy, NGL Consulting concluded that "video retail is tending to follow cinema exhibition trends" (NGL, 1992: vi). Its study suggested that the best

Table 6-2
Average Television Audience for Selected Canadian
Feature Films (CBC, Cinema Canada)

1992–93 Season (10:00 P.M.) Film Title	Average Audience (000)
One Magic Christmas	643
Dead Ringers	477
Roadkill	374
The Grey Fox	366
Une Histoire inventée	365
Jesus of Montreal	362
Life Classes	345
Bye Bye Blues	333
I've Heard the Mermaids Singing	301
Night Zoo	296
Speaking Parts	294
Audience Average for 23 Titles	*(340)*

1993–94 Season (11:00 P.M.) Film Title	Average Audience (000)
Chain Dance	429
Forbidden Love	413
Milk & Honey	345
Dead Ringers*	304
Hounds of Notre Dame*	294
Termini Station	254
Clearcut	241
Decline of the American Empire	236
Masala	180
Grocer's Wife	171
Les Bons Debarras	151
*aired at 10:00 P.M.	
Average Audience for 26 Titles	*(209)*

Source: CBC Audience Research.

vehicle for the exhibition of Canadian feature films is conventional TV, especially the CBC. It noted: "The premiere showing of Canadian feature films on CBC reaches an average of over 500,000 Canadians and, by the second showing, over 1 million viewers. This reach exceeds the combined viewership of theatrical, home video and pay-TV by roughly four times (approximately 30,000 moviegoers see a $2000K box-office film; plus 150,000 viewers will watch videos based on 2000 video copies of the film; and approximately 100,000 viewers will see it on pay-TV)" (NGL, 1992: 122).

Table 6-2 provides a sample of audience figures for Canadian films shown on the CBC English network's Cinema Canada series during 1992–93 and 1993–94. It suggests that the NGL statistics are an overestimate. It also indicates the importance of scheduling practices in reaching audiences; in 1992–93 Cinema Canada was aired at 10:00 P.M. and reached an average audience of 340,000; in 1993–94, the films were aired at 11:00 P.M. and reached an average audience of 209,000.

Private-Sector Distribution

Analysis of the market for film (and video) production must include a discussion of the distribution system. Distributors serve primarily as brokers between producers and the various sites of exhibition; in many cases, they also function as investors and producers as well. Hollywood's international success, especially in the feature film market, is tied to the distribution activities of the major studios. Hollywood studios not only produce and distribute their own feature films; they also distribute a good number of feature films produced by independents outside of the studio system. Because feature film-making is such a costly and risky venture, control over the circuit of distribution is vital to long-term financial success; a few blockbuster hits can compensate for the majority of films, which barely recoup production and marketing costs.

The Canadian distribution market is dominated by a small number of American companies. In 1989–90, fifteen American subsidiaries operating in Canada together generated 85 per cent of the total profits from film and video distribution (Groupe Secor, 1994: 48). In 1991–92, the American subsidiaries received a little more than 83 per cent of the total revenues from movie theatres, and 51 per cent of the revenues from home entertainment. As Table 6-3 also shows, most of the revenues from distribution in Canada are generated by foreign productions. Because the American majors consider Canada to be part of their domestic market, they typically include Canadian distribution rights in their negotiations with independent (i.e., non-studio) producers. In effect, Canadian distributors have access only to those films that have been picked over by the large U.S. distributors; thus, the lion's share of the distribution revenues in Canada flows south

Table 6-3
Domestic and Foreign Share of Distribution Revenues in Canadian Market, 1987–88 to 1991–92 (by Primary Market)

	1987–88	1988–89	1989–90	1990–91	1991–92
Primary Market ($ millions)					
Theatrical	168.5	158.7	225.5	193.4	184.6
Home entertainment	288.2	306.4	398.2	437.8	435.9
Foreign-controlled Share (%)					
Theatrical	87.5	83.6	85.5	84.0	83.4
Home entertainment	54.6	50.1	49.0	47.7	47.6
Proportion of Receipts from Canadian Productions					
Theatrical	4.4	4.9	4.3	5.8	6.4
Home entertainment	7.9	8.5	10.2	12.7	14.7

N.B. the primary market of a company is that in which the largest number of titles are distributed.

Source: Statistics Canada, 1994a: 33.

of the border, contributing further to the undercapitalization of Canadian production activities.[4]

Industry Structure

The Public Sector: The National Film Board of Canada

The NFB was created by the federal government in 1939 with a mandate "to produce, distribute and promote the production and distribution of films designed to interpret Canada to Canadians and other nations." In the 1980s, its mandate was altered to emphasize the production and distribution of "films and videos which focus on contemporary problems which reflect the social and cultural concerns of a growing number of Canadians" (NFB, 1987). The NFB is more than a producer and distributor of films and video; it is also a training and research facility committed to advancing the art and technology of audiovisual communications. While the NFB's activities are centred in Montreal, the development of regional productions is a major priority for the NFB, through the provision of technical services and co-production activities with the private sector. The

Table 6-4
Canadian Film and Video Production Summary
1987–88 to 1991–92

	1987–88	1988–89	1989–90	1990–91	1991–92
Number of Producers (by specialization)					
Theatrical features	18	13	20	19	20
Conventional and pay-TV	96	86	92	119	137
Advertising	64	73	61	61	58
Gov't and educational	84	105	103	123	123
Industry	136	138	127	183	182
Other	154	207	199	236	222
Total	552	622	602	741	742
Number of Productions					
Theatrical features	334	46	48	54	56
Television					
Under 30 min.	...	...	...	...	2,223
30-74 min.	...	...	...	...	4,867
75 min. or more	...	...	...	...	414
TV commercials	4,065	4,366	4,728	3,619	3,929
Music videos	92	80	157	217	209
Corporate videos	...	...	...	...	4,069
Home videos	...	...	...	...	141
Educational	...	...	...	...	262
Other	2,423	3,032	1,806	987	3,721
Total	16,040	18,802	17,181	17,634	19,891
Employment					
Total	3,391	4,593	4,283	18,973	14,108
Salaries and Wages ($ millions)					
Total	172.4	205.5	205.1	243.1	208.1

Table 6-4 (cont.)
Canadian Film and Video Production Summary
1987–88 to 1991–92

	1987–88	1988–89	1989–90	1990–91	1991–92
Production Revenue (by client type) *($ millions)*					
Distributors					
Theatrical features	10.4	27.7	10.3	17.0	8.5
Other placements	25.3	48.1	1.9	12.3	74.2
Conventional TV	91.0	89.9	91.4	149.4	138.0
Pay-TV	6.8	3.1	6.3	32.5	33.9
Non-theatrical					
Advertising	120.5	143.1	134.3	131.9	137.0
Government	20.2	37.8	31.1	38.0	45.0
Educational	3.8	2.4	2.9	5.0	3.5
Industry	69.0	77.9	80.7	95.1	78.1
Sub-total	213.4	261.2	249.0	270.0	263.6
For Other Producers	68.2	65.9	85.9	89.3	50.2
Other	20.0	37.0	37.7	14.0	13.3
Total	435.4	532.8	499.6	584.5	581.8
Exports *(included in total)*	62.8	80.6	116.1	80.6	82.8
Total Revenue	517.7	629.4	583.6	703.8	688.2
Total Operating Expenses	494.0	606.8	567.8	693.5	611.9
Profit Margin	4.6%	3.6%	2.7%	1.5%	11.1%

Source: Statistics Canada, 1994a: 14. Total Revenue includes
government loans and investments.

NFB operates six regional distribution and marketing centres and maintains partnerships with over 400 libraries and community centres throughout Canada.

On average, the NFB is involved in the production of between 80 and 100 films a year; more than 80 per cent of the audience for these films finds them on television. In 1994–95, the NFB will operate with a budget of $81.1 million and is slated to produce 88 films (51 English, 37 French). Of these films, 60 per cent will be documentaries, 25 per cent will be animations, and 10 per cent will be dramas (*Playback*, 9 May 1994: 2). Included within the NFB's annual expenditure is a $5 million fund to co-produce culturally relevant films — especially feature films and documentaries — with independent Canadian producers. The NFB's concentration on documentaries and experimental animation (for which it has received numerous international awards) is a significant contribution to the overall diversity of film production in Canada, since these are precisely the kinds of projects not undertaken by private-sector producers because of the financial risks involved. Likewise, the NFB's New Initiatives in Film, an internship program designed to address the misrepresentation of aboriginal women and women of colour in Canadian film, reflects the NFB's interest in productions that probe the underexplored dimensions of Canada's social and cultural diversity.

Private-Sector Production

Data compiled by Statistics Canada provided a useful overview of private-sector film and video production in Canada. In 1991–92, there were 742 film and video production companies operating in Canada, a 34-per-cent increase since 1987–88. They paid more than $208 million to over 14,000 workers (more than 60 per cent of which were freelancers). The average profit margin in 1991–92 was 11.1 per cent, up substantially from 4.6 per cent in 1987–88, and 1.5 per cent in 1990–91 (see Table 6-4).

Total revenues for film, video, and audiovisual productions in 1991–92 were $688.2 million on operating expenses of $611.9 million. Exports accounted for $82.8 million of total revenues. The theatrical market contributes a little more than one per cent, or $8.5 million, to total production revenues. The non-theatrical market, which consists of advertising, government, educational and industrial clients, continues to be the largest market for Canadian film production, accounting for 45 per cent of total 1991–92 production revenues. The home entertainment market, which includes video sales

Table 6-5
Financing of Production and Development Budgets of Canadian and Co-production Feature Films and Television Productions

	Canadian		Co-production	
	1991–92	**1992–93**	**1991–92**	**1993–94**
Feature Films				
Number of productions	56	35	11	4
Financing ($ millions)				
Public	25.7	16.8	6.4	*
Private				
Canadian	22.6	16.4	7.4	7.8
Foreign	9.1	19.4	3.4	15.8
Total	57.4	54.4	17.3	23.6
Television				
Number of Productions	7,504	7,414	43	47
Financing ($ millions)				
Public	86.8	69.9	6.5	14.0
Private				
Canadian	174.0	137.4	6.9	31.8
Foreign	62.0	111.9	19.7	52.3
Total	323.0	326.8	33.1	105.5

Source: Statistics Canada, 1994b: 9.
All figures in current dollars.
* confidential to meet secrecy requirements of the Statistics Act.

and rentals, as well as conventional and pay-television, accounted for 42 per cent of total production revenues. Preliminary data for 1992–93 indicate little change in the overall pattern of production revenues, with the exceptions that revenues from theatrical feature films dropped to $4.1 million and revenues from exports rose substantially to $132 million (Statistics Canada, 1994b: 8).

The 1991–92 data show that production companies tend to specialize in a single market and that there is considerable discrepancy in overall profitability among producer types. In 1991, 20 producers specialized in theatrical productions. On total revenues of $10.9 million, the average profit margin for theatrical producers was -22.6 per cent (Statistics Canada, 1994a: 22-26). Producers of industrial films and videos and advertising had the highest profit margins, at 17.8 per cent and 16.5 per cent respectively. Producers of conventional and pay-television had an average profit margin of 10.4 per cent in 1991–92, up substantially from the 4.6 per cent in 1989–90 and 0.7 per cent in 1990–91.

Table 6-5 provides an overview of public-sector funding for film and video production in Canada. Considering the industry as a whole, public-sector funding accounted for 20-25 per cent of all production and development budgets in 1991–92 and 1992–93. This figure reflects the fact that public-sector funding to non-theatrical producers is low. For theatrical feature films and television productions, public funding represents a far larger total of budgets: in 1992–93, public funds accounted for 31 per cent of total budgets for feature films, and 21 per cent of total budgets for television productions; in 1991–92 the figures were 45 per cent and 27 per cent respectively. If anything, these figures underestimate the importance of public-sector funding for those feature films and television programs that make use of them. For feature films that receive government loans and investment, the average public contribution to total budgets is greater than 50 per cent and in many cases reaches above 70 per cent.

It is also worth noting that the foreign share of private investment in Canadian feature films and television programs almost doubled between 1991–92 and 1992–93, while Canadian private investment dropped by more than 20 per cent. In the case of feature films, private foreign investment went from $9.11 million in 1991–92 to $19.4 million in 1992–93 (Table 6-5). If the financing of co-productions for feature films and television is included in the calculations, total private Canadian investment in 1991–92 and 1992–93 amounted to $404.3 million, while total foreign investment amounted to $293.6 million.[5] These figures undoubtedly underestimate the importance of foreign investment to film and television production in Canada because they do not include the value of strictly American productions that are shot on location in Canada or American-Canadian joint ventures (since there is no co-production treaty between Canada and the United States). In 1994, for example, foreign productions spent more than $140 million on location in Ontario alone (11 feature films and 25 TV projects) (*The Globe and Mail*, 4 January, 1994: C3). Although precise figures are difficult to come by, total foreign production in Canada has been estimated at more than $200 million a year (Audley, 1991: 63)

The Emergence of Core Companies

While the absolute number of film and video production companies is high, many of them are small operators. In 1990–91, 80 per cent of the companies had a turnover of less than $1 million. On average, these companies accrued losses of 30 per cent. Fifteen per cent of the companies in 1990–91 had a turnover of between $1 and $5 million; their average profit margin was 11.0 per cent. Of the 741 companies that operated in 1990–91, only 29 had more than $5 million in turnover, with combined expenditures of $333.6 million and a profit margin of 7.9 per cent (Groupe Secor, 1994: 38). One interpretation of these data is that film and video companies are often established to produce a single project and then disbanded; they are designed as limited partnerships and reflect the complex financial arrangements used by producers. At the same time, the data reveal the emergence of a core group of film and video companies that has achieved considerable industry prominence.

This trend has continued. One of the most noteworthy developments in 1993–94 was the growing number of companies who successfully issued public share offerings: Paragon Entertainment ($4.0 million), Malofilm Communications ($13 million), Cinar ($13.5 million), Nelvana ($28.8 million), Alliance Communications ($34 million) and Atlantis Communications ($36.5 million). Astral Communications, which has traded as a public company for some years, also issued a $23-million common share offering in 1993.

The emergence of a small group of well-financed and diversified production companies signals an important shift in the Canadian film industry. These companies have benefited greatly from the combined policy measures introduced by the federal and provincial governments to spur independent production in Canada. They have also taken advantage of the U.S. industry's new-found interest in foreign partnerships and foreign productions. A number of factors are at work here. Canada's relatively cheap dollar has made it an attractive site for the production of films and television programs destined for the U.S. market. At the same, the maturation of cable-delivery systems in the U.S. and the concomitant increase in specialty channels and pay-television has led to a growth in demand for film and television programs. The proliferation of channels has also had the effect of reducing the average profit margin on television programming, because the audience is much more fragmented than before. In general, Hollywood needs to make more for less; and Canadians can make the product that Hollywood thinks it needs, at a reduced price. Finally, partnerships between American and Canadian producers can still take advantage of Canadian government financial incentives, provided that minimum rules with respect to Canadian content and expenditures in Canada are met. What is true of the U.S. market is also true of the global marketplace for film and television productions. Canadian companies are now attractive partners to a large number of foreign producers, and Canadian film and television programming sell well in these markets. A closer look at some of the industry's key players reveals the extent to which they have been integrated into the global marketplace for film and television production.[6]

Alliance Communications
Alliance is Canada's leading fully integrated producer and distributor of television programs and feature films. Aside from its near-frantic production schedule, Alliance operates as a domestic distributor (Alliance Releasing) and international distributor (Alliance International Releasing) of film and television productions, and through a licensed subsidiary (Equicap), it arranges and markets structured financing for the Canadian production industry. Alliance also owns 55 per cent of the Showcase Network, a Canadian specialty cable channel. The company's revenues have increased annually. In 1989, Alliance reported revenues of $43.6 million on expenses of $41.5 million. At its year-end of 31 March 1993, the company reported revenues of $132.1 million on expenses of $125.4 million. Cineplex Odeon is one of the company's principal shareholders, owning about 8 per cent of the company's stock.[7]

Since 1985, Alliance has produced, or co-produced, close to 450 hours of television programming, including the series *Night Heat*, *Bordertown*, *E.N.G.*, *Counterstrike* and *North of 60*. *Night Heat* and *Bordertown* have been sold in strip syndication (the lucrative aftermarket where the program is sold to different broadcasters and scheduled into daily runs over a period of months). *E.N.G.* has been sold in almost fifty countries, and there are enough episodes of *E.N.G.* (95) and *Counterstrike* (66) to exploit the strip syndication market. Alliance has also produced a number of successful movies for television and mini-series, among them: *Family of Strangers*, which ranked third among movies for television shown in the United States in the 1992–93 season, and *Woman on the Run: the Lawrencia Bembenek Story*. In 1996, Alliance has roughly 15 projects either shooting or in the development stage with a variety of U.S. broadcasters and cable networks, including ABC, CBS, Fox, USA Network, Family Channel, Nickelodeon and MTV. In 1993, Alliance contracted with Harlequin Enterprises (a subsidiary of Torstar) to produce and distribute television movies based upon Harlequin's extensive library, as part of an effort to establish a romance fiction syndicate of international broadcasters. The contract called for an initial six movies to be shot in Canada in the summer of 1994 (each with a budget of $3 million). In September 1994, Alliance's *Due South* became the first Canadian-produced series to be broadcast during network prime time in the U.S.. Alliance sells about two-thirds of its television production in the United States (*The Globe and Mail*, 10 December 1994: C4).

Television is not only a lucrative market for Alliance, it is also, relatively speaking, a safe one. Alliance will not normally start production until 80 per cent of the costs have been covered by a combination of licence fees from television services (in the United States and Canada), contributions from co-producers, presales of foreign distribution rights and government incentives. For the fiscal year ended 31 March 1993, of $81 million spent on television program production, approximately $17.3 million or 22 per cent was financed through government incentives (Alliance, 1993: 13). In other words, government equity investments, grants and tax abatements play a crucial role in the financial underpinning of Alliance.

Unlike a number of the other major production companies in Canada, Alliance is active in feature film production as well as television programming. In 1991, Alliance produced *Black Robe*, a $12-million Canada-Australia co-production that won six Genies. In 1994, Alliance produced Atom Egoyan's Genie and Cannes-award-winning *Exotica*, and Léa Pool's *Mouvements du Désir*. These ventures notwithstanding, Alliance is not particularly bullish when it comes to the feature film market. Given Hollywood's dominance over screen time in most of the major markets, Alliance sees itself as producing "specialty films designed for niche markets" (Alliance, 1993: 14). These ventures rely heavily upon government financial incentives. According to Alliance's prospectus, the budget of a recent feature film received approximately 50 per cent of its funds from Telefilm and 27 per cent of its funds from the Ontario Film Development Corporation. Alliance paid itself 13 per cent to acquire worldwide distribution rights to the film, and the remaining 10 per cent was financed by the deferral of fees payable to creative personnel. As long as government agencies continue to subsidize close to 75 per cent of the costs of Canadian feature film production, it seems reasonable to conclude that Alliance will continue to support the development of Canadian projects.

In April 1994, Alliance signed a deal to co-produce three $10-to-$15-million feature films with Universal Studios. The deal marks the first time that a major American studio and a Canadian company have signed a multi-picture agreement. Alliance has also taken the plunge into the big-budget, video-game-film-making market. In affiliation with Sony, Alliance produced a $30-million science-fiction thriller, *Johnny Mnemonic* (starring Keanu Reeves), which coincided with the release of a CD-ROM game by the same name.

Atlantis Communications
Founded in 1978, Atlantis has concentrated its production activities in television programs, rather than feature films destined for the cinema (Atlantis, 1993: 4). Atlantis has produced over 60 titles encompassing more than 400 hours of programming. Some of its more notable series titles include *Neon Rider, Maniac Mansion, The Ray Bradbury Theatre* and *Destiny Ridge.*

Atlantis's business plans reveal a company eager to exploit foreign markets and to break free of any dependence upon government financing. Atlantis has entered into a strategic relationship with the U.S.-based Interpublic Group of Companies (IPG) and Freemantle Corporation. IPG is one of the largest advertising organizations in the world, with agencies operating in over 75 companies, including McCann Erickson Worldwide, Lintas Worldwide, and the Lowe Group. IPG also owns 80 per cent of Freemantle International, the world's leading producer of television game shows. Freemantle International is affiliated with Freemantle Corporation, a major international distributor of television programs and now the subdistributor of Atlantis's programs in South America. The relationship with IPG gives Atlantis access to the growing market for barter television programming in which advertising is prepackaged for would-be broadcasters (Atlantis, 1993: 12).[8] For Atlantis, as for the other major independent Canadian production companies, many of the broadcasters who play this formative role are foreign. In the period between 1990 and 1993, close to 68 per cent of the licence fee revenue received by Atlantis came from broadcasters and distributors outside

Canada. In 1994, it sold roughly half of its television product in the United States, with the other half split equally between Canada and European markets (*The Globe and Mail*, 10 December 1994: C4).

Nelvana Ltd.

In business since 1971, Nelvana is Canada's leading producer of animated television programs and feature films. Nelvana's revenue for 1993 was $19 million; the company has forecast revenue $27.7 for 1994 and a profit of $3.6 million (Nelvana, 1994; *The Globe and Mail* 1994, 19 March: B20). Nelvana's lineup of animated shows includes *Babar, Care Bears, Tales from the Cryptkeeper, Jim Henson's Dog City, Eek the Cat* and *Cadillacs and Dinosaurs*. The company has also produced three Care Bear movies and the live-action series, *The Edison Twins, T and T* and *The Twenty-Minute Workout*. In keeping with the marketing strategy of most U.S. children's programming, Nelvana has entered into master toy licence agreements for *Cadillacs and Dinosaurs* and *Tales from the Cryptkeeper*. In the fall of 1993, Nelvana signed a multi-year deal to produce five animated feature films for Paramount Pictures. The first two features began production in the summer of 1994; both are budgeted at approximately $20 million (*Playback* 1993, 8 November: 4). Nelvana relies heavily on the U.S. and international market for its success. In 1993, 61 per cent of its revenues came from the United States; in total, 92 per cent of Nelvana's revenues came from sources outside Canada.

Independent Feature Film Producers

The growth of companies such as Alliance, Atlantis and Nelvana has to be contrasted with the continuing saga of most Canadian feature film production. As noted above, the core companies have focused their business strategies on television production. In the case of Alliance and Nelvana, they have also joined forces with American companies to produce a limited number of feature films. While the budgets for these films (e.g., Alliance's three-picture deal with Universal at $10-$15 million apiece) are small by Hollywood standards, they are quite large when compared to the average budgets of Canadian feature films, which have hovered around $2 million over the last ten years.

Most Canadian feature films are cobbled together by independent producers, a term which belies their heavy dependence upon government funds. As Michael Posner (1993) has shown in his revealing study of 10 recent Canadian feature films, government funds often account for more than 70 per cent of total budgets. As noted above, the profit margin for companies that specialize in feature film production is an abysmally low -22.6 per cent. While the core companies strike potentially lucrative deals to produce feature films with American partners, most Canadian feature film-makers still struggle, first to arrange government financing, and second to find the private money that makes up the last 30 per cent or so of production budgets.

Policy Structure

The Pre-CFDC Era

The establishment in 1918 of the Canadian Government Motion Picture Bureau, the first state-sponsored film production unit in the Western world, reflected the Canadian government's early interest in film as means of publicity, especially to encourage immigration and foreign investment (Morris, 1978). The bureau did nothing to promote the production of feature films, and private-sector activities centred on short films sponsored by industry (mostly, for training and publicity), and until the mid-1950s, newsreels for theatrical distribution. While the Canadian government was conscious of both the economic and cultural costs of Hollywood's dominance in Canada, it did virtually nothing to challenge the status quo (Magder, 1993). Hollywood was made to feel right at home; so much so that it counted Canada as part of its domestic market, a practice that continues to this day.

The establishment of the NFB in no way challenged Hollywood's theatrical dominance, nor did it seek to. Under the leadership of John Grierson, the film board did become a powerful agent of wartime propaganda; it also developed an innovative distribution system that reached into schools, community centres and factories and encouraged audience discussion. But Grierson was loathe to encourage the production of fictional feature films (Morris, 1986, 1987). Over time, Grierson's didactic approach to film-making and his emphasis on documentaries as an ongoing set of lessons in civics was supported by Canada's cultural elite. Indeed, the Massey report crystallized what had become something of a cultural and political quandary. It went something like this: NFB films were good because they were educational, while popular Hollywood films threatened to undermine the very existence of a Canadian identity; the federal government should support only those cultural activities that are educational and thus make a meaningful contribution to Canadian identity; state support for popular fictional feature films was untenable because popular culture did not serve an educational purpose.

The Early Years of the CFDC

This dead-end logic was successfully challenged in the 1960s. At the NFB's twenty-fifth anniversary, in 1964, the federal government announced plans to provide financial aid for the production of private-sector Canadian feature films. The Canadian Film Development Corporation began operations in 1968 with a mandate to "foster and promote the development of a feature film industry in Canada" through the provision of loans, grants and awards to Canadian producers and film-makers. Unlike the NFB, the CBC or the Canada Council, the CFDC — with its initial budget of $10 million — was expected to become self-financing. From its inception, the CFDC was conceived as a commercial agency, interested as much (if not more) in the profitability of the films it supported as in their contribution to Canada's cultural life. As the CFDC's first chair, Georges Emile Laplame, remarked: "We are not film-makers. We're just investing money and making loans ... If we were to judge our scripts from an intellectual and cultural point of view we would not be a bank anymore." (Magder, 1993: 134)

By 1971, the CFDC had invested $6.7 million in 64 projects and recouped barely $600,000 or roughly 9 per cent of its investments. In keeping with its commercial orientation, the CFDC had contributed to a number of films that came to be referred to as "maple-syrup porn," movies such as *Love in a Four Letter World*. (Magder, 1993: 136). At the same time, the CFDC had contributed to a number of films that have come to be regarded as early Canadian classics, films such as *Goin' Down the Road*, *Les Mâles* and *Kamouraska*.

In November 1971, the federal cabinet approved a second allotment of $10 million for the CFDC. For the next six years, the CFDC struggled to establish guidelines to accommodate its commercial and cultural objectives. By then it had become clear that the structures and practices of film distribution and theatrical exhibition were a major stumbling block to the CFDC's efforts. Given that Canada was still the second-largest foreign market for Hollywood films and given the increasing competition from television, neither the Hollywood majors nor Canada's major theatrical chains would easily accommodate demands to make more space available for Canadian films.[9] In 1973, and again in 1975, the federal government and the major theatrical chains negotiated a scheme of voluntary exhibition quotas to ensure minimum screen time for Canadian films. The 1975 quotas were set at four weeks of Canadian films per theatre per year. Neither Famous Players nor Odeon fully co-operated with the quota, and since the quota was applied to theatres not screens (at a time when both chains were in the midst of multi-plexing their theatres), its impact was negligible.

During this period, the federal government was lobbied extensively by industry representatives. In terms of the CFDC's development strategy, two options emerged. One option, which would have transformed the CFDC into something of a Canada Council for feature films and brought it closer in line with the mandate of the NFB, was to rechannel the CFDC's money into a system of grants for the production of a small number of Canadian films a year. The other option was to rechannel the CFDC's priorities toward the production of feature films with strong box-office potential, in particular films that would be attractive to the Hollywood majors.

The Tax-Shelter Boom

This second option became viable after changes in tax regulations were followed by a change in the CFDC's financial practices. In 1974 the Capital Cost Allowance (CCA) for Canadian feature films was extended. Instead of writing off capital costs at a rate of 30 per cent a year, investors were allowed to write them off in one year. In 1978, the CFDC shifted its focus from the provision of equity financing for low and medium-budget Canadian films to the provision of bridge financing for projects that were designed to take advantage of the tax shelter. The number of productions and average budgets soared. In 1975, 18 certified films were produced with an average budget of roughly $350,000. By 1979, at the height of the boom, 66 certified feature films were produced with an average budget of $2.6 million (Pendakur, 1990: 172). Measured in terms of employment and total dollars spent, the tax-shelter boom was a success. But many of the films produced during this period were never distributed; many of those that did receive distribution were second-rate efforts that were, as Nat Taylor had earlier suggested, practically indistinguishable from American ones (notable examples include *Meatballs* and *Running*).

By 1980, there was growing criticism of the direction taken by the CFDC, particularly from French-Canadian producers and film-makers who benefited far less than their English-Canadian counterparts from the CFDC's shift in investment priorities. The tax-shelter boom came to a crashing halt in 1980. By 1982, only 30 certified feature films were produced, with an average budget of a little more than $1 million. Federal policy-makers were equally unsatisfied by the tax-shelter boom. Over the course of the 1980s, the CCA provisions were revised twice, in each case after substantial opposition from Canadian producers. In 1983, the CCA was reduced from 100 per cent in one year to 50 per cent in the first year and 50 per cent in the second year. In 1988, the CCA was further reduced to 30 per cent per year.

Telefilm: Putting Television before Film

Easily the most significant policy innovation since the establishment of the CFDC was the establishment of the Canadian Broadcast Program Development Fund in July 1983. The fund has four overall objectives: a) to stimulate production of high-quality, culturally relevant Canadian television programs in targeted categories (drama, children's, documentary and variety programming); b) to reach the broadest possible audience with those programs through scheduling during prime-time viewing hours; c) to stimulate the development of the independent production industry; and, d) to maintain an appropriate regional, linguistic and private-public broadcaster balance in the distribution of public funds (NGL, 1991). The fund had an initial budget of $254 million spread over five years. In 1988, the budget for the fund was made permanent, with annual funding at $60 million. In 1989, the fund was supplemented by an auxiliary fund of $16.5 million per annum. To reflect this shift in investment priorities, the CFDC was renamed Telefilm Canada in February 1984.

A 1991 review of the fund concluded that it "has been enormously successful in achieving its original objectives" (NGL, 1991: xi). In 1986–90, for example, the fund helped finance close to $800 million in total production volume of 2,275 hours of original television programming, of which more than 1,000 hours consisted of drama programs exhibited during peak viewing hours. In terms of audience reach, viewing of Canadian programs in peak time increased substantially between 1986 and 1990. For English television, viewing of Canadian programs during peak time went from 19.6 per cent in 1984–85, to 25.4 per cent in 1988–89, while viewing of drama programs went from 2.4 per cent in 1984–85 to 4.0 per cent in 1988–89.

It is worth noting that the fund's objectives do not include any provisions regarding Telefilm's return on investments. Certainly, there is no expectation that the fund can or should be self-financing. From the fund's inception to 31 March 1990, Telefilm participated in the financing of approximately one-third of the budgets for Canadian programs and recouped roughly 14 per cent of its investments in English productions and 7 per cent of its investments in French productions (NGL, 1991: 32).

Table 6-6 provides a breakdown of financial participation in Broadcast Fund programming. Since the NGL report, the most notable change has been in the contributions from other government sources; between 1986 and 1990 they averaged roughly 4 per cent of budgets; over the last two years they have averaged 12 per cent. Also notable is the significant role played by the CBC/SRC and provincial educational broadcasters; their combined contributions outstrip the contributions of Canada's private broadcasters (though in 1993–94 there was a dramatic increase in the latter's participation). If the contributions from public broadcasters are added to those from Telefilm and other government sources, the combined outlay is close to 58 per cent of total budgets.

The Feature Film Fund

In an attempt to redress the shift toward television production that resulted from the Broadcast Fund, the federal government introduced the Feature Film Fund in July 1986 to "promote the production and theatrical distribution of high-quality dramatic films with a high level of Canadian content" (Telefilm, 1994: 2). Telefilm may (by way of equity investment, secured loans or non-interest bearing advances), finance up to 49 per cent of a project's production budget and will not normally invest more than $1.5 million in any given project.

In 1993–94, Telefilm provided $21.8 million towards the development and production of Canadian feature films. As Table 6-7 shows, of this amount, $19.4 million was allocated to the production of 26 feature films, which included *Exotica*, *Whale Music* and *Louis 19, le roi des ondes*. Telefilm's financial contribution averaged 39.4 per cent, while other government sources provided 28.3 per cent of total budgets, making the total contribution from government sources close to 70 per cent.[10] Over this period, there has been a significant drop in the contributions from the private sector, reflecting the reduced value of the Capital Cost Allowance as a financial instrument. At the same time, contributions from other government sources have increased by roughly the same amount. In other words, Telefilm-

Table 6-6
Financial Participation: Canadian Broadcast Program Development Fund: Production Only
(Thousands of Dollars)

	1993–94	1992–93
Number of projects	107	80
Hours	531	458
Telefilm	66,587 (41.5%)	63,689 (34%)
Other Government Sources		
Quebec Tax Credit	13,288	12,699
Other	12,365	9,956
Total	25,653 (12.5%)	22,655 (12.0%)
Broadcasters		
CBC/SRC	20,667	23,006
Educational	4,849	1,681
Private	21,980	12,408
Total	47,496 (23.2%)	37,095 (19.0%)
Private Sector		
Producers	8,387	7,045
Private Investors	23,474	36,271
Other	2,885	4,239
Total	34,746 (16.9%)	47,557 (25.0%)
Distributors	10,134 (4.9%)	4,773 (3.0%)
Foreign		
Co-producers	2,979	1,763
Broadcasters	15,863	12,691
Distributors	1,164	177
Other	403	0
Total	20,409 (10.0%)	14,631 (8.0%)
Total*	205,025	190,399

*Total does not include the foreign share of co-production budgets in which Canada is an equal or minority partner (1993–94: $30.9 million; 1992–93: $8 million)
Source: Telefilm Canada, *Annual Reports*.

supported Canadian feature film production is now more dependent than ever on direct government contributions.

Provincial Funding of Film and Video

The inception of the Feature Film Fund coincided with the emergence of funding agencies in a number of English-Canadian provinces. The Ontario Film Development Corporation was established in 1986–87 to provide equity investment in feature film and television productions based in Ontario.[11] In 1992–93, the OFDC committed $3.9 million to six feature films and 15 television productions (OFDC, 1994). Since 1989, the OFDC has also operated the Ontario Film Investment Program (OFIP), which provides cash rebates to Ontario investors of 15-20 per cent for television productions and 20-25 per cent for feature films. Eligible projects must have significant Canadian content, and at least three-quarters of their budgets must be spent in the province. In 1992–93, the OFIP gave rebates totaling $14.1 million to Ontario investors in 37 film and television productions. In its first three years of operation, the OFIP supported more than 70 per cent of independent productions in Ontario (with the exception of variety shows). On average OFIP funding represents 17 per cent of production financing (*The Globe and Mail*, 9 December 1994: D2).

The emergence of the OFDC reflects an important trend in Canadian cultural policy. As the federal government has reduced its financial commitment to the independent production sector, much of the slack has been taken up by provincial governments. Between 1988–89 and 1992–93, provincial expenditures in the film and video sector more than doubled, from $32 million to $82 million (Statistics Canada, 1994c: 41), and interprovincial rivalry is now an important facet of the policy process. For example, the OFIP was in part a response to Quebec's decision in 1988 to extend its lucrative tax write-offs for film and television productions to Ontario-based producers. Clearly, more is at stake here than culture. The OFDC has estimated that it anchored over $125 million worth of independent production in 1992–93; the OFDC has also calculated that over the next three years its programs will support roughly 6,000 jobs in the industry. According to figures released by the Ontario government, the OFDC's programs not only generate jobs, they also generate direct tax revenue equal to $1.23 for every $1.00 spent (*The Globe and Mail*, 9 December 1994: D2).[12]

Table 6-7
Financial Participation: Telefilm-Supported Feature Films: Production Only
(Thousands of Dollars)

	1993–94	1992–93	1991–92	1990–91	1986–90 (4-year totals)
No. of projects	26	23	24	26	104
Telefilm	19,411 (39.4%)	20,450 (35%)	18,191 (36%)	27,511 (30.0%)	94,400 (39%)
Other Gov't Sources	13,940 (28.3%)	18,085 (31%)	12,834 (25%)	13,128 (14.0%)	39,300 (16.0%)
Distributors	5,696 (11.6%)	5,106 (9.0%)	5,889 (12%)	7,491 (8.0%)	18,000 (7.0%)
Private Sector	5,036 (10.2%)	5,380 (9.1%)	6,959 (14.0%)	18,482 (20.0%)	51,900 (22.0%)
Broadcasters	672 (1.4%)	910 (2.0%)	2,160 (4.0%)	2,160 (2.0%)	7,400 (3.0%)
Foreign	3,963 (8.1%)	7,624 (13%)	4,251 (8.0%)	22,492 (35%)	28,300 (12.0%)
Total*	49,217	58,153	51,144	91,267	239,200

*Total does not include the foreign share of co-production budgets in which Canada is an equal or minority partner (e.g. 1993–94: $10.4 million; 1992–93: $5.2 million)
Source: Telefilm Canada, *Annual Reports;* Groupe Secor, 1991: 26-8.

Current and Future Issues

Distribution/Exhibition

The most successful measures to increase market share for Canadian feature films and dramatic television programs have been in the broadcasting sector, most notably the Canadian-content regulations, and the existence of public broadcasters (the CBC and the various provincial outlets). But the Canadian content regulations for broadcasting are not inviolable. Since their introduction, Canadian private broadcasters have regarded the regulations as a cost of doing business and there is now considerable political pressure to have them reassessed. While smaller, independent Canadian producers of feature films and television programs depend in no uncertain terms on the existing regulations, the core companies, such as Alliance, Atlantis and Nelvana, have evolved to the point where they can survive without them. In other words, while the reduction of Canadian-content regulations would undoubtedly reduce the number of Canadian productions, it would not dismantle that part of the industry now heavily involved in the global marketplace for film and video products.

For the theatrical and home video markets, quotas (for screen time or display space in video stores) to improve the Canadian market share are now both unworkable and impractical. Instead, since the early 1980s, the federal government has been prodded into considering measures to increase the share of distribution revenues that flow to Canadian firms. In 1987, Communications Minister Flora MacDonald proposed to limit foreign distributors to those films or videos for which they held world-distribution rights or those films that they themselves produced (Bergman, 1988; Magder, 1993: 215-230). The proposal would have transferred approximately 7 per cent of the majors' revenues in Canada to Canadian distributors, a major boost to the capital base for the production of Canadian films and videos.[13] Amidst a flurry of high-level lobbying (including American threats to abandon the Free Trade Agreement during the final stages of negotiation), the proposal was abandoned. A watered-down version was introduced the following year, requiring only that the majors enter into separate negotiations to distribute independent films in Canada: the net effect would have been more paperwork for the majors. Perhaps mercifully the bill that included these proposals died on the order paper before the free trade election.

After Viacom's 1994 takeover of Paramount Communications in the United States, the Directors' Guild of Canada, together with nine other organizations, asked the federal government to instruct Viacom to divest the Famous Players theatre chain to Canadians and to limit itself to distributing only those films that it produced. Viacom responded by establishing Viacom Canada and promised to dole out $5 million over five years to Canadian arts organizations. Eventually, the federal government and Viacom struck a deal that permitted Viacom to keep its Paramount holdings in Canada (which included Canada's Wonderland, Ginn Publishing and Maxwell Macmillan Publishing, as well as Famous Players) in exchange for a commitment to invest $377 million in film and television production by 1999. About two-thirds of Viacom's financial promise includes money that its production arms (Paramount Pictures, Showtime Network and Spelling Television) had already committed to productions in Canada (*The Globe and Mail*, 17 December 1994). The Viacom deal signifies the growing importance of joint ventures between Canadian and American firms and of location shots by American firms in Canada to the economic base of Canada's production industry.

Production

Of the growth areas in film and video production, none perhaps hold more promise than the fields of advanced special effects and interactive media. The video-game production industry alone has been estimated to be worth over $10 billion worldwide (*Playback*, 24 October 1994: 1,12). Canadian production companies and Canadian talent are well-situated to take advantage of these trends. We have already noted that Alliance completed *Johnny Mnemonic*, a co-venture with Sony that included a feature film and video segments for a new CD-ROM game. In the fall of 1994, Paragon Entertainment completed production in Toronto on the live-action segment of *Fahrenheit*, a new video game to be released by Sega. Of the four largest computer animation houses in North America, three are located in Canada: Alias Research and Side Effects Software, both in Toronto, and Softimage, located in Montreal and recently acquired by U.S.-based Microsoft.[14] Alias Research, for example, has grown substantially over its last four fiscal years: its revenues went from $12 million in 1990 to $38 million in 1994. Alias targets its products and technologies to three markets: industrial design, graphic design and entertainment. For the entertainment market, Alias creates animation and special effects for motion picture, television, video games and theme-park rides (Alias, 1994). Alias distributes its products in over 30 countries, and close to 40 per cent of the company's sales are in markets outside of North America. In March 1995, Alias accepted a $135-million friendly takeover by U.S.-based Silicon Graphics (*The Globe and Mail*, 7 March 1995: B5).

Conclusion

Since the establishment of Famous Players in the 1920s and Canadian-born Mary Pickford's rise to Hollywood stardom, Canadian capital, Canadian artists and Canadian culture have been inexorably entwined with Hollywood's dream machine. In the 1990s, the likes of Cineplex, Alliance and Alias continue the tradition of Canadian capital, seeking profit by cozying up to the Hollywood nexus, and a new generation of Canadian-born talent, actors, screenwriters and animators have made a home for themselves in Beverly Hills and Bel Air. Despite all its foibles, the Canadian government's policy initiatives in the film and video sector have helped to nurture and consolidate a Hollywood North, though it must be said that the integration of Canada's production industry into the Hollywood nexus has much to do with factors beyond the range of Canadian cultural policy, such as the relative decline in the value of the Canadian dollar and the proliferating demand for inexpensive film and video programming in the United States and elsewhere. Culture and industry have collided again and again in the making and administering of public policy in the film and video sector. The net result of the policies and practices over the last generation has been an industry with two faces: one, tanned by the California sunshine, poised, eager and able to exploit the international marketplace with film, television and video (and multimedia) productions that, in many cases, seem to be Canadian only by virtue of the workers they employ; the other, hardened by the chill of the Canadian winter, resolute, eager and able to explore the dramatic diversity of everyday life in Canada. It is pointless to enter into a debate about which face is more revealing and more authentic; each speaks to different dimensions of Canadian cultural life. It is, however, important that each face be given an opportunity to show itself.

The most significant question now facing Canadian policy-makers and the community of film and video-makers is the extent to which the allure of Hollywood and global markets will influence the full range of creative and financial decisions. Canadian public policy in the film and video sector is in danger of succumbing to the strict logic of commercialism. Over time, the financial contributions from Telefilm and other government sources, the environments of the NFB and CBC, the Canadian-content regulations for television, have each contributed to the promotion of a diversity of Canadian idioms and styles. It is imperative that Canadian cultural policy continue to protect and to promote independent Canadian voices, in all languages and in all narrative forms. The emergence of a small group of financially successful production companies, more and more oriented to foreign markets, should in no way obscure the need to maintain policy instruments to support film and video productions that offer only marginal commercial returns. If anything, now is the time to reorient the financial contributions of Telefilm and other government agencies to ensure that they do not become cashcows for the major Canadian production companies. The bias of the market is both palpable and seductive, but it should not be permitted to determine the future course of Canadian cultural policy.

Notes

1. While a number of Hollywood studios are now owned and controlled by foreign companies (e.g., News Corporation owns Twentieth-Century Fox, Seagram's owns MCA, and Sony owns Columbia), Hollywood is still the focal point for virtually all film and television productions undertaken by the majors. Foreigners, including a great number of Canadians, have always occupied key creative roles in Hollywood. To a large extent, Hollywood's continued success is related to its ability to siphon talent from around the world.
2. This chapter does not include production activities undertaken in-house by Canadian broadcasters, including the CBC.
3. For a discussion of the Canadian television audience, see chapters 7, 8, and 9 in this volume.
4. Some Canadian distributors have negotiated exclusive subdistribution deals for the Canadian market with foreign distributors. Alliance, for example, recently signed a deal to release fifty Miramax titles over the next five years.
5. Co-productions are projects that involve producers from two or more countries that have signed a legal accord to permit the pooling of creative, technical and financial resources. Canada has signed co-production treaties with 23 countries (C. Hoskins and S. McFadyen [1993]; Canadian Film and Television Production Association [1994]).
6. The section that follows is an updated version of material first published in Magder (1995) (with permission).
7. Alliance recently served notice that it was interested in expanding into music publishing, new media and animation. In October of 1994, Alliance made good on that promise by purchasing Toronto-based Partisan Music Productions (*Playback*, 4 October 1994, 10 October 94).
8. Atlantis has also embarked on a buying spree. In the summer of 1994 it purchased a minority position in two smaller Canadian production companies (Halifax-based Salter Street Films and Edmonton-based Great Northern Communications), as part of its strategy to create a cross-Canada company. Atlantis also completed a 100-per-cent acquisition of Soundmix, a post-production facility located in Toronto (*Playback*, 9 August, 1994: 1, 6).
9. Between 1975 and 1984, Canadian film rental revenues for U.S. product grew faster than the revenues from any other export market: from $63.2 million to $111.0 million, an increase of roughly 75 per cent. By comparison, Japan experienced the next highest increase (36.0 per cent), while Australia recorded a decrease of 11 per cent (NGL, 1991: 14-15).
10. Since 1988, Telefilm has also operated the Feature Film Distribution Fund to assist Canadian distribution companies in their marketing, rights acquisition and corporate development activities. In 1993–4, Telefilm disbursed $13 million to 12 companies, all of whom are integrated distribution-production firms.
11. All together, seven provinces now operate film and television loan and investment agencies. Aside from the OFDC, they are: La Société générale des industries culturelles (Quebec); British Columbia Film; Manitoba Cultural Industries

Development Office; SaskFilm; Nova Scotia Film Development Corporation; and the Alberta Motion Picture Development Fund. The Canada Council and Ontario Arts Council also provide grants to independent film-makers for projects of an innovative and experimental nature.

12. In 1995 August the new Progressive Conservative government in Ontario froze the OFDC's budget, including $8 million not yet handed out for the fiscal year 1995–96. The decision is particularly damaging to new film-makers and small, independent producers, but its impact will spread across the industry as certain projects are cancelled, while others are relocated, and still others are reconceived to appeal to non-Ontario and non-Canadian capital sources.

13. The Quebec government passed and implemented its own distribution bill in 1986. With only minor adjustments, the MPAA companies have been able to conduct business-as-usual in Quebec. Ironically, the most significant effect of Bill 109 was to prohibit all non-Quebec based Canadian distributors from doing business in Quebec (Houle [1987]; Magder [1993]).

14. The largest computer animation house in North America is Industrial Light and Magic in San Francisco; its chief animator is Steve Williams, a Toronto native who graduated from Sheridan College's pioneering computer animation program. Sheridan, together with other college and university programs in Canada, and the NFB, make Canada a world-leader in animation research and training (Mazurkewich [1995]).

References

Alias Research. 1994. "Form 10-K: Annual Report to Securities and Exchange Commission, Washington D.C." (File number: 0-18614).

Alliance Communications. 1993. "Prospectus for Initial Public Offering." 20 July.

Atlantis Communications. 1993. "Prospectus for Initial Public Offering." 3 December.

Audley, Paul. 1983. *Canada's Cultural Industries*. Toronto: Lorimer.

Audley, Paul and Associates. 1991. "Film and Television Production in Canada: Trends to 1989 and Projections to 1995." Study commissioned by the Alliance of Canadian Cinema, Television and Radio Artists (ACTRA) and Communications Canada with support from the Ontario Film Development Corporation and the National Film Board.

Bergman, Michael. 1988. "The Real Cost of the Federal Distribution Deal." *Cinema Canada*. No. 157, November.

Berton, Pierre. 1975. *Hollywood's Canada: The Americanization of Our National Image*. Toronto: McClelland and Stewart.

Canada. 1951. Royal Commission on National Development in the Arts, Letters and Sciences (Massey commission). *Report*. Ottawa: King's Printer.

Canadian Film and Television Production Association. 1994. *The Guide: 1994*.

Cineplex Odeon. 1994. *Annual Report 1993*.

Clandfield, David. 1987. *Canadian Film*. Toronto: Oxford University Press.

Ellis, David. 1992. *Split Screen: Home Entertainment and New Technologies* Toronto: Friends of Canadian Broadcasting.

Groupe Secor. 1994. *Canadian Government Intervention in the Film Industry*. Prepared for the Department of Canadian Heritage.

————. 1991. "Evaluation of Telefilm Canada Feature Film Fund." Prepared for Telefilm Canada.

Hoskins, C., and S. McFadyen. 1993. "Canadian Participation in International Co-productions and Co-Ventures in Television Programming." *Canadian Journal of Communication*, 18 (2), Spring.

Magder, Ted. 1995. "Making Canada in the 1990s: Film, Culture, and Industry." In K. McRoberts, (ed.). *Beyond Quebec: Taking Stock of Canada*. Montreal: McGill-Queen's University Press.

————. 1993. *Canada's Hollywood: The Canadian State and Feature Films*. Toronto: University of Toronto Press.

Mazurkewich, Karen. 1995. "The Great Canadian Cartoon Conspiracy." *Take One*, no. 7, winter.

Morris, Peter. 1987. "Rethinking Grierson: The Ideology of John Grierson." In P.Véronneau et al. (eds.). *Dialogue*. Montreal: Mediatexte.

————. 1986. "Backwards to the Future: John Grierson's Film Policy for Canada." In G. Walz, (ed.). *Flashback: People and Institutions in Canadian Film History*. Montreal: Mediatexte.

————. 1978. *Embattled Shadows: A History of Canadian Cinema 1895–1936*. Kingston: McGill-Queen's.

NGL Consulting. 1992. "Evaluation of the Feature Film Distribution Fund." Prepared for Telefilm Canada.

————. 1991. "Evaluation of the Canadian Broadcast Program Development Fund." Prepared for Telefilm Canada.

Nelvana Ltd., 1994. "Prospectus for Initial Public Offering." 17 March.

Pendakur, Manjunath. 1990. *Canadian Dreams and American Control*. Toronto: Garamond.

Posner. Michael. 1993. *Canadian Dreams: The Making and Marketing of Independent Films*. Vancouver: Douglas and McIntyre.

Statistics Canada. 1994a. *Film and Video 1991–92*. Catalogue 87-204. Ottawa: Minister of Industry, Science and Technology.

————. 1994b. *Focus on Culture*. Catalogue 87-004. Ottawa: Minister of Industry, Science and Technology.

————. 1994c. *Government Expenditures on Culture 1992–93*. Catalogue 87-206. Ottawa: Minister of Industry, Science and Technology.

Telefilm Canada. 1994. "Feature Film Fund: Policies 1994–5."

————. Various years. *Annual Report*.

The Wall Street Journal. "Global Entertainment" (special section). 26 March 1993.

7

Public Television

Marc Raboy

To many observers, the terms *cultural industry* and *public broad-casting industry* are oxymorons. Perhaps in no other area is the inherent conflict between culture and economics as evident as it is here (Raboy, Bernier, Sauvageau and Atkinson, 1994).

Yet, upon minimal investigation and reflection, one finds that public broadcasting is on the cutting edge of this conflict. Contrary to most European examples, public broadcasting in Canada has al-ways been an enclave within a broader industry. Its main instrument, the Canadian Broadcasting Corporation, has never been entirely shel-tered from the industrial aspects of broadcasting (although the CBC enjoyed a monopoly in television during most of the medium's first decade, and CBC radio, since 1974, has been commercial-free). On the other hand, as a *regulated* industry, no sector of broadcasting can claim to be entirely independent of public purpose, and indeed, according to the Broadcasting Act of 1991, all broadcasting in Can-ada constitutes "a public service essential to the maintenance and enhancement of national identity and cultural sovereignty" (Statutes of Canada 1991: art. 3.1.b).

Canadian broadcasting is a hybrid system. This means that there are two ways to look at the developments of the past fifteen years. On the one hand, there has been a definite shift towards privatization, as commercial and budgetary pressures on the CBC force it to adopt a posture increasingly resembling that of the private sector, as more and more of its production activities are farmed out to privately owned companies, and as public funding that used to go to the CBC is diverted to subsidize private broadcasters via Telefilm Canada's broadcast development fund. On the other hand, these developments can also be seen as a "public-ization" of the private sector, insofar as that sector has become increasingly reliant on public funding and public policy measures, not only the Telefilm fund, but also various CRTC regulations and the protection afforded Canadian cultural industries under the Canada-U.S. Free Trade Accord, the North American Free Trade Agreement and the General Agreement on Tariffs and Trade.

So, as the multichannel environment continues to expand, as the relationship between audiovisual production and distribution takes on a new shape and form, and as the policy apparatus redefines its role under the guise of adapting to the so-called information highway, the question of the future of public broadcasting has to be repositioned. The starting point is to recognize that there is far more at stake than the institutional future of the CBC. The Broadcasting Act is not naive when it describes all of Canadian broadcasting as a public service, but the system governed by the act has been inconsistent and, at times, incoherent, in operationalizing that description.

The most striking example of this is the chasm between Parliament's mandate for the CBC and the government's refusal to provide the resources the CBC needs to do its job. But there is more. Community broadcasting, legally recognized since 1991 as one of the three component parts of the Canadian system, along with the public and private sectors, has as its only institutional base (in television anyway), the obligation of cable companies to provide a community access channel. Strange bedfellows, to say the least. Educational broadcasting has become a viable complement to public and private broadcasting in some parts of the country, in spite of the fact that its structure has more to do with the bizarre peculiarities of the Canadian political system than the public service requirements of broadcasting. The policy discourse continues to emphasize access — surely the core element of any public service — but concrete developments and innovations are increasingly tied to some variant of the consumer model, where the quality of service is invariably tied to the ability to pay.

The debate on the information highway is illuminating in this respect. In the face of the new technological context, conventional television, both public and private, faces a serious challenge. The key to success in this environment will be quality of content and efficiency of delivery. The old formulas based on brand (channel) loyalty, which allowed conventional broadcasters to get away with packaging trash alongside popular programs, will no longer work. In fact, many fear that the conventional broadcasting model itself will no longer work. As a result, we have seen some scrambling. In a rather original move, a coalition of Quebec francophone broadcasters, public and private, presented a common brief to the CRTC's information highway hearings in March 1995; their *porte-parole* was the Radio-Canada vice-president in charge of television, Michèle Fortin, a strong advocate of generalist, mainstream popular television. At the same hearings, the Canadian Association of Broadcasters — which has represented the interests of private broadcasters since 1926, making it the oldest organization in Canadian broadcasting — presented itself as the champion of Canadian content, which, if memory serves correctly, it had at one time eschewed (McCabe, 1995).

Yes, the lines between public and private broadcasting are increasingly blurred. It is a paradoxical situation indeed. But, like the psychologist's reversible goblet, the picture can be looked at two ways. The key question is which is the object and which is the illusion.

The period since the early 1980s has witnessed a generally recognized worldwide crisis of public broadcasting (Rowland and Tracey, 1990), brought on by the simultaneous erosion of political commitment on the part of governments, the ballooning fiscal crisis of the state, a changing technological environment and mutations in audience expectations.

In Canada, this has been felt most acutely in the angst surrounding the financial and existential crisis of the CBC, as it careens like a corporate Titanic on the verge of capsizing. But public broadcasting in Canada is far more than the CBC, and if public broadcasting in Canada is to have a future, it will most likely be through new and alternative forms of broadcasting — including several that can still involve a revitalized and rejuvenated CBC.

In the recent intense debates on the future of Canadian broadcasting, there has been a palpable shift from the traditional idea that public broadcasting should refer exclusively to a national broadcasting service. The Canadian Broadcasting Corporation remains the centrepiece and most important single institution of the Canadian broadcasting system, but the space it occupies continues to shrink. At the same time, however, the total space occupied by public-service broadcasting in Canada has been enhanced by the addition of public educational broadcasting services, by the formal recognition of community broadcasting as a distinct and legitimate part of the system and by the active involvement in the policy-making process of representative organizations from dozens of less-than-national publics. The CBC itself has moved into specialty broadcasting, and

Table 7-1
Canadian Television Economy

Public Spending on Television	
Ottawa	
CBC	985m (CBC Annual Report, 1994)
Telefilm	95m (Telefilm Annual Report, 1994)
NFB	66m (NFB Annual Report, 1994; based on est. that 80% of NFB production ends up on TV)
TVNC	3,5m (ATEC, 1993)
Subtotal	1,147m
Provinces	
Educational TV	230m (ATEC, 1993)
Total	1,377m
Television Commercial Revenue in Canada (Statistics Canada. *Radio and television broadcasting 1992*, Cat. no. 56-204; *Cable television 1993*, Cat. no. 56-205.)	
Advertising	
CBC	309m (1992)
Private TV	1,341m
Subtotal	1,650m
Cable subscription	
Basic	1,700m (1993)
Discretionary	471m
Subtotal	2,171m
Total	3,821m
Economy of Canadian Television, 1994 (Author's Compilation)	
Public funding	1,377m
Advertising	1,650m
Cable subscription	2,171m
Total	5,198m

Sources: As indicated above.

the CRTC has in some cases (albeit rare ones) insisted on holding private broadcasters to their public-service obligations. Independent television production is increasingly reliant on public funds. All of these developments require a new conceptual and strategic approach to public broadcasting in Canada. Typically, this has been slow to emerge, as public debate tends to focus narrowly on the CBC. The public-service commitment of Canadian broadcasting faces grave challenges, in spite of the rhetorical reassurances enshrined in the legislation governing it.

Here Canada is not alone. The worldwide evolution of broadcasting was marked in the 1980s by the convergence of two parallel sets of changes, one technological, the other ideological. While broadcasters became equipped with unprecedented capacity for the production and distribution of audiovisual material, political leaders subscribed to the idea that this new capacity should be used for market-based broadcasting. Canada provided a particularly interesting vantage point for observing these changes, because the issues have been with us for such a long time — in fact, since the beginning of broadcasting. What is the appropriate mix of public and commercial broadcasting activity within a single system? What is the appropriate relationship of foreign to domestic programming? What is the appropriate social role for broadcasting?

While the basic nature of broadcasting has usually been posed as a dichotomy in western Europe (broadcasting: public service *or* business), in Canada, since 1932, broadcasting has been a hybrid entity (public service *and* business) (Atkinson, 1993). Despite what we say (often at great length), business has most of the time held the upper hand. Yet, *all* broadcasting is deemed responsible to a principle of public service and can be challenged, at least formally, to meet that obligation.

Any consideration of public broadcasting in Canada must obviously begin with, and focus at length on — although not necessarily end with — the CBC.

Background

To a remarkable extent, the major defining issues of Canadian broadcasting have remained unchanged since the late 1920s (Raboy, 1990). In 1932, a Conservative government adopted Canada's first national broadcasting legislation, creating the Canadian Radio Broadcasting Commission (CRBC), which became the Canadian Broadcasting Corporation (CBC) in 1936. While the legislation did provide for the CRBC, and then the CBC, to establish a national public-service monopoly, no move was ever made to limit the expansion of private, commercial broadcasting. In 1958, the legislation was finally changed to reflect the reality of the "mixed" ownership system.

Provincial authorities were completely excluded from any official role, and indeed, explicitly prohibited from operating broadcasting stations until educational television — provincial, as opposed to federal, public broadcasting — was licensed in the early 1970s. While official policy documents emphasized the importance of a publicly owned national corporation funded by a licence fee, advertising (and therefore competition with the private sector) was to play an important part from the beginning. And, while the entire strategy was centred on creating an authentic, autonomous Canadian broadcasting system on the periphery of the United States, that system would become a vehicle for introducing American broadcasting content into Canada.

By the mid-1930s, therefore, the major themes that characterize Canadian broadcasting had been established. These can be summarized as three sets of tensions: a) between private capital and the state, over the economic basis of broadcasting; b) between the state and the public, over the sociocultural mission of broadcasting; c) between dominant and alternative visions of the state, over the relationship of broadcasting to the politics of Canadian nationhood. Overriding these are the constant pressures of North American continentalism against the desire that Canadian broadcasting be *Canadian*; and the tendency of each succeeding wave of technological change to re-introduce problems that the system thought it had resolved.

In the 1940s, following the massive expansion of the CBC as one of the government's leading information instruments in the war effort (another one being the National Film Board), the system appeared to have reached a workable equilibrium. The CBC was clearly the dominant element in the system, charged with realizing the national purpose in broadcasting. It had achieved a significant degree of success in involving community organizations in rural and urban areas in public-interest programming and organizing participatory listener groups. Its leadership in newsgathering was unchallenged. Its signal was the only one available in many parts of the country, and it was moving towards full coverage of the territory, in both English and French.

In 1948, the CBC was mandated to develop and introduce television as a public-service monopoly — a policy position endorsed by the 1951 Royal Commission on National Development in the Arts, Letters and Sciences (the Massey Commission) (Canada, 1951). When it began broadcasting in 1952 and, for the rest of the decade, Canadian television was strictly a public affair, as the government pursued a single-station policy, in which no more than one station (in each language) would be licensed in any community, either to the CBC or a privately owned affiliate.

Soon after CBC television began broadcasting, it became clear that the service could not be supported by the licence fee, even when supplemented with advertising. In fact, the high cost of television had led to creation of the affiliate system in the first place, whereby private corporations were allowed to own and operate stations dedicated to distributing the CBC signal. The licence fee was abolished and an annual grant from Parliament was introduced to balance the CBC's budget. This formula remains in effect to this day, despite repeated calls for multi-year funding.

A major shift occurred in 1958, following the election of the Diefenbaker government. In a new broadcasting act, the private sector finally got the independent regulatory authority it had been arguing for since the end of World War II. The act created the Board of Broadcast Governors (BBG) (which became the Canadian Radio-television Commission [CRTC] in 1968 and, in 1976, the Canadian Radio-television and Telecommunications Commission). One of the first acts of the BBG was to authorize commercial television, which began operating in major cities in 1960, and as a national network in English in 1961. The public cost of public television rose steadily through the 1960s, at the same time that the purpose of public broadcasting moved to the centre of national political debate. The emergence of radical nationalism in Quebec in the 1960s called Canadian political unity into question. The federal government determined to use cultural policy and the CBC in particular as a strategic instrument (Raboy, 1990: chapter 4).[1] Paradoxically, the discovery of a political purpose for public broadcasting was a financial boon for the CBC, while it sowed discord between the politicians and professionals working in television. The CBC went through a series of melodramatic crises in attempting to define and play out its proper role — with the net result of a serious loss of credibility, particularly in Quebec. When the broadcasting legislation was updated in 1968, the government wrote in a clause obliging the CBC to "contribute to the development of national unity and Canadian identity" — a measure that was widely seen as threatening to turn the corporation into a propaganda vehicle. The act still defined the CBC as Canada's national, not public, broadcaster.

Industry Structure and Policy

The 1968 Broadcasting Act set out the basic principles and structures of Canadian broadcasting as a single system comprising public and private elements, under the supervision of an independent, public regulatory authority, the CRTC. But on the margins of the system, social pressure from the youth and oppositional movements that grew up in the 1960s led to a range of community broadcasting initiatives in radio, video and television. Community radio stations were set up in cities such as Vancouver and Montreal, on college campuses, in rural Quebec, and in northern native communities. Community media began to attract strategic institutional support: in Quebec, for example, the government decided to finance community radio and television as one way of occupying space in this sphere of federal jurisdiction; later, the federal secretary of state would fund minority-language community media as well as autonomous native broadcasting initiatives.

All of these forms of broadcasting clearly fit the definition of "public" broadcasting (Salter, 1988). At the same time, political pressure to redefine the nature of the Canadian state led finally to the first provincial incursions into public broadcasting, in the guise of educational television networks set up, first in Quebec and Ontario, later in Alberta and British Columbia, and eventually in Saskatchewan and the north. By 1992, educational television accounted for some $233 million in public spending (Association for Tele-Education in Canada, 1993).

Public dissatisfaction with the increasingly bureaucratic and centralized structure of the CBC poured out at CRTC hearings in 1974, at which the regulator rapped the knuckles of the public broadcaster and suggested that it seek a new relationship with its public as the best way to distinguish itself from the dominant North American commercial mould. One upshot was the abolition of advertising on CBC radio; despite the exhortations of the CRTC, the CBC was unable to reduce its dependence on advertising in television. Advertising on CBC television reached a peak of $309 million in 1992, accounting for 22 per cent of the corporation's total budget (around 31 per cent of the budget for television) (CBC, 1994a). This has reinforced the view that the CBC should be more properly seen as a hybrid or semi-private broadcaster.

The government's commitment to the CBC was shaken in the late 1970s by the perception that public broadcasting had not fulfilled its

Table 7-2
Spending on Public Educational Television, 1992

Alberta (Access Network, est. 1973)	18.8m
British Columbia (Open Learning Agency, est. 1988)	31.4m
Quebec (Radio-Québec, est. 1968)	80.4m
Ontario (TVOntario, est. 1970)	90.6m
Saskatchewan (Sask. Comm'ns Network, est. 1989)	8.35m
Northern Canada (Federal) Television Northern Canada, est. 1989)	3.5m
Total	233m

Source: Association for Tele-Education in Canada, 1993. *Creating Access to Tele-Education*. Burnaby: ATEC.

role as a contributor to national unity. Following the election of a Parti Québécois government in Quebec in 1976, Ottawa instructed the CRTC to conduct an inquiry into the CBC's news operations. The CRTC exonerated the CBC of exhibiting unfair bias, but found its French and English operations in fact demonstrated the non-communication between Canada's "two solitudes." Nonetheless, only the CBC covered the entire territory in both official languages — one of the fundamental distinguishing marks of a public broadcaster.

Canada's geographical and linguistic requirements made the CBC arguably the world's biggest and most complex television broadcaster. By the mid-1960s, the CBC was producing more in English than any of the American networks and more in French than the national system in France (Nash, 1994a: 374). But the Americanization of Canadian television continued nonetheless. As the share of American programs on Canadian prime time reached an estimated 80 per cent in 1970 (Hardin, 1985), the CRTC stiffened the rules to require 60 per cent Canadian content in prime time. Paradoxically, it continued to license more private stations, increasing the competitive pressure on the CBC and the tendency towards homogenized commercial formats across the public and private television schedules.

The implications for public broadcasting were manifest in the report of the Federal Cultural Policy Review Committee (Applebaum-Hébert) which, in 1982, endorsed a new economistic thrust, and made recommendations to shift the emphasis in public funding from the CBC to the private sector. Leaning on the Broadcasting Act's requirement that the system as a whole should provide a balanced program schedule, the committee suggested that the role of the CBC should be to serve as "an alternative to private broadcasters" (Canada, 1982: 273).

Sceptics recalled that the public broadcaster was supposed to be the central agency of the Canadian system and not a kind of "PBS north," but a possibly irreversible process had begun. The committee proposed that the CBC reduce its reliance on advertising revenue (an ambiguous proposal because it could lead to improved quality only if the government increased public funding) and eliminate in-house production in favour of contracting out to private producers in all areas but information programming.

The minister of communications integrated many of the committee's proposals into a policy document (Canada, 1983). The paper outlined a new strategy for broadcasting, whose central point was to promote the private sector's capacity to produce high-quality television that Canadians would watch and that could be marketed worldwide. To aid this, the government created the new Broadcast Program Development Fund, administered by Telefilm Canada, to subsidize independent production for broadcast on both public and private sector television. The role designated for the CBC was to be a *provider* of Canadian programming produced in the private sector with the assistance of Telefilm. In other words, the government was shifting its support for Canadian television production and programming from a public corporation to private companies. In real terms, this meant the privatization of a large part of the production activity formerly performed by the CBC — production which is now done by private production companies using public funds, and in many cases for the benefit of private broadcasters. Since the late 1980s, the broadcast fund injected some $140 million a year into the system, and it is not stretching things to characterize Canadian private broadcasting as semi-public (Groupe Secor, 1994).[2]

But the new environment now included not only traditional over-the-air private broadcasters (generally outnumbering the CBC two-to-one in every market); it also included, for the growing number of cable subscribers, the full gamut of U.S. networks, a range of pay-TV (since 1982) and specialty services (since 1987).[3] It also included the underdeveloped alternative public services provided by provincial educational and community broadcasters.

The Conservative government of Brian Mulroney, elected in September 1984, was committed to rolling back the public sector. One of its first moves was to instruct the CBC to cut its budget by about 10 per cent. In April 1985, the new minister of communications, Marcel Masse, set up the Task Force on Broadcasting Policy (Caplan-Sauvageau) to propose "an industrial and cultural strategy to govern the future evolution of the Canadian broadcasting system through the remainder of this century." A key part of its mandate was to take account of "the need for fiscal restraint" (Canada, 1985; Canada, 1986).

The Caplan-Sauvageau task force took to its role in the fine tradition of Canadian broadcasting inquiries since the 1920s. Although the minister had asked for a quick and expeditious report, the task force held public meetings around the country and solicited public input from interested parties, while conducting an ambitious research program. Finally, it produced an 800-page report, with more than 100 recommendations, in which the essential public-service nature of Canadian broadcasting was reaffirmed, and the key role of both new and old public broadcasting institutions (not only the CBC, but the provincial, community and native broadcasters) was reasserted.

The task force proposals were referred to the parliamentary committee on communications and culture, which repeated the process with its own round of hearings and consultations, refining the proposals while maintaining the overall thrust favourable to support for public broadcasting. The government then introduced legislation to replace the outdated Broadcasting Act, and this was referred to yet another parliamentary committee, which conducted yet another round of public hearings (Canada, 1988; Communications Canada, 1988).

The result was a genuine public debate over the social purpose and structure of broadcasting, in which hundreds of organizations and thousands of individuals got to speak out and present visions that corresponded to their own interests. The powerful broadcasting organizations, both public and private, were compelled to take part in the process as well, in order to maintain their credibility (while obviously continuing their habitual behind-the-scenes lobbying activity) (Raboy, 1995a; 1995b). Eventually, a new broadcasting act was adopted, basically reaffirming the mandate of the CBC, and introducing the notion that all broadcasting in Canada was a public service.

It is important to recognize, however, that while the public debate about future legislation was being carried on in the essentially symbolic sphere of policy discussion, the system was evolving according to the government's broad agenda. The new Broadcasting Act clearly affirmed the public nature of all Canadian broadcasting, but from that declaration to the actual realization of public-service objectives was a long way indeed. Public broadcasting, since the mid-1980s, has received declining support from public funds while public funds have flowed, through independent producers, to private broadcasting; meanwhile, private broadcasters and their upstart cousins, the cable distributors, have been subjected less and less to public-service obligations.

One example serves to illustrate the general problem. The CBC's mandate under the Broadcasting Act of 1991 is to

be predominantly and distinctively Canadian ... reflect Canada and its regions to national and regional audiences ... strive to be of equivalent quality in English and in French ... contribute to shared national consciousness and identity ... (and) reflect the multicultural and multiracial nature of Canada (Statutes of Canada 1991: art. 3.1.m).

One important aspect of this broad and detailed mandate is the requirement to serve the regions. The challenge of balancing national and regional program requirements has always been a strain on CBC management. National programming has a higher and more easily identifiable profile. It is prestigious and, to a certain extent, marketable internationally. It is based in two major production centres, Toronto (English) and Montreal (French), and can be more easily attuned to the expectations of national politicians in Ottawa.

Regional programming, on the other hand, is not so transparent. Its effect is difficult to measure. Closer to the population it serves, it often reflects the potentially divisive undercurrents of regional politics and is often out of tune with national policy objectives. Good, popular public broadcasting in a region also threatens the financial security of local private broadcasting outlets.

The CBC virtually eliminated its regional television services in December 1990, closing eleven stations in different parts of the country and reducing non-national programming to two daily newscasts in each province. These cuts provoked a massive public outcry, not only in regions with a long tradition of contesting Ottawa's centralism, such as the prairie provinces and Quebec, but even in the Ontario heartland of Windsor. City councils sought injunctions to require the CBC to fulfil its legal mandate, mayors petitioned members of Parliament, laid-off CBC employees and their unions prepared proposals to purchase their stations and run them as co-operatives, and users took to the streets. For many Canadians, the elimination of local and regional CBC programming has come to symbolize the hubris and, to some, the passing of the CBC (Skene, 1993).

Future Policy Issues

The election of a Liberal government in October 1993 was supposed to reverse this tendency, but unsurprisingly, it did not. During the nine years of Tory government, cumulative cuts had reduced the CBC's base funding by $276 million (CBC, 1993). Despite Liberal campaign promises, and post-election public assurances by heritage minister Michel Dupuy, the federal budget of February 1995 added further cuts which, according to CBC president Anthony Manera, increased the 1985–97 reduction to $350 million. In a rare display of public dignity surpassing corporate loyalty, Manera, looking for all the world like Gorbachev trying too hard, too late to salvage the organization to which he had dedicated his career, resigned. He had repeatedly stated that he would not manage further funding cuts but, apparently, no one had believed him.

Just how serious was the CBC's financial situation? It quite depends on how one looked at it. According to author Wayne Skene, who observed the beast from within during twelve years as a producer and middle-level manager, the problem was not so much in the amounts cut by government as in how those cuts were applied (Skene, 1993; 1994). As anyone who has ever tried to read a CBC financial statement can attest, budgetary sleight-of-hand appears to be one of the corporation's most valued administrative qualities.

Reduction in service has been apparent at many levels, however. The shutdown of local stations, trimming of staff, cancelled programs, increased reliance on advertising and farming out of production have all translated into a less distinctive, less popular personality, which the encroaching 500-channel universe continues to undermine.

Table 7-3
CBC, 1993–94

Spending on Operations		$1,482m (1,303 "requiring current operating funds")
	Television	985m (67%)
	Radio	325m (22%)
	Newsworld	47m (3%–offset by revenue)
Revenue		1,329m
	Parliament	955m (72%)
	TV advertising	299m (22%)
	Other revenue	75m (6%– including Newsworld)
Staff		9,117 employees in March 1994 (12,183 in March 1984)
English TV		
	11 owned and operated stations	
	22 private affiliates	
	438 CBC and 172 private and community rebroadcasters	
Average Prime Time Canadian Content in 1994		80% (65% over the day; 86% from 6 PM-midnight; regular season Canadian content in prime time: 88%)
Viewing of Canadian Programs, 1991–92, 7-11 P.M.		
	CBC	78%
	CTV	19%
	Global	17%
Audience Share, 24 Hrs, 1993–94		
	CBC	13.9% (without Newsworld)
	Other Canadian	42.6%
	U.S.	25.1%
	Pay/specialty	18.4%
	Newsworld	0.7% with average weekly reach of 91% of cabled households

Source: CBC. *Annual Report, 1993–94.*

But the CBC is still a considerable enterprise. In 1992, it accounted for 40 per cent of the total spent on radio and television in Canada, 25 per cent including subscription revenues flowing through the cable industry.[4] It still received nearly $1.1 billion from Parliament in 1994–95 (about $950 million for operations and $140 million for capital expenses), and anticipated another $300 million in television advertising revenue. This represented one-third of all federal spending on heritage and cultural programs, and made the CBC the largest single player in the system.

Despite the increased visibility of publicly funded Canadian programs on private television, and the diminishing role of the CBC as the principal producer of Canadian programs, the CBC is still by far the largest exhibitor of Canadian programs. In 1994, Canadian content on CBC television was about 85 per cent in prime time, while the total across the entire system was about 25 per cent (CBC, 1994b).[5] The CBC's preponderant contribution to a Canadian screen presence continues to be a major aspect of its role as a public broadcaster.

Meanwhile, however, the CBC's total space in the system is progressively shrinking. While 89 per cent of Canadians still claimed to tune in CBC television at least once a week, English TV's share had plunged to 13.6 per cent by the fall of 1993 (Kiefl, 1994). Even Radio-Canada sank to an all-time low of 22 per cent in the fall of 1994, before rallying back to 25 per cent in spring 1995 (*Le Devoir* 1995a; 1995b).[6]

As the CBC's ship rocked unsteadily in increasingly stormy seas, the overall environment of Canadian broadcasting was shifting as well. Here too, the CBC's place was ambivalent. As the CRTC identified and addressed the presumed threat of U.S. direct-to-home satellites by licensing new specialty services, the conventional television market continued to fragment. At the same time, the CBC was actively involved in developing new services, with new corporate partners. This again raised two distinct spins with regard to its mandate: should the CBC concentrate on providing a distinctive, streamlined public service on the margin of an increasingly commercial television market, or should it participate in expanding the public-service horizons of broadcasting?

The problem was a combination of money and political will. These two issues were at the heart of a long round of parliamentary committee hearings held during the fall of 1994, at which the CBC's mandate and funding formula were scrutinized once again (Canadian

Heritage, 1994). Proposals put before the committee ranged from privatization of all or parts of the CBC's activities to simply increasing its parliamentary appropriation, but some pointed to new approaches to the perpetual problems of Canadian public broadcasting.

The main question facing Canadian public broadcasting in 1995 was, simply stated: what should it be doing (mission), how (content) and with what funds (financing)? In its own submission to the parliamentary committee, the CBC presented a three-pronged strategy, aimed at programming, accountability and financial security:

The commitment that we offer is to create a new CBC — a CBC that provides more service, and better service; a CBC that is more open and transparent — but a CBC that costs fewer tax dollars. The commitment we seek is the tools to do the job. We need funding that is dependable and diverse (CBC, 1994b: 1).

The CBC would be more Canadian (95 per cent in prime time and 80 per cent throughout the day) and less commercially driven, "devoted to public service rather than to private profit"; striving to do more than just "provide a pastime, it [would] also contribute actively to the quality of Canadians' lives *as citizens*" (CBC, 1994b: 5. Emphasis in original).

The most fundamental distinction between the CBC and the private sector is that public broadcasting is driven by values of service rather than profit. Our programming must be more thoughtful. It must provide the kind of text and context that empower citizens to make informed choices in a democratic society. It must move and amuse them with programs that best reflect their own values and experiences (CBC, 1994b: 12).

This was as good a definition as any of public broadcasting, but good intentions aside, the CBC was unfortunately ill-equipped to turn it into something concrete.

Meanwhile, it was put clearly before the parliamentary committee that there was essentially no way to maintain public expectations of the CBC without the government biting the bullet by continuing to provide significant public funding. As the CRTC stated in its 1994 decision renewing CBC network television licences, "At issue is the extent to which the objectives for the corporation set out in the act are realistically achievable" (CRTC, 1994). But the issue of alternative financing, outgoing CBC chairman Patrick Watson told the committee, was "a red herring ... A decisive minister committed to leadership and clarity of vision would, in my judgment, say to his officials, come to me with a proposal that works and we'll do it" (Watson, 1994: 49:7).

And proposals there were, but most of them were unlikely to sit well with a government single-mindedly focused on deficit-paring and program-dismantling. Consultant Paul Audley pointed out that "from 1984–85 to 1993–94, CBC funding grew at half the rate of increase in the defence budget, half the rate of growth in (federal) program spending, and half the rate of inflation" (Audley, 1994: 30:45). Or, as Tony Manera repeated persistently, if the federal government had controlled its spending to the extent that the CBC had since the mid-1980s, there would be no federal deficit today.

Indeed, regardless of how one sliced it, maintaining the traditional policy objective of a strong Canadian screen presence meant finding more money, not less, for public television. Ken Goldstein, from the Winnipeg consulting firm Communications Management Inc., told the committee: "As long as the economic engine for Canadian content is fuelled primarily by advertising and government appropriations, you might anticipate modest increases in spending on Canadian programs over the next decade, but likely not at the pace required to maintain the current relative position of Canadian content in the overall television and video system" (Goldstein, 1994: 47:5).

Therefore, even assuming government funding and advertising at existing levels, more money needed to be found simply to maintain the existing level of Canadian screen content. Where could this possibly come from? Goldstein suggested "a rebalancing of revenue sources and program responsibilities within the regulated component of the Canadian video system" could be possible, by introducing a system of "compensation for carriage," whereby conventional broadcasters, both private and public, "could receive a meaningful portion of the subscriber fees Canadian consumers pay to the cable television industry every month." In other words, "make the rich pay," as some used to say in the 1970s.

And why not? As Goldstein's study showed, cable subscription was currently the only source of new revenue in the Canadian broadcasting system. Yet, the cable industry, with 38 per cent of total broadcasting revenue, accounted for only 6.4 per cent of the amount spent on Canadian programming (essentially in local community broadcasting. The CBC, in comparison, with 20 per cent of the total revenue — 13 per cent from its parliamentary appropriation and 7 per cent from advertising — accounted for 42 per cent of spending) (Communications Management Inc. 1994, based on Statistics Canada data).

Indeed, by mid-1995 it was clear that the only "solution" to the financing of public broadcasting lay in taking the Broadcasting Act at its word, and adopting a holistic approach to the economics and policy expectations of the system as a whole: stop treating a cable franchise as a licence to print money, stop agonizing over the fiscal bellyaching of both private broadcasters and the CBC and insist they meet their respective mandates, and open up new windows of public service in the expanding media environment.

Some of this had begun gingerly with the creation of Newsworld and, eight years later, its French-language equivalent, RDI. Fitting into the CRTC's logic of using the cable service as a locomotive for adding new user-financed specialty services, Newsworld and RDI were vibrant, apparently meaningful additions to the environment, at no direct public cost (the services are financed exclusively by cable fees and advertising, although they benefit from CBC infrastructures and news staff). According to research done for the CBC, Newsworld was the only specialty service for which more than 50 per cent of subscribers felt that they were getting what they paid for (Kiefl, 1994).

One path to the future was for the CBC to continue branching into additional specialty services, while maintaining its generalist channels. The corporation was institutionally prepared to go this route, which had the advantage of "unbundling" its services, to use a term introduced by David Ellis (Ellis, 1994: 36), and requiring separate services to seek an accommodation with a particular segment of the public. The CBC, in 1993, was associated with no less than six specialty licence applications; it was awarded one on its own and a second in partnership with the private sector. One could not have expected more, given the prevailing logic of the mixed-ownership system, but the overall result was not particularly edifying for broadcasting's public-service objectives.

The unbundling principle could also be applied to the CBC's conventional services, heretical as this might sound. The CBC's corporate reflex, historically, has been to retrench against criticism and position itself as a vital national institution, and so it is. But there is no reason for all services to be on a single corporate flow chart. National and regional services, English and French language serv-

ices, television and radio, could all be unbundled so that each operated autonomously with a statutory budget envelope reflecting their
mandate. No less an authority than the CBC's emeritus journalist
Knowlton Nash, reborn as the corporation's latest historian, has
stated that decentralization would be the surest way of increasing
creativity in the CBC (Nash, 1994b).[7] Unbundling would take it a
major step further by making it possible for programmers and their
publics to meet on the common ground of specific services, without
referring to a single encompassing corporate structure.[8]

The result would be a radically different CBC — but one that
would be *recognizably* different in a positive sense. In terms of
accountability and community participation, the possibilities are enticing.

But the parliamentary committee also had to juggle proposals to
sell off CBC's owned-and-operated stations, to take the main television services off the air and distribute them by cable only, to get out
of sports and other programming highly attractive to the private
sector and, generally, to redefine the CBC as an up-market provider
of edifying fare. The committee's chair, Toronto Liberal MP John
Godfrey, professed a definite affinity to the PBS model. Buttressed
by the much more favourable position of Radio-Canada in the francophone television market, the Bloc Québécois supported maintaining the CBC's historic generalist mandate. The Reform Party,
meanwhile, pegged broadcasting as another fiscal problem area in its
crusade to mow down every federal program that lay in the way of
reducing the deficit.

By May 1995, it appeared unlikely that the committee would be
able to agree on a single report. The committee finally reported in
June 1995 (Canada, 1995). Whether out of impatience, or whether it
knew something the rest of us didn't, the government short-circuited
the process by naming yet another committee, headed by former
CBC president Pierre Juneau, to review the mandates of the CBC,
Telefilm and the National Film Board (Canadian Heritage, 1995).
Since leaving the CBC in 1989, Juneau had become an energetic
global proponent of public-service broadcasting as founder and head
of the UNESCO-backed World Radio and Television Council. His
committee could be expected to hand in a report highly supportive
of the traditional functions and institutions of Canadian public broadcasting. The Mandate Review Committee, consisting of Juneau,
TVOntario president Peter Herrndorf and Simon Fraser University

Table 7-4
Where Your Television Dollar Goes
(Author's Compilations)

Public expenditure as percentage of overall economy of television	27%
Average annual expenditure of a cabled household for basic service	$300
Average annual expenditure by advertisers per television household	$200
Average annual public expenditure per household for CBC television	$123
Average annual public expenditure per household for Canadian television production via Telefilm	$12
Average annual public expenditure per household for NFB production destined for television	$8
Average annual public expenditure per Ontario household for TVOntario	$36

Sources: CBC, Telefilm, and NFB Annual Reports for 1994; Statistics Canada. *Radio and television broadcasting 1992* Cat. no. 56-204 and *Cable Television 1993* Cat. no. 56-205; Association for Tele-Education in Canada. 1993. *Creating Access to Tele-Education*. Burnaby: ATEC.

professor Catherine Murray, reported in January 1996 (Canada, 1996).

Technical and Cultural Issues

Between the parliamentary committee and the Juneau committee, the government would probably find itself with authoritative backing to do just about whatever it pleased. The point is, after all that had been said and learned about public broadcasting in the previous ten years, it was time the government went beyond policy-talk and did *something*. With the exception of the largely symbolic Broadcasting Act, one had to go back to 1983 to find a major government policy that had left its mark on broadcasting. On the public side, broadcasting had been victimized by federal fiscal policy and the higher mission of industrial development. Yet, incredibly, people still believed in public broadcasting, and, to the extent that the system allowed, some even tried to practise it. Canadian supporters of public-service broadcasting could be heartened by the fact that broadcasting could still be deemed to have a civic purpose. Not only in its traditional baili-wick of Western Europe, but also in the emerging democracies of the former socialist bloc and the developing world, finding appropri-ate new ways to meet the social and cultural objectives traditionally associated with public broadcasting was on the agenda.[9]

In Canada, the key to resituating public broadcasting for the twenty-first century, therefore, lay in integrating the following:

- a redefined mandate, structurally recombining national, re-gional, local, generalist and specialized services, including those offered via the CBC and other institutions;

- funding based on a more appropriate distribution of the wealth and resources generated by the broadcasting system, supple-mented by public subsidy and strategically targeted advertising;

- programming that met definable audience needs and interests, as opposed to mere addition of more and more entertainment;

- public accountability, through mechanisms that established a two-way flow of information and communication between broadcast professionals and their audiences.

Broadcasting in Canada has developed as a hybrid creature — to the point where, today, it can best be described as a semi-public, semi-private system. Although most of the arguments raised against en-hancing the public dimension of the system tend to be economic, the real obstacles are political. The simple fact is that the principal shareholders of the private sector and a certain public-sector estab-lishment share a vested interest in the prevailing structures, despite their differences. The public interest demands that neither should be sacrosanct.

Repositioning public broadcasting needs to be approached first of all as an exercise in constructing an ideal type, where hard questions can be asked and radical proposals put forward. Regarding financing, for example, why must we take for granted the private sector's hold on broadcasting activities that are able to turn a profit? Assuming that broadcasting generates a range of products, some of which cost more to produce than others, some of which are more attractive to advertisers than others, some of which can be financed by subscrip-tion while others must, in the interest of equity, be supplied free of charge ... assuming all of this, and remembering that broadcasting is a public service, why shouldn't the profits generated by certain activities be used to subsidize the rest?

Regarding structure, why must we continue to protect the institutional framework of the CBC, rather than broaden the horizons of public broadcasting? This has occurred to a limited extent, as I have shown earlier, but real innovation would require a lot more imagination, political will and tenacity on the part of the government and the CRTC. As it now stands, by insisting that the CBC, as the main corporate embodiment of public broadcasting in Canada, compete with the private sector directly for audiences, for advertisers and now for access to cable channels and their value-added subscriber base, we risk painting public broadcasting into a corner.

Finally, regarding content. Here the question of taste and the role of the system's various gatekeepers will inevitably continue to clash with audience figures, budget projections and the availability of cheap American programs. Some admirable progress has been made in the quality of Canadian program production over the years, but let us recall again that none of this would have been possible without public subsidy. We do have a public broadcasting *system* in Canada, which means that we, the public, are entitled to insist that public broadcasting be more than an anachronistic oasis of political correctness in a postmodern cultural desert.

Notes

1. A particularly candid and revealing statement of government policy on this point is to be found in Canada 1964–65: 10080-10086 (summarized in Raboy [1990: 158-160]).
2. According to this report, the Canadian independent production industry was a $688 million business in 1991–92.
3. From a humble 20.5 per cent in 1970, to 60.8 per cent in 1984, cable penetration of Canadian households had reached 74.1 per cent by 1994 (Statistics Canada, 1994).
4. Compilation based on Statistics Canada data (Statistics Canada, 1992, 1993, 1994).
5. According to this document, 90 per cent of the CBC's spending on programming went to Canadian production, as opposed to 55 per cent in the private sector.
6. The 1994–95 fluctuations in the francophone markets had analysts perplexed: among other things, the spring 1995 figures showed Radio-Canada ahead of its principal rival TVA in prime time, with eight of the top-ten rated programs, while TVA's news programming was attracting more viewers than Radio-Canada's.
7. "I don't look upon decentralization as a way of saving money, but as a way of increasing creativity in the CBC. I think creativity is much more vibrant when

you are able to disperse power down into the program regions, down into the network and down into the regions" (Nash, 1994b: 49:20).

8. Full development of such a model is beyond the scope of this chapter, but let us mention a few non-Canadian examples such as Britain's Channel 4, Australia's Special Broadcasting Service and the French-German arts channel, Arte, as services with public-service briefs created outside the corporate structures of national public broadcasters. Perhaps the most extensive example of unbundling is the French example, where the monopoly public-service broadcaster ORTF was "exploded" (*éclaté*) into seven distinct corporations in 1974.

9. See, for example, the December 1994 statement of the Committee of Ministers of the Council of Europe, which included a nine-point mission statement of public-service broadcasting, "stressing the importance of public-service broadcasting for democratic societies ... and underlining the vital function of public-service broadcasting as an essential factor of pluralistic communication accessible to everyone" (Council of Europe, 1994).

References

Association for Tele-Education in Canada, *Creating Access to Tele-Education.* ATEC: Burnaby, 1993.

Atkinson, Dave. 1993. *La crise des télévisions publiques européennes: Ou la propagation du "syndrome canadien."* Quebec City: Institut québécois de recherche sur la culture.

Audley, Paul. 1994. Parliamentary Standing Committee on Canadian Heritage, 5 October.

Canada. Department of Communications. 1985. "Review of the Canadian Broadcasting System: Terms of Reference for the Task Force." Ottawa: DOC Information Services, 9 April.

———. Department of Communications. 1983. *Towards a New National Broadcasting Policy.* Ottawa: Minister of Supply and Services Canada.

———. Federal Cultural Policy Review Committee. 1982. *Report.* Ottawa: Minister of Supply and Services Canada.

———. House of Commons. Standing Committee on Canadian Heritage. 1995. *The Future of the Canadian Broadcasting Corporation in the Multi-channel Universe.* Ottawa: Public Works and Government Services Canada.

———. House of Commons. Standing Committee on Communications and Culture. 1988. *A Broadcasting Policy for Canada.* Ottawa: Queen's Printer.

———. House of Commons. *Debates* (Hansard). 1964–65.

———. Mandate Review Committee. 1996. *Making Our Voices Heard: Canadian Broadcasting and Film for the 21st Century.* Ottawa: Minister of Supply and Services Canada.

———. Royal Commission on National Development in the Arts, Letters and Sciences. 1951. *Report.* Ottawa: King's Printer.

———. Royal Commission on Radio Broadcasting. 1929. *Report.* Ottawa: King's Printer.

———. Task Force on Broadcasting Policy. 1986. *Report.* Ottawa: Minister of Supply and Services Canada.

Canadian Broadcasting Corporation (CBC). 1994a. *A New Commitment*. Submission to the Parliamentary Standing Committee on Canadian Heritage, 1 November.

————. 1994b. *Annual Report 1993–94*. Ottawa: CBC.

————. 1993. "1985–1997 Budgetary Cuts as at April 26, 1993." Internal document. Ottawa: CBC.

Canadian Heritage. 1995. "Minister Dupuy names the members of mandate review of CBC, NFB and Telefilm Canada." News Release, 2 May.

————. 1994. "Minister Dupuy announces details of review of the role of the CBC by Standing Committee." News release, 26 August.

Canadian Radio-television and Telecommunications Commission (CRTC). 1994. Decision CRTC 94-437, "Canadian Broadcasting Corporation." Ottawa, 27 July.

Communications Canada. 1988. *Canadian Voices Canadian Choices: A New Broadcasting Policy for Canada*. Ottawa: Minister of Supply and Services Canada.

Communications Management Inc. 1994. *The Changing Economic Structure of the Canadian audio/video Industry: Implications for Public Policy*. Ottawa: CBC and Department of Canadian Heritage.

Council of Europe. 1994. *The Media in a Democratic Society*. Draft Resolutions and Draft Political Declaration, 4th European Ministerial Conference on Mass Media Policy, Prague, 7-8 December 1994. Document MCM-CDMM (94) 3 prov 1. Strasbourg: Council of Europe.

Le Devoir. 1995a. "Un automne désastreux pour la SRC." 6 January.

————. 1995b. "La SRC forte en soirée, mais faible en information." 5 May.

Ellis, David. 1994. *The CBC & Alternative Revenue-Generating Mechanisms: A Conceptual Analysis*. A Report for the Department of Canadian Heritage. Ottawa.

Goldstein, Ken. 1994. Parliamentary Standing Committee on Canadian Heritage, 22 November.

Groupe Secor. 1994. *Canadian Government Intervention in the Film and Video Industry*. Montreal, October.

Hardin, Herschel. 1985. *Closed Circuits: The Sellout of Canadian Television*. Vancouver: Douglas and McIntyre.

Kiefl, Barry. 1994. Parliamentary Standing Committee on Canadian Heritage, 22 September.

McCabe, Michael. 1995. "CRTC should make sure Canadian content isn't run off info highway." *The Gazette*, 10 May.

Nash, Knowlton. 1994a. *The Microphone Wars: A History of Triumph and Betrayal at the CBC*. Toronto: McClelland and Stewart.

————. 1994b. Parliamentary Standing Committee on Canadian Heritage, 24 November.

Raboy, Marc. 1995a. "The Role of Public Consultation in Shaping the Canadian Broadcasting System." *Canadian Journal of Political Science* 28: 3, pp. 455-477.

————. 1995b. "Influencing Public Policy on Canadian Broadcasting." *Canadian Public Administration*, 38: 3, pp. 411-432.

————. 1990. *Missed Opportunities: The Story of Canada's Broadcasting Policy*. Montreal: McGill-Queen's University Press.

Raboy, Marc., Ivan Bernier, Florian Sauvageau and Dave Atkinson. 1994. "Cultural Development and the Open Economy: A Democratic Issue and a Challenge to Public Policy." *Canadian Journal of Communication* 19: 3/4, pp. 291-315.

Rowland Jr., Willard D. and Michael Tracey. 1990. "Worldwide Challenges to Public Service Broadcasting." *Journal of Communication*, 40: 2, pp. 8-27.

Salter, Liora. 1988. "Reconceptualizing the Public in Public Broadcasting." In Rowland Lorimer and Donald Wilson (eds.). *Communication Canada: Issues in Broadcasting and New Technologies*, Toronto: Kagan & Woo, pp. 232-248.

Skene, Wayne. 1994. Parliamentary Standing Committee on Canadian Heritage, 17 November.

————. 1993. *Fade to Black: A Requiem for the CBC*. Vancouver: Douglas and McIntyre.

Statistics Canada. 1994a. *Cable television 1993*. Cat. no. 56-205. Ottawa: Minister of Supply and Services.

————. 1994b. *Household Facilities and Equipment 1994*. Cat. no. 64-202. Ottawa: Minister of Supply and Services.

————. 1994c. *Radio and television broadcasting 1992*. Cat. no. 56-204. Ottawa: Minister of Supply and Services.Statutes of Canada. 1991. *Broadcasting Act*, 38-39 Elizabeth II, c. 11.

Watson, Patrick. 1994. Parliamentary Standing Committee on Canadian Heritage, 24 November.

8

Private Television and Cable

Liss Jeffrey
Assisted by Fraser McAninch

Introduction

Canada's television broadcasting system has undergone a fundamental transformation over the past fifteen years, and there's much more to come: increased competition and viewing choices; rival technologies and disputes over international trading agreements; conflicts pitting advocates of deregulation against advocates of government regulation and pro-national cultural policies. These and other forces are reshaping the business behind the box, and what's on the screen.

Conventional broadcasters in the "free-TV" business — those who transmit programs and commercials over the air to rooftop antennas — currently face unprecedented competition for audiences and advertising revenue. Nearly three-quarters of all households pay the cable companies to deliver their TV signals and receive in return a choice of up to 60 domestic and foreign services. This expanded choice has led to a decline in the total audience share for all conventional broadcasters. The CBC has been the hardest hit. Since their debut in 1985, Canadian specialty channels such as MuchMusic and The Sports Network (TSN) have succeeded in attracting subscribers and sponsors by "narrowcasting" programs that appeal to specific groups, and marketing these viewers — in this case fans of new music and sports — to advertisers who wish to target precisely these audiences. Cable also delivers an array of non-programming services including home shopping, real estate and (coming soon) subscription video games.

Broadcasters also face competition from alternative media (Table 8-1). Eighty-two per cent of households own VCRs, and VCR viewing has taken five per cent of audience share. Increasingly, households (29 per cent in 1994) are equipped with personal computers, and four out of ten of these have modems, which permit connection to the Internet via telephone lines. By one estimate, video game units can be found in 85 per cent of households occupied by males under 20. Three per cent of all households officially receive television via satellite, a figure that probably underestimates the "grey market" for unauthorized U.S. satellite signals. This pirate underground is plainly visible in non-urban areas where backyard satellite dishes sprout just as urban homes once bristled with antennas. Since the early 1990s, cable operators have warned that direct-to-home U.S. satellites, or "death stars," threaten to bypass the regulated broadcasting system. Their dishes are harder to see because they are smaller, but their presence on the landscape could profoundly alter the mediascape.

Over the longer term, the one-way broadcasting system will be transformed into a two-way "cybersystem" by the entry of competitors from the giant foreign and domestic telephone and telecommunications companies. These companies have announced plans to construct an information highway to deliver video and other services to the home. During the current transitional period, all media and telecommunications companies are eyeing one another's businesses, while consolidating their operations through mergers and strategic alliances. Bell Canada, a leading telecommunications firm, has established a subsidiary to produce multimedia content. Along with its industry allies, the largest cable operator, Rogers Communications, intends to compete with the telecommunications companies to provide telephone service. Rogers has teamed up with Microsoft to offer its customers a high-speed broadband cable link to the information highway and has set up its own multimedia production division. Full-scale competition between the cable and telephone companies will commence whenever the federal government and the regulator change the rules governing the broadcasting system.

New and old media are colliding in the home, where Canadians spend an ever-increasing portion of their leisure time (Statistics Canada. Household, 1995: 11). For conventional broadcasters, the message of the converging media environment is blunt: adapt or disappear. Already rival media are forecasting television's demise. One leading computer magazine ran a cover story in early 1996 proclaiming, "Toss your tube: How the Internet will replace broad-

Table 8-1
Penetration of Household Equipment as a
Percentage of All Homes

	1984	1989	1994	1995
Telephone	98.6	98.7	99	98.5
Radio	98.9	98.9	98.9	98.9
Colour TV	88.5	96.1	98.2	98.5
VCR	12.6	58.8	79.2	82.1
Cable Television	60.1	70.8	74.1	73.4
Compact Disc Player	*	11.6	40.8	47.4
Personal Computer	10.4	12.6	25	28.8
Modem	*	*	8.4	12.1

* Data not available for that year.
Source: Statistics Canada. Catalogue 84-202. *Household Facilities and Equipment.*

casting" (*BYTE*). Given the popularity of watching television, audience habits will not likely change overnight. Since 1984, however, average per capita hours of television viewing have fallen slowly but steadily. VCRs, video games, CD-ROMs, computers and on-line services such as the Internet and World Wide Web offer alternatives for audiences, a trend that will accelerate. The steepest declines in TV viewing are reported for children and teenagers, groups most likely to use alternative media.

In the age of cyberspace, the fundamental question for broadcast policy makers has as much relevance today as it did when first raised by cultural nationalists back in the radio days of the late 1920s: how to ensure that Canadians receive a choice of domestically produced programming from their broadcasting system, given the abundance of American shows available from Canadian and U.S. stations. Broadcasting shares this perennial conundrum with Canada's other cultural industries, notably English-language film and publishing. The problem is structural. U.S. producers enjoy competitive advantages because they can recover most of their production costs in a market ten times the size of Canada's and have established vertically integrated conglomerates (like Time Warner and Disney) to produce, distribute and promote their exports globally.

New media technologies will not alter these structural and competitive advantages in the immediate future. But the current upheavals within the broadcasting system threaten to subvert Parliament's intention (as expressed in broadcasting acts dating back to 1932) to ensure that the system offers a choice of Canadian shows and contributes to national identity and cultural sovereignty. The prospect of two-way interactive media also awakens hopes and fears: hopes that new media can serve as instruments for nation building, for connecting communities and households and for generating new wealth; fears that the nation may not survive, that jobs may be lost and that information have-nots may be created. To quote Canada's pre-eminent media theorist, Marshall McLuhan (1964): "[I]t is the framework that changes with new technology, and not just the picture within the frame." These controversies over the future of broadcasting are only superficially about programming. In the Canadian context, they challenge the capacity and the willingness of the nation to continue to use broadcasting — the most pervasive and popular of the cultural industries — as a means to foster its own distinctiveness and cultural development.

This chapter will review the key shifts that are affecting the market, industry structure and policy environment for private broadcasting and cable. The next section situates television broadcasting within a global and historical context and examines what is at stake in debates over broadcast policy and Canadian production from an English Canadian, cultural-nationalist perspective.

Historic Debates about Broadcasting as a Cultural Industry

The Canadian broadcasting system, like Canada itself, is the product of public and private enterprise. In the nineteenth century, the decision was made to confederate as a nation, and the railroad became the techno-cultural instrument and symbol of this defiance of geography. In the twentieth century, the nation became independent, no longer a British colony. The electronic railroad — the CBC — became an instrument and symbol of an evolving process of nation building; a hopeful sign that a collective consciousness might emerge out of the national conversation over the public airwaves, a national dream in defiance of the tensions among the regions and the pull of our powerful southern neighbour. If policy is — as Thomas Dye has suggested (in Aucoin, 1979: 2) — whatever governments choose to do or not to do, then both the broadcasting system and the nation share self-conscious moments of birth as products of public policy. The first private Canadian radio station began broadcasting in 1919. During the 1920s, unregulated U.S. signals bombarded the country and threatened to drown out domestic voices. Persuaded by citizen activists in the Canadian Radio League, Parliament declared the airwaves public property in the Broadcasting Act of 1932 and established the Canadian Radio Broadcasting Commission, precursor to the CBC, signalling a national determination to guarantee Canadians ownership and control of their broadcasting system. Private-sector radio stations continued to operate. From this point on, the Canadian broadcasting system was composed of both public service and private commercial stations and featured U.S. as well as home-grown programming. In sharp contrast, the U.S. Communications Act of 1934 confirmed the predominant status of commercial broadcasting and marginalized public-sector and educational stations (McChesney, 1993).

Like radio before it, television began as a business built around the invention and sale of equipment and, once widely diffused, became both a cultural and economic force (Jeffrey, 1995b). The CBC launched the first Canadian television stations in 1952, four years after U.S. networks began regular broadcasting into Canada. This delay meant that an estimated 100,000 Canadian households first received television from U.S. border stations. CBC reached a national audience through stations it built and by paying private affiliates to carry network programming. When the privately owned CTV network made its debut in 1961, the distinctively Canadian mixed system of public and private stations also became predominant in television.

Historically, the tension between private profits and public service has supplied the dynamic for Canadian broadcasting policy. It is, and has always been, cheaper and less risky for Canadian broadcasters — with a market one-tenth the size of the U.S., two official languages and easy cross-border reception of U.S. stations by most of the Canadian population — to import U.S. dramatic programs and benefit from American stars and promotional efforts. The English-language private broadcasters became rich by selling audiences for imported U.S. shows to advertisers, not by producing or purchasing shows of comparable quality in Canada, nor by promoting homegrown stars. Cable system operators profited from importing and selling clear reception of U.S. signals, which were already spilling over the border, not by encouraging Canadian stations or production.

From the first Broadcasting Act of 1932 to the current act of 1991, the federal response has remained consistent: license broadcasters and allow them to import popular U.S. programs, while requiring them to use a portion of the resulting revenues to carry, produce or purchase domestic content. The early CBC radio network reaped the rewards of delivering *Amos 'n Andy* to every region, just as the CBC television network did later by carrying *Dallas* to every home. When the cable companies were officially recognized within the broadcasting system in the 1970s, the *quid pro quo* was mandatory carriage of local Canadian channels. The cable companies also agreed to protect the rights of domestic broadcasters to import U.S. shows by means of "simulcasting," which requires the cable operator to substitute a Canadian for a U.S. signal when the show for which the Canadian broadcaster has purchased rights airs at the same time. If the intention was to preserve domestic markets, the unintended consequence has been that program schedules for Canadian stations mirror those of their U.S. counterparts and include fewer Canadian shows in prime time.

Historically, Canadian broadcasters and cable operators have played the role of middlemen, brokering the flow of programs from U.S. producers to Canadian consumers. So far, this "intermediary" strategy (as we might call it) has protected Canadian broadcasters and their markets. It has also amounted to what critic Hershel Hardin (1985) has called "Canadianization through Americanization." Majority Canadian ownership is crucial to this strategy, based on the fact that Canadian companies are more likely to employ Canadian talent and fund Canadian productions. Foreign investors were prohibited from owning more than 20 per cent (now 33 per cent) of licensed Canadian broadcasters. But restricting ownership did not succeed without additional policies, because the immediate profits to be made from importing expensive U.S. dramatic series at a fraction of the production cost proved irresistible. This short-sighted and unimaginative response was partly due to the scarcity of entrepreneurs with production as well as business and engineering talent in the boardrooms of the private broadcasters.

Ensuring a choice of Canadian content on the broadcasting system — a goal supported in principle by most Canadians — has required repeated government intervention, beginning with radio and extending to television. Some of the major initiatives over the years include establishment of the Canadian Radio Broadcasting Commission (1932), the CBC (1936), the Board of Broadcast Governors (1958), content regulations (1959), the CRTC (1968), revised content regulations (1970), income tax advantages for companies advertising on Canadian media (1976), direct subsidies for independent producers through Telefilm Canada's Broadcast Fund (1983) and requirements that private broadcasters fund underdeveloped program genres, especially dramatic entertainment and children's shows (1979; 1989). Cable operators now also contribute to a production fund (1994).

At one level the intermediary policy has succeeded: things might have been worse! Private broadcasters are required to meet Canadian content quotas of 60 per cent of the daily schedule and 50 per cent of evening (6-12 P.M.) programming. Even allowing for the oddities (such as counting the Academy Awards because of their interest to Canadians), the Canadian presence in the regulated system far exceeds that on the unfettered movie screens of the nation, where Canadian content is shown during an estimated five per cent of screen time. Made-in-Canada TV news (usually aired at 6 and 11 P.M.) has always been genuinely popular with audiences and provides the major source of local and world information for most citizens (TVB. Television Bureau of Canada, 1995: 14). Thanks to Telefilm Canada, in recent years there have been encouraging signs in dramatic production, such as the successful series *Street Legal*, aired on CBC; *Due South*, aired on CTV and CBS; and *Traders*, aired on the CanWest Global system. Independent producers have also created critically acclaimed made-for-TV movies such as *Conspiracy of Silence*, *Love and Hate*, and *The Boys of St. Vincent*, all of which were sold and aired worldwide (and in the U.S.) after scoring ratings hits when aired on the CBC.

Canadian ownership policies, content rules and the CBC laid the groundwork for the survival of a Canadian broadcasting system known for excellence in news and public affairs; Telefilm Canada supplied the missing ingredient — targeted funds — that fostered an independent production industry capable of producing high-quality drama popular with audiences (Canada. "Mandate," 1996; Audley 1993). Both private and public broadcasters have contributed to achieving this policy-driven outcome. To qualify for funding, an independent producer must secure a commitment from a conventional broadcaster to pay a licence fee for a show that must be scheduled during prime time. If there were no control over the system — in this case the Canadian broadcasters — just as there is no control over movie screen owners, then viewers would be denied a choice of Canadian shows. Here the "intermediary" policy has begun to achieve its desired effect.

The imminent threat to the Canadian broadcasting system is that new technologies and international trading agreements are combining to knock out the props for this intermediary approach, just as it appears to be working. If U.S. producers reach and bill Canadian households directly, whether by satellite, telephone or the information highway, then this approach to preservation of a choice of Canadian voices will no longer be viable. Using North American (NAFTA) and world (GATT) trading agreements as battering rams, the U.S. is presently attempting to topple Canada's cultural industries policy framework. U.S. trade representatives insist that cultural industries are businesses like any others, and Canada's protections for its cultural industries (which the Americans call entertainment industries) constitute unacceptable trade barriers, requiring economic retaliation. This pro-market position has appeal on both sides of the border, but especially for those companies who wish to do further business in the U.S.

The resolve to create a national space using the broadcasting industry as an instrument of cultural sovereignty has been renewed repeatedly, most recently when the federal government renegotiated the exemption for Canada's cultural industries while NAFTA was extended to include Mexico. Public opinion polls have historically shown support for policies to protect the cultural industries. A 1991 "Media Study" conducted by Environics found that 70 per cent of Canadians believe Canada has a distinct culture, while 60 per cent agreed that more should be done to develop a separate cultural identity from the Americans. A 1991 Goldfarb report discovered that 81 per cent of Canadians support Canadian ownership of Canada's cultural industries. In English Canada, 70 per cent of adults believe that preservation of Canadian heritage is more important than preservation of their own ethnic heritage, while the response was 50-50 in Quebec (Canada. Standing Committee on Communications and Culture, 1992: 112). Among major public concerns over the information highway, Andersen Consulting found that more than half of respondents worried about the threats posed to Canada's cultural identity, and 62 per cent believed government should be responsible for protecting that identity (Rowan, 1995: B1). Will this approval continue? More recently, the public appears ambivalent: in no mood to support any government expenditures, yet supportive in principle of defending Canadian culture. The gravest threat to the continuance of the Canadian broadcasting system will come from within, if arguments that have historically been persuasive in linking broadcasting and the Canadian nation lose their force.

Canadian Policy Debates in a Global Context

Beginning in the 1930s, Canada opted for a middle way between the state monopoly of Britain and the purely commercial model of the United States. Since 1980, the broadcasting systems of most countries (except, of course, the U.S.) have come to resemble the Canadian mixed model. Private and public broadcasting cohere into distinctive institutional and programming arrangements within each country (Noam, 1991). Most have policies regarding entry into national markets and protection of domestic audiovisual space. Globalization, evident in the proliferation of satellite broadcasting, the relaxing of domestic barriers to foreign programs and ownership and the continued expansion of transnational media and marketing conglomerates, has meant that Canada's cultural industries problem — how to ensure a choice of domestic programs when faced with cheap and popular foreign competition from transborder and domestic sources — is now widely shared. There has been a worldwide decline in audience share for the state public broadcasters as they lose their monopolies and adapt to increased competition with the private sector.

What makes the Canadian case of global interest is that English Canada (but not French Canada) is the only known broadcast market in the world where local dramatic production is not necessarily preferred over foreign content of comparable quality (Tracey and Redal, 1995: 361). This point is contentious. Some have argued that the problem is strictly one of availability, because Canadian shows with high production values perform well with audiences and on occasion outdraw the foreign competition. This refutes the often-repeated falsehood that Canadians always dislike Canadian programming; it also contradicts the mistaken impression that contemporary cultural nationalists are actually trying to force "high culture" upon their fellow citizens. Given the slim chance of recovering the costs of production (averaging over $1 million per episode for a continuing dramatic series) within the Canadian market, however, the volume of expensive Canadian dramas (the kind most attractive to audiences) will remain modest. Others have argued that there is no problem, reasoning that English Canada's acceptance of American productions is due to a deep similarity between English Canadian and American values and cultural preferences. This opinion seems to justify something that requires explanation. Arguably, this anomaly could just as easily be explained as the result of sixty years of cross-border and domestic broadcasting of popular U.S. shows, particularly to children, a process that began with radio but accelerated with the advent of television in the 1950s. In any case, due to an accident of geography, English-speaking Canada has the longest-known exposure to the direct and indirect output of the U.S. media, and its fate offers a timely reminder of the possible long-term consequences of opening borders to the products of another culture's imagination.

There are serious issues at stake. In the aftermath of the cold war, entertainment and information products have overtaken armaments as a major source of export revenue growth. As a global entertainment economy has developed and the globalization of broadcasting has accelerated, cultural industries policy has become a source of persistent international friction. This deeply ideological debate pits those who regard cultural industries and their products in purely economic terms against those who consider the cultural industries to have sufficient national importance that regulatory and legislative measures are required to defend them.

The U.S. is the leading proponent of the unrestricted markets argument. The Americans are highly successful at the business of commercial television and are proven masters at creating and marketing cultural goods to international audiences. U.S. export revenues from cultural products and services rank second only to aerospace and show faster growth. The U.S. supports its position on the ideological grounds that open markets benefit all nations and that broadcasting is a business like any other. No amount of protection should be allowed to compensate for market failure and a "weak" culture. The U.S. buttresses this position by invoking the cause of freedom of expression. Thus, the wide range of available U.S. stations and programs is not enough; Canadian content quotas constitute a form of censorship.

On the other side of the debate, represented by Canada and France, broadcasting is viewed as a strategic industry, with a significant role to play in cultural development and national life. This argument for cultural sovereignty affirms that nations are entitled to enact policies and legislation to ensure that audiences can receive news from domestic sources and that citizens can reach their fellow citizens with

Table 8-2
Non-Canadian Satellite Services
(Eligible for Carriage in Canada)

WTBS Atlanta
WGN-TV Chicago
WWOR-TV New York City
WPIX New York City
WSBK-TV Boston
KTLA Los Angeles
Cable News Network (CNN)
CNN Headline News (CNN-2)
The Nashville Network (TNN)
The Arts and Entertainment Network (A&E)
CNBC/FNN*
The Weather Channel (TWC)
Cable Satellite Public Affairs Network (C-SPAN)
The Silent Network
The Learning Channel
Black Entertainment Television (BET)
Lifetime Television
Comedy Central

* 6 A.M.–7 P.M. (ET) Mon-Fri programming component only
Source: CRTC.

the products of their imagination. In defence of these cultural objectives, it is argued that no nation has the right to regard another nation as an automatic extension of its own market. This happens, for example, when U.S. film distribution companies sell rights to North America and do not sell Canadian rights separately. Canadian cultural nationalism hinges on a sense of community preservation — a pale version of nationalism — and a belief in the legitimate power of the nation state to promote its own cultural industries by limiting foreign competitive advantages where necessary. Cultural sovereignty has also been defended on the positive grounds of preservation of cultural diversity. At a 1995 G7 conference, for instance, then heritage minister Michel Dupuy took the position that protecting cultural diversity — which in North America could include protection of any minority culture, whether English Canadian, Francophone or native — can legitimately take precedence over pro-market ideology.

In North America, the conflict between the two positions is written into the language of NAFTA, which permits the U.S. to retaliate economically if it believes that Canada's cultural industries policies have damaged U.S. trade interests (Comor, 1991). The U.S. seems determined to make an example of Canada, accusing it of hiding "a culture of greed" behind a façade of cultural policy. U.S. complaints include the 1995 removal by the CRTC of the U.S. Country Music Television channel (but not the U.S.-based Nashville Network) from an official list of approved satellite services available for carriage by Canadian cable companies (Table 8-2). The U.S. company knew when it commenced service in Canada that if a viable domestic competitor received a licence, the Canadian licensee was entitled to request deletion of the U.S. service. Yet U.S. interests argued that this action represented a form of "expropriation," and that Canada should not be permitted to set a poor example for the rest of the world. The U.S. government threatened to initiate trade retaliation before a proposed settlement was reached that allowed the U.S. country channel to own the maximum permissible share of the Canadian New Country Network — a kind of reverse takeover. These conflicts will escalate.

Opposition to cultural industries regulation gained ground in academic and pro-market political circles (left and right) during the 1980s. Some opponents champion "consumer sovereignty," which means that the individual consumer interest in lower prices is best served by deregulation and unfettered competition. From this perspective, historical attempts to support and promote Canadian cultural production are dismissed as economically inefficient. From a populist perspective, the complaint is that government should not be allowed to dictate what viewers watch. Another charge is that policies to encourage Canadian content in the private broadcasting sector have failed. Broadcasters, producers and cable companies, it is argued, along with a tiny cultural elite, have been the main beneficiaries of such policies, with consumers picking up the bill, in the form of a "hidden tax." The cultural sovereignty position is also attacked by those who contend that the linkage between broadcasting Canadian content and promoting national cultural identity is weak and unquantifiable (e.g., Collins, 1990). Furthermore, it is argued that technologies such as satellites and the Internet make the nation state obsolete, and render all pro-national policies based on cultural sovereignty ineffective.

The resilient nation state has numerous powers to enforce its sovereignty, if the citizens are willing and the politicians persuaded. The cultural sovereignty position recognizes the contribution of broadcasting to citizenship, which is more difficult to quantify than consumer welfare (Jeffrey, 1994: 497). What is at stake is the kind of community and nation that the communications system will support. In Canadian debates, the cultural sovereignty position highlights three key points: the linkage between identity formation and exposure over time to television; the linkage between television and cultural diversity, as audiences from different regions and ethnic and linguistic backgrounds are included in a fluid national mosaic; and the linkage between political unity and a broadcasting system that is predominantly Canadian. These hopeful aspirations collectively aim at a unified nation composed of diverse communities sharing common values, within what Powe (1993) has called a communications state. This English Canadian, cultural-nationalist position promotes the heritage of the past and the cultural development of the future and regards Canada as a process, not a product. "Canada's cultural diversity should enhance and enrich our potential for cultural growth and identity, both individually and collectively" (Standing Committee on Communications and Culture, 1992).

These linkages lie at the core of Canadian broadcast policy making, as expressed in section 3 of the Broadcasting Act (1991), which says in part, "the Canadian broadcasting system, operating primarily in the English and French languages and comprising public, private and community elements, makes use of radio frequencies that are public property and provides, through its programming, a public service essential to the maintenance and enhancement of national identity and cultural sovereignty." Within this visionary framework, it is expected that the pragmatics of regulation, broadcasting and viewing proceed. This distinctive English Canadian visionary pragmatism strives for a broadcasting system that combines public-sector commitments and private-sector entrepreneurial energies, each contributing to nation building by providing the collective instruments to express that hoped-for unity within diversity. This technological nationalism — as it has been disparagingly called — may be unfashionable, liberal or romantic, yet it offers a historical ground and principled inspiration for Canada and the broadcasting system that serves all Canadians.

The fundamental policy problem has not changed, but upheavals in the broadcasting system and new media technologies on the horizon offer opportunities to renew or to destroy the conscious public policy decision to use media technologies as instruments for nation building. This may explain why citizen groups — like their predecessors of the 1920s — once again are emerging to ensure a public space, this time on the information highway (Canada. Industry Canada, 1995). But the environment for policy making differs this time around. The increasing blare of pro-market calls for deregulation focuses the debate on the costs while downplaying the values at stake, or what may be lost if Canada abdicates its cultural sovereignty. In the 1990s, the acceptable policy options may have been narrowed irrevocably — along lines that echo American debates.

Market Analysis

Conventional television broadcasting is a mature industry poised for transition. Colour television sets saturate the market, and nearly half of all households own two or more. On the horizon are two-way interactive media, which could enable consumers to become producers and transform the broadcasting system into a cybersystem. It is widely speculated that some hybrid of a computer and television may emerge as the "smart" home entertainment appliance of the future (e.g., Gilder, 1994).

On the demand side, available viewing time is a finite resource, and the proliferation of alternatives to television broadcasting has cut into this time. A national survey conducted by Statistics Canada in 1992 found Canadians enjoyed an estimated 4.7 hours per day of leisure time, down from 5.5 hours in 1986 (Statistics Canada, 1995: 16). Most consumers will require major incentives in price, content or use value if they are to be tempted to abandon the familiar habit of watching TV. Already, hours of viewing have dropped from an average of 24.3 hours per week in 1984; yet watching TV remains the number one leisure activity at 22.7 hours weekly. Viewing habits differ across audience subpopulations, by region and by season, plummeting in the summer. Viewing time is lower in B.C. and Alberta, and highest for French-speaking Quebec audiences, at 26.3 hours per week (ibid: 83). Young females (18-24) watch four hours more television weekly than do their male counterparts. Between 1986 and 1994, TV viewing among children fell from 22 to 18 hours weekly; for teens the decline was from 20 to 17 hours weekly (ibid: 82). Much of this time is reportedly spent playing video games or using computers.

Figure 8-1
Stations Tuned Per Week

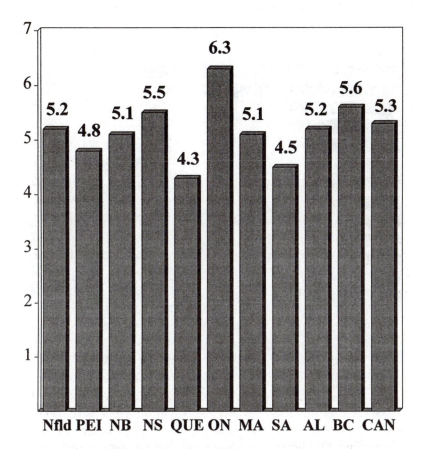

Source: Television Bureau of Canada. 1996. BBM Fall 1994 Sweep Survey in *TV Basics 95/96*.

Canada's audiences are concentrated in 42 major markets across the country, each with distinctive characteristics, and some with two or more language communities. Fewer than one quarter of all households receive their signals over the air from conventional broadcasters, which is too large an audience to abandon, but costly to serve. These issues will become pressing as broadcasters make the costly shift from delivering analogue to digital services. Two-thirds of subscribers receive more than 45 channels, yet in 1994 an average viewer watched 5.3 stations per week (Figure 8-1). The more chan-

Figure 8-2
Canadian Specialty Services Viewing Statistics
English TV Specialty Services (Anglophones 2+, Winter 1995)

Average Weekly Share among Cable Households

3.5		YTV
3.0		TSN
1.5		NewsWorld
1.5		Discovery
1.0		MuchMusic
0.8		New Country Network
0.6		Bravo
0.6		Showcase
0.5		Weather Network
0.5		Vision
0.5		Life Network
0.4		WTN
0.1		Cdn. Home Shopping

%   1   2   3   4

Share of hours (%) — The percentage of time spent viewing a particular network or station.
Data: A.C. Nielsen.
Source: CCTA 1995.

nels available, the more are watched, yet the increase is slight. In the Toronto-Hamilton market, the sixth largest in North America, an average of 6.8 stations were tuned in (TVB 1996: 20).

An international comparison among the Toronto-Hamilton and New York, Los Angeles and London (U.K.) markets concluded that competition has major effects: the share of audience delivered by the domestic conventional stations was much lower in Toronto-Hamilton, at 49 per cent, compared to 79 per cent in New York, 81 per cent in L.A. and 90 per cent in London (Marchant, 1995: 24). Higher Canadian cable penetration levels meant that clear U.S. signals were more readily available. Whereas in the foreign markets domestic conventional stations compete only with pay, specialty or satellite services, Canadian conventional stations compete with U.S. stations for share

Figure 8-2 (cont.)

Average Weekly Reach among Cable Households

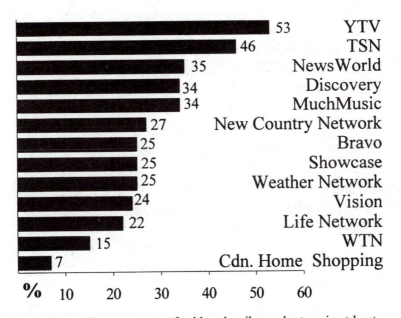

53		YTV
46		TSN
35		NewsWorld
34		Discovery
34		MuchMusic
27		New Country Network
25		Bravo
25		Showcase
25		Weather Network
24		Vision
22		Life Network
15		WTN
7		Cdn. Home Shopping

% 10 20 30 40 50 60

Reach (%) — The percentage of cable subscribers who tune in at least once a week.
Data: A.C. Nielsen.
Source: CCTA 1995.

of a smaller audience (due to a less concentrated population). Toronto-Hamilton may be the most competitive market in the world, concluded the study authors, but the world may now be catching up.

Canadian conventional stations have learned to cope with a highly competitive marketplace, but the pressures are increasing. The cable industry has tended to expand the number of channels offered on the basic service, charging the subscriber an average $4.62 per month on top of a $17.75 average monthly rate for this discretionary or "extended basic" tier (CCTA, 1995: 4). 91 per cent of subscribers offered this option had taken it by 1994. (One reason is that — except in Quebec where the practice is illegal — the customer received a rate increase without notification of a choice, a practice known as "negative option marketing" and discussed further below.) Until 1995, cable operators were permitted to link two American services

Table
Share of Hours of TV Viewing by Station

	1983	1984	1985	1986
Canadian Conventional Stations				
CBC O&O	10.4	10.4	10.1	10
CBC AFFILIATES	6.6	6.6	6.1	5.8
CBC TOTAL	17	17	16.2	15.8
CTV	25.2	22.5	22.3	20.2
INDEPENDENT ENGLISH	9.9	10	8.3	9.5
GLOBAL	3.7	3.6	3.8	4.3
RADIO CANADA O&O	6.2	6.2	6.3	6.4
RADIO CANADA AFFIL	3	2.7	2.5	2.6
RADIO CANADA TOTAL	9.2	8.9	8.8	9
TVA	8.2	10.1	11.1	10.9
RADIO QUEBEC	0.9	1	1.2	1.3
QUATRE SAISONS	N/A	N/A	N/A	1.1
Total Canadian Con. Stns.	**74.1**	**73.1**	**71.7**	**72.1**
U.S. Conventional TV				
U.S.: ABC AFFIL	N/A	N/A	N/A	N/A
NBC AFFIL	N/A	N/A	N/A	N/A
CBS AFFIL	N/A	N/A	N/A	N/A
INDEPEND	N/A	N/A	N/A	N/A
PBS	N/A	N/A	N/A	N/A
Total U.S. Con. Stns.	23.7	**23.3**	**23**	**22**
Non-Conventional TV				
CABLE	0.3	0.2	0.4	0.3
PROV	0.1	0.1	0.2	0.2
VCR	0.6	1.3	2.2	2.6
CAN SPECIALTY	0.9	1.4	1.7	1.9
U.S. SPECIALTY	0.2	0.4	0.4	0.4
OTHERS	0.1	0.2	0.4	0.5
Total Hours (Millions)	**578.4**	**579.2**	**593.2**	**599.5**

Source: BBM. 1994.

8-3
Group, 10-Year Trends, All Persons 2+

1987	1988	1989	1990	1991	1992	1993
9.4	8.9	9.3	8.6	8.2	6.7	6.6
5.7	4.1	3.9	3.5	3.3	3.1	3.2
15.1	13	13.2	12.1	11.5	9.8	9.8
19.7	18.7	16.9	18.6	18.4	18.3	18.3
10.3	10.5	11.1	11.1	11.8	11.8	11.5
4.2	4.4	4.9	4.8	4.7	4.8	4.6
5.5	5.5	4.9	5.3	4.8	4.8	5.2
2	1.8	1.6	1.7	1.5	1.5	1.6
7.5	7.3	6.5	7	6.3	6.3	6.8
9.8	10.3	9.6	9.7	9.9	8.4	10.1
1.3	1.2	1.2	1.1	1	1	0.8
3.5	3.8	4.5	4.2	3.5	3.7	3.7
71.3	**69.2**	**67.8**	**68.6**	**67**	**64.2**	**65.5**
N/A	N/A	4.7	4.2	3.9	3.8	3.2
N/A	N/A	5.1	4.6	4.4	4	4.3
N/A	N/A	5.4	5.1	5.1	4.9	4.2
N/A	N/A	3.2	3.2	4.1	4.2	3.8
N/A	N/A	2.1	2.2	2.1	2.3	2.3
22.1	**20.6**	**20.5**	**19.3**	**19.6**	**19.3**	**17.8**
0.4	0.3	0.3	0.4	0.4	0.3	0.3
0.2	1	1	0.8	0.9	0.8	0.8
3.1	3.4	3.3	3.4	3.9	5.4	5.1
2	4.2	5.3	5.6	5.8	6.3	6.5
0.5	0.5	1	1.3	2.3	3	3.1
0.4	0.8	0.7	0.6	0.1	0.8	0.9
583.1	**590.9**	**595.5**	**595**	**610**	**619.1**	**623.1**

Table
Percentage Distribution of
by Origin and Type of Pro
Fall 1993 Canada, Anglo

TYPE OF PROGRAM	ALL TELEVISION STATIONS		
	Canadian Programs	**Foreign Programs**	**Total**
News & public affairs	15	7.9	22.8
Documentary	0.5	1.5	2
Instruction			
Academic	0.4	0.7	1
Social	0.5	1.1	1.7
Religion	0.2	0.1	0.3
Sports	5.2	2.7	7.9
Variety and games	0.7	6.2	6.8
Music and dance	0.4	1	1.4
Comedy	0.4	16.2	16.6
Drama	2.3	29.5	31.8
Other	—	7.7	7.7
TOTAL	**25.5**	**74.5**	**100**

Figures may not add to totals due to rounding.
Source: Statistics Canada. Catalogue 87-208.

to one Canadian service, on the (intermediary policy) assumption that U.S. services would sell the combination. Currently the linkage ratio is one for one, thus permitting more Canadian specialty channels. The first pay-TV movie services were licensed in 1982, and the six current pay-TV services had a 12.4 per cent penetration rate in 1994. Viewers Choice, a pay-per-view service (partly owned by Rogers) featuring variable starting times for movies and events such as sports — which on some systems took up 18 channels — reported a reach of 900,000 customers in winter 1995 (CCTA,1995: 7) and revenues of $9.8 million with a seven per cent profit margin before interest and tax (CRTC. "Statistical Summaries," 1995).

Since 1985, subscriptions to discretionary services have increased, resulting in profits for their owners, and major revenue and profit

8-4
Television Viewing Time
gram and Origin of Station
phones, 2 years and older

FOREIGN STATIONS	CANADIAN STATIONS		
All Programs	All Programs	Cdn. Programs	Foreign Programs
4.4	18.4	15	3.4
1.3	0.7	0.5	0.2
0.6	0.5	0.4	0.1
0.8	0.8	0.5	0.3
—	0.2	0.2	0.1
1.4	6.5	5.2	1.3
2.2	4.6	0.7	3.9
0.8	0.6	0.4	0.2
5.2	11.3	0.4	11
10.4	21.4	2.3	19.1
0.9	6.8	—	6.8
28.1	**71.9**	**25.4**	**46.5**

growth for cable companies. This sign from the market has stimulated further applications to launch specialty services. As Figure 8-2
shows, the percentage of cable subscribers tuning in is small. Other
data show viewers spend twice as much time watching Canadian as
U.S. specialty channels (BBM, 1995). Much but by no means all of
the programming on the specialty channels is foreign. The measure
of reach, in the second graph of Figure 8-2, or the percentage of
subscribers who tune in weekly, has become a more significant
indicator, as advertisers seek exposure on channels that draw small
but dedicated target audiences.

The much-feared direct broadcast satellite (DBS) remains on the
horizon. Current (C band or big dish) satellite penetration is greatest
in remote regions unserved by cable and reaches a high of eight per

Table
Percentage Distribution of
by Origin and Type of Pro
Fall 1993 Canada, Franco

TYPE OF PROGRAM	ALL TELEVISION STATIONS		
	Canadian Programs	Foreign Programs	Total
News & public affairs	25	1.4	26.3
Documentary	1.4	0.4	1.7
Instruction			
Academic	1.6	0.1	1.7
Social	1.1	0.2	1.3
Religion	0.3	—	0.3
Sports	5.7	0.7	6.4
Variety and games	15.7	1.9	17.6
Music and dance	1	0.2	1.2
Comedy	2.7	8	10.7
Drama	10.4	18.1	28.5
Other	—	4.2	4.2
TOTAL	**64.9**	**35.1**	**100**

Figures may not add to totals due to rounding.
Source: Statistics Canada. Catalogue 87-208.

cent of households (in Dawson Creek) but averages three per cent
nationally (TVB, 1996: 18). As with the early days of cable TV,
households that receive television from satellite watch more U.S.
channels than they do Canadian channels (BBM, 1994). This may
change when a Canadian DBS service is launched, which will make
more Canadian channels available.

The market formula for conventional broadcasters consists of assembling mass audiences for general interest programs and selling
these audiences to advertisers. This practice occurs when advertisers
require mass exposure (or gross rating points). The situation is more
complex for the specialty channels, which market themselves to the
cable companies, to potential and actual viewers, as well as to the
advertising community. They have succeeded despite their small

8-5

Television Viewing Time

gram and Origin of Station

phones, 2 years and older

FOREIGN STATIONS	CANADIAN STATIONS		
All Programs	All Programs	Cdn. Programs	Foreign Programs
0.8	25.6	25	0.6
0.2	1.6	1.4	0.2
0.1	1.6	1.6	—
0.1	1.2	1.1	0.1
—	0.3	0.3	—
0.3	6.1	5.7	0.4
0.8	16.8	15.7	1.1
0.1	1	1	—
0.7	10	2.7	7.3
1.9	26.6	10.4	16.2
0.6	3.7	—	3.7
5.6	**94.4**	**64.9**	**29.5**

viewership numbers in part through their use of audience research. Advertisers can be persuaded to buy when narrowcasting is more cost effective in reaching desirable viewers. Youth Television (YTV), for instance, reports that advertisers "want assurances that you absolutely know who your target audience is, and you understand who they are as a consumer, and that you know the characteristics of these eyeballs, as it were, that you're bringing to the table" (*Strategy*, 1995: 21). Station branding — as with the production and marketing of lines of T-shirts, toys and other merchandise — becomes a way for both conventional and specialty channels to build audience loyalty, which attracts sponsors.

In a more competitive environment, all broadcasters stress knowing their audiences. Computer-aided technologies (such as "people

Table 8-6
Viewing of Canadian Programs on English TV,
7 P.M. to 11 P.M.

	1984–85	1985–86	1986–87	1987–88	1988–89	1989–90*
CBC	12.2	13.1	13.6	13.5	14.0	12.3
CTV	4.5	5.1	4.4	4.8	5.3	4.0
Canadian independent	2.4	2.9	3.4	4.5	4.1	3.8
Other **	0.5	1.1	1.3	1.8	2.0	4.7
Total	19.6	22.2	22.7	24.6	25.4	24.8

Data: CBC Research (A.C. Nielsen, Sept-March), excludes coverage of 1988 Olympics.
* Indicates an estimate
** Includes Pay-TV & Specialty Services
Source: Audley 1993.

meters") permit more detailed tracking and analysis of audience behaviour (Jeffrey, 1994). The eventual shift to "pick-and-pay" transactional services, possible when cable companies supply "addressable decoders," will permit greater choice for audiences but also increased monitoring of preferences. This prospect pleases advertisers and raises concerns about privacy. Another major concern is that certain desirable programs may migrate from free to pay services, as the pay subscriber base expands, and thus will be unaffordable for some audience members. Ellis (1992) has noted the trend, as first-run programming rights gravitate towards the greatest revenue source.

The specialty channels have contributed collectively to a decline in audience share for conventional broadcasters (Table 8-3). In 1994, the national viewing share was divided among Quebec French-language, 21.1 per cent; non-conventional, 18.7 per cent; CTV, 17.6 per cent; U.S. conventional, 16.5 per cent; independent English, 16 per cent; and CBC, 10.1 per cent. U.S. conventional station share has dropped dramatically, as has that of CBC. From a 98 per cent share in 1983, total conventional share dropped to 83 per cent in 1993. Most viewing time continues to be spent with conventional television. However, this figure reveals another important trend for English-language broadcasters: the increase in audience share for the independent stations. Beginning in 1988, the Global Television network in south-

Table 8-7
Viewing Time for Canadian and Foreign Programs, 7 P.M. to 11 P.M.

Station Category	1984–85		1992–93	
English	*Canadian*	*Foreign*	*Canadian*	*Foreign*
CBC	62.0%	38.0%	81.7%	18.3%
CTV	20.8%	79.2%	17.3%	82.7%
GLOBAL	7.9%	92.1%	17.4%	82.6%
Independent	16.4%	83.6%	17.9%	82.1%
French				
SRC	72.1%	27.9%	90.9%	9.1%
TVA	46.2%	53.8%	66.3%	33.7%
TQS*	54.8%	45.2%	47.6%	52.4%

* The first year data shown are for 1986–87.
Data: CBC Research (A.C. Nielsen)
Source: Canada. Mandate Review Committee.

ern Ontario and the independents in major metropolitan areas across the country captured a greater share of total hours viewed than the public-sector CBC.

Among Anglophones, three-quarters of all television viewing — whether from U.S. or Canadian stations — is of foreign (i.e., over-whelmingly U.S.) programs (Table 8-4). Of the top ten regularly scheduled network shows viewed by Canadians in 1993, only CTV National News was Canadian, placing eighth (TVB, 1995: 21). Among the top ten Canadian network shows, only sporting events made it onto the chart that year. News, public affairs and sports remain the most popular Canadian content categories, consistent with previous trends. This finding must be kept in context by comparing it to the viewing habits of Francophones, where these genres are also popular, but where nearly two-thirds of total viewing is devoted to domestically produced shows (Table 8-5). On all indicators, the behaviour of Francophone viewers demonstrates Quebec's distinctiveness. Where language supplies a common bond, television has proven to be an instrument for building community and identity, and not simply an industry to market goods to consumers. But an increasingly competitive marketplace can create additional pressures. The tiny Quebec market was fractured by the addition of a private-sector

Table
Percentage Share of Viewing
English Language

	Can.	Atlan.	Que. (T)	Que. (E)
English provincial	1			
CTV	18	26	6	34
Global	5			1
CBC total (Eng)	10	16	2	12
English independent	12	19		
Total % share	46	61	8	47

T = Total, E = English, F = French

English independent includes: ASN, CFMT, CFPL, CFRE, CRSK,
CHCH, CHML, CHWI, CICT, CIHFNB, CIHFNS, CITV, CITY,
CKND, CKNX, CKVU.
Source: 1993 Fall BBM Sweep Survey.

third network, Télévision Quatre Saisons (TQS). Partly as a conse-
quence, spending on independently produced domestic drama in
Quebec has fallen by more than half from 1991 levels (Mandate
Review Committee, 1996: 224).

Viewing tends to follow availability, but the relationship is far
from exact. David Ellis (1991) found that the availability of Canadian
content in the Toronto-Hamilton market exceeded audience viewing
levels at the private-sector stations, but not at the CBC (1991: 59).
Paul Audley (1993) studied national data from the Canadian
English-language conventional stations (including CBC) from 1982–
1991 and found that availability of Canadian shows as a percentage
of all programs increased from 51 to 55 per cent. Viewing of Canadian content increased from 36 to 40 per cent (Audley, 1993: 9-3;
9-5). During prime time (7 to 11 P.M.), Audley found that CBC
attracted nearly half of the total viewing of Canadian content, with
the private broadcasters (CTV, Global and the independent stations)
averaging less than five per cent each (Table 8-6). In this study,
prime-time Canadian viewing increased from 20 to 25 per cent. More
recent figures indicate that the English-language private broadcasters
attract 17 to 18 per cent of prime-time viewing of Canadian shows,
compared to 82 per cent for the CBC (Table 8-7). This study also
reported that private conventional broadcasters had increased their

8-8
for 2+ Population,
TV Stations

Que. (F)	Ont.	Man.	Sask.	Alta.	B.C.
	2			1	1
2	19	20	38	27	28
	13				
1	11	15	21	16	12
	16	28	11	20	9
3	61	63	70	64	50

English provincial includes: Access, TVO, KNOWLEDGE,
MEMORIAL UNIVERSITY, SASKATCHEWAN CABLE NETWORK.

share of prime-time viewing of Canadian drama, up from an average per station of 2.7 per cent in 1984–5 to 7.8 per cent in 1992–3 (Mandate Review Committee, 1996: 222). There is modest progress.

Tables 8-6 and 8-7 indicate that both viewing and availability of Canadian content are very low in the category most popular with English-language viewers, dramatic fictional entertainment. Policy efforts during the 1980s were directed at increasing the choice of Canadian dramatic content in prime time, when most viewers are available. Choice and quality of Canadian content, or Cancon (as it is sometimes less than affectionately known), has indeed increased. As these figures also demonstrate, the intermediary policy has meant that Canadians watch their U.S. shows on Canadian stations. In 1993, CTV, with its consistent track record of airing commercial U.S. programming during prime time, was the most watched station in every market across the country, except Manitoba (Table 8-8). CTV's major competitor, CanWest Global, has succeeded in large part due to smart purchases of U.S. shows and simulcasts of shows from the fourth U.S. network, Fox.

The public takes its television very seriously, a point convincingly made in early 1995 when consumer activism boiled over against the cable practice of "negative option marketing." Rogers Communications was forced to issue a public apology for rearranging familiar

Table 8-9
Revenue Trends, Cable, Television, and Specialty
Services: 1981–91

	1981	1987	1989	1991[P]
($ millions)				
By Revenue Source				
Advertising	703.4	1,226.5	1,503.3	1,630.8
%	44.3	41.1	41	38.2
Subscriptions	378.3	997.2	1,329.1	1,664.8
%	23.8	33.4	36.3	39
Parl. app. to CBC[1]	405.5	545.2	559.3	683.3
%	25.6	18.3	15.3	16
Other	98.9	214.9	273.3	287.2
%	6.2	7.2	7.5	6.7
By Industry Component				
Privately owned TV	652.4	1,065.9	1,276.0	1,377.8
%	41.1	35.7	34.8	32.3
CBC TV[2]	528.7	804.5	900.6	1,012.6
%	33.3	27	24.6	23.7
Cable TV[3]	405	997	1,272.6	1,520.0
%	25.5	33.4	34.7	35.6
Pay TV	—	79.1	86.2	84.2
%	—	2.7	2.4	2
Specialty Services	—	37.2	129.6	271.5
%	—	1.2	3.5	6.4
Total	**1,586.2**	**2,983.7**	**3,665.0**	**4,266.0**
%	100	100	100	100

P: Preliminary
Note 1: Estimated by Communications Management Inc.
Note 2: Excludes Newsworld in 1990 and 1991.
Note 3: Revenues are net of amounts paid to Canadian pay and specialty services.

Data: Statistics Canada, CRTC, CBC, Communications Management Inc.
Source: HRDC 1993.

channel positions to make room for newly licensed Canadian specialty channels. Several popular U.S. specialty services (including Arts and Entertainment on Rogers) were shifted, in order to link them with the unknown Canadian services and boost the new channels' appeal. Customers objected to being charged more for services they had grown accustomed to, packaged with new services they had not requested. These mobilized citizen consumers telephoned, cancelled their cable service and had their letters printed in the newspapers. There was satisfaction across the country as Rogers was forced to back down. This display of consumer anger warned the cable companies that they could not take their market for granted and put the regulator on notice that consumer protection issues could not be ignored.

These market developments confirm the power shift from broadcasters to cablecasters, following the decline of over-the-air TV signal delivery. Traditionally, advertising has represented the major revenue source for conventional broadcasting, but the expected changes in the market have been clearly identified by one observer: "Instead of advertisers pushing messages through communications channels, consumers will be pulling in messages from their end. Consumers will control the entertainment and the advertising they watch" (*Financial Times of Canada*, 1994: 6). An interactive model will some day replace the old one-way, point-to-mass broadcasting model, driven by audience demand for more genuine control, which originated with the remote control and VCR. But not overnight. These developments also flag a neglected aspect of the current transitional period: the broadcasting system has a long way to go yet before achieving a genuine transactional (pick-and-pay) model. Ellis (1992) has characterized the current period as transactional because consumers pay for services that were previously free. At the moment, however, subscribers still predominate. For a flat monthly fee, subscribers pay the cable companies, who then act as brokers, buying and selling tiers of programming. As broadcasters arrange their program line-ups and schedules, the cable operators now negotiate and arrange their tiers of services and channels, including broadcasters. Power in the marketplace may eventually devolve to the consumer, but for the moment, the cable companies have taken charge.

Industry Structure

The private broadcasting and cable industries are currently restructuring under the combined pressures of economics, globalization,

Table 8-10
Cable Television Revenues

	1990	1991	1992	1993	1994
Basic Cable ($ millions)					
Subscription revenues	1,295	1,414	1,518	1,608	1,687
Revenues	1,357	1,478	1,588	1,681	1,759
Expenses	1,174	1,298	1,343	1,498	1,535
Net profit before taxes	191.8	186.9	253.3	194.7	274.5
Salaries paid	320	331	347	366	369
Employees	8,951	9,043	8,455	8,684	8,844
Number of subscribers	7.1	7.3	7.5	7.7	7.8
Discretionary Services					
Subscription revenues	227	250	282	386	478
Revenues	285	312	358	471	570
Expenses	226	232	258	401	465
Net profit before taxes	59.4	80	100.5	70.9	110.3
Salaries paid	27	25	24	20	22
Employees	848	715	657	527	541
Number of subscribers	2	2.3	4.5	5.3	5.4

Data: Statistics Canada, Cable Television

Private Television Revenues

	1990	1991	1992	1993	1994
Sales of air time*	1,248	1,263	1,341	1,330	1,371
Operating revenues	1,365	1,378	1,460	1,464	1,490
Operating expenses	1,374	1,394	1,407	1,387	1,413
Net profit before taxes	14	-70	57	90	82
Salaries & other staff benefits	406	421	425	428	444
No. of employees (weekly average)	8,673	8,524	8,297	8,158	8,273

* Excludes CBC.
Data: Statistics Canada, *Radio and Television Broadcasting Annual Returns*.
Source: Statistics Canada. *Canada's Culture* 1995.

Table 8-11
Multiple-System Operators

Company	Systems	Subscribers	% of Total Subscribers
Rogers Cable TV	50	2,519,616	31.5%
Shaw Cablesystems	96	1,523,597	19.0%
Videotron	45	1,175,654	14.7%
Cogeco Cable Inc.	45	442,735	5.5%
CF Cable TV Inc.	80	413,341	5.2%
Moffat Communications	8	169,652	2.1%
Fundy Cable Ltd.	82	145,722	1.8%
Cable Atlantic	13	78,183	1.0%
Total	419	6,468,500	80.8%

Data: MediaSTATS September 1994.
Source: CCTA 1995.

new technologies and audience demand. In 1991, the share of total broadcast system revenue accounted for by cable subscriptions surpassed advertising for the first time (Table 8-9). Private television revenues grew 55 per cent between 1981 and 1986, and 37 per cent between 1986 and 1991. Since the nosedive of 1991 (during the recession), advertising expenditures have recovered (more slowly outside central Canada) but average revenue growth and profit are flat or modest for most conventional broadcasters (Table 8-10). There are 108 conventional private broadcast stations that originate programming or sell ads nationwide, with total operating revenues of nearly $1.5 billion, almost all of which comes from airtime sales. Basic cable subscription and discretionary services revenues (from subscriptions and advertising) continue to show significant increases in revenue and profits.

After the recession of 1991, the broadcasting and cable companies consolidated their operations before embarking on expansion strategies. Corporate concentration increased dramatically in the cable industry. With the blessing of the CRTC — which encouraged consolidation as a response to competition anticipated from foreign sources and the telephone companies — Rogers Communications succeeded in a $3.1 billion hostile takeover of venerable Maclean Hunter, a diversified communications corporation with vast holdings

Table
Broadcasting

Company and Year End	Revenue		Profit	
	$000	% Change	$000	% Change
Rogers Communications (De94)	1,482,755	25	-168,013	41
Groupe Videotron (Au94)	646,340	8	20,462	-18
WIC Western Int'l. Commun. (Au94)	393,028	14	9,807	227
Canadian Broadcasting Corp.(Mr94)	374,410	0	-152,376	-99
Shaw Communications(Au94)	288,789	24	33,280	35
CanWest Global Communications(Au94)	273,396	1	44,716	72
Baton Broadcasting (Au94)	253,346	12	3,411	100
Standard Broadcasting Corp.(Au94)	239,560	5	2,867	185
CHUM Ltd.(Au 94)	202,585	-1	8,448	-43
Cogeco Inc.(Au94)	194,612	-7	10,712	-52
CFCF Inc.(Au94)	175,642	9	8,019	-33
Tele-Metropole Inc.(Au94)	165,929	-1	218	-97

Source: *Report on Business Magazine*. 1995.

in cable, publishing (including the national newsmagazine *Maclean's* and the *Sun* newspaper chain) and broadcasting (CFRN Calgary was sold to CanWest Global Communications in 1995). By 1994, Rogers controlled cable franchises covering 32 per cent of all subscribers (Table 8-11) and 43 per cent of English-language subscribers. Rogers sold off its substantial U.S. interests in order to consolidate by region in Canada and continued this strategy by swapping properties with Shaw Cablesystems of Edmonton. In 1995–96, Quebec cable giant Videotron proposed an exchange of its interests in private broadcaster Tele-Metropole for the cable holdings of Montreal-based CFCF, which also owns the third French-language network Télévision Quatre Saisons. Cogeco, another major Quebec broadcaster and cable operator, slowed down this deal in the courts, but was ultimately unsuccessful.

8-12

and Cable

Return on Capital		Assets		Cash Flow	Capital Spending	
1-Yr%	5-Yr%	$000	% Change	$000	$000	% Change
4.18	3.08	6,128,627	54	274,817	3,374,709	1,080
6.29	7.68	2,028,455	34	130,588	319,989	40
9.87	10.28	691,868	-1	62,777	19,096	7
-12.32	-10.9	1,582,041	0	13,671	137,531	-76
14.93	17.48	825,163	11	79,811	91,507	-70
21.94	19.86	625,496	20	40,986	5,110	-16
7.12	2.83	323,918	3	24,748	20,736	-51
8.54	10.91	129,654	-13	19,772	3,726	445
9.15	18.51	199,591	3	16,882	15,433	126
9.83	9.44	476,639	2	36,349	29,609	115
11.97	5.1	352,352	34	36,171	76,018	153
6.15	3.84	226,321	3	9,385	9,383	58

There are more than 1,800 cable systems operating in Canada, and well over two-thirds offer their customers 30 to 45 channels (CCTA, 1995: 6). Among Canada's multiple system owners, Rogers predominates because of its market power and entrepreneurial flair. Its diverse strategies include a plan to supply its subscribers with high-speed modem connections to the Internet, a cellular phone franchise (Cantel), a video rental chain, a multimedia division and the multicultural broadcaster CFMT in Toronto. Recently Rogers wrote off its interest in telephone long-distance supplier Unitel. Not far behind Rogers are other large cable operators. Videotron has launched an experimental two-way TV trial, called UBI, in Chicoutimi, as a joint venture with companies including Canada Post; an earlier experiment called Videoway allowed audiences to control the viewing angle on sports events. Shaw Cablesystems now owns part of YTV and has joined with partners in a proposed non-commercial children's specialty channel. The cable industry contributes a community channel as a required public benefit, although this has been criticized for not permitting sufficient community control (Surman, 1995). In addition, CPAC, the excellent Parliamentary and public affairs channel, carries speakers and conferences (sometimes in French) on highly relevant matters of public debate when the House of Commons is not in session.

It is useful to keep the scale of the coming competition in mind: Rogers' revenues led all Canadian broadcasting and cable companies for 1994 at $1.5 billion (Table 8-12), compared to telephone behemoth BCE's $22.4 billion, which ranks first in the country and first in profitability (*Report on Business Magazine*, 1995). Publicly traded Rogers practises old-fashioned debt financing for expansion and does not report a profit.

The prolonged uncertainty surrounding the publicly funded Canadian Broadcasting Corporation (CBC) has affected every aspect of the system. Conventional private broadcasters include the 25 affiliates of the CBC (five are Francophone), who reach that 16 per cent of the population not otherwise covered by CBC and receive $15 million annually to carry network programming. The once predominant CBC suffers from declining audience share, diminished public funds and vacillating political support (Skene, 1993). Criticized by public broadcasting supporters as too commercial, by private stations as redundant in major sports and local news and by pro-market politicians as too costly, the CBC appears to lurch from crisis to crisis. Considered the heart of a distinctively Canadian system, CBC continues to air the majority of available Canadian dramatic programming. It also earned advertising revenues of $292 million in 1994 (Statistics Canada, 1995: 80). The Mandate Review Committee (established to review the CBC) has recommended that commercials be eliminated from the CBC, which would open up opportunities for the private sector. CBC's beleaguered status has tipped the system's uneasy balance between private and public sectors definitively towards the private sector.

Like the cable industry, broadcasters have consolidated and are engaged in diverse expansion strategies. These include attempted takeovers, new channels, new technologies, new territories, new network strategies and export of Canadian expertise. Network affiliations are well-established strategies to obtain rights to desirable programs and spread the costs by expanding the broadcast market.

Table 8-13
Major Market Private Television Stations

Location	POP.2+ (000)	Cable %	Satel- lite%	VCR %	Hours per capita	Station Call	Affiliation	Corporate Owner
Vancouver	2,557	90	2	75	20	CHAN	CTV	WIC
						CKVU	IND	CW\G
Victoria						CHEK	CTV	WIC
Edmonton	1,241	70	4	75	20.5	CFRN	CTV	ELECTRO
						CITV	IND	WIC
Calgary	1,043	74	4	75	19.7	CFCN*	CTV	MH
						CICT	IND	WIC
Regina	302	64	4	69	22.2	CKCK	CTV	BATON
						CFRE	IND	CW/G
Saskatoon	314	44	3	68	20.2	CFQC	CTV	BATON
						CFSK	IND	CW/G
Winnipeg	832	72	4	78	22.5	CKY	CTV	MOFFAT
						CKND	IND	CW/G
Toronto	5,358	85	2	76	21.1	CFTO	CTV	BATON
						CIII	IND	CW/G
						CITY	IND	CHUM
						CFMT	IND	ROGERS
Hamilton						CHCH	IND	WIC
Kitchener	894	71	2	80	21.8	CKCO	CTV	ELECTRO
London	804	67	5	73	21.1	CFPL	IND	BATON
Ottawa-Hull	1,155	76	2	77	22	CJOH	CTV	BATON
Montreal	3,965	66	2	71	24.2	CFCF	CTV	CFCF
						CFTM	TVA	T-M
						CFJP	TQS	TQS(CFCF)
Quebec City	966	65	3	73	25.1	CFCM	TVA	T-M
						CFAP	TQS	TQS(CFCF)
						CKMI*	CBC	T-M
Moncton	534	73	4	71	24.1	CKCW	CTV	CHUM
St. John						CHSJ	CBC	CW/G
Halifax	600	79	3	76	25	CJCH	CTV	CHUM
St. John's	478	81	3	71	23.3	CJON	CTV	NFLD.
Total Can.	27,507	73	3	74	22.7			

* Pending CRTC approval owner becomes CanWest/Global.
Note: T-M=Tele-Metropole, ELECTRO=Electrohome, MH=Maclean
Hunter, CW/G=CanWest Global, NFLD=Newfoundland Broadcasting
Co. Ltd.
Data: CRTC, BBM 1993.

Figure 8-3
Growth of English-Language Market

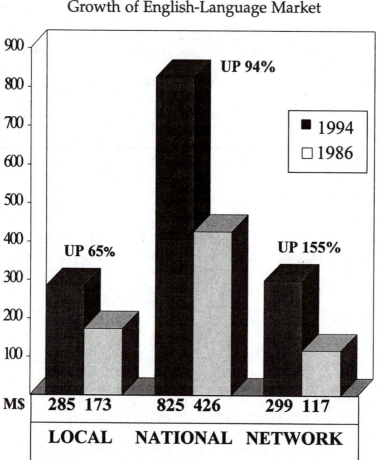

* Network in the context of TV advertising means the segment of the
market which is sold on a national coverage, 52-week, discounted basis.
** Specialty channels are included in National.
Data: CRTC
Source: Marchant.

Table 8-13 presents the pattern of local private broadcaster affiliations in major markets. Clearly indicated is the growing number of
second-wave independent stations (licensed beginning in the 1970s)
that are owned by quasi-networks and share program buying relationships.

CanWest Global of Winnipeg has applied to the CRTC to establish what it calls a "national system" from coast to coast, consisting of stations it owns and stations it seeks regulatory approval to purchase in Quebec and Alberta. A family-run company started in the mid-1970s by entrepreneur Israel (Izzy) Asper, the highly litigious CanWest took over the Global Television Network in 1990. The business case for this third English mini-network stems from the advantages of purchasing program rights (mainly from the U.S.) for high-population major markets and cooperation in advertising sales (Marchant, 1995: 3). This system could offer multinational advertisers attractive domestic options for their global ad campaigns. The context for this strategy is the recognition that ad revenues for the Canadian TV broadcasting system compare poorly with such revenues outside Canada, at least on a per capita basis. In 1994, ad revenues were $62 per capita in Canada, $147 in the U.S., $74 in the U.K., $105 in Australia and $104 in New Zealand (TVB, 1995: 35-36; in Cdn $).

CanWest Global's proposal — whatever its fate before the regulator — highlights two trends: growth of the national advertising market (Figure 8-3) and the repositioning of conventional broadcasters in response to the success of the Canadian specialty channels. It should be noted that specialty channels and network licensees are prohibited from selling local advertising, a *quid pro quo* granted to local broadcasters in return for fulfilling their public service and Canadian content obligations. One result of this policy of protection for local markets (a variant of the intermediary strategy) has been the emergence of regionally based and publicly traded broadcasting powerhouses, including CanWest Global (Winnipeg and Toronto), WIC Western International Communications (Vancouver) and Allarcom (Edmonton).

The push to consolidate regional and national purchasing power and markets has led to intense corporate manoeuvring. The joke of 1995 was that more Canadian drama was taking place in courtrooms and corporate boardrooms than on the screen. CanWest Global Communications, Canada's most profitable broadcaster, attempted to take over WIC Western International Communications, Canada's richest private broadcaster (see Table 8-12). The Allard family company, Allarcom, now owned by WIC, had previously tried a similar tactic, but stood with WIC against CanWest Global. The courts awarded this round to WIC's founding family, the Griffiths. In Toronto, the Eaton family launched an unsuccessful bid to take control of and

Table 8-14
Net Advertising Volume for Canada
Millions of Dollars (Domestic Currency)

		1983	1985	1987	1989	1991	1993
Television	Total	835	1,055	1,215	1,499	1,618	1,709
	National	473	599	673	786	859	898
	Local	186	223	291	355	357	375
	Network	176	228	239	328	330	339
	Specialty	-	6	12	30	72	97
Daily Newspaper	Total	1,233	1,475	1,761	2,068	2,002	1,863
	National	230	312	359	420	420	391
	Local	724	803	919	1,053	1,021	950
	Classified	279	360	483	595	561	522
Weeklies/Semi-Tri	Total	289	399	324	466	537	552
Radio	Total	480	566	648	751	741	722
	National	127	140	153	181	168	167
	Local	353	427	495	570	573	555
General Magazines	Total	229	215	224	265	256	252
Business Papers	Total	137	133	165	194	174	173
Other Print	Total	64	86	93	91	125	116
Outdoor	Total	77	93	104	102	108	123
MAJOR MEDIA	SUB	3,344	4,022	4,534	5,436	5,561	5,510
Catalogues/Direct Mail	Total	873	1,135	1,363	1,589	1,742	1,968
TOTAL ADVERTISING $	100%	4,596	5,626	6,495	7,770	8,141	8,333

Data: Television: Statistics Canada
          Specialty: TVB, Radio-Quebec included since 1985
          Newspapers: CDNA
          Radio: Statistics Canada
          Print: *TV Basics 95/96.*
          Outdoor: OACC
Source: Television Bureau of Canada. 1996.

privatize Baton Broadcasting, the largest shareholder within the CTV network, and owner of stations across the country. The Eatons let it be known that broadcasting had more of a future than department stores. Baton's holdings were consolidated into the BBS regional network in Ontario and Saskatchewan. After years of squabbling, the CTV network restructured itself from a cooperative of 25 private stations into a centralized business operation. Rogers was prevented from sitting on the board of CTV when it divested CFCN Calgary from its corporate empire, a deal that, if approved, would give the place to CanWest Global. When they stopped fighting among themselves, these publicly traded broadcasters were repositioning to meet new and old competition. The debt loads resulting from these manoeuvres siphoned off funds for programming.

Broadcasters are diversifying their sources of revenue in an attempt to reduce their dependence on airtime sales. They are motivated to seek alternatives given a relatively modest growth rate in ad revenues. Compared to other major media, television ad revenues have recovered (Table 8-14). In 1993, $1.7 billion was spent on television advertising, up from $835 million in 1983 (TVB, 1995). Newspapers command higher total ad revenues than television; however, their rates of growth are declining. Television advertising accounted for 31 per cent of ad dollars spent in major media, and 21 per cent of total advertising.

The strategic approach of Toronto-based CHUM, owned by the Waters family, involved allying itself with an innovative upstart and building from the previous consolidation of its traditional broadcasting interests. In the late 1970s, CHUM purchased Citytv, the first of the second-wave metropolitan independent UHF/cable stations to be licensed (in 1971). Under founding president and executive producer Moses Znaimer, City has attracted many imitators for the young, multicultural and intensely local format that it markets internationally. Operating out of the historic Ryerson Press building, which contains no conventional studio, CHUMCity now houses specialty channels MuchMusic and Bravo! (arts and culture). MuchMusic is carried on cable systems in the U.S., Mexico and South America. It half owns and has marketed its format to MuchaMusica in Argentina. An early champion of the niche specialty service concept, CHUMCity, Znaimer and other partners also own 50 per cent of MusiquePlus in Montreal, MuchMusic's Francophone sister station, and have expanded into educational broadcasting with the takeover (for $1) of Access Alberta. A producer of stylish, inexpensive programming,

CHUMCity syndicates locally produced shows globally, including *MediaTelevision, Fashion Television,* and *Electric Circus.* Major revenues to support this creative operation flow from simulcast and syndicated U.S. programming, especially movies. CHUMCity has established itself as a rights packager capable of assembling impromptu mini-networks across the country.

A former CBC producer, Znaimer's philosophy of television (uniquely presented in 1995 as a three-hour prime-time special on CBC called *TVTV*) was applied by CHUMCity to a makeover of CHUM's Barrie station, CKVR, which reaches the Toronto market and mid-Ontario. CKVR disaffiliated from the CBC and was transformed into a station brand known as "the new VR," which specialized in sports by obtaining broadcasting rights to a new basketball team, the Toronto Raptors. CHUMCity also operates a new media division, CityInteractive, which has launched a Canadian partnership between MuchMusic and America Online (called AOL-Canada), and a distribution arrangement for CD-ROMs with Voyager of New York. Many broadcasters now have sites on the Internet, which serve mainly as promotional vehicles. CHUMCity simulcasts online and offline productions. CHUM's repositioning has come at a cost. Profits dropped in 1994, due in part to the poor fortunes of its extensive radio broadcasting holdings.

Among the expansion strategies for WIC Western International Communications is a wireless transmission technology called cellularvision, which is in test markets in Calgary in 1996. WIC believes that this alternative technology can cut into the cable and telephone markets at one-tenth the cost of hard wiring. According to WIC, a microwave network can blanket a city and deliver 400 TV channels, videoconferencing, phone and high speed Internet access. Once regulatory approval is secured, WIC plans to launch its technology in 30 cities. WIC has also ventured into satellite broadcasting and is a part owner of Cancom, supplier of satellite signals to remote and underserved regions, and also (with telecommunications giant BCE) owns part of the DBS service, Expressvu. When it purchased Allarcom, WIC obtained licences to several pay-TV movie channels covering the territory west of Ontario.

There are many different approaches to the question of how the conventional broadcasters will survive the challenges of the transitional period. Colourful entrepreneurs such as Moses Znaimer and Izzie Asper found themselves temporarily frustrated in their aspirations to expand further into the domestic marketplace. Znaimer has long wanted to launch Citytv as a superstation and is currently seeking to expand into Ottawa and Vancouver, as well as on satellite services. Both Znaimer and Asper lost bids to start up operations in Britain. Asper has expanded by purchasing a majority position (58 per cent) in Network Ten Australia and a minority position (20 per cent) in a New Zealand broadcaster, commenting that, "We have to be part of a much larger family than just Canada" (*Financial Times of Canada*, 1994). Paul Taylor (1993) has observed that CanWest Global's forays into international expansion and co-productions represent market-based solutions to the problem of how to recoup program production costs despite the small Canadian market. He observes further that such activities demonstrate the inadequacy of regulatory measures to achieve domestic cultural objectives. The question is familiar: what does the system get in return for providing licences to public airwaves?

Znaimer, who believes in Canadian cultural imperialism, prefers to reframe the fundamental question for broadcasting and insists that, "Broadcasting is not a problem to be solved; it is an instrument to be played." Thus he places the onus on the producers and entrepreneurs, rather than on the state. Given Canada's historic struggles to ensure domestically produced content on the airwaves, such a strategy depends on convincing broadcasters to play this instrument instead of letting others take the risks while creaming off the rewards. Such a producer-oriented strategy can only succeed if some broadcasters learn how to play and profit at the same time, as Znaimer and his partners have done. Producer/entrepreneurs such as Znaimer are still rare in the boardrooms of the private broadcasters. Perhaps new circumstances will dictate new attitudes towards risk. Should the intermediary strategy fail, one way Canadian channels can distinguish themselves and win audiences will be by producing and marketing distinctive programming.

On the supply side, rights to U.S. shows are more expensive in Canada than elsewhere due to the competition among stations for rights. A show costing $1 million to produce can obtain a substantial licence fee in pre-sales within the domestic U.S. market, where the costs of production can be nearly recouped. The same show can be sold, or rights licensed, to Canadian broadcasters for a fraction — as low as 10 per cent — of the cost of production. Some Canadian broadcasters have tried to persuade the CRTC of the hardship they suffer as a result of the Canadian content obligations. Whereas the CRTC and cultural policy makers calculate the contributions of the

Table 8-15
Pay and Specialty Channels in Canada

Service	Ownership	Launch Date	Systems Carrying	Subscribers	Hr. viewed 1994	Hr. viewed 1995
Bravo	CHUM	1995	125	5,232,280	1.2	1.6
Canal D	Astral	1995	87	1,649,632	*	*
Canal Famille	Astral	1988	319	1,901,771	*	*
CBC Newsworld	CBC	1989	898	7,077,241	1	0.8
The Discovery Channel	Labatt Comm.	1995	261	6,429,374	**	0.8
Fairchild Colorvision	Fairchild Holdings	1985	20	130,320	*	*
Life Network	Atlantic Comm.	1995	152	6,149,157	**	0.4
MeteoMedia Weather Channel	Pelmorex Comm.	1988	93	1,637,661	0.4	0.4
			570	6,088,086	0.3	0.3
MoviePix	TMN	1994	99	184,033	*	*
MovieMax	WIC/ALLARCOM	1994	40	94,088	*	*
MuchMusic	CHUM	1988	1,359	6,160,274	0.5	0.5
MusiquePlus	CHUM/Radio-mutuel	1988	418	2,594,616	0.6	0.6
NewCountry Network (NCN)	Rawlco Comm.	1995	713	6,874,031	**	0.8
RDI	Societe Radio-Canada	1995	164	5,102,816		1
RDS	Labatt	1984		1,998,400	*	*
Showcase	Alliance Comm.	1995	133	4,562,996	**	0.6
SuperChannel	Astral	1983	360	238,496	*	*
SuperEcran	Astral	1983	345	243,038	*	*
Talentvision TV (formerly Cathay)	Fairchild Holdings	1985	5	18,517	*	*
Telelatino	Telelatino	1984	41	1,620,960	*	*
TMN The Movie Network	Astral	1983	373	444,373	*	*
TSN The Sports Network	Labatt Comm.	1984	1,606	6,333,763	1.2	1.6
Vision	Non-Profit/Charitable	1988	394	6,037,698	0.5	0.5
WTN	Moffat Comm.	1995	108	4,693,106	**	0.5
YTV	Rogers/Atlantis/Shaw	1988	1,099	7,179,911	1.3	1.4

Data: *Matthew's Media Directory* & CATV Directory, CCTA 1995, 1996.
* Not Supplied   **New Channel

private sector to the system, some broadcasters calculate how much profit they forego in order to meet their Canadian content requirements. The "opportunity cost" is what broadcasters figure they lose in revenues when broadcasting Canadian shows. CTV estimated in 1991 that while a low-rated U.S. series provided $1.94 in revenue for every $1 of cost, an hour of Canadian entertainment programming returned 62 cents on the dollar. CTV argued that broadcasting three hours of Canadian programming per week in prime time lost it more than $15 million a year. Global estimated that replacing one hour of an average-rated U.S. network program during prime time would have an opportunity cost of $2.9 million over the course of a year (unpublished CRTC data). The market lesson has always been that it is only possible to stay in business and run Canadian shows by making profits brokering U.S. shows. Critics charge that the problem is that it is cheaper to ask for relief from the regulator than to learn how to master successful Canadian production for domestic and global markets.

The specialty channels (Table 8-15) have two streams of revenue, from portions of the cable subscription fees and national ads. MuchMusic and The Sports Network (TSN) astonished observers by becoming profitable by 1985, the first year. The attempt to tap into the growth of subscription and advertising revenues for specialty services means that conventional broadcasters are heavily represented in the latest round of applications (in May 1996). The licensing of the specialty channels amounts to a kind of rebirth of the broadcasting and cable industries, paradoxically widening the pool of owner companies in broadcasting, while encouraging vertical integration. Two successful and highly creative independent production companies, Alliance Communications (Showcase) and Atlantis (Life Network and part of YTV) now own channel licences. By stressing "financial viability" in its licensing decisions, the CRTC has shut out very small entrepreneurs, while rewarding middle-size players in the industry.

Conventional broadcasters have discovered that in addition to the profits to be made, there may be attractive features for ad sales similar to the network strategy resulting from the addition of specialty channels. The reason is that the specialty channels are narrowcast networks and transmit to cable via satellite. Although the reasoning remains somewhat arcane, the CRTC grants specialty licences where applicants can demonstrate financial viability, that they are committed for the long run and have identified a programming niche and market demand that is not filled by conventional broad-

Table 8-16
Expenditure by Private Canadian TV Broadcasters on Canadian and Foreign Programs, 1994
($ millions)

	Canadian Independent Production	Other Canadian	Total Canadian	Foreign	Total
Drama	37.3	14.8	52.1	‹193.3	245.4
Music and variety	10.3	15.8	26.1	2.9	29
News and information	5.4	267.6	273.0	15.7	288.7
Sports	3.8	74.4	78.2	10.8	89
Game shows	5.1	4	9.1	11.2	20.3
Human interest	3.9	28.9	32.8	21.4	54.2
Total	**65.8**	**405.5**	**471.3**	**255.3**	**726.6**

Note: "Other Canadian" production includes in-house production, programs produced by an affiliated production company, programs acquired from other stations, network programs, and programs from other sources.
Data: Statistics Canada Annual Broadcasting Survey, special data provided by the Department of Canadian Heritage.
Source: Canada. Mandate Review Committee.

casters. They also must prove that they will not siphon off ad revenues from conventional stations. Successful examples include Vision TV's religious programming, the licensing of The Women's Television Network (WTN), Bravo! (arts and culture) and the Canadian version of the Discovery channel.

In this transitional period, the question of access to scarce cable capacity continues to dominate discussions. Historically, scarcity referred to the limited number of clear broadcast frequencies available on the electromagnetic spectrum; for the moment the issue is capacity on the cable systems. By regulation, cable must carry all local domestic broadcasters. So far, the CRTC has rejected the broadcasters' request for retransmission fees — revenues that U.S. local broadcasters enjoy from American cable companies. Cable serves as a gatekeeper, controlling access by program or service providers and also by viewers to channels. In response to various complaints, including the problems encountered by the specialty channels, which must negotiate individually with each cable operator, the CRTC has required the cable industry to adopt an access code. Digital video

Table 8-17
Film, Video and Audiovisual Production

Indicator	1990–91	1991–92	1992–93	1993–94	% change 1992–93 to 1993–94
Number of producers	741	742	667	743	11.4
Number of productions					
Theatrical features	54	56	31	44	41.2
Television productions[1]	—	7,504	7,181	8,498	18.3
TV commercials	3,619	3,929	3,908	3,637	-6.9
Other productions	—	8,402	4,993	4,605	-7.8
Total productions	17,634	19,891	16,113	16,784	4.2
Production revenue ($millions)	584.5	581.8	586.4	733.9	25.2
Other revenue ($millions)	119.3	106.4	111	262.6	136.6
Total revenue ($miilions)	703.8	688.2	697.4	996.5	42.9

[1] Excludes TV commercials.
— Figures not appropriate or not applicable.
Source: Statistics Canada. *Focus on Culture*, Winter 1995.

compression and other technologies are expected to alleviate the problem of scarcity; however, the new questions concern "shelf space" or how the Canadian services can be featured prominently.

The financial contribution of the private broadcasters to production has grown in recent years, due mostly to the incentives offered by Telefilm Canada (Table 8-16). Yet the fees paid by Canadian TV broadcasters to license independent dramatic film productions are lower than elsewhere and amount to less than one-third of production costs. TV broadcasters in Britain and France supply an average of 24 per cent of the sources of revenue for feature films that receive public support, compared to two per cent in Canada (Groupe Secor 1994: 63). One reason for the discrepancy is that public support has been more generous in getting Canadian projects under way. With respect to made-for-TV production, there are encouraging signs that the independent Canadian production industry may have gained a more solid foundation (Table 8-17). In 1993–4, several of the largest independent production companies, including Alliance, Atlantis, Paragon and Nelvana, began trading on the stock exchange. Canadian independent producers are aggressively seeking domestic and international partners and sales. In the 1994–5 season, *Due South*, a co-production between Alliance Communications and the CTV Network, became the first Canadian-produced dramatic series to break into U.S. prime time, on CBS.

The need for financing solutions has motivated the federal government to arrange, and the independent production companies to enter into, co-productions and pre-sales to foreign investors and broadcasters. According to Ellis (1992), where broadcasters were once expected to drive the system, now they are minor players in arranging serious dramatic production. Financial expertise has migrated to independent producers who put deals together with multiple partners. One auspicious sign is that the specialty services have contributed to independent production, in fact and by condition of licence. According to the Canadian Association of Broadcasters, in 1993–4 there were an estimated fifty production funds worth $374 million, aimed at support for the Canadian film and video sector (CAB, 1995). The cable fund alone is expected to generate $300 million over five years. Private-sector broadcasters call for a removal of the rules restricting them from equity ownership of productions and the ability to enter into program distribution.

Critics object that co-productions should be more authentically Canadian. Current certification criteria are based on industrial criteria of employment of key personnel and salary size. No one has yet proposed acceptable alternative criteria. The current guidelines have at least allowed Canada to develop production expertise and infrastructure to support its cultural objectives, and Canadian independent production reportedly now ranks number two internationally in English-language exports. Having prepared the base, a creator may emerge who can (as Znaimer puts it) play this instrument. In the meantime, the framework for broadcasting ensures that Canadians have an increasing choice of Canadian shows.

Policy and the Future of Regulation

"If Canadians want a Canadian broadcasting system, we have to have some rules." — Bud Sherman, Vice-Chair, CRTC.

Broadcasting has been the centrepiece of federal cultural policy since the creation of the Canadian Broadcasting Corporation in the 1930s. The federal government has jurisdiction and statutory authority over broadcasting and telecommunications. Operating at arm's length, but subject to federal direction, the CRTC regulates both systems under the Broadcasting Act (1991) and Telecommunications Act (1993). The changes expected en route to the convergence of broadcasting and telecommunications will mean further collision between the forces of the market and the national system goals.

The turbulent environment for policy making stems from the numerous changes within the market and broadcasting and cable industries, but also at the government level. In 1996, the federal government will release a policy on Canada's information highway. It is also examining the mandate of the CRTC and will shortly appoint a new chairman, who will steer the CRTC through the challenges of harmonizing the broadcasting and telecommunications systems. Government and regulator are addressing the old cultural industries problem within this new environment.

In 1986, the report of the Task Force on Broadcasting restated the enduring question for the system: "[H]ow can Canadians be offered a serious choice of Canadian programming in a system in which a) American influences are inescapable, b) market forces dictate American programming, through both production costs and advertising benefits, and c) Canadians themselves want access to Canadian as well as American programming" (1986: 17). The report concluded that the CBC was "the very heart of Canadian culture" and repeated the "harsh judgements" of previous inquiries on the contribution of private broadcasters, pointedly observing the minimal Canadian programming in the schedules of English-language broadcasters, and limited financial commitments to program expenditures on Canadian shows (ibid: 418).

The report called for a more substantive contribution from private broadcasters to new English Canadian programming: "The appropriate objective for public policy in the face of the technological challenge from American television is to offer Canadians compelling home-made alternatives so that they will choose to resist the foreign seduction." This recommendation became cautiously worded legislation: "Private networks and programming undertakings should, to an extent consistent with the financial and other resources available to them, (i) contribute significantly to the creation and presentation of Canadian programming, and (ii) be responsive to the evolving demands of the public" (Broadcasting Act 1991, s.3 (1)[s]).

A variety of strategies have been tried by the regulator to accomplish these legislative and policy goals, and above all to ensure a system that will maintain and enhance national identity and cultural sovereignty. Beginning in 1979, the CRTC recognized that time quotas for Canadian content had resulted in cheap and unappealing programming. Since then, the CRTC has imposed a formula of program expenditure requirements on broadcasters. These have varied and were first applied to networks, later to local stations. CTV took the CRTC to court in 1982 to contest its power to impose such regulations; the courts ruled that the CRTC had full authority. By the early 1990s all private stations earning more than $10 million in revenue were asked to contribute as a condition of licence. The CRTC continues to insist that local broadcasters reflect their communities, which they mainly do in news broadcasts, and grants them protection from competition in their ad markets as the *quid pro quo*; it has added to this incentives to form joint buying networks to pool the resources of smaller stations and contribute to production, especially of dramatic and children's shows.

The Broadcasting Act of 1991 altered the ground rules. The Act reflects the reality of a fractured "single system" in which the public-sector national broadcaster no longer predominates. The CRTC has interpreted the act as conferring a strong mandate for regulatory flexibility and has tailored its regulations to fit the particular sector or problem at hand. For example, in the 1994 licence renewal decisions for local private broadcasters, the CRTC offered broadcasters a choice of regulatory mechanisms — content quotas or proportion of program spending in specific target program areas (CRTC 1995–48). Regulatory flexibility has also meant that different expectations apply to the different elements in the system. One trendsetting example is the "exemption" rule, which permits the CRTC to decide that a service may be offered without formal regulation, and without content quotas, so long as specified criteria are met. A video-on-demand service and a new video-games channel have received exemptions. Some object to this approach, arguing that it creates a two-tiered system of regulation that amounts to *de facto* deregulation; other observers have commented that they doubt the CRTC will be able to exercise supervision over the exempt services. The CRTC takes the position that it is possible to insist upon compliance with regulations in order to grant the exemption, while demonstrating the flexibility that the new Act requires.

The CRTC has shifted its approach away from "micromanagement" of the system and is seeking ways to combine encouragement of competitive market forces with its supervisory obligations. The disputes that can be expected concern how quickly the regulator should abandon all attempts to achieve public service goals, leaving them to a market that is increasingly competitive with the addition of new entrants, notably the telephone companies. From the perspective of the CRTC, the regulatory dilemma has always involved striking a balance among conflicting objectives — those objectives increase with the addition of the very different telecommunications regime. In 1996, the CRTC is struggling to find a balance between consumer choice and the system goals of promoting and nurturing Canadian programming, while protecting the broadcasting and cable industry as they encounter increased competition. At the end of the day, the CRTC must also meet the demands of conflicting political masters.

The 1991 Broadcasting Act strengthened the federal cabinet's power to issue directives to the CRTC. Long accused of relinquishing policy formulation to the CRTC, the cabinet set about using its powers to send back CRTC decisions on DBS service and telecommunications rate increases. Many observers believe that an erosion of the traditional arm's length relationship between broadcasting and government is dangerous. All systems have rules; if the rules are not made by an independent regulatory agency, then critics fear that the rules will be made in the political backrooms and corporate boardrooms. Who will then speak for the public interest?

The environment for policy making and regulation also changed significantly as a result of internal government reorganization. In 1993, the Conservative government split the Department of Communications into Industry Canada and the Department of Canadian Heritage. This reinforced the tension between industrial and cultural objectives and gave it a political spin. The environment in which the CRTC operates continues to be volatile, polarized between the requirements under the Act to uphold cultural objectives and the pro-market objective to reduce government costs and involvement in industry.

Despite its shift to regulatory flexibility, the CRTC, under outgoing chairman Keith Spicer, announced that it will exert influence on socially significant matters. This continued a policy evolved during the 1980s, whereby codes of conduct were developed on sex role stereotyping, violence and abusive programming and employment equity (Jeffrey, 1995b). The CRTC prided itself on bringing complainants (members of the public and advocacy groups) together with the industry to fashion a self-regulatory response that encouraged the industry to police itself and pay for the policing. Trimble (1992) concluded that the result was confusing for all parties.

More recently, CRTC chairman Keith Spicer has been a major proponent of measures to address the issue of violence on television, organizing conferences, speaking and visiting Washington. The V chip, a Canadian technology that permits parents to block unwanted signals, offered a deceptively simple technological fix for a contentious problem. It was endorsed by President Bill Clinton, who ordered all new television sets sold in the U.S. to feature V chips within two years of passage of the U.S. Telecommunications Act of 1996. The violence issue once again starkly raised the structural problems faced by Canada in attempting to implement any national policies. Spicer's answer was to lobby in Washington. Again, a compromise was worked out: in this instance, U.S. broadcasters were persuaded (in an election year) to reverse their opposition to the V chip as a violation of freedom of speech and agreed to work on a ratings system for TV shows similar to that for movies.

Globalization poses significant challenges for the Canadian broadcasting system. The merger of Rogers and Maclean Hunter signalled the acceptance by the CRTC of the argument that global realignments required large homegrown corporate entities to withstand the challenges of megamedia firms such as Time Warner. As a result of this decision to sanction concentration of ownership and cross-ownership, the CRTC will now need to focus its attention on consumer protection and the issue of affordable access. It was possible to presume universal service when telephone rates were cross-subsidized (a practice that is ending) and when cable rates remained low. In the transition from free TV to the information highway, these assumptions are under siege.

The entry of telecommunications companies into broadcasting erodes previous distinctions between content and carriage and poses the major long-term threats and opportunities. One particular issue concerns how the new media services will be classified: if they are considered broadcasting services, then they fall under NAFTA's cultural industries exemption; if they are considered new telecommunications services, then Canada will not be allowed to promote its own cultural objectives. The greatest challenge to the CRTC lies in forging a balanced approach to regulation of the coming cybersystem, which will emerge as a hybrid out of the convergence of broadcasting and telecommunications. Ultimately, however, the federal government must wrestle with these problems, due to their ramifications for the international trading agreements and for the nation as a whole. It will be up to the federal government (and the citizens and corporations who lobby it) to decide what price the nation is prepared to pay in order to maintain its values as a culturally sovereign nation.

Hoskins and McFadyen (1980) concluded their study of broadcasting with the then heretical observation that regulation incompatible with private broadcasters' interest in making money would fail. In a sense the observation is true, as the history of Canadian broadcast policy making shows that bureaucratic rules that do not match the realities of the business of broadcasting inevitably are adjusted in practice. Canada's long history of muddling through by compromise is well illustrated in broadcasting. Yet in a more important sense this conclusion misses the point, since there would be no Canadian broadcasters, no domestic profits and no serious Canadian jobs in the industry, if there were no rules for the system. No Canadian content means no reason to protect the broadcasters. The private sector is well aware of this point and has in recent years done a remarkable about face, shifting from a call for an end to regulation to a call for continued protection. The threats to the intermediary policy may be having the effect that years of regulation could not: acting as an incentive to convince private broadcasters to produce and exhibit high-quality Canadian production.

The key policy question for the future is whether the U.S. can bypass or overturn the Canadian intermediary policy, which would bring an end to the Canadian system. The question becomes how vulnerable the federal government is or will be to pressures to abandon Canada's cultural industries policy framework and its broadcasters. Strategies to support the diversity of Canadian culture within a globalizing media system will require the intelligent design of policies that are cognizant of history, suited to the unfolding media environment and flexible enough to cope with constant change. But only if there is a shared commitment by citizens to Canada's national experiment in unity through diversity will it be possible to stand up to the U.S. and preserve what has been attained, while addressing the challenges for the future posed in this transitional period. Without the persuasive visionary pragmatism of Graham Spry and the Canadian Radio League, there would not be a public sector in broadcasting and little to distinguish the broadcasting systems of the two sovereign nations. As Marshall McLuhan observed, "Nothing is inevitable so long as we are prepared to pay attention."

References

Aucoin, Peter. 1979. "Public Policy Theory and Analysis." *Public Policy in Canada: Organization, Process, and Management*. G. Bruce Doern and Peter Aucoin (eds.). Toronto: Gage.

Audley, Paul. 1993. *Human Resource Study of the Cultural Sector: Cultural Sector Profile*. Ottawa: Employment and Immigration Canada.

———. 1983. *Canada's Cultural Industries: Broadcasting, Publishing, Records and Film*. Toronto: James Lorimer & Company.

BBM (Bureau of Broadcast Measurement). 1994. "TV Info ... on Specialty Services." Toronto: BBM.

BYTE. 1996. "Toss your TV: How the Internet Will Replace Broadcasting." *BYTE*. (February) Peterborough, N.H.: The McGraw-Hill Companies.

Canada. CRTC. 1995. *Public Notice CRTC 1995-48: Introduction to decisions renewing the licenses of privately owned English-language Television Stations*. Ottawa: CRTC.

———. 1994. *Cable Television Statistical and Financial Summaries 1988–93*. Ottawa: CRTC.

———. 1994. *Pay and Specialty Services Statistical and Financial Summaries 1988–93*. Ottawa: CRTC.

———. 1994. *Radio and Television Statistical and Financial Summaries 1988–93*. Ottawa: CRTC.

———. House of Commons Standing Committee on Communications and Culture. 1992. *Culture and Communications: The Ties that Bind*. Ottawa: House of Commons.

———. HRDC. (Employment and Immigration Canada). 1993. *Human Resources in the Canadian Broadcasting Industry*. Ottawa: The Canadian Broadcasting Industry Human Resources Steering Committee.

———. Industry Canada. Information Highway Advisory Council. 1995. *Access and the Information Highway: Public Submissions and Comments — Summary of Comments by Topic*. (Prepared by Peter Brandon and Jens Laursen). Ottawa: Industry Canada.

———. Mandate Review Committee. 1996. *Making Our Voices Heard: Canadian Broadcasting and Film for the 21st Century*. Review Committee chairman was Pierre Juneau. Hull, Quebec: Minister of Supply and Services.

———. Statistics Canada. 1995. *Canada's Culture, Heritage and Identity: A Statistical Perspective*. Cat. 87-211. Ottawa: Minister of Supply and Services.

———. 1994–1995. *Household Facilities and Equipment*. Cat. 64-202 Annual. Ottawa: Minister of Industry, Science and Technology.

———. 1987. *Vital Links*. Ottawa: Minister of Supply and Services.

———. Statutes of Canada. 1991. *Broadcasting Act*. 38-39 Elizabeth II. c.11.

Canadian Cable Television Association. 1996. *Cable TV Facts 1995–96*. Ottawa: CCTA/ACTC.

———. 1995. *Cable TV Facts 1994–95*. Ottawa: CCTA/ACTC.

Collins, Richard. 1990. *Culture, Communication & National Identity: The Case of Canadian Television*. Toronto: University of Toronto Press.

Comor, Edward. 1991. "The Department of Communications Under the Free Trade Regime." Hoskins, Colin and Stuart McFadyen. (guest editors). *Canadian Jour-*

nal of Communication: International Market for Television and Film. 16: 239-262.

Ellis, David. 1991. *Networking: How are Canada's English TV Networks Performing?* Toronto: Friends of Canadian Broadcasting.

———. 1992. *Split Screen: Home Entertainment and the New Technologies.* Toronto: Friends of Canadian Broadcasting.

Financial Times of Canada. 1994. "Channel Champs: Why CanWest and WIC are winning on the airwaves." *Financial Times of Canada.* (November 5-11.) Toronto: 1,6,7.

Gilder, George. 1994. *Life after Television: The Coming Transformation of Media and American Life.* Revised edition. New York: W.W. Norton & Company.

Groupe Secor. 1994. *Canadian Government Intervention in the Film and Video Industry (final report).* Quebec: Groupe Secor, October 19.

Hardin, Herschel. 1985. *Closed Circuits: The Sellout of Canadian Television.* Vancouver/Toronto: Douglas & McIntyre.

Jeffrey, Liss. 1995a. "Progress in Canada Toward Women's Equality and the Media: Access to Expression and Decision Making 1980–94." Ottawa: Status of Women Canada.

———. 1995b. "Opening the Doors of Reception." *Watching TV: Historic Television and Memorabilia from the MZTV Museum.* Toronto: Royal Ontario Museum/MZTV Museum.

———. 1994. "Rethinking Audiences for Cultural Industries: Implications for Canadian Research." *Canadian Journal of Communication.* 19 (Summer/Autumn): 495-522.

Marchant, C.K. 1995. *Economic Implications of a third National Television System.* Toronto: The Marchant Practice. Filed with the C.R.T.C. on 9 January 1996 as an addendum to CanWest Alberta Television Inc.: Application to Obtain a Licence to Carry on a Programming Undertaking: Television Station, Application Nos. 952788800 (Calgary) and 952924900 (Edmonton), submitted to the C.R.T.C. on 27 November 1995, hearing date 15 July 1996.

Matthew's Media Directories. 1995a. *Matthew's Media Directory.* Toronto: Canadian Corporate News.

———. 1995b. *Matthew's CATV Directory.* Toronto: Canadian Corporate News.

McChesney, Robert W. 1993. *Telecommunications, Mass Media, and Democracy: The Battle for the Control of U.S. Broadcasting, 1928–1935.* New York: Oxford University Press.

McFadyen, Stuart and Colin Hoskins. 1980. *Canadian Broadcasting: Market Structure and Economic Performance.* Montreal: Institute for Research on Public Policy.

McLuhan, Marshall. 1964. *Understanding Media: The Extensions of Man.* New York: McGraw Hill.

Noam, Eli. 1991. *Television in Europe.* New York: Oxford University Press.

Powe, B.W. 1993. *a tremendous Canada of light.* Toronto: Coach House Press.

Raboy, Marc. 1990. *Missed Opportunities: The Story of Canada's Broadcasting Policy.* Montreal & Kingston: McGill-Queen's University Press.

Report on Business Magazine. 1995. *The Top 1000.* Toronto: The Globe and Mail.

———. 1996. "Izzy Vision." Toronto: The Globe and Mail.

Rowan, Geoffrey. 1995. "Canadians Fear Info Highway a Threat to Culture." *Report on Business: The Globe and Mail.* April 20: B1.

Skene, Wayne. 1993. *Fade to Black: A Requiem for the CBC.* Vancouver & Toronto: Douglas & McIntyre.

Surman, Mark. 1995. "From VTR to Cyberspace." Toronto: (unpublished).

Strategy. 1995. "TV: Focus on Audience Research. Specialty services qualify their existence." 13 November: 21,24.

Taylor, Paul W. 1993. "Third Service, Third Network: The CanWest Global System." *Canadian Journal of Communication.* 18 (Autumn): 469-477.

Television Bureau of Canada. 1996. *TVBasics 95/96.* Toronto: TVB.

———. 1995. *TVBasics 94/95.* Toronto: TVB.

Tracey, Michael and Wendy W. Redal. 1995. "The New Parochialism: the triumph of the populist in the flow of international television." *Canadian Journal of Communication.* 20 (Summer): 343-365.

Trimble, Linda. 1992. "Coming Soon to a Station Near You? The CRTC Policy on Sex-Role Stereotyping," in *Seeing Ourselves: Media Power and Policy in Canada.* Helen Holmes and David Taras (eds.). Toronto: Harcourt Brace Jovanovich.

9

Narrowcasting: Home Video and DBS

Paul Attallah

Over the past decade, broadcasting has been joined by a new form of audience contact, *narrowcasting*. They differ in how they understand audiences, construct messages and deploy technology.

Broadcasting vs Narrowcasting

The modern media, whether metropolitan dailies, films, best-selling novels or popular music, were mostly conceived on the broadcast model. They create products (movies, books, songs) in centralized locations, often at great effort and expense, and distribute them to as many people as possible.

The modern television network illustrates this well. A network assembles programs in a central location for broadcast to the largest audience possible. It also ensures that the same program reaches everyone at the same time. Broadcasting, therefore, puts large audiences in simultaneous contact with a single, centrally created product. This is its main advantage. Broadcasting can be a powerful tool for co-ordinating mass movements, popular sentiments, political and economic forces, etc., and has been used as such by governments, industries, political parties and so on.

The broadcast model, however, also raises certain intractable questions. How can broadcasters be sure that everyone understands the message in the same way? Indeed, how can they even be sure that people are paying attention? Generally, they can be sure of neither. Consequently, broadcast messages — i.e., TV shows aimed at large audiences — assume certain characteristics. In order to attract and hold audience attention, broadcast messages must be appealing and attractive, in some cases even spectacular. In order to guarantee understanding, they must strive for maximum clarity and transparency. However, they cannot be so transparent as to insult the audience or so enticing as to provoke condemnation. Broadcasting, therefore, balances attractiveness with a sense of propriety, and understanding with a sense of worthiness.

Two basic assumptions underlie the broadcast model: the same content will, more or less, interest everyone; and an appropriate and adequate manner of expression, intelligible to all and alienating to none, exists for this purpose. These assumptions limit what may legitimately be said in public and constitute a theory of the socially approved way to reach large numbers of people.

Such assumptions, when combined with the high visibility of television, generate debate. Consequently, television programs — their content and style, their placement and mode of address — come under constant scrutiny. The ongoing debate on television violence illustrates this process.

Finally, because of its assumptions, broadcasting also requires a specific deployment of technology. For example, although the technology used at the point of manufacture tends to be sophisticated, delicate and expensive — printing presses, movie studios, computer systems — the final product tends to be quite affordable. Hence, the cost of a newspaper, novel, record or movie ticket bears little relationship to the cost of the original artifact. Indeed, the need to amortize the discrepancy is one of the main forces behind the quest for large audiences. Additionally, lavish expense can help stimulate audience interest by promising a unique or superlative experience.

Ideally, then, broadcasting favours a limited range of consumer options to ensure both maximum exposure to available products and maximum profitability. Some media (radio and TV) even give their content away free, thereby removing any remaining barriers to attention and consumption. This requires that when technology moves into the home, it be extremely easy to operate. Hence, as personal computers move into the home, they become more user-friendly.

Nonetheless, there have always been two main criticisms of broadcasting. First, in its attempt to reach everyone, it necessarily reduces everything to the lowest common denominator. Second, because universal appeal is fundamentally impossible, certain audiences, taste-cultures and points of view are invariably and systematically excluded. Narrowcasting emerged as a response to these criticisms. Its success, however, has altered the ecology of television.

Home video and direct broadcast satellites (DBS) illustrate the general principles of narrowcasting. These industries address not a single mass audience but multiple, fragmented micro-audiences. They therefore assume that a single style or content cannot reach everyone. Narrowcasting assumes that audience members derive greater satisfaction from the pursuit of private interests than from the sharing of collective experience. Hence, its main appeal lies in the promise of individual gratification.

Additionally, since narrowcasting aims at micro-audiences, the central concerns of broadcasting — legitimacy, intelligibility, acceptability — become secondary. The audience is assumed to possess the skills and attitudes needed to appreciate the content because they actively seek it out. Hence, whereas broadcasting strives to be appealing and acceptable, universal and intelligible, narrowcasting can be highly specialized, arcane and particular. It need interest no one beyond the micro-audience. As a result, the only typical characteristic of narrowcast messages is their implicit appeal to individual gratification.

Audience fragmentation may have two main effects. The first is liberation. Narrowcasting effectively liberates individuals from the tastes, concerns and judgments of others. In the logic of broadcasting, controls on content express a concern for the public good. In the logic of narrowcasting, they simply express unprincipled meddling in the pleasures of others. Regulations cease to represent concern for public life and begin to embody a denial of freedom.

The second effect is disorientation. Broadcasting confronts everyone's private taste with a publicly visible norm, the television program that everyone watches. It helps form a collective taste by providing a common experience. Narrowcasting, however, ensures precisely that no taste need ever be confronted by any other. All taste is private and measured only against itself. The measure of taste ceases, therefore, to be its relationship to others and becomes the effectiveness with which it can be satisfied. The public that shapes taste through common experience undergoes a relative atrophy. People become less aware of what others like and less able to understand their own taste in terms of a larger context; they are thrown back increasingly upon themselves. The criterion of acceptability ceases to be that which can be shared and becomes that which is most individual. Narrowcasting forms not so much taste as a taste for novelty. Perhaps predictably, then, as narrowcasting multiplies viewing options, the complaint is increasingly heard that there is nothing to watch.

Narrowcasting also involves a direct financial transaction with the consumer. Content is rented or bought individually, on a pay-per-view (PPV) or pay-per-channel basis. The user-pay relationship represents the direct sanction of the market and directly measures the worth of various content types. It ultimately displaces reliance upon surveys and audience measurement techniques.

The user-pay system also introduces price and usage discrimination. For example, although not all films cost the same to make, all movie tickets cost the same to purchase. Likewise, not all TV programs are equally enjoyable, but they all occupy time in precisely the same manner. Narrowcasting allows viewers to exercise discretion over their expenditures of time and money. A special sporting event may be highly priced on a satellite service whereas a video store may rent old movies more cheaply than new movies. Likewise, viewers can fast-forward through a rented video, thereby giving a more precise value to their time than the formats of network TV allow. The ability to discriminate constitutes a more direct and more accurate valuation of content types. It also eliminates many grounds for complaint: consumers watch only what they want.

Narrowcasting also uses technology for specific purposes. The logic of broadcast technology (superlative production, ease of consumption) does not entirely hold with narrowcasting. Since it seeks out micro-audiences presumed to want the content, narrowcasting can offer less lavishly packaged content. Indeed, micro-audiences will accept and expect lower production values. Hence, makers of lower-budget material — Canadian or alternative film-makers, makers of specialty genres — can gain easier access to narrowcasting than to broadcasting. Finally, whereas broadcast technology makes everyone simultaneously present for a common, centrally produced message, narrowcast technology disconnects everyone from the centre and from simultaneity. With narrowcasting, viewers remove themselves from the schedules and rhythms of centralized broadcasters and follow the vagaries of individual motivation.

Broadcasting's audience is weakly differentiated with respect to age, race, sex, income, education, habits etc. To a weakly differentiated audience, it proposes weakly differentiated content — the same styles, modes of address, viewing times, intelligibility etc. Broadcasting tends towards broadly shared and weakly differentiated cultural referents. Narrowcasting's audience is highly differentiated accord-

Table 9-1
VCR Penetration of TV Households in Canada, by Year

Year	VCR Penetration	Year	VCR Penetration
1983	6.4%	1989	58.8%
1984	12.6%	1990	66.3%
1985	23.5%	1991	68.6%
1986	35.4%	1992	73.8%
1987	45.2%	1993	77.3%
1988	52.0%	1994	79.2%

Source: Statistics Canada. 1994. *Household Facilities Survey.*

ing to age, race, sex, preferences, interests etc. To a highly differentiated audience, it proposes content highly differentiated as to its mode of delivery, style, intelligibility, price, mode of consumption etc. Narrowcasting tends towards privately held cultural practices.

Home Video

The video cassette recorder (VCR) was the first TV peripheral device to gain widespread acceptance. Its acceptance also challenged broadcast TV.

The first successful mass-market, stand-alone VCR was the Betamax, introduced by Sony Corp. in 1976. In 1977, JVC followed suit and launched its own VHS (video home service) recorders in the United States under the RCA label. They proved even more successful than the Betamax because of lower prices and longer recording times and within a decade had established themselves as the home standard.

The rate of VCR penetration grew in Canada from 6.4 per cent in 1983 to approximately 80 per cent in 1994 (see Table 9-1). This compares with a cable subscription rate of 80 per cent and a TV penetration rate of 95 per cent.

VCR usage has settled into three major categories: time-shifting, library building, and playback of pre-recorded material.

Time-shifting

For VCR users, time-shifting (recording a program for later viewing) is a great convenience and was one of the reasons for which VCRs

Table 9-2
Type of Program Typically Time-Shifted
(% of VCR owners)

Type	Total
Feature films	88%
Drama series	71%
Documentary/education	62%
Situation comedy	59%
Sports	49%
Variety	44%
Music videos	37%
News & public affairs	34%

Source: Gallup. 1992.

were originally promoted. Time-shifting allows viewers to remove themselves from the constraints of television networks and exercise ultimate control over the time, speed, sequence and context in which programs are watched. The convenience of viewers, however, breeds considerable upset in advertisers and audience surveyors. It is simply impossible to know if the commercials embedded within time-shifted programs are actually watched or if viewers fast-forward through them, an activity known as zipping. Likewise, it is extremely difficult to determine exactly the size of a time-shifted audience. Does the time-shifted content get watched in whole or in part or does it simply languish only to be erased at a later date?

It is perhaps worth noting that the introduction of the VCR coincides quite precisely with the decline of network TV in North America, although it is hardly the only cause. For example, in 1976 the three U.S. networks controlled 92 per cent of the viewing audience on a typical night. By 1984, they controlled 75 per cent. By the 1990s, the number had fallen to less than 60 per cent (see Auletta [1991]).

In Canada, fully 81.4 per cent of VCR users engage in time-shifting, with younger viewers doing so more than older viewers. However, not all programs are time-shifted equally. Eighty-eight per cent of all time-shifting is devoted to feature films, whereas only 34 per cent is devoted to news and public affairs (see Table 9-2).

Library Building

Library building is an activity that worries copyright holders. If material (film, TV shows, sporting events etc.) is broadcast on TV or rented or bought on cassette, the owner of the material (movie studio, production company etc.) receives a payment or royalty. If, however, home videotapers record the material and watch it again at their leisure or show it and lend it to friends, then a number of potential royalty payments are foregone. This is aggravated when the source of the material is not the airwaves but a rented video cassette that is copied and kept, shared or resold by home tapers. Strictly speaking, this last activity (copying commercial videotapes) is known as video piracy.

In Canada, unlike the United States, home videotaping is illegal, although the law is not enforced against individuals unless they are conducting a large-scale piracy operation. Furthermore, the magnitude of the problem and the revenues lost through home videotaping are difficult to measure. Indeed, the marketplace may actually encourage home videotaping.

For example, unlike audio recordings, which can be heard off-air and purchased in stores, television programs can generally only be seen on-air, since no network of retail outlets exists for viewers to purchase programs which they particularly like. Additionally, many broadcasters encourage viewers to set their VCRs so as not to miss a special event or movie, thereby stimulating the very behaviour they reprove. Finally, many retailers make available devices such as the VCRplus, which makes setting VCRs easier and which requires newspapers to print special VCR codes.

At the present time, the federal government is considering a videotape tax to compensate Canadian copyright holders. This would be similar to a tax on audio tape for the same purpose and is a technique adopted by many countries. Significantly, although the tape may not be used to record Canadian content, the tax would be remitted to Canadian copyright holders.

Statistics indicate that 16 per cent of VCR owners build video libraries, with teenagers and pay-TV subscribers being the most assiduous collectors. The incidence of library building is also reflected in blank tape purchases. If users simply time-shifted without collecting, a handful of tapes per household would suffice. In 1991,

Table 9-3
Type of Program Typically Included in Video Libraries
(% of VCR owners)

Type	Total
Feature films	71.3%
Drama series	58%
Documentary/education	50.1%
Situation comedy	47.3%
Sports	40%
Variety	36%
Music videos	29.7%
News & public affairs	27.5%

Source: Denton Consultants. 1992.

however, VCR users purchased approximately 42.8 million blank videotapes worth approximately $245 million. It is estimated that, on average, they recorded 8.49 hours monthly or 101.88 hours annually (see Denton Consultants [1992]).

As Table 9-3 shows, inclusion in video libraries by program type closely matches the frequency of time-shifting. It is also worth noting that for both time-shifting and collecting, feature films occupy the top spot. Traditionally, it is the movie studios who have felt most aggrieved by, and received the greatest benefit from, the VCR. It is also around their product that the largest sector of the video industry, sales and rentals, has developed.

Video Sales and Rentals

The software of choice for VCR owners is pre-recorded movies. Individual owners rent on average 4.65 pre-recorded videos per month or 55.8 videos per year. For all owners combined, the total is 378 million pre-recorded video cassettes per year (see Denton Consultants [1992]). In 1993, film attendance generated $400-500 million but video rentals generated $1.6 billion (Brehl, 1994b).

Not all movies, however, are equally popular nor do they contribute equally to video store revenues (see Table 9-4). Additionally, not all pre-recorded movies carry the same potential for profit. This is due to the process by which video cassettes are manufactured and

Table 9-4
Video Rentals by Type and by Contribution to Revenues

Type	% of rentals	% of revenues
Feature films (old & new)	69%	75%
Adult	13%	9%
Children	12%	9%
Special interest	3%	2%
Music	3%	2%

Source: Griffin. 1990.

marketed. Movie studios shoot the movies and hold the copyrights. They transfer their films to cassette by licensing video cassette manufacturers, essentially large factories capable of striking thousands of copies from a single master. The video cassette manufacturers then sell the cassettes outright to wholesalers who supply the retail outlets frequented by VCR owners.

A video cassette's profitability depends upon the price which the wholesaler charges the retailer. The cost to a video store of a single cassette can range from as little as $15 to as much as $200. A very popular recent film would be sold at the highest price whereas a lesser-known film could be sold at the lowest. If a retailer purchases a single video cassette at $200, it will require 67 rentals, at $3 each, before returning a profit. A hit film, however, can easily be rented a minimum of 100 times before losing its hit status. Furthermore, even when it loses its hit status, it continues to be rented and to generate profit. Nonetheless, a cheaper film might only require five rentals to return a profit. Obviously, wholesalers charge retailers according to a film's theatrical track record. Some box-office hits, however, fail to rent adequately whereas others with poor box-office sales rent extremely well. Large video chains are estimated to earn an annual profit of about 30 per cent (see Crosariol [1991]).

The sums involved in the video industry — the North American market is currently estimated at $U.S. 15 billion — have drawn big players. Blockbuster Video, the world's largest video chain, began in 1987 with 19 stores. By 1994, it had 37,000 outlets worldwide and was acquired by Viacom (owner of Paramount Pictures, MTV and

Simon & Schuster) for $U.S. 8.7 billion. Its revenues grew from $U.S. 7 million in 1987 to $U.S. 3 billion in 1994. Blockbuster and two Canadian companies, Jumbo Video and Rogers Video, control 20 per cent of the Canadian video rental market. The remainder belongs to regional chains (such as Videotron in Quebec), convenience stores, independent outlets, "mom-and-pop" operations and so on.

A small video store or convenience kiosk may carry as few as 200-300, usually recent, titles. Superstores belonging to giant chains stock 10,000-12,000 titles across a huge range of taste categories. Since 56 per cent of customers enter a video store with no particular title in mind, superstores allow them to browse and be tempted. They typically provide informed employees who can direct customers to suitable titles, offer promotions and giveaways (e.g., free popcorn), carry more copies of each title, allow for reservations and provide faster check-out.

The very success of video rentals has also altered the behaviour of movie studios. As noted above, video rentals return roughly three times the revenue of box office. Hence, rather than let wholesalers and retailers reap the benefits of their films, studios are now attempting to control the industry by producing directly for video.

For example, Paramount Pictures' control of Blockbuster guarantees it a video window for all of its products, both old and new. Studios, however, are generally attempting to develop the "sell-through" market, getting individuals to purchase rather than rent video cassettes. Studios currently realize their profit when they license titles to video cassette manufacturers. If, however, they sell films directly to consumers, this allows them to eliminate the video rental outlet and keep more profits for themselves. As a result, the cost to consumers of pre-recorded video cassettes has fallen throughout the 1980s from about $100 to less than $25 (see Table 9-5).

The figures involved can be quite staggering. *Jurassic Park*, for example, grossed $900 million at the box office worldwide and sold $1 billion in merchandise. It is expected to sell 20 million video cassettes which, at $25 each, means an additional $500 million. Walt Disney's *Aladdin* has already sold over 24 million cassettes and *Snow White* is expected to sell another 20 million. The *Flintstones*, which earned $126 million at the box office is expected to sell 15 million cassettes worth at least $300 million (see Nichols [1994]).

Families with children are the likeliest to purchase video cassettes as a safe programming alternative. Additionally, studios promote

Table 9-5
U.S. Video Sell-Through, 1987–91

Year	Units (millions)	Average Unit Price ($)	Total Market ($billions)
1987	115.6	21.23	2.47
1988	147.7	19.53	2.89
1989	195.5	17.83	3.49
1990	231.0	16.14	3.73
1991	290.7	15.93	4.63

Source: Ellis, 1992: 112.

children's content because of the merchandising tie-ins, television spinoffs, theme park possibilities, novelizations and the fact that this undemanding audience renews itself roughly every seven years, thereby restarting the cycle.

Studios, therefore, are now producing films direct to video. For example, Disney's *The Return of Jafar*, the sequel to *Aladdin*, was never distributed theatrically but went directly to video. It cost $U.S. 5 million and returned $U.S. 120 million in cassette sales. The direct-to-video trend is increasing and opens opportunities for producers with smaller budgets. It also demonstrates the extent to which video has become an alternative programming choice alongside television, cable, pay-TV etc. Indeed, video may eventually replace movie theatres as the first window for new product.

Not only major studios, however, benefit from the home video market. One-time "B" studios such as Republic Pictures have also successfully produced for the home video market. Additionally, makers of films which would normally receive only spotty distribution — i.e., first films, low-budget horror/slasher and science-fiction films, biker films, specialty topics, NFB productions etc. — actually receive sufficient distribution through video to sustain a minor industry from which major talents may emerge.

Video has brought about a reversal in the relationship between film and television. From the very beginning, television was decried for destroying film. Not only had it damaged film attendance, but television had also insidiously altered the integrity of film. Films on TV were mercilessly edited, interrupted by commercials, squeezed into small frames, colourized and otherwise denatured. Television even caused films to be shot differently to accommodate its own small, low-definition screen. As a result, the wide-angle shot and deep focus were gone, moving spectacle and meaningful performance forgotten, in favour of television's own shallow style and comedic rhythms. The VCR, however, is film's revenge on television. Films constitute the overwhelming number of cassettes rented and purchased. They displace TV's own content and cultivate a taste for stories and styles not available on TV. Equally, the VCR wrenches viewers away from the rhythms and patterns of television and turns the television set into an independent programming source, no longer tied to the exigencies of networks.

The next logical step would seem to involve the elimination of the video retailer altogether through electronic home delivery of movies. This is certainly the strategy behind pay-TV channels, whether delivered via cable, fibre optic or satellite. Movie studios and the companies that control the delivery vehicles harbour great hopes for the future of video on demand as they expect to displace video retailers almost entirely and deliver more profits into their own hands.

The pleasures of video rental, however, should not be underestimated. People have already invested time and money in VCRs, building libraries and enjoying their convenience. Any alternative technology will have to provide the same benefits at comparable or lower prices. Additionally, people genuinely enjoy the shopping experience of video stores, a fact of which the stores are increasingly aware as they improve their marketing through promotions and giveaways and redesign their spaces to be bright, clean and safe. There are few shopping experiences as suitable for the entire family where consumers are exposed to so great a choice. Going to the video store can be an outing for the family, a way to get children out of the house, to institute a family ritual, to expose family members to each other's tastes and to pick a viewing alternative directly approved by parents.

Video stores are also comparable to book stores. All readers could join book clubs and have their books delivered to the door. This would be like subscribing to a video-on-demand service. Home consumption is clearly linked to convenience and a feeling of safety but also allows pre-selection by the delivery vehicle: not all books are offered and the delivery vehicle has an interest in promoting some books over others. Book clubs, therefore, have not caused the disappearance of book stores or libraries, although they can serve as a useful supplement.

The book store analogy may go even further. Book selling is a culturally unregulated industry. For example, no literary equivalent of the CRTC licenses book sellers, imposes quotas, requires must-carry rules etc. This in turn raises serious questions about cultural regulation generally. Why can home video be unregulated whereas cable and broadcast TV are subject to extensive regulatory intervention?

There would seem to be two types of regulation: industry regulation and audience regulation. Industry regulation involves fairness and access. For example, the regulation of cable costs may be in the public interest if it guarantees all people access to a service deemed socially desirable. Audience regulation, however, is concerned with the nature of the audience's response. It seeks to police behaviour in order to make it conform to a pre-existing norm. For example, licensing practices seek specifically to channel audiences towards approved choices by eliminating others, by imposing costs on some, by linking less approved choices to more approved choices etc.

The difference in regulatory types, however, might lead us to ask why audience response is a good indicator in one part of the industry — home video — but bad in another part — broadcast, satellite, cable TV. Why can audience judgment so easily be replaced by regulatory judgment? The substitution of regulatory judgment for audience judgment can cause resources to be channelled to projects in which the audience has no genuine interest. This results in audiences being offered what authorities say is good for them rather than what audiences themselves say is good for them. Narrowcasting undermines the paternalism of this position.

Direct Broadcast Satellites (DBS)

Where home video provided the example of an unregulated industry, DBS provides the example of an industry caught between increased regulatory intervention and growing deregulatory pressure.

Satellites have several implications for television. First, a single satellite's "footprint" can cover 40 per cent of the earth's surface. Satellites are said to be distance-insensitive because they can reach all points in their footprint at exactly the same cost. Satellites, therefore, possess the potential to render obsolete distance-sensitive systems such as coaxial cable, telephone lines, microwave relays, fibre optics and so on.

Second, satellite signals undergo very little degradation over extreme distances. They are an ideal medium for introducing advanced television display systems such as HDTV, which in itself will cause enormous upheaval in the television industry.

Third, like cable TV or any other high-capacity vehicle, satellites introduce channel overcapacity. For example, each Anik satellite carries at least 12 channels; just two Anik satellites provide many more channels than are available over the air in virtually any city. The overcapacity eventually generates pressure for more content providers, if only to avoid waste. And as with cable, the step from satellites as redistributors to satellites as originators of content is but a small one. In fact, since satellites matured as an industry after cable, they drew upon the model of cable from their very inception.

Fourth, the demand for new channels creates opportunities for content providers who might not be able to break into other delivery systems or who wish to establish themselves in as many systems as possible. But satellites may create opportunities in an unprecedented manner. Their ability to assemble isolated pockets of widely dispersed viewers into relatively large audiences at no extra cost makes niche programming highly feasible. Home video achieves a similar result with a much lower order of technology.

Fifth, satellites affect cable TV. On the one hand, many of the most desirable cable services are distributed via satellite and cable companies make heavy use of them. On the other hand, just as sell-through allows studios to eliminate video retailers, DBS allows satellites to eliminate cable companies.

Sixth, satellites constitute a challenge to home video. As we have seen, the ability to provide video on demand may eliminate the home video industry.

Ted Turner was probably the first person to learn the lesson of satellites when, in 1978, he turned his low-rated Atlanta television station WTBS into the first superstation, a local station retransmitted via satellite. Cable operators downlink and resell it to their customers. The superstation charges higher advertising rates due to the size of its satellite/cable-enhanced audience but in order to be nationally attractive, it must be prepared to offer network-style programming — feature films, major sporting events, news etc. — or a niche service. Superstations also demonstrate that traditional terrestrial networks with their complex systems of affiliates, time zones and technical links are no longer necessary. A new network can be started with a single station and a satellite.

Channel overcapacity also moved the Department of Communications (now the Department of Heritage Canada) in 1978 to explore pay-TV. Pay-TV channels and subsequent specialty services, licensed by the CRTC from 1982 onwards, would be distributed by satellite to cable operators in order to strengthen the cable companies, to legitimate the satellite industry and to stimulate the production industry. As a result, satellites are now more used, cable has more subscribers and bigger profits, and more television than ever is being produced.

Rise of the Satellite TV Market

TV networks and cable companies, however, are not alone in their ability to receive satellite signals. So, too, can anyone with the appropriate antenna array, and, since the late 1970s, a growing army of satellite TV enthusiasts has been doing precisely that by means of *TVRO* (television receive only) earth stations, the large parabolic antennas or dishes which take up whole yards.

TVROs can be constructed for as little as $100 but most are professionally installed at a cost of $2000-$5000. Their size — roughly one to three metres in diameter — is a function of the power of early satellites (usually two to 60 watts) and of their relative earth position. TVRO owners can watch at least 200 television channels and listen to numerous audio services from any of about 30 satellites of various national origins. The TV signals are devoid of commercials and viewers get to see all the technical manipulations which are usually hidden from audiences. There are approximately 500,000 TVROs in Canada and some four million in the United States. They created the satellite TV market.

Two fairly predictable phenomena have accompanied the emergence of the satellite TV market: signal encryption and high-power DBS. Program providers who transmitted their signals to cable companies via satellite came to see their reception by non-paying TVROs as a form of foregone revenue. Consequently, in 1986 HBO and other program providers began to encrypt their signals. This forced TVRO owners to acquire descramblers and subscribe to the services as though they were cable subscribers. Encryption in turn produced a trade in pirate decoders.

If TVRO owners with ungainly, expensive dishes are willing to subscribe to encrypted services, then the next logical step is to upgrade the whole process of satellite reception so that everyone will want satellite TV. This is where direct broadcast satellites come in.

DBS extends the idea of home-satellite TV by adding three key refinements: ease of use, aesthetic appeal of the apparatus and heavy promotion.

DBS, the Domestication of Satellite TV

In technical terms, DBS refers simply to a class of high-powered satellites operating at 120-200 watts in a part of the radio spectrum specifically reserved for direct-to-home (DTH) TV, the Ku-band. Their high power makes them receivable by small 27-40 cm dishes that are the size of a large pizza and can be mounted on a window ledge, balcony or rooftop. Because they are discrete, owners generally find them more aesthetically pleasing than TVROs and they generate fewer complaints from neighbours.

DBS also uses digital video compression (DVC), a technique for squeezing more channels into the same bandwidth. This allows satellites to deliver 150-200 channels. Cable companies can achieve similar results with the same technology.

All DBS transmissions are encrypted. The DBS dish therefore also includes an integrated addressable decoder. This allows the DBS operator to transmit a coded signal which activates only specific decoders for the reception of specific channels, movies, sporting events and so on. Addressable decoders, therefore, make possible highly targeted transmissions to widely dispersed audiences without bothering in the least other DBS subscribers who have chosen to watch other content.

It is important to remember, however, that the DBS decoder is effectively tuned to the satellite of the DBS operator. Hence, DBS is quite different from TVROs. TVRO owners can point their dish at any satellite in the sky. DBS owners can only point theirs at the satellite of their service provider. For this reason, DBS has been likened to a cable company in the sky, albeit with vastly improved choice, PPV ability and digital quality sound and image.

Permanent tuning to a single satellite, however, can also be an advantage. First, since the receiver does not swing around to locate satellites, installation and operation are extremely easy. Second, permanent tuning allows the satellite provider to incorporate a sophisticated graphical user interface — an elaborate electronic TV guide — to help viewers navigate through the enormous number of offerings. These factors — ease of installation and operation, graphical user interface — effectively domesticate satellite technology for huge categories of users.

In North America, DBS will necessarily be engaged in a struggle for market share with cable TV, since both offer similar services. This struggle will, at least initially, tend to lower subscription costs as both services attempt to attract or conserve subscribers. It will also induce an upward spiral in the number of channels offered as each system attempts to demonstrate its superiority. It will likely also accelerate the adoption of new technologies (addressable decoders, DVC, HDTV) and non-programming services (data connections, home banking etc.) as each service attempts to anticipate the grounds on which it could be challenged. For these reasons, the Canadian cable industry immediately dubbed the new satellites "deathstars." The fact of the matter, however, is that they represent the first competition cable has ever known.

In the longer term, DBS may have other effects. Channel abundance is likely to produce a lowering of overall production values as advertising dollars are spread over more and more outlets. It is not clear what effect lower production values will have on audiences. The adoption of new technologies will likely also impose new costs on consumers. Ultimately, the cost of watching television will increase for all consumers and the notion of "free" TV will atrophy.

The first successful DBS system in North America, DirecTV, was launched in the U.S. in June 1994. It has to date exceeded by a wide margin even the most optimistic projections. Since it offers some 150 channels, it poses an interesting problem: how to fill them? Many of its channels are devoted to films, which start approximately every 15 to 30 minutes. However, DirecTV also offers three Canadian services — Newsworld International, MuchMusic International and Trio (a selection of CBC programs) — and other Canadian services could be added. MuchMusic in particular has emerged as a sophisticated alternative to MTV, and DirecTV estimates that by the year 2000 it will remit $400 million to these three services (Brehl, 1994a).

This creates an unanticipated situation. For years, nationalists have decried American television and the fact that Canadians subsidize it through imports. Now, via DBS, Americans are importing and subsidizing Canadian TV. Furthermore, DBS raises some interesting statistical possibilities. The CBC is currently watched by 10-15 per cent of the population, representing 1 to 1.5 million of the 10 million homes with TV (2.4 to 3.6 million viewers). If DBS gives the CBC only one per cent of the 100 million U.S. homes, representing some 270 million viewers, the CBC would effectively reach 1 million homes or 2.7 million viewers. Hence, its U.S. audience could actually be larger than its Canadian audience. The situation would also give the CBC a double revenue stream, advertising plus DBS subscription fees, and would allow the CBC to raise its advertising rates. DBS represents, therefore, an unprecedented opportunity for Canadian TV to reach an audience 10 times larger than usual.

The Urge to Regulate

The minutiae of Canadian DBS development will likely be lost to history. Nonetheless, an overall pattern can already be discerned.

Home satellite TV has so far been unregulated in both Canada and the United States. As a result, Canadian TVRO owners are free to subscribe to encrypted U.S. services, which are not licensed by the CRTC. Indeed, the owners' biggest problem lies not in circumventing the CRTC but in concealing their location from the U.S. satellite operator. A U.S. operator will not knowingly activate a decoder located in Canada if it does not hold distribution rights. If it did so knowingly, it would expose itself to legal action from the legitimate rights holder. Fortunately for the owners of decoders, several private post offices will maintain legitimate U.S. mailing addresses which can be forwarded to the U.S. satellite operator for billing purposes. Hence, although the decoder is located in Canada, the operator bills a U.S. address. This is possible because decoders are activated by serial number rather than location.

Distribution rights are extremely important to the film and TV industries because they determine who gets what share of revenue. Ultimately, these have more force and meaning than government regulation. DBS highlights the problem of rights with the simple fact that satellite footprints spill across borders into territories for which the operator may not hold rights. The CRTC does not and cannot regulate such rights. They grow out of commercial agreements between suppliers and distributors.

The CRTC, however, can and does want to regulate the consumption of DBS, although this is difficult precisely because of the nature of footprints. Nonetheless, the CRTC has undertaken a number of steps to extend to DBS the rules which govern cable.

The stakes for the CRTC are simple and blunt. Its legitimacy is on the line. After years of regulated cable choice, the possibility exists that Canadians may prefer DBS to cable, disconnecting from cable or greatly reducing their reliance upon it. In the process, they would plug into a system, DBS, which is essentially international in scope and beyond the regulatory reach of the CRTC. Canadians would choose content on the basis of their own judgment rather than on the basis of a system of managed choice. This would effectively render the CRTC redundant and underscore the restrictive nature of its regulatory framework.

To maintain its credibility and legitimacy, the CRTC needed a policy on DBS. A DBS policy, however, requires a Canadian DBS supplier. Indeed, this fact seemed all the more urgent as, in March 1993, the U.S.-based DirecTV announced plans to launch a service in Canada, without seeking CRTC authorization, although it did wish to include some Canadian services in its lineup. The question became, therefore, who in Canada can possibly launch or manage a direct broadcast satellite?

At the time, only one Canadian company, Canadian Satellite Communications Inc. (Cancom), was licensed to distribute television via satellite. However, it served 1,526 small cable systems as well as some 31,000 TVRO owners with a mixture of 12 CRTC-approved Canadian and American services (Enchin, 1994). This was far short of a DBS service.

Nonetheless, in early 1994, the CRTC turned to Cancom and the cable companies to create a Canadian DBS service. By late May, they had created a consortium called Expressvu (originally DTH Canada). However, when questions were raised as to whether such a consortium violated the rules of competition, the cable companies withdrew.

During roughly the same period (March-April 1994), DirecTV joined with Power Corporation of Montreal to form Power DirecTV, thus bringing it into line with Canadian media ownership regulations. With the presence of two potential suppliers, the opportunity now existed for DBS to compete with cable and for DBS providers to compete with each other. The CRTC's actions, however, muddled the situation to the benefit of one potential operator only.

In response to the fear that Canadians would disconnect from cable in favour of DBS, and in order to prevent U.S. suppliers from serving the market, the CRTC had ruled, in late 1993, that any DBS provider using exclusively Canadian satellites (and meeting certain other requirements) would be exempted from the need to obtain a licence. The ruling was surprising because cable companies regularly receive some of their services from U.S. satellites. Indeed, as a rule, Canadian satellites are used only for the delivery of Canadian services; it would be wasteful and expensive to duplicate on Canadian satellites foreign services available on foreign satellites. Furthermore, the ruling obviously favoured Expressvu, whose formation the CRTC had favoured, since it obviously used only Canadian satellites. As a result, Expressvu would be allowed to launch its service whenever it wished without obtaining a licence, whereas all other hopefuls would be required to go through the official licensing procedure.

The ruling, however, was not left unchallenged. The Bureau of Competition Policy noted that the satellite requirement was contrary to the rules of competition and was unlikely to encourage a strong DBS sector or make a strong contribution to Canadian broadcasting. Consequently, the government established a DBS policy review panel, which concluded that the CRTC's exemption order had the immediate effect of creating a *de facto* monopoly in the Canadian satellite TV market (Government of Canada, 1995a). Indeed, as a member of the panel stated, "Monopoly privileges can no longer be justified at a time of rapid technological change and expanded channel capacity" (Government of Canada, 1995b).

Another panel member pointed out that the CRTC had erred in underestimating the importance of DBS:

The CRTC should exempt from licensing only those broadcasting entities that do not have a significant impact on the Canadian broadcasting system. Satellite TV clearly will be an important part of Canada's broadcasting system, and as such should be licensed (Government of Canada, 1995b).

Following the review panel's repudiation, the federal cabinet took the unprecedented step, in July 1995, of overturning the CRTC's exemption decision and ordering it to hold formal licensing hearings. The CRTC complied but not without a petulant outburst from its chairman, Keith Spicer.

Immediately, Expressvu warned that the rules exempting it from licensing could not be changed without providing it grounds for legal recourse. A compromise was necessary. Expressvu's exemption would be maintained until the end of the licensing procedure, at which point it would no longer be exempt and would be required to seek a licence. Logic dictated, therefore, that it apply for a licence along with all other applicants, albeit in the full knowledge that it could launch its service before the end of the hearings.

Three main applicants sought licences: (a) Expressvu, owned jointly by Western International Communication Ltd., Bell Canada Enterprises and Tee-Comm Enterprises; (b) Power DirecTV, 80 per cent owned by Power Corporation and 20 per cent by DirecTV, a subsidiary of Hughes Corporation; and (c) HomeStar, a cable consortium led by Shaw Communications, Canada's second-largest cable operator. A fourth applicant, Star Choice of Lindsay, Ontario, missed the application deadline.

In December 1995, the CRTC awarded licences to Expressvu and Power DirecTV. Both companies use different encryption standards but both use Canadian satellites for the delivery of Canadian services. Both must also contribute five per cent of gross revenues to a Canadian production fund.

Their basic line-ups are substantially similar and mirror the channels approved by the CRTC for cable. Furthermore, they are subject to the same tiering and substitution rules as cable operators. This could be a problem, as satellites broadcast everywhere irrespective of time zones, making simultaneous substitution highly problematic. One obvious solution is to exclude certain regional services likely to request substitution, such as Global Television, from the satellite line-up altogether.

Their PPV lineups, however, are quite different. Expressvu will offer 22 PPV channels drawn from existing Canadian suppliers. Power DirecTV, however, will be able to draw upon the pool of services offered by DirecTV and will provide 60-70 PPV channels. Indeed, it is likely that Power DirecTV will have greater purchasing power than Expressvu, will be able to draw upon a larger pool of services and may even be able to buy up North American rights for certain films, sporting events, music specials etc. (see Visser and Barr [1995]).

The CRTC will entertain new DBS applicants six months after the existing licensees begin taking subscription orders. Somewhat surprisingly, however, the president of Power DirecTV, Joel Bell, announced in late 1995 that his service would not be launched unless DBS's startup costs — in part related to the differing encryption standards — were subsidized by cable. This would, in his view, create a level playing field. The CRTC ignored the demand, but Power DirecTV now has a licence that it might not use.

Conclusion

The industries examined in this chapter both share one thing: as narrowcast technologies, they detach audiences from centralized sources and deliver them to their own preferences. They are characterized by an inflation of the individual and of individual choice. The increasing importance of individualism is not merely a byproduct of narrowcast technologies but appears to be a feature of modern society. Of course, the centralized sources are fighting back with more or less vigour, depending on the industry and the perceived stakes.

Nonetheless, if the role of narrowcasting continues to grow, television might evolve towards a newsstand or library model. Like the racks of a newsstand, it might well consist of a large array of discretely consumable titles. The criteria governing choice will then be individual interest and ability to pay. And, as size of holdings is often a criterion of a library's quality and social utility, so too might the sheer variety of choice serve as a marker of the value and desirability of television. Indeed, we already value video stores according to this criterion.

Should this come about, the role of regulation might well be confined to matters of public interest, such as guaranteeing fairness and access. At the present time, there appear to be two main types of regulation, industry regulation and audience regulation. It might well become as intolerable to regulate viewing habits as it would be to oblige library patrons to borrow books from predetermined categories. Even so, we may still want the television equivalent of the public library.

The passing of broadcast TV need hardly move us. It has not always existed and need not always exist. Our attachment to it may come to seem quaint. It is equally likely, however, that narrowcasting will not totally displace the broadcast model any more than automobiles eliminated walking or television eliminated film. They will likely co-exist and come to some accommodation.

References

Brehl, Robert. 1994a. "Satellite ruling will hurt Canadians, U.S. firm says." *Ottawa Citizen*, 6 September, p. E6.

———. 1994b. "We're not ready for last rewind, video stores insist." *Toronto Star*, 9 November, p. B1.

Crosariol, Beppi. 1991. "Now Playing: Attack of the Killer Video Chains." *Financial Times*, April 29/May 5, pp. 12-14.

Corcoran, Terence. 1995. "Beam up the competition, Scotty." *The Globe and Mail*, 14 January, p. B2

Canadian Radio-television and Telecommunications Commission. 1994. Public Notice 1994-111. *Exemption Order Respecting Direct-to-Home (DTH) Satellite Distribution Undertakings*.

———. 1993. "Consumer-Drive TV: A Canadian Bridge to the Future." *News Release*, 3 June, Ottawa: CRTC.

————. 1993. Public Notice 1993-74. *Structural Public Hearing.*

T.M. Denton Consultants Inc. March 1992. *A Report on Home Taping of Audio and Video Products in Canada and Copyright Régimes in Other Countries Dealing with Home Taping.* Ottawa: For the Director General, Cultural Industries, Department of Communications.

Ellis, David. 1992. *Split Screen, Home Entertainment and the New Technologies.* Toronto: Friends of Canadian Broadcasting.

Enchin, Harvey. 1995a. "Canadian firms threaten suit to keep out deathstar." *The Globe and Mail,* 11 January, p. B10.

————. 1995b. "Satellites beam savings, DirecTV says." *The Globe and Mail,* 24 January, p. B8.

————. 1994. "Cancom pledges price cuts — with a hitch." *The Globe and Mail,* 5 October.

Gallup Canada Inc. 1992. *National Video Home Recording Survey — Final Report.* Ottawa: For the Film, Video and Sound Recording Policy & Programs Directorate, Communications Canada.

Gooderham, Mary. 1995a. "Why it's not the viewer's choice." *The Globe and Mail,* 13 January, p. A10.

————. 1995b. "Some not hesitating to sneak a peek behind CRTC's back." *The Globe and Mail,* 18 January, p. A5.

Government of Canada. 1995a. *Ministers Dupuy and Manley Receive Report on Direct-to-Home Satellite Distribution.* Ottawa. News Release 7239.

————. 1995b. *Competition in Satellite Broadcasting Will Bring Increased Choice for Consumers, New Funds for Canadian Program Producers.* Ottawa. News Release 7237.rel.

Griffin, Jeff. 1990. "Here Come the Superstores!" *Montreal Gazette,* 3 November, pp. D1, D8.

Hofmeister, Sally. 1994. "Appeal of 'Direct-to-Video' Grows Among Film Studios." *The New York Times,* November 8, p. D1.

Kainz, Alana. 1994. "Satellite Wars." *The Ottawa Citizen,* 23 December, p. E1.

Lardner, James. 1987. *Fast Forward, Hollywood, the Japanese, and the Onslaught of the VCR.* New York: W.W. Norton & Company.

Lewis, Claude W. 1994. *Satellite Broadcasting in North America.* Ottawa: Cancom.

Mayson, Guy and Karyn Rathwell Wichers. April 1994. *The Film and Video Industry in Canada: An Overview.* Ottawa: Department of Heritage Canada, The Film and Sound Recording Policy Research Project.

Nichols, Peter M. 1994. "Dopey takes on the T-rex." *Globe and Mail,* September 12, p. A10.

Peterson, Richard R. 1994. "US High Power DBS Frequently Asked Questions List," version 21, 28 December. The DBS Connection: 1480 Lark Avenue, Maplewood, MN 55109. Internet: rich@ncs.com.

Visser, Pat and Bill Barr. 1995. "Canadian Licenses for Digital DTH Issued." *Digital Satellite Facts,* volume 1, issue 17, December 21.

Wall, G., R. Poirier, A. Boucher. 1992. *The DBS Report.* Ottawa: Canadian Cable Television Association.

Part Four

Policy

10

Convergence and the New Technologies

Robert E. Babe

Over the last two or three years media attention has focused on the supposed imminence of an "information highway." *The Globe and Mail* alone published some 513 articles during 1994 containing the words *information highway* (Keenan and Pitts, 1994: p. B1). Defined by Industry Canada as "a network of networks," the information highway is anticipated to meld diverse communication systems into "a seamless Canadian information and communications infra-structure ... linked and integrated with the networks of our trading partners as part of a seamless, global information infrastructure" (Canada, Industry Canada, 1994: 13, 25).

Undergirding the new investment, the industry restructurings and the revised regulatory policies that accompany and indeed comprise information highway initiatives, however, is the notion of conver-gence.

Convergence

The term *convergence* summarizes the blurring of industry or sector boundaries in the communication field. According to the Organiza-tion for Economic Co-operation and Development (OECD), conver-gence has technical, functional and corporate dimensions (Canada, Industry Canada, 1992: 40).

Technical convergence means that increasingly a single mode of transmission (for example a coaxial or fibre optic cable) simultane-ously transmits diverse information: voice, text, data, sound, image. An important contributor to technical convergence has been the digi-tization of information whereby various types of messages (video, sound, text) are converted into patterns of on/off electronic pulses. All forms of information capable of being transmitted electronically can be so digitized.

The second dimension set forth by the OECD is *functional convergence*. Sometimes referred to as "multimedia," functional convergence points to new, hybrid services that combine voice, data, text and/or image. Electronic encyclopedias, for example, combine text, video and sound. While closely allied to technical convergence, functional convergence nonetheless is distinct insofar as this latter term emphasizes services and products as opposed to carriage or modes of transmission.

For some, technical and functional convergence are central (Irwin, 1984: 3; de Sola Pool, 1990: 17-18). Limiting analysis to technical and functional aspects, however, is equivalent to accepting the doctrine of technological determinism (see Babe [1990]; Winner [1977]). *Corporate convergence*, the third dimension recognized by the OECD and Industry Canada, however, belies that position. Corporate convergence refers to mergers, amalgamations and diversifications whereby media organizations come to operate across previously distinct industry boundaries. Time Warner, for example, operates in such previously distinct communication sectors as book and periodical publishing, recorded music, movie production and cable TV (Litman and Sochay, 1994: 237). Other examples include Rupert Murdoch's News Corporation, Sony, Disney, Bertelsmann and Matsushita (Barnet and Cavanagh, 1994). In Canada, Rogers Communications, Inc. is active in newspaper and magazine publishing, long-distance and cellular telephony, cable TV and radio/television broadcasting. Corporate convergence indicates that factors other than merely technical ones are entailed in the blurring of industry boundaries; this is a major theme of the chapter.

Business activity of course takes place only within a legal/policy framework. Convergence therefore, is to be understood as taking place within a context of law and policy. Since law and policy, however, can either encourage or discourage convergence, the deeper question to be explored concerns what factors influence or determine government policy.

Convergence, arguably, is the single most important communication policy issue of the 1990s. This is because convergence relates closely to such basic geopolitical trends and issues as the erosion of national sovereignty and the concomitant growth in transnational corporate power; the controversy over whether government should be a major policy planner as opposed to merely a market facilitator; the debate over whether information/communication are to be treated as instruments of social/political/cultural policy, or merely as commodities; questions of continued universal access to telecommunications and information in the context of widening gaps between the information-rich and the information-poor, both domestically and internationally. Elsewhere I have suggested that convergence also has important environmental implications (Babe, 1995).

To understand convergence in all its aspects — including the technical, functional, corporate and legislative/regulatory — a historical perspective is required on how a *diverged* communication industry structure emerged. Historical *di*vergence, therefore, is addressed next.

Divergence

Traditionally, information/communication have been thought to embrace three distinct sectors: publishing (that is, periodical and book publishing, and by extension movie production); telecommunications (the postal service, telegraphs, telephones and more recently computer-communication networks); and broadcasting (the radiation by transmitter of radio and television signals). These three sectors, although distinct for decades, did not however arise as singular entities. Nor did an inherent technological imperative dictate their segregation. Rather, the three sectors were initially conjoined, and segregation was effected through conscious acts by corporate players and government officials; as a result analysts today should look first to government policy and the exercise of corporate power to explain convergence, rather than to technological or engineering factors.

Divergence of Telecommunications and Publishing (1910)

The daily press and the telegraph emerged together in the 1840s. From the outset, they were reliant upon one another for development. The press required the immediacy of the telegraph to obtain dispatches about faraway events that had occurred within the previous twenty-four hours. The telegraph, on the other hand, was financially dependent on the daily press as its single largest class of customer.

Customer-supplier dependencies made functional and corporate integration profitable. Indeed from the 1850s until 1910, apart from a few professional journalists in the major cities, the only news correspondents were telegraph operators (Rutherford, 1982: 10).

This meant that the only Canadian newswire services in these developmental years were ones provided by telegraph companies (Nichols, 1948: 10). When, in 1895, Canadian Pacific Telegraph Company (aligned with the railway) secured exclusive Canadian rights to the American Associated Press newswire, virtually every Canadian daily thereafter needed to subscribe to Canadian Pacific's news service and to utilize its telegraph lines. Canadian Pacific's exclusive right to the AP newswire, in other words, helped extend its dominance not only in collecting and selling Canadian news but in transmitting journalistic messages as well: CP adroitly bundled its telegraphic press transmission and its news services together so that one could not be procured without the other. Likewise in the United States, restrictive arrangements between the dominant telegraphic interests (viz., Western Union) and the dominant newswire service (Associated Press), were implemented to subdue and eliminate competition in both fields (Harlow, [1936] 1971).

Canadian Pacific dominated newsgathering in Canada until 1910, at which time the Canadian Railway Commission, upon complaint of three Winnipeg dailies, ruled that Canadian Pacific Telegraph's press rates were unduly discriminatory and hence unlawful, whereupon Canadian Pacific and its major rival, the Great North Western Telegraph Company, abandoned the newsgathering field, giving rise to Canadian Press as a newspaper-owned, newsgathering cooperative. Thus was inaugurated the era of the communication common carrier.

Divergence of Broadcasting and Telephony (1923)

The initial high degree of corporate, functional and technical integration between telephony and broadcasting in the United States, and its subsequent dissolution, have been described by a number of commentators (Danielian, [1939] 1974; Harlow, [1936] 1971; Barnouw, 1978; United States, Federal Communications Commission, [1939] 1974; and Kern, 1983). Less well known, however, is the parallel history in Canada.

Prior to World War I, wireless transmissions were termed "radio telegraphy" and "radio telephony." Radio at the time, in other words, was conceived as being merely a mode of point to point (primarily ship-to-shore) communication — an extension of wire telephony and wire telegraphy.

Electronic point-to-multipoint communication, on the other hand, what we today refer to as "broadcasting," at that time was a service offered occasionally by telephone systems. Telephone companies sometimes diffused operas, sermons, election returns, popular entertainment, and news to their subscribers, thereby prefiguring modern cable television systems by seventy years or more.

With the armistice in 1918, however, radio equipment manufacturers in both the United States and Canada became interested in new markets to offset dwindling military sales. First to experiment with radio for direct-to-home transmissions were Canadian Marconi (operating XWA, later CFCF, Montreal) and Westinghouse (owner of KDKA, Pittsburgh). Full development of radio as a mode of point-to-multipoint transmission was stymied, however, on account of a patent deadlock among telephone, radio equipment manufacturing and radio-transmitting interests. American Telephone and Telegraph Company (AT&T), for instance, which had proprietary and patent links to the Bell Telephone Company of Canada, envisaged monopoly control over radio broadcasting, which it termed toll broadcasting, a field it foresaw as developing in accordance with the principles of the common carrier.

For the U.S., the patent dispute was resolved partially in 1920 and more fully in 1926 when rivals pooled their patents and split markets. In Canada, a similar settlement was signed in 1923 by subsidiaries and affiliates of foreign-owned firms. As described in the Bell Telephone Company of Canada's *Annual Report to Shareholders* for the year 1923,

An agreement has been concluded with the Canadian General Electric Company, the Northern Electric Company, the Marconi Wireless Telegraph Company, the Canadian Westinghouse and the International Western Electric Company, covering the use by all for radio purposes of the respective patents of each concern. Under the terms of the agreement, each of the companies agrees to the use of its patents within the natural field of such other company.

The Marconi Company will have the use of all the patents for wireless telegraph purposes; The Bell Telephone Company of Canada for the purposes of public telephone communication; and the manufacturing companies, including the Marconi Company, for the purposes of manufacture and sale (Bell Telephone Company of Canada, 1923: 8).

Table 10-1
Characteristics of the Classic, Three-Sector Communication Field

	Publishing	Broadcasting	Telecommunications
Technology	Printing press, hard copy distribution	Transmitters	Wires, cables, satellites, switching centres
Competition and Entry Conditions	Easy entry, market forces	Limited entry through restricted licensing of radio frequencies	Monopolistic; licences, franchises and charters; high entry barriers
Vertical Integration	Complete between carriage and content	Complete between carriage and content	Absent, common carrier only, not a content originator
Regulation and Special Legislation	Market forces (Competition Act), copyright law; S. 19(1) of Income Tax Act favouring advertising placed in domestic media	Cultural regulation, licensing; Radiocommunication Act, Broadcasting Act, S. 19(1) of the Income Tax Act favouring advertising placed in domestic media	Public utility regulation of prices and profits; Railway Act (now the Telecommunications Act), and company charters
Services	Information distributed from central point to customers who pay directly, frequently financed also by advertising	Information radiated spatially; financed by advertisers or taxation	Transport of messages originated by customers who pay directly
Nature of the Communication	Point to mass, largely one-way	Point to mass, one-way	Point to point, two-way
Aims of Public Policy	Marketplace of ideas; protection of authors' rights. Canadian ownership favoured through Income Tax Act (Bill C-58); promotion of an indigenous industry	Nation-building, social and cultural improvement, marketplace of ideas; universal service. Canadian content and other regulations; Bill C-58	Just and reasonable access; no undue preference or unjust discrimination; low cost, efficient, universal service; common carriage; profit regulation

Source: Adapted from Robert E. Babe. 1990. *Telecommunications in Canada: Technology Industry and Government*. Toronto: University of Toronto Press, 17.

That agreement was the primary cause of the technical, functional and corporate divergence in Canada between broadcasting and telecommunications. Not only were facilities thereafter segregated and deployed for distinct services, in 1932 a unique legal/policy/regulatory framework for broadcasting was created as well.

Diverged Industry Characteristics

Table 10-1 summarizes features of the classic, diverged, three-sector communication field. The remainder of the section describes and amplifies these features.

Publishing

Historically, the publishing industry has centred on the printing press. The publisher's role has been to select and assemble texts from various contributors for distribution and sale to customers.

In the newspaper industry, the arrangement between publisher and contributor has frequently been that of employer-employee, but not always: letters to the editor represent publishers' discretionary inclusion of unremunerated content from readers, while commissioned and syndicated materials are procured in the absence of an employer-employee relationship. In addition, and most significantly, advertisers pay publishers to carry messages of the advertisers' choosing, albeit subject to the publishers' discretion. Since the owner of the means of production/distribution retains discretionary control over what materials are included and excluded (subject, of course, to laws regarding national security, police matters, obscenity and defamation), vertical integration between content and carriage, that is, common control over both the message and the medium, characterizes publishing.

For publishing, vertical integration between content and carriage traditionally has been justified by the liberal or libertarian presumption of effective competition. This doctrine assumes that the marketplace for commoditized information will generally be sufficient to constrain, at least to tolerable levels, control over flows of knowledge or information by individual publishers. Despite the existence of a highly concentrated daily press in Canada (Babe, 1988: 1321-2; Babe, 1996; Winter, 1994), proposals for reform, for example the ones set out by the Royal Commission on Newspapers (Canada, 1981: 237-255), remain to be implemented, and the presumption of effective competition remains.

Besides highly concentrated control, there are other reasons for questioning the liberal position. The presumed identity of, or at least consistency between, the Miltonian ideal of a marketplace of ideas and the economic marketplace for commoditized information, that is the presumed consistency between dialogue, debate and dialectic in the pursuit of truth on the one hand and the pursuit of profit on the other, needs much more thorough and critical scrutiny than it has received hitherto. The series of media books and articles by Noam Chomsky and Edward S. Herman, for instance, has documented significant omissions and biases in the coverage of international news by America's elite media, coverage upon which the rest of America's mainstream media rely (see, for example, Chomsky [1989]; Chomsky and Herman [1979]; Herman [1989]; and Herman [1994]; see also Ginsberg [1986]; and Badikian [1990]). Likewise for Canada, some perceive a distinct class bias in the reporting of news (Winter, 1992; Hackett, 1991). In this context, political econo-mist Dallas Smythe's observation that for an advertiser-financed press system consumer sovereignty resides much more with adver-tisers than with readers is most instructive (Smythe, 1981).

Broadcasting

Over the years broadcasting has shared certain characteristics with publishing. For both sectors, a central node gathers messages for distribution to multiple points. Moreover, both sectors have been characterized by vertical integration whereby control over the means of distribution has carried with it control over content. Furthermore, both sectors have accepted payment in return for diffusing messages (advertising).

There have been, however, important differences. Whereas pub-lishing has centred on the printing press, broadcasting has been based on the transmitter. The radio frequency spectrum used in over-the-air broadcasting is a finite and scarce resource that can be and is put to alternative uses (mobile communication, telephony and so forth). In Canada, this radio frequency resource has been declared public prop-erty, and therefore non-market mechanisms — licensing and public ownership — have been used to apportion it among uses and users (Babe and Slayton, 1980; Babe, 1979: 173-209). Furthermore, for privately owned Canadian broadcasting, a *quid pro quo* has been exacted by government in return for derogating publicly owned radio frequencies to the pursuit of private gain. The federal government, through its regulatory board, the Canadian Radio-television and

Telecommunications Commission, has required private broadcasters to comply for instance with Canadian-content quotas in order that broadcasting might help "safeguard, enrich and strengthen the cultural, political, social and economic fabric of Canada" (1968 Broadcasting Act).

Competition in broadcasting, therefore, far from being envisaged as ensuring a "marketplace of ideas" as in publishing, has been viewed more sceptically. Competitive entry into profitable programming niches, it has been maintained, inevitably decreases overall profits, making it difficult to sustain cross-subsidies for "meritorious" but inherently unprofitable programming. Indeed, Keith Spicer, chairman of the CRTC, speculated in a 1994 speech to communication students at the University of Ottawa that the commission would be unable to sustain Canadian-content regulations in the years to come on account of the proliferation of competing television and radio outlets, including cable-only specialty channels and direct-broadcast satellite channels. If Spicer is correct, the policy framework for broadcasting will approach more closely the one for publishing, with market forces becoming ever more decisive.

Another noteworthy difference is that publishers retain direct contact with the reading public, or at least with retailers, whereas broadcasting signals historically have been diffused rather indiscriminately for general reception by audiences that remain anonymous, except in a statistical sense. From this perspective, therefore, signal scrambling and descrambling, characteristic of pay-television and specialty channels delivered by cable or satellites to paying subscribers, converge publishing and broadcasting, pointing to heightened commodity (or user-pay) treatment of broadcast-type information.

Telecommunications

Historically, much of telecommunications has been considered to be "naturally" monopolized on account of purportedly large economies of scale. The presumed natural monopoly properties of telecommunications led in turn to enactments of special legislation to regulate profits and prices. Rates charged to the public by federally regulated telecommunication carriers, for instance, became subject to regulatory approval by predecessors of the CRTC in 1906, while public ownership was sometimes introduced at provincial and municipal levels as an alternative or complementary mode of protecting the public (Babe, 1990).

A second distinction between telecommunications and broadcasting/publishing stems from the instantaneous, bidirectional, point-to-point nature of telecommunications. Both publishing and broadcasting, in contrast, historically have been predominantly one-way, point-to-multipoint communication services.

Perhaps the most striking difference, however, has been the absence, by and large, in telecommunications of vertical integration between carriage and content; indeed telecommunications firms offering service to the public have been treated as common carriers, meaning that they must accept, without discrimination, all message senders who pay the government-approved tariffs. Furthermore, as common carriers, they have not been permitted to alter messages originated by others for transmission over their facilities. The concern has been that, without such safeguards, monopoly might be extended from ownership of facilities to message originations (for example, into the news agency business, or newspaper publishing or into broadcast programming). Telephone companies to date have been explicitly precluded by legislation and regulatory policy from holding broadcasting (including cable TV) licences.

Finally, in telephony, universal service has historically been pursued through principles of cost averaging and cross-subsidization, somewhat analogous to the pursuit of the "public-service" or "nation-building" ethic characterizing broadcasting. Whereas in competitive, "market-driven" situations, proponents maintain, prices tend to be driven by costs, for historically monopolized telephony high profit centres (such as long distance) have been used to cross-subsidize rural and basic local service. While cost averaging and cross-subsidization have undoubtedly been instrumental in achieving near universality of service, there have been other consequences as well. As noted elsewhere, cross-subsidies can and have been used to extend dominance from the original monopoly into other domains through non-compensatory (predatory) pricing (Babe, 1990).

Three Instances of Convergence (Re-convergence)

Cable TV and the Convergence of Telephony with Broadcasting

Cable television is an early, and continuing, instance of technical (but, to date, suppressed functional and corporate) convergence. Since its inception in the early 1950s, cable TV has proven to be problematic for maintaining the bifurcation between the telecommunications and broadcasting sectors. On the one hand, cable television's historic *raison d'être* has been to rediffuse off-air broadcasting signals to the home. Consequently, even though cable TV itself radiates no signals, legislation enacted in 1968 declared cable to constitute a component of the Canadian broadcasting system (Broadcasting Act, 1968), and the industry has been regulated under authority of the Broadcasting Act ever since: renewable licences are issued to cable firms; Canadian content-requirements, in terms of priority of signals, are applied to the industry; larger cable systems are required to contribute financially to the production of Canadian television programs.

On the other hand, in providing a direct wire connection to the home, cable TV has resembled telephone systems, and indeed in recognition of this fact, a form of price regulation, albeit not nearly as stringent as in the case of the telephone industry, has been applied to cable TV. Moreover, the cable industry has been dependent upon telephone companies for poles, ducts and rights-of-way to lay its coaxial cable network.

Telephone companies, recognizing early on the potentially rivalrous nature of cable TV, took advantage of the latter's need for telco pole and duct access to enforce technical segregation. In federally regulated territories until 1977, and in some other jurisdictions until much later, telephone companies granted cable companies access to duct and pole space only under conditions that precluded all forms of service competition. By telephone company fiat, cable companies were prohibited from attaching their own cables to telephone company property; cable systems were required to lease cables (and in some cases amplifiers and other equipment) from telephone companies. Retaining ownership of cables enabled telephone companies to prohibit certain modes of message transmission. Typically precluded were: (1) material not part of or ancillary to broadcasts or cablecasts; (2) messages for distribution point-to-point, or to only a portion of the network (for example pay-television and certain educational and industrial programming); (3) bidirectional messages and conversations; and (4) facilities used in conjunction with, or interconnected to, telephone switching centres. A telco-cable TV contract dating from the late 1960's is reprinted in Babe ([1972] 1974: 429-469); the arrangements are discussed also in Babe, (1974, 1975).

In 1977, however, for Bell Canada's territory at least, such restrictions were terminated by the CRTC, which ordered Bell to permit reasonable pole access by cable companies in Ontario and Quebec, thereby enabling cable systems to begin offering pay-television, specialty channels, and an increasing array of non-programming services, all previously precluded by telephone company rules. Restrictions were subsequently lifted in other jurisdictions as well, paving the way for greater technical and functional convergence between broadcasting and telecommunications.

The federal government to date has helped preserve corporate divergence, however, by refusing to issue cable TV licences to telephone companies, a policy that seems likely to be lifted within the foreseeable future (CRTC, 1995b: 7). In the United States, the ban on telephone companies owning and operating cable systems in locations other than where they currently offer telephone service has already been lifted (Reuters, 1994: B16). In its September 1994 Review of Regulatory Framework decision, the CRTC advocated direct competition between cable and telephone companies for both local telephone service and video programming/distribution (CRTC, 1994: 45-51). Likewise, in its 1995 report to the government on the information highway, the CRTC declared:

> There should be no fixed transition period before telephone companies are permitted to compete in the core cable business. They should be permitted to enter the cable business as soon as barriers to effective competition in the local telephone business are removed (CRTC, 1995: 7).

Similarly, the Information Highway Advisory Council recommended that competition between telephone and cable companies be inaugurated quickly as an essential element of an information highway strategy (Canada, Information Highway Advisory Council, 1995: 100-101).

Moreover, the legal, regulatory and policy frameworks for telecommunications and broadcasting are converging not only with one another, but also with the framework long associated with publishing, which is to say a market-based framework for the sale of commoditized (user-pay) information. Indeed the very goals for broadcasting and telecommunications are increasingly seen by policy-makers as synonymous with whatever the market and technology may bring (Babe, 1995: chapter 5). In its landmark 1994 regulatory framework decision, for example, the CRTC declared:

Evolving communications technologies will continue to provide the potential for services, both social and commercial, to be offered in a variety of new ways. Use by individuals, businesses and institutions of Canada's communications systems is creating electronic marketplaces and virtual communities that transcend geographic boundaries and which are increasingly interactive and transactional in nature. Underlying these phenomena is a political, economic and cultural revolution, in which Canadians are redefining themselves and their business, social and institutional environment in ways that outpace the ability of regulators to recognize and define, let alone control (CRTC, 1994: 49).

In this extract the commission stated, in effect, that it is powerless to affect matters substantially, given the omnipotent forces of market, technology and evolution.

Likewise, in opening the CRTC's hearings on the information highway, chairman Keith Spicer intoned,

This hearing comes at a critical time in the history of communications. Within a very short period of time, we've witnessed the virtual explosion of information technologies that will someday no doubt reshape our lives in ways that even the richest and wisest entrepreneurs haven't begun to dream of. And Canada is at the forefront of this technological revolution that seemed a long way off only a short time ago (Spicer, 1995).

Such an unadulterated, if not indeed blind, faith in the inevitable beneficence of technological outcomes can only be described as technological determinism.

Satellites and the Converging of Telephony and Broadcasting

Like cable TV, communication satellites are seemingly another instance of a technology challenging historical demarcations among communication sectors. Communication satellites are used to diffuse broadcasting material from origination points to television networks, to broadcasting stations and cable systems and even directly to home receivers. They are also used to transmit voice and data as components of larger, point-to-point messaging systems. For print periodicals, such as *The Globe and Mail*, satellites relay editorial content to printing presses at diverse locations. As was the case with cable television, however, so too do communication satellites point to the centrality of both public policy and private corporate powerplays in setting in motion and maintaining processes of divergence and convergence.

When incorporating Telesat Canada by act of Parliament in 1969, the government took steps to ensure a degree of technical and corporate segregation between satellites and telephone systems. In its white paper (Canada, Department of Industry, 1968) the government stated that it wanted to maintain the possibility of competition between the media. Nonetheless, in response to representations from the telephone industry, and cognizant that for financial viability Telesat needed lots of business from telephone companies, the government agreed that Telesat would be precluded from leasing channels to parties other than common carriers and those non-carrier entities prepared to lease full transponders (equivalent to 960 voice telephone channels) on long-term (five-year) contracts, without possibility of resale or sharing of channels. As well, the government allowed terrestrial telecommunication carriers to subscribe to fifty per cent (less one share) of Telesat's stock, the federal government retaining the other fifty per cent (plus one share).

In 1976, Telesat needed to plan for a new generation of satellites as its existing capacity was scheduled to become obsolete within a few years. At this point the telcos informed the satellite company that they would not renew their leases unless Telesat joined their consortium (then called the TransCanada Telephone System or TCTS, subsequently renamed Telecom Canada, and today known as Stentor). By joining TCTS, Telesat obtained a guaranteed rate of return on investment, courtesy of the telephone companies, irrespective of whether its facilities were used or not. In return, however, Telesat ceded control over the planning and operation of its ground stations to the telcos, and was officially designated a carriers' carrier, that is, it was thereafter to be prohibited from leasing channels directly to third parties such as the CBC. While the Telesat-TCTS agreement was rejected by the CRTC after lengthy public hearings, the federal cabinet overturned the commission's decision, and the agreement was allowed to stand.

Over the next few years, the CRTC issued a number of decisions designed to reassert a degree of independence for Telesat's management, endeavouring to promote a form of corporate divergence. In 1981, for instance, it ordered Telesat to open up its customer base to all potential clients, and as well no longer to refuse to lease partial channels, a decision that was, however, overturned by the federal cabinet. Again, in 1984, the CRTC ruled that Telesat had to permit licensed broadcasters to resell excess capacity to other broadcasters, while in 1986, the commission approved a revised connection agreement between Telesat and TCTS (at the time, Telecom Canada) whereby Telesat's customer base would no longer be limited to broadcasting undertakings and specified common carriers.

While these regulatory measures served to separate Telesat somewhat from the telephone operating companies, the initiatives were largely negated on 23 October 1991 when the federal government tabled in the House of Commons Bill C-38, the Telesat Canada Reorganization and Divestiture Act. That act provided for the divestiture of the government's approximately 50 per cent ownership of Telesat. As forecast (Babe, 1991), sale of the government's stock to the highest bidder resulted in Telesat being enfolded more completely within the managerial control of the telephone industry. The successful bidder for the government's shares was Alouette Telecommunications Inc., a consortium of major telephone companies plus Spar Aerospace (manufacturer of Telesat's satellites). Also as forecast (Babe, 1991), Telesat immediately underwent downsizing. For 1992, Telesat posted losses of $30 million and projected further losses of $60 million over the next two years. Soon Telesat dismissed 250 of its workers, reducing employees to 580 by early 1993 (Goff and Lacasse, 1993: 1). By January 1994, firmly under telephone industry control, a diminished Telesat retained only 520 employees (Hill, 1994: G1).

Meanwhile, satellites are also becoming increasingly integrated into the broadcasting system. The CBC utilized satellites even in Telesat's early years. Since that time television networks such as TVOntario and Global also have been using Telesat to distribute signals to transmitters for broadcast. Another important customer for Telesat has been Cancom (Canadian Satellite Communications Inc.), licensed initially to provide a package of U.S. and Canadian off-air signals to remote areas for rediffusion by small cable systems. In more recent years, virtually all Canadian cable systems have come to rely on satellites for reception of an array of American and Canadian specialty channels and for distant superstations. Advanced techniques permit digital video compression (DVC), whereby as many as five digitized channels can be squeezed onto the bandwidth required by one conventional (analogue) channel (Kainz, 1994: C3).

At the time this chapter was being prepared, the CRTC was holding hearings on the licensing of direct-to-home (DTH) satellite broadcast operations, posing thereby a major challenge not only for traditional broadcasters, but for the cable-television industry as well. One of the principal concerns seeking a licence is controlled by Bell Canada.

Information Highway and Media Re-Convergence

In October 1993, hard on the heels of U.S. Vice-President Al Gore's promotion of an information highway for the United States, the consortium of Canada's major telephone companies (Stentor Telecom Policy Inc.), announced the Beacon Initiative, a plan to build "a national information highway capable of carrying voice, text, data, graphics and video services to and from all Canadians," also providing "universal access to basic and advanced communications and information services through a network of many networks, owned and operated by different service providers" (Stentor, 1993a: 5). The information highway is the next and perhaps ultimate chapter in the convergence saga.

In contemplating the integration of networks "owned and operated by different service providers," this Beacon Initiative departed significantly from previous telephone company recommendations. During the 1970s, telcos had advocated implementation of a Single Integrated Network (SIN) under their control whereby they would lease capacity on (upgraded) local distribution facilities to, *inter alia*, licensed cable television companies. In the 1980s, telcos, now emphasizing digitized communication, renamed their proposed monopoly ISDN (Integrated Services Digital Network) (Babe, 1990: 217, 243). The most recent strategy, however, envisages a "network of networks" to be comprised of many smaller networks owned by various parties but integrated with facilities controlled by the telephone companies.

It is imperative, Stentor admonished, that action proceed immediately on implementing an information highway, the gains being so immense and the costs of delay so gargantuan. On the one hand, according to Stentor, an information highway will provide "an economic opportunity by delivering heightened competitiveness, new revenue sources and greatly enhanced market reach to businesses of all sizes and scope of operation, regardless of geographic location; it will herald a new world for the educational and cultural industries by eliminating the restrictions of time and distance; and it holds the potential of helping to ensure our national health care system and other governmental services remain universal and viable." Conversely, "to not act on this vision, is to sabotage our own future" (Stentor, 1993b).

Soon the telephone companies had enlisted the enthusiastic support of the government. The January 1994 Speech from the Throne announced the government's intention to develop a Canadian strategy for an information highway. Shortly thereafter, Industry Minister John Manley established the Information Highway Advisory Council, consisting of nineteen business persons (largely CEOs from such vested interests as Bell, Stentor, IBM, Unitel, broadcasting and cable companies), and eleven representatives from labour, consumer, education, computer network and public interest groups. One of the ironies of this council was the holding of its deliberations in camera. In September 1994, the CRTC published its Review of Regulatory Framework decision designed to help telephone companies put in place an information highway. On October 11, 1994, the Governor-in-Council issued Order-in-Council P.C. 1994-1689 outlining the government's current policy framework for new communication technologies, and also ordering the CRTC to report "on a number of wide-ranging questions covering three broad areas, namely facilities, content and competition." In ordering this review the government stated that "the convergence of media as well as technologies has huge implications for both Canadian culture and our economy" (Canada Gazette, Part 1, 29 October 1994: 4321). On 19 May 1994, the CRTC published its report on the information highway (CRTC, 1995b.; see also CRTC, 1995a), envisaging full competition between telephone and cable companies in both the local telephone exchange services market and in the market for cable TV services. As well, the CRTC foresaw the likelihood that telephone companies would enter program origination and other content services activities. Then, in September 1995, the government's Information Highway Advisory Council issued its final report, advocating direct competition wherever possible. There can be little doubt, then, that in the eyes of the federal government, convergence and the information highway are not only imminent, but are to be welcomed and supported.

The Political Economy of Re-convergence

Radical changes are afoot for the policy framework within which Canadian information/communication industries operate. A few of the interrelated terms describing these changes are: convergence, deregulation, privatization, market-driven, user-pay and, of course, information highway. In fact, convergence is by and large a code word for the deregulation of capital flows in media industries. It is to be emphasized that convergence, information highway, and associated trends and phenomena have wide-ranging implications, and are key components of broader geopolitical trends that encompass free trade agreements, growing divisions between the world's rich and poor, environmental stress, the enfeebling of national governments and the concomitant ascendancy of transnational corporate power (Babe, 1995). Among the groups with keen interest in processes of convergence or re-convergence are Canadian telephone and cable companies; Canadian and foreign program suppliers; transnational businesses; and all others who would further commoditize information.

Canadian telephone and cable companies

As we have seen, Canada's telephone and cable companies have for years been locked in a struggle over the size and nature of their respective domains. Pro-competitive telecommunications policies, particularly in the U.S. and increasingly in Canada, indicate that it is exceedingly unlikely that policy makers in the near and medium terms will permit telephone companies simply to assimilate cable operations in their own territories, as telcos so vigorously recommended for the three decades leading into the 1990s. Meanwhile, computerized scrambling, descrambling and storage devices, bidirectional distributional techniques, digitization, and expanded-channel fibre optics, in conjunction with satellite communications, are making it increasingly lucrative to offer a panoply of pay-per-view and other on-demand informational services over a wide geographic expanse. In this information age, information and communication sectors are among the most rapidly growing, and prospects of greater user-pay, in place of (or, more likely, in conjunction with) advertising, can make plain old telephone service seem decidedly uninspiring.

In Canada, the push for a "network of networks" (information highway) came initially from the telephone companies, zealous to enter video distribution and new on-demand markets, yet fearful lest fibre-using cable systems, perhaps aligned with independent long-distance carriers like Unitel, pre-empt telco participation in the emerging "pay-per," switched, broadband field. Pre-emption from the emerging field by cable TV has been a real concern for telephone companies, despite the latter's disproportionate size, on account of government proscriptions limiting them to common carriage and precluding them from holding broadcasting licences. These restraints, from the telephone company perspective, have necessitated a fundamental revision to the telecommunications regulatory framework, a revision which the CRTC, in its "regulatory framework" decision of 1994, delivered. From a telephone company point of view, it is far better to "converge" industries, and even encounter a degree of "competition," than it is to maintain previous distinctions and thereby be barred from participating in seemingly immensely lucrative emerging markets. The more levels at which telephone companies are permitted to participate — program transmission, advertising, information storage and retrieval, program creation, program scheduling, program exhibition, marketing, billing, switching, provisioning of requisite household equipment and so forth — the better, from the standpoint of corporate growth and profitability.

Canadian and foreign program suppliers

At one level, the interests of program suppliers in expanded broadband, interactive, switched transmission capability are obvious enough: increased transmission capacity should improve terms and likelihood of access, while direct payments by users, possibly in conjunction with advertising, should multiply revenues severalfold. Canadian program creators and other domestic informational providers should be cautioned, however, that access to the emerging information superhighway, as a practical matter, may not be all that easy, or at least lucrative. Information is characterized by almost inexhaustible economies of scale; it is infinitely reproducible at very low incremental cost; moreover, information can be used by some without detracting from use by others. These characteristics mean that enterprises marketing informational products globally have distinct economic and financial advantages over those confined locally, regionally or nationally (Babe, 1995). Hence, the emergence of concentrated, global, media-based conglomerates, as noted in a previous section. These latter media complexes can be expected to gain disproportionately from heightened convergence, as embodied in an internationally interlinked, seamless information highway.

Transnational business

Convergence (re-convergence) and the information highway support trends apparent since the 1950s towards the aggrandizement of transnational corporate power and the concomitant lessening of national sovereignty, the weakening of labour, and the comparative diminution in the relative strength of domestic-only businesses. In a prophetic speech delivered in 1969, Jacques Maisonrouge, then president of IBM World Trade Corporation, opined: "The world's political structures are completely obsolete; the critical issue of our time is the conceptual conflict between the global optimization of resources and the independence of nation states ... For business purposes the boundaries that separate one nation from another are no more real than the equator" (quoted in Barnet and Müller, 1974: 14; and in Mulgan, 1991: 220).

Advanced telecommunications permit transnationals to administer, in real time, activities of foreign divisions from central locales — gleaning information and monitoring activities electronically, dispensing orders and exploiting international divisions of labour (Hepworth, 1990, 1994; Hills, 1994). Modern telecommunications enable transnational managers hastily to relocate production to non-unionized sites where wages are a small fraction of those in Canada, and where transnational companies can benefit from more favourable tax laws, from lax but "business-friendly" environmental standards and from "pro-business" health and safety regulations. As explained by William H. Melody,

As TNCs [transnational corporations] expand through the use of information technologies, they can reduce their dependency upon any single resource supply or production location, thereby enhancing their negotiating power with individual governments, unions, and other groups ... The information technologies become a major tool for TNCs to enhance both their market power and their autonomy in negotiating with all nation-states, whether hinterland producers or home governments ... A revised model of dependency may have to focus on TNCs at the center, and how affected nations relate to them from different positions of dependency (Melody, 1991: 35).

In this regard it is instructive to note some observations by the 1994 Special Joint Committee of the House of Commons and Senate reviewing Canada's foreign policy. According to the Joint Committee, "globalization is erasing time and space, making borders porous, and encouraging continental integration." "Globalization," the report continued, means that "national sovereignty is being reshaped and the power of national governments to control events, reduced" (Canada, Special Joint Committee, 1994: 1). Inducing globalization, in the view of the Joint Committee, has been an "explosion of technology ... a revolution in transportation, communications and information processing." But behind these technologies, the joint committee remarked, stand transnational corporations. Furthermore, the joint committee remarked astutely,

> The transnational mobility of capital generates pressures for deeper harmonization of national policies. In the competition for comparative advantages governments must deal with pressures to cut back on social and environmental programs that may raise the cost of producing goods and services, and to lower corporate taxes (1994: 4).

General Motors, for instance, seeking competitive advantages, by 1992 had closed 12 of its 21 plants in Canada and the U.S. while opening 37 plants (employing more than 42,000 workers) in Mexico's infamous maquiladora free-trade zone, where wages are less than 10 per cent of comparable U.S. wages, and where companies can get away with ecocide due to negligible health and environmental standards. According to Susan Meeker-Lowry, rocks tossed into canals of the Rio Grande cause "black globules [to] bubble from the bottom, releasing an eye-stinging chemical stench" (Meeker-Lowry, 1992: 30). Proliferation of free-trade treaties, when combined with expansive computer/telecommunications networks, such as the projected, globally interconnected information highway, threaten to turn much of the industrialized world into one global maquiladora.

Convergence and the information highway, like free trade, are about reapportioning power from government to business, from domestic to transnational enterprises, from labour to capital, from consumers and producers of public services to consumers and producers of private commodities.

The Information Commodity

We live both in the Information Age and in a new Golden Age of Global Capitalism, a veritable New World Order. But these "ages" are contradictory: as noted above, information's epiphenomenal character is fundamentally inconsistent with commodity treatment.

Historically, information/knowledge has been afforded treatment as a public good and as a community resource, not merely as a commodity: folklore, public education, libraries, museums, access to information legislation, sponsorship of the arts, public broadcasting, freedom of speech and of the press — all these exemplify this non-market tradition of information as a community resource and as a public good, as well as a fundamental human right. Convergence and the information highway, however, and the accompanying de-regulation/privatization of communication sectors, are enhancing the powers of those who desire to turn information further into a commodity at the expense of its being a public resource. The information highway makes it much more feasible than hitherto to deliver for a fee specific bundles of information to target audiences. Ability to pay will surely come to be of even greater significance in future years, giving rise to even sharper divisions between the world's information rich and the poor. The poor face the risk of being more stringently excluded unless steps are taken to *de*commoditize information — steps, however, that are incongruent with the very logic of an information highway.

Canada, being a net importer of information from the U.S., is likely to suffer financially from the expanded transmission capacity and the enhanced capabilities to make information a commodity — the very essence of the information highway and of convergence. These features will dramatically magnify Canada's trade imbalance. According to Rohan Samarajiva, Canada has for years experienced rapidly growing deficits in services. Canada's deficits in the balance of trade due to royalties, patents and trademarks amounted to $800 million to $1 billion per year for the period 1983–87, while trade in films and broadcasting accounted for a further $160 to $180 million per year over the same period (Samarajiva, 1993: 166-8). No wonder the U.S. withdrew from UNESCO when that body insisted that information be treated more as a resource than as a commodity (Preston, Herman and Schiller, 1989). Canada, by contrast, in welcoming uncritically convergence and the information highway, acts perversely.

Conclusion

Convergence and new communication technologies, as epitomized by information highway initiatives, are part and parcel of a neo-conservative, transnational corporate agenda of globalization, de-regulation, privatization and the further unleashing of augmented, unencumbered market forces. It is important that they be understood in these terms, rather than (as so much of the convergence and information highway literature and policy posturing would have us believe) as inevitable consequences of technological evolution.

References

Andres, Edmund L. 1994. "Stepping Into an Uncertain Future: Bell Atlantic Ready to Provide Films, TV Programming." *Ottawa Citizen*, 29 October, p. F 7.

Babe, Robert E. 1996 "Canada." In *Media Ownership and Control, Global Report Series*, edited by Vicki Macleod. London: International Institute of Communications.

————. 1995. *Communication and the Transformation of Economics: Essays in Information, Public Policy, and Political Economy*. Boulder, Colorado: Westview Press.

————. 1994. "The Place of Information in Economics." In *Information and Communication in Economics*. Robert E. Babe (ed.). Boston/Dordrecht/London: Kluwer Academic Publishers, pp. 41-67.

————. 1991. Testimony Before House of Commons Legislative Committee on Bill C-58, Re Telesat Canada, 3 December 1991.

————. 1990. *Telecommunications in Canada: Technology, Industry and Government*. Toronto: University of Toronto Press.

————. 1988. "Media Ownership." *Canadian Encyclopedia*. Edmonton, Alberta: Hurtig Publishers, pp. 1321-2.

————. 1979. *Canadian Television Broadcasting Structure, Performance and Regulation*. Ottawa: Supply and Services for the Economic Council of Canada.

————. 1975. *Cable Television and Telecommunications in Canada*. East Lansing, Michigan: Bureau of Business and Economic Research, Michigan State University.

————. 1974. "Public and Private Regulation of Cable Television: A Case Study of Technological Change and Relative Power." *Canadian Public Administration* 17 (2), pp. 187-225.

————. [1972] 1974. *The Economics of the Canadian Cable Television Industry*. Ph.D. thesis, 1972, Michigan State University. Ann Arbor, Michigan: University Microfilms.

Babe, Robert E. and Philip Slayton. 1980. *Competitive Procedures for Broadcasting — Renewals and Transfers*. Study prepared for Department of Communications.

Badikian, Ben H. 1990. *The Media Monopoly*. 3rd edition. Boston: Beacon Press.

Barnet, Richard J., and John Cavanagh. 1994. *Global Dreams: Imperial Corporations and the New World Order*. New York: Simon and Schuster.

Barnet, Richard J. and Ronald E. Müller. 1974. *Global Reach: The Power of the Multinational Corporations*. New York: Simon and Schuster.

Barnouw, Eric. 1978. *The Sponsor: Notes on a Modern Potentate*. New York: Oxford University Press.

Bell Telephone Company of Canada. 1923. *Annual Report*.

Canada. 1992. *Convergence: Competition and Cooperation — Policy and Regulation Affecting Local Telephone and Cable Networks*. Report of the Co-chairs of the Local Networks Convergence Committee. Ottawa: Minister of Supply and Services.

Canada. Canadian Radio-television and Telecommunications Commission. 1995a. *Public Hearing on Convergence: Overview of Issues*. 6 March.

————. Canadian Radio-television and Telecommunications Commission. 1995b. *Competition and Culture on Canada's Information Highway: Managing the Realities of Transition*. Ottawa: Public Works and Government Services Canada.

————. Canadian Radio-television and Telecommunications Commission. 1994. "Review of Regulatory Framework." Telecom Decision CRTC 94-19, 16 September.

————. Department of Industry. 1968. *White Paper on a Domestic Satellite System for Canada.* Ottawa: Queen's Printer.

————. Industry Canada. 1994. *The Canadian Information Highway: Building Canada's Information and Communications Infrastructure.* Ottawa: Supply and Services.

————. Information Highway Advisory Council. 1995. *Final Report: The Challenge of the Information Highway, Connection Community Content.* Ottawa: Minister of Supply and Services.

————. Royal Commission on Newspapers. 1981. *Report.* Ottawa: Supply and Services.

————. Special Joint Committee of the Senate and the House of Commons Reviewing Canadian Foreign Policy. 1994. *Canada's Foreign Policy: Principles and Priorities for the Future.* Ottawa: Publications Service, Parliamentary Publications Directorate.

Chomsky, Noam 1989. *Necessary Illusions.* Toronto: CBC Enterprises.

Chomsky, Noam, and Edward S. Herman. 1979. *The Political Economy of Human Rights* (2 volumes). Montreal: Black Rose Books.

Danelian, N.R. [1939] 1974. *AT&T: The Story of Industrial Conquest.* New York: Arno Press.

de Sola Pool, Ithiel. 1990. *Technologies Without Boundaries: On Telecommunications in a Global Age.* Eli M. Noam (ed.). Cambridge, Massachusetts: Harvard University Press.

Ginsberg, Benjamin. 1986. *The Captive Public: How Mass Opinion Promotes State Power.* New York: Basic Books.

Goff, Kristin, and Dominique Lacasse. 1994. "Telesat Cuts 200 Workers." *Ottawa Citizen,* 5 March, p. 1.

Harlow, Alvin F. [1936] 1971. *Old Wires and New Waves.* New York: Arno Press.

Hackett, Robert A. 1991. *News and Dissent: The Press and the Politics of Peace in Canada.* Norwood, New Jersey: Ablex Publishing Corporation.

Herman, Edward S. 1989. "U.S. Mass Media Coverage of the U.S. Withdrawal From UNESCO." In William Preston, Jr., Edward S. Herman, and Herbert I. Schiller (eds.). *Hope & Folly: The United States and Unesco 1945–1985.* Minneapolis: University of Minnesota Press., pp. 203–284.

Herman, Edward S. 1994. "All the Editorials Fit to Print: The Politics of 'Newsworthiness.'" In *Information and Communication in Economics.* Robert E. Babe (ed.). Boston/London/Dordrecht: Kluwer Academic Publishers, pp. 177-199.

Hepworth, Mark. 1990. *Geography of the Information Economy.* New York/London: Guilford Press.

Hill, Bert. 1994. "Satellite Troubles Add to Woes." *Ottawa Citizen,* 22 January, p. G1.

Hills, Jill. 1994. "Communication, Information, and Transnational Enterprise." In *Information and Communication in Economics.* Robert E. Babe (ed.). Boston/Dordrecht/London: Kluwer Academic Publishers, pp. 293_320.

Irwin, Manley. 1971. *The Telecommunications Industry.* New York: Praeger.

Kainz, Alana. 1994. "CRTC Frees Telesat to Set Digital Fees." *Ottawa Citizen*, 4 October, p. C3.

Keenan, Greg, and Gordon Pitts. 1994. "Who? What? How Much? A Quiz." *The Globe and Mail Report on Business*. 24 December, pp. B1 and B15.

Kern, Stephen. 1983. *The Culture of Time and Space, 1880–1918.* Cambridge: Harvard University Press.

Litman, Barry R., and Scott Sochay. 1994. "The Emerging Mass Media Environment." In *Information and Communication in Economics*. Robert E. Babe (ed.). Boston/Dordrecht/London: Kluwer Academic Publishers, pp. 233-268.

Markoff, John. 1993. "Big Guns Stake Out New TV Frontier." *The Globe and Mail Report on Business*, 7 April, p. B4.

Meeker-Lowry, Susan. 1992. "Maquiladoras: A Preview of Free Trade." *Z Magazine*, October, pp. 25-30.

Melody, William. 1991. "The Information Society: The Transnational Economic Context and its Implications." In *Transnational Communications: Wiring the Third World.*" Gerald Sussman and John A. Lent (eds.). Newbury Park/London/New Delhi: Sage Publications, pp. 27-41.

Mulgan, G. J. 1991. *Communication and Control: Networks and the New Economies of Communication.* New York/London: Guilford Press.

Nelson, Joyce. 1989. *The Sultans of Sleaze. Public Relations and the Media.* Toronto: Between the Lines.

Nichols, M. E. 1948. *(CP): The Story of Canadian Press.* Toronto: Ryerson.

Reuters. 1994. "U.S. West Continues Cable Quest." *The Globe and Mail Report on Business*. 16 July, p. B16.

Rutherford, Paul. 1982. *A Victorian Authority: The Daily Press in Late Nineteenth Century Canada.* Toronto: University of Toronto Press.

Samarajiva, Rohan. 1993. "Down Dependency Road? The Canada-U.S. Free Trade Agreement and Canada's Copyright Amendments of 1988." In *Illuminating the Blindspots: Essays Honoring Dallas W. Smythe*. Janet Wasko, Vincent Mosco and Manjunath Pendakur (eds.). Norwood, New Jersey: Ablex Publishing Corporation.

Schumacher, E.F. 1974. *Small Is Beautiful: A Study of Economics as if People Mattered.* London: Abacus.

Smythe, Dallas W. 1981. *Dependency Road: Communications, Capitalism, Consciousness, Canada.* Norwood, New Jersey: Ablex Publishing Corp.

Spicer, Keith. 1995. "Opening Remarks at the Public Hearing on the Information Highway." Hull, Quebec, 6 March.

Stentor Telecom Policy Inc. 1993a. *The Information Highway, Canada's Road to Economic and Social Renewal: A Vision Statement.* October.

———. 1993b. *The Beacon Initiative: Backgrounder, Building a Stronger Canada Through The Beacon Initiative.*

Suzuki, David. 1994. *Time to Change.* Toronto: Stoddart.

United States, Federal Communications Commission [1939] 1974. *Investigation of the Telephone Industry in the United States.* House Document No. 340, 76th Congress, 1st Session. New York: Arno Press.

Winner, Langdon. 1977. *Autonomous Technology.* Cambridge, Mass.: MIT Press.

Winter, James. 1992. *Common Cents: Media Portrayal of the Gulf War and Other Events.* Montreal/New York: Black Rose Books.

———. 1994. "Building Babel." *Canadian Forum*, January/February, pp. 10-17.

11

Copyright and Trade Regimes Governing Print, Television and Film

Keith Acheson and Christopher Maule[1]

Viewers, listeners and readers have a rapidly changing set of options. Compact disks have relegated vinyl to a niche in the recording industry. Books, magazines and newspapers are being delivered both electronically and in their traditional format. Direct broadcast satellites compete with expanding cable systems. Today more movies are viewed on video players than in movie theatres and more encyclopedias are sold in CD-ROM format than in book form.

Behind this pervasive change lies a much more stable set of national laws, norms and international treaties that govern the commercial and not-for-profit media. The new technologies make exciting initiatives possible, but it is contracts that coordinate the transformation of potential into reality. In each of the cultural industries, contracts link creative people, sources of finance, manufacturers, printers and distributors that deliver content to consumers. Copyright and trade regimes establish the rules within which contracts are written and enforced. Without the copyright and trade regimes, the communication highways would carry far less traffic.

Laws and international regimes are not static. They evolve to accommodate emerging practices and address new problems. Each technology creates an adjustment challenge for domestic copyright law, commercial and nonprofit producers and the international regimes co-ordinating domestic responses. In this chapter, we examine the role of copyright in the cultural industries, the issues posed by new technologies for copyright and selected aspects of international arrangements governing trade, investment and the movement of labour. We begin by describing the importance of international linkages for the cultural industries.

International Dimensions of the Audiovisual Industries

All of the cultural industries have an incentive to market their output internationally. The additional costs of, for example, making a television program available in another viewing market are small compared to the costs of creating, writing and producing the show. This is also true in the film, book and record industries. The low cost of further dissemination provides a strong incentive to market widely.

Production and distribution have a strong international dimension. A Canadian publisher may produce the work of a foreign author and have the books printed in Asia. The international aspects of production in the film industry are even more complex. Concepts for a film may originate with foreign-authored material, be translated into scripts by foreign writers, be co-produced using a mix of nationalities and receive funding from private and public sources in different countries. Production and post-production is internationally footloose and worldwide distribution can involve versions dubbed or subtitled in different languages.

Some figures from the film industry illustrate this. From 1990 to 1993, international co-productions as a percentage of total productions rose from 4.8 per cent to 17.8 per cent. For 1992, total production for 54 surveyed countries was 3,052 feature films, of which 273 or 8.9 per cent are listed as co-productions. The principal partnerships are between countries within the European Union (EU), and between these countries and other European countries. Canada is actively engaged in co-productions mainly with European countries. Foreign markets are particularly important for the American film industry. In the United States, 38 per cent of total film revenues were generated abroad and 55 per cent of this total came from western Europe (*Screen Digest*, July 1994: 153-160). These figures are even more startling when one considers that piracy results in substantial revenue losses.[2]

Whether the medium is a book, film, television program or recording, protection against illegal copying or piracy is required for the money paid by consumers to filter back through the chain of contracts to those involved in production and distribution. Although it is difficult to quantify the extent of piracy, the development of photocopying, printing and taping technologies has made illegal copying by organized bootleggers and by individuals a serious problem for all the cultural industries.

Copyright

A Primer on Copyright

Copyright is granted for the expression of an idea and not for the idea itself. An expression cannot qualify for copyright if it is a copy of an existing expression. This distinction is informative but puzzling. If an author is aware of another work, how different must his or her expression be to qualify for a copyright? How is the expression, which is protected, separated from the idea, which is not? Legislation and the courts answer these questions. Judges interpret generally worded laws in deciding specific cases and give form to the domain of copyright. Unfortunately, the boundary set by court precedents is not a bright line. The polar cases are clear. A novel that is identical to an existing novel except for incidental detail does not qualify for copyright. A novel that has the same general plot but different characterization and setting as an existing novel does qualify. In between there are many ambiguities.

Copyrights are generally granted only to individuals in Canada. Corporations can own a copyright but cannot receive a copyright as an original author. A corporation obtains copyrights by purchasing them directly or indirectly through the terms of its contracts with employees. In the latter case, copyrights that are technically granted to employees are immediately transferred to the corporate employer. This arrangement is particularly important in the software industry.

Although registration is advised, a copyright need not be registered. If a copyright holder takes legal action against someone copying his or her material without permission, proof that the expression was in existence and known to the copier is sufficient to determine infringement.

Copyright grants a right that is limited in time and is subject to a number of conditions. The time limit is called the duration of the copyright. For a book, copyright lasts for the life of the author plus fifty years in Canada. The dominant current view in North America is that the duration of copyright should be chosen to balance, at least crudely, the incentive to create and the inefficiency of denying access to a work for which there are individuals willing to pay the marginal costs of reproduction.

For example, while a book's copyright is in effect, it will be sold at a price set by the publisher, constrained by what the market will bear. The social cost of the copyright during this period is the denial of a pleasurable reading experience to individuals who would be willing to pay more for the book than the cost of making an additional copy available to them, but are not willing to pay the price set by the publisher. From this description it may sound as if the publishing house is gouging, but that need not be the case. The publisher has to set the price above the cost of printing to cover its other costs. When copyright has lapsed, anybody can print and sell the content. If the book is still sufficiently popular to warrant publishing, competition will set the price.

All of the cultural industries confront risk. A publisher does not make the same return on each separately authored book. Unforeseen circumstances make a few books commercial winners while many others fail to generate sales and lose money. To survive, commercial publishers depend on printing sufficient winners to offset the losers. Even a discerning and well-managed publishing house can have a run of bad luck and difficulty financing its activities.

During the period in which copyright is valid, copyright law shapes and disciplines this contractual and institutional nexus. By giving the copyright holder the right to prevent reproduction of the work, the law makes legally enforceable a contract requiring someone to pay for reproducing the work. In the absence of copyright, a cartel of publishers could control commercial reproduction by agreeing not to produce a book that "belonged" to another member of the club. Cartels are often unstable, so it is doubtful that private arrangements for creating property of this type could work effectively in many countries or for a sustained period of time.

Not only is the right created by copyright law restricted in duration, the breadth of coverage also varies. For some purposes, such as personal scholarship, Canadian copyright law grants an exemption from copyright. One can photocopy any amount of work for personal scholarship and not have any obligations to pay the owner of the copyright. The courts can also decide that using or producing a work without permission of the copyright owner is not an infringement because the fair-dealing defence applies. In practice, the defence applies if the courts believe that the circumstances and purpose of access have a sufficiently significant social purpose to warrant suspending the rights of the copyright holder.

Fair dealing in Canada is similar in concept but different in detail to fair use in the United States. Fair use was a crucial part of Sony's defence in an important suit brought by American film interests in the early 1980s against the Sony Corporation. The plaintiffs hoped to have the court rule that the video recorder was a burglary tool designed to trespass on the copyrights of film and television program owners. The Supreme Court of the United States ruled in Sony's favour by the narrowest of margins (Lardner, 1987).

In the book trade, a publisher earns revenue by selling books that contain the copyrighted material. In television the rights for a television broadcaster to show a program at a certain time in a specified location will be licensed. A distributor of a film negotiates with a movie house to show a film. The box-office revenue will be shared between the distributor and the cinema according to complex formulas set out in the contract. In some instances, contracts between those who obtain access and the copyright owners are too expensive to negotiate. Collective arrangements are substituted for individual contracts. In the print media, universities sign contracts with a reprography collective representing a set of copyright holders. The universities pay an amount determined by the amount of photocopying done on campus to the collective which then allocates it among its members.

Similarly, a collective represents composers and the publishers of their music. Broadcasters and other users pay a levy for the right to play the composers' music. The collective, the Society of Composers, Authors and Music Publishers of Canada (SOCAN), allocates the funds collected to its members. The amount paid by the user group for a right administered collectively is determined either by negotiation, a government tribunal or by legislation. For example, the amount paid by broadcasters and other beneficiaries of playing music is set by the Copyright Board of Canada.

As well as governing reproduction, copyright protects what are called the moral rights of authors or creators. Moral rights embrace a number of different rights. The right of paternity requires that the author be identified, while the right of integrity prevents the owner of the work from altering it to the detriment of the reputation of the author. Other moral rights are designed to protect the commercial interests of the creators. They require that the author or artist receive payment for particular uses of the work by its current owner. In some jurisdictions, such as Canada, moral rights can be waived while in others, such as France, they are inalienable.

Laws that have international application and common commercial conventions are necessary for strangers from different cultures to deal with each other and understand what they will receive and what they are required to deliver. The agent of a Canadian author of children's books can reach an agreement with a publisher's representative from another country, who has just introduced himself or herself at a trade show, because both parties believe that the terms of a licence can be enforced in court, should that prove necessary.

International Copyright Regimes

Because of the international dimension of the cultural industries, copyright laws that differ considerably from country to country create significant enforcement problems. Consider duration. If a book is no longer under copyright in country A but is in country B, a publisher in country B will be plagued by cheaper copies seeping into the home market from country A. A drastic version of this problem occurs when one country provides no effective copyright protection at all. International distribution is facilitated by international agreements in which each country extends reasonably uniform protection to works of creators from other countries.

If more homogeneous copyright laws are desirable, what common level of protection should be provided? Countries with undeveloped cultural industries benefit less from more protective copyright regimes, as they buy more copyrighted material than they sell. Understandably, their copyright protection is often weak. Consumers like the lower prices associated with weak protection. Commercial print shops may also benefit from the lack of national protection as they produce works previously published and sell them domestically and abroad. On the other hand, creators in countries with little protection suffer, as do producers who nurse creative works through the chain from concept to book, film, television program or record.

The "free-rider" incentive also encourages weak copyright laws. A free-riding country relies on consumers in countries with more protective laws paying higher prices to support a flow of new published works. Its citizens will then enjoy cheap access to works, the development costs of which have been paid by others. If all countries reason this way, little protection will be provided anywhere and there will be few works to copy. Differences in commercial interests plus the free-rider incentive make international agreements constraining national copyright laws difficult to reach and to enforce.

Despite these problems, by the end of the nineteenth century, the major European countries had negotiated an international governance structure for copyright, the Berne Convention. Canada has been a member of Berne since its inception, but until 1989, the United States had refused to join. Berne has been frequently revised to accommodate new technologies and changing opinions about the appropriate degree of protection. Each revision is called a protocol. At any one time, different members of Berne may be committed to different protocols.

For many aspects of copyright, accession to Berne requires "national treatment" of foreign creators, i.e., a foreign creator will be treated in the same way as a domestic creator with respect to domestic copyright law. Berne also imposes minimum requirements on national laws with respect to coverage, duration, the absence of formal notification procedures for obtaining copyright and the moral rights of patrimony and integrity. The stipulations with respect to coverage are ambiguous, allowing countries to modify coverage with respect to new technologies. Berne has no effective way of punishing a member country that fails to meet its obligations.

A number of recent trade treaties have also addressed copyright. Under the Canada-United States Free Trade Agreement (FTA), Canada was obliged to create a copyright structure for the retransmission by cable companies of distant signals that did not discriminate by nationality. Canada did so and in October 1990, the Copyright Board of Canada (1990) set a benchmark royalty rate of 70 cents per month per cable subscriber.[3] This benchmark was later lowered by 50% for francophone systems to reflect the lesser value of distant signals to these systems.[4] The cable companies pay into a fund and collectives representing the owners of the programming shown on the distant signals draw from it. Each collective's share depends on a formula based on the number of eligible channels and the viewership of programs. Current Canadian viewing patterns dictate that a large proportion of the fund is disbursed to foreigners.

The thrust of the North American Free Trade Agreement (NAFTA) chapter on copyright was to bring Mexico's laws into greater conformity with those of the United States. Although Canada exempted its cultural industries in the NAFTA negotiations, this exemption had no effect on copyright law. Our current law plus the commitments made under the recent General Agreement on Tariffs and Trade/World Trade Organization (GATT/WTO) negotiations comply with the requirements of the NAFTA chapter.

The GATT/WTO agreement of 1994 includes important copyright commitments. The agreement adopts Berne principles and extends copyright coverage, reduces differences in national copyright laws, introduces the most-favoured-nation commitment to the copyright area, makes GATT/WTO's dispute resolution mechanisms and enforcement procedures apply to copyright, and expands the number of countries covered by Berne-style copyright commitments.

As a result of the agreement, Canada must accede to the more demanding 1971 Paris protocol of Berne, except for its moral rights provisions. GATT/WTO countries must, as Canada has, extend copyright to cover computer programs, which are at the core of new media initiatives. Under the GATT/WTO agreement, a minimum duration for sound recordings (50 years) and for broadcasts (20 years) is established. Members of GATT/WTO must adopt transparent procedures for actions against infringement of copyright. Penalties for infringement have been strengthened and member countries have agreed to enhance their enforcement efforts. Most importantly, perhaps, a process for dealing with countries that are not meeting their GATT/WTO copyright commitments has been adopted. If a review panel confirms noncompliance, a measured retaliation by the complaining party will be permitted.

In the GATT/WTO negotiations, the less-developed countries argued that GATT/WTO should concentrate solely on the issue of counterfeit trade and leave other intellectual property issues out of the negotiations. In contrast, the developed countries were unified in supporting more protection and the adoption of a GATT/WTO-style dispute settlement mechanism. They succeeded on both accounts.

Other international conventions deal with specialized rights that relate to copyright or augment the more general copyright conventions on specific issues. Of these the most important are the Rome Convention, which protects neighbouring rights;[5] the Geneva Convention,[6] which covers records, tapes and cassettes; and the Brussels Convention,[7] which requires members to be responsible for unauthorized distribution of programs by satellite. At the end of 1994, Canada belonged to none of these conventions. Canada may join some of these conventions in the near future, depending on how it resolves issues discussed in the next section.

Current Copyright Issues with an International Aspect

In the past, moral rights were adjudicated mainly with respect to visual art. A colourful case involved the suit brought by Canadian artist Michael Snow to prevent the Eaton Centre from putting red ribbons at Christmas time around the necks of his sculptured snow geese, which were suspended over an open area of the mall.[8] Snow claimed that this action violated his right of integrity and the Canadian courts agreed. A number of equally interesting cases have occurred in Europe. Despite the intriguing philosophical and economic issues raised by the right of integrity, its exercise by artists and sculptors has had almost no effect on international trade and only a small impact on the domestic market for such works. However, the exercise of this right with respect to audiovisual works, particularly films and television programs, could have a more significant impact.

Potential integrity violations occur when films are altered by colourization, are shown on a television screen that has a different aspect ratio than a cinema screen, are altered in length to match traditional time slots in television or are interrupted to permit commercials. Not being able to compress programming to fit traditional time slots and to insert commercials would have a significant economic effect on broadcasters. These issues are currently before the courts in European countries with strong moral rights traditions (Geller, 1990: 426). Our expectation is that if the courts rule in favour of the moral rights of the author in this situation, legislation will be passed to allow broadcasters to carry on business according to the traditional practices of the country.

The development of direct-broadcasting satellite services, which can deliver service packages comparable to those offered by a modern cable system, has brought a murky area of copyright to the forefront of policy debate. We understand that if a satellite service delivers signals directly to a home in Canada, copyright clearance must be obtained in the country from which that signal emanates. For example, Cancom and First Choice are licensed to deliver encoded signals to Canadian homes and since their signals emanate from Canada, Canadian copyright clearance is required. If those signals had originated in the United States, American copyright clearance would have sufficed. If the signal is not delivered directly to the home, but is received by a cable company, which then transmits it to the viewer's set, the copyright jurisdiction is altered. Clearance of copyright in the receiving country, Canada, has to be obtained for the programming. Copyright issues are important in this context, but they pale in comparison to the challenges posed by foreign direct-broadcasting satellites, such as the recently launched American DirecTV service.

As mentioned above, the composer and the publisher of his or her music are the only parties who have a public performing right that entitles them to a share of royalties collected from broadcasters, taverns, concerts, "elevator" music operators and other users. In Canada, new legislation extending coverage of the public performance right to include record companies and performers has been promised despite broadcasters' opposition.

Studies commissioned by the Department of Consumer and Corporate Affairs in the early eighties argued against the granting of such a public performance right for performers and for record companies (Globerman and Rothman, 1981; and Keon, 1980) on the basis that their interests were better served by the existing structure. The main argument on the pro side is that performers face a bargaining disadvantage in dealing with the record companies. Smith (1988) disagreed that performers faced the same contracting difficulties as composers and argued that, unlike the interests of composers and lyricists, those of performers can be effectively addressed by individually or collectively negotiated contracts. This appears to have been the case in the past, but there is some concern that recent technological developments, such as digital broadcasting and taping, may have a significant effect on the revenues of recording producers and make ineffective the current process for remunerating performers. Advocates of the new rights emphasize this forecasted problem of commercial decline of the recording industry, but at the time of writing, there was no evidence of declining profits by the recording companies. Indeed they appear to be more economically viable than the radio broadcasters, who would have to pay the levies under the new rights structure.

A contentious international issue raised by a Canadian public performance right for performers and record companies is the treatment of foreign performers and record companies. Many of the performers of recorded music broadcast in Canada are foreign, largely American, and the record companies are predominately foreign-owned. Some policy advisers have argued against including foreigners; others have recommended reciprocity on this issue. Anything short of nondiscriminatory access by performers and record companies broadcast in Canada will face opposition from the United States.

The fourth topic of current interest is copyright and the information highway. The growing popularity of the Internet and the explosion of bulletin boards and databanks have raised concerns about the

Table 11-1
Internet and Copyright Issues

Characteristic	Copyright Question
The Web increasingly has multimedia works posted.	Does the protection of a compilation under the Copyright Act provide adequate protection for such works?
The network encourages "browsing."	Can a work be "browsed" without infringing copyright?
Works in digital form can be readily altered.	How is the moral right of an author affected if someone downloads a graphic and then posts an altered version?
Many texts posted on bulletin boards are in hypertext form — broken into concise parts that can be accessed separately.	Is access to part of an article an infringement of copyright?
In forums on the Internet or on commercial bulletin board services content is typically provided by subscribers.	Is the co-ordinator of the activity on which a subscriber posts content liable if the material is posted without the permission of the copyright owner?
Enforcement of copyright by individual owners may be prohibitively costly on the Internet.	Should a compulsory licensing system be introduced with the resulting revenue distributed to the owners of posted works according to, for example, the number of downloads?

Source: Acheson and Maule.

protection granted posted works under existing law. To summarize a complex topic we list characteristics of the new technology and corresponding questions for copyright posed by them in Table 11-1.

There is no shortage of questions. Government departments, advisory committees and task forces will struggle with developing answers and the amendments to the Copyright Act or distinct legislation. Business and user groups will compete to influence the process. This process has already begun in Canada. In December 1994, the Copyright Subcommittee of the Advisory Council on the Information Highway issued a draft report on copyright and the information highway. Interested parties were asked to submit their reactions.

International Trade, Investment and Labour

Canada has largely excluded the cultural industries from the international trade and investment provisions of the FTA, NAFTA and GATT/WTO.[9] That culture was not on the negotiating table was and still is the official Canadian position, except for four provisions in the FTA.[10] What this actually means will become clearer as the processes for resolving trade disputes between Canada and other countries in these exempted activities are revealed by experience. Currently a number of disputes with the United States have arisen with respect to the cultural industries. The most significant involve Country Music Television (CMT), a Canadian split-run published by Sports Illustrated and direct-to-home satellite broadcasting.[11] Because there is no formal dispute resolution mechanism for cultural issues, these disputes are handled in the political arena where Canada deals one on one with its much larger trading partner. While Canada argues that the cultural exemption allows it to do what it wants, it also permits the United States to act in a manner that could be harmful to Canada. The CMT case is one illustration of this informal dispute resolution process.

Country Music Television

In 1994, the CRTC announced the removal of the American specialty channel, Country Music Television (CMT), from Canadian cable television services and its replacement by a Canadian-owned service, the New Country Network (NCN). A dispute arose and has been handled in several fora. First, CMT appealed the regulatory decision in the Canadian courts. It lost its appeal in the Federal Court of Appeal and was refused the right to appeal to the Supreme Court of Canada. Next, CMT filed a 301 petition to the United States Trade Representative (USTR) complaining of its treatment in Canada. The USTR responded on February 6th, 1995, stating that Canada had acted in an "unreasonable and discriminatory" manner and called for public comment within thirty days. Various stories appeared in the press about possible areas for American retaliation in both cultural and noncultural areas.

The USTR wrote to the Canadian Minister of International Trade asking whether Canada is likely to make a practice of delisting foreign cable services, and indicating that even if there is a minimal response in the CMT case, this may not be so in the future. At the same time, CMT and NCN were pursuing a possible collaboration. On the day the USTR was due to announce its findings and possibly make recommendations for retaliation, NCN and CMT announced the formation of a commercial partnership that would create a new service, meeting Canadian-ownership requirements.

It has been suggested that both governments encouraged the firms to resolve the dispute, as neither side wanted to test the meaning of the cultural exemption in the NAFTA. By placing cultural industries outside trade agreements, Canada has opted to continue to use an informal corporate-political resolution process to address conflicts in the cultural industries. Smaller countries are generally better protected by embracing internationally agreed law, which all small countries can influence, than relying on a bilateral process that is subject only to the law of power.

Investment

In this section we highlight aspects of an emerging international regime for investment that has special relevance to the cultural industries. One of the features of the audiovisual sector, remarked on above, is the growing importance of co-productions between firms in different countries. Co-productions are attractive because they allow the producers to raise private money in different countries, often in conjunction with the sale of distribution rights to persons in these countries, to qualify for subsidized government funding and to be considered as national product for content quotas in the participating countries. Joint funding may also improve the commercial performance of a film or program in different countries where financial interests have some input into the type of product made. It may also be a recipe for a bland pudding. Europeans have coined the word "Europudding" to describe some of their less successful joint ventures.

Canada has signed official co-production treaties with a number of other countries. Aside from these official treaties, there are many unofficial co-productions, or what we will call here co-ventures, taking place because of the commercial advantages that accrue from co-operation in this sector. Canadian firms are heavily engaged in co-ventures with partners in countries such as the United States, where there is no treaty, and in Europe, where there is a treaty but the parties seek more flexibility in their arrangements than they would have in forming an official co-production. The Canadian regulatory and financing authorities, such as Telefilm Canada, have extended the privileges of treaty co-productions to projects that are structured in a similar manner, but are produced and financed with partners from countries with which Canada has no treaty.

Canada signed its first co-production treaty with France in 1963. By July 1994, the total had risen to 23. The partner countries are in Europe, Asia and Latin America. The treaties specify restrictions with respect to financing and the nationality of personnel used in the productions. While a fairly rigid framework is imposed, some flexibility is achieved through permitting third-party countries to participate, and allowing the project to include stars from other countries.[12]

To accommodate the growing importance of television, the co-production treaties, which originally covered only film, have typically been redrafted to include both feature films and television programs. By far, the most activity has occurred under the Canada-France agreement. One natural advantage that Canada has been able to exploit is its position as a gateway to the American market, particularly for French producers. This helps to explain the surprisingly large number of Canada-France co-productions that have been shot in English (Acheson and Maule, 1989: 54-5; Hoskins and McFadyen, 1992: 17, 19). As American broadcasting interests begin to pursue joint ventures with European partners, this Canadian advantage may erode.

Increasingly co-productions and co-ventures are likely to present problems for those determining the national content of films and programs in order to enforce content quotas.[13] Even with some of the existing co-production treaties, one side may not recognize a project for national quotas. *Black Robe,* for example, is an official Canadian-Australian co-production. The story deals with French missionaries in Canada interacting with native peoples. The main Australian ingredient is the director, Bruce Beresford, together with some financing. In Canada the film is considered as Canadian content but we have been informed by the Australian Broadcasting Authority that it will not qualify as Australian content when shown on television by an Australian broadcaster.

In broadcasting, international investment is constrained by national-ownership restrictions. The general tendency has been to relax those constraints and Canada has recently announced that it will adopt for broadcasting the more relaxed national-ownership constraints now in place for telecommunication companies. Foreign interests have assumed the allowed minority positions in a number of Canadian specialty cable channels.

In publishing, Canada's Baie Comeau policy requires that if a foreign company owning a Canadian publisher is sold to another foreign owner, the new owner must sell the Canadian publishing subsidiary to Canadian interests. A clause in the FTA, inserted at American insistence, requires that such a divestiture be executed at fair market value. In bookselling, there has been concern about the expansion of foreign chains in Canada. Some of this concern is voiced by Canadian publishers who anticipate the disruption of traditional patterns of distributing foreign books, which have been commercially rewarding to the participants. The entrants obviously feel that consumers will welcome the prospect of cheaper books even if they have to contend with longer commutes to the megastore locations.

Labour Issues

As co-productions in the audiovisual industries increase and different locations become economically attractive for offshore productions, the terms and conditions for persons to work in foreign countries become increasingly important. A 1994 report on the industry in Ontario notes that the current attraction of Toronto as a production site is due to a cheap Canadian dollar, good-quality production and post-production facilities, an active film commission and favourable provincial government policies.[14]

While labour permits are dealt with primarily by domestic immigration authorities, an international organization, the International Labour Organization (ILO), monitors the interests of labour in all industries. A 1992 survey by the ILO entitled *Conditions of Employment and Work of Performers* triggered a response from the Canadian government on a wide range of topics (Chartrand, 1992). The Alliance of Canadian Cinema, Television and Radio Artists reported to Labour Canada that,

> it is virtually impossible for a Canadian performer to work in the recorded media in other countries on a single contract. As a result, some Canadians have chosen to move permanently to other countries, primarily the United States, in order to pursue careers (Labour Canada, 1992: 26).

A fairly complex procedure has been devised by the unions in conjunction with record, film and television producers and immigration and employment authorities regarding permits for performers to work in foreign countries.

Our understanding is that the unions in different countries have agreed to recommend the use of foreigners as performers, directors and technicians under certain conditions. These are written into agreements with producers and form the basis of recommendations to immigration authorities as to whether foreigners should be issued work permits. The official procedure involves authorities from Citizenship and Immigration Canada consulting with officials of Human Resources Development Canada concerning the availability of domestic workers.[15]

De facto, a special regime for movement of performers is evolving about which little information is publicly available concerning the negotiations between the unions and government. Outside of North America, cases are documented of foreigners only being allowed entry to a country if they first pay a sum of money equal to the wages that would have been paid to domestic workers but for the use of foreigners. In effect, the producer pays twice and probably more as the unit becomes hostage to the country once shooting has begun (Boorman, 1985).

Conclusion

Copyright has always been a fluid body of law. New technologies generate both a commercial potential and related piracy challenges. The law adapts by balancing the interests of creative producers and users in the new context. The challenges raised by the new technologies of the mid-nineties concern the effect of the right to integrity on the owners, creators and licensees of films and television programs; the legal status of audiovisual material delivered by satellite; the ability of contracts to reward adequately the performers of recorded music for public performances of their work by broadcasters and others; and the emerging role of copyright on the information superhighway.

Each of these issues has an important international aspect. For example, there are significant trade policy issues associated with how audiovisual content made available through the information highway is treated. The Canadian government will have to decide whether it will treat that material in a manner similar to the detailed regulation of television broadcasting, or to the relatively unregulated manner in which books, magazines or videos are bought or rented. In the former case, providers will have to be approved by a board serving the same functions as the CRTC. Only Canadian firms will be licensed and Canadian-content provisions will be imposed on the subject matter. In the latter case, entry will be open, and users of the highway will have the same freedom of choice and absence of regulation experienced in a magazine or video rental store.

Canadian policy choices concerning the information highway, public performing rights for performers and record companies, direct broadcast satellites and moral rights will affect other countries. Canada and most of its important trading partners are constrained in their copyright policy options by the Berne convention, the GATT/WTO and regional trade pacts. Canada is restricted in its own choices but gains from the discipline imposed on the policies of other countries by these agreements.

Trade regimes pose a similar array of issues. Adherence by countries to the provisions of the GATT/WTO signifies the first step towards an international agreement for trade in services, which now stands where trade in goods stood fifty years ago with passage of the original GATT. Canada has made a minimal commitment for its cultural industries, but this stance will have to be reviewed over the next ten years. Canada, as a small country, will benefit greatly if resolution of international conflicts in the cultural area can be negotiated with the parties disciplined by possible appeal to a formal multilateral dispute resolution mechanism.

Notes

1. The authors would like to thank Gary Hufbauer, John Sigmund and Doug Smith for their comments on earlier drafts of this chapter.
2. Of the 36 countries (the EU is listed as one country) noted under the Special 301 provisions by the United States Trade Representative, estimated losses due to piracy are $U.S. 1.2 billion for each of the motion picture and record/music industries (International Intellectual Property Alliance. 1994. Press Release. April 30th.).
3. Cable systems with less than 6000 subscribers pay a lower subscription according to a tapered schedule.
4. In a 1993 decision, the Copyright Board of Canada stated: "The figures advanced by various parties may differ; however, they all confirm that whether one looks at prime time, off-prime or full time, distant signal viewing as a percentage of hours tuned to cable is between 14.9 and 17.7 per cent for Canada, 18.3 and 21.5 per cent for Canada excluding Quebec, and only between 4.4 and 5.2 per cent in Quebec" (1993: 48).
5. The Rome Convention's formal name is the International Convention for the Protection of Performers, Producers of Phonograms and Broadcasting Organisa-

tions, adopted at Rome on 26 October 1961. Neighbouring rights are distinct from but related to copyright.

6. Convention for the Protection of Producers of Phonograms against Unauthorized Duplication of their Phonograms, Geneva, 1971.

7. Convention relating to the distribution of program-carrying signals transmitted by satellite, Brussels, 21 May 1974.

8. *Snow v. The Eaton Centre Ltd.* (1982), 70 C.P.R. (2d) 105 (Ont. High Ct.).

9. The treatment of culture in the three trade agreements is dealt with more fully in Acheson and Maule (1994a).

10. The four are: the elimination of tariffs for goods used as inputs to the cultural industries; removal of a requirement that magazines must be published in Canada in order to gain tax benefits; a commitment to make copyright payments for cable redistribution of distant signals; and an assurance of the receipt of fair market value for the divestment of foreign assets required by Canadian ownership restrictions in the cultural industries.

11. For a more detailed discussion of these three cases and their implications for cultural and international policy in Canada see Acheson and Maule (1995a, 1995b).

12. For more details on co-productions, see Acheson and Maule (1989); Hoskins and McFadyen (1992); Paul Audley and Associates (1989); Telefilm, (1987), (1989).

13. Michele Cotta, a French journalist and television producer questions the current relevance of quotas in Europe and notes the problem of enforcing "... a regulation which the broadcasters go out of their way to disobey ..." (Report by the Think Tank, 1994, 61).

14. See *Hollywood Reporter*. 1994. Weekly International Edition, Sept. 6th, S-1 to S-44.

15. Citizenship and Immigration Canada. *Immigration Manual*. Sec. 15.38, 3c, 38.

References

Acheson, Keith, and Christopher Maule. 1995a. "Trade Disputes and Canadian Cultural Policies." Paper presented to a conference on Media Policy, National Identity and Citizenry in Changing Democratic Societies: The Case of Canada, Canadian Studies Center, Duke University, October 6-7th, 1995.

————. 1995b. "International agreements and cultural industries." Paper presented to CSIS workshop in Washington D.C. on November 14, 1995.

————. 1994a. "International Regimes for Trade, Investment and Labour Mobility in the Cultural Industries." *Canadian Journal of Communications*, 401-421. Vol. 19. 3/4

————. 1994b. "Copyright and Related Rights: The International Dimension." *Canadian Journal of Communications*, pp. 423-446. Vol. 19. 3/4

————. 1989. "The Higgledy-Piggledy Trade Environment for Films and Programs, The Canadian Example." *World Competition*, pp. 47-62.

Benko, Robert P. 1987. Protecting intellectual property rights: issues and controversies. Washington: American Enterprise Institute.

Blomqvist, Ake G. and Chin, Lim. 1981. *Copyright, Competition and Canadian Culture: The Impact of Alternative Copyright Act Import Provisions on the Book Publishing and Sound Recording Industries.* Ottawa: Supply and Services.

Bloom, Glen A. 1991. Copyright in the visual arts. In *Copyright: new developments, new costs.* Mississauga: Insight Press.

Boorman, John. 1985. *Money Into Light, The Emerald Forest: A Diary.* London: Faber and Faber Ltd.

Canada. Copyright Board of Canada. 1993. *Statements of royalties to be paid for the retransmission of distant radio and television signals.* Ottawa: Copyright Board of Canada.

————. Copyright Subcommittee of the Advisory Council on the Information Highway. 1994. *Draft Final Report,* Ottawa.

————. Copyright Board of Canada. 1990. *Statements of royalties to be paid for the retransmission of distant radio and television signals.* Ottawa: Copyright Board of Canada.

Canada-United States Free Trade Agreement Implementation Act. *Canada-United States Free Trade Agreement Implementation Act.* 1988. S.C., 1988, C.65

Chartrand, Harry H. 1992. Intercultural affairs, a 14 country survey. *Journal of Arts Management Law and Society,* pp. 134-154. Vol. 22 No. 2.

Geller, Paul Edward. 1990. "Can the GATT incorporate Berne whole?" *European Intellectual Property Review,* pp. 423-28. Vol. 12. 11.

Gibbens, R. D. 1989. "The Moral Rights of Artists and the Copyright Act Amendments." *Canadian Business Law Journal,* pp. 441-70. Vol. 15.

Globerman, Steven, and Mitchell P. Rothman. 1981. *An economic analysis of a performers' right.* Ottawa: Minister of Supply and Services.

Hahn, R. Richard. 1988. "An analysis of Bill-C60: an act to amend the Copyright Act and to amend other acts in consequence thereof." *Canadian Intellectual Property Review,* pp. 154-168. Vol. 5. 1.

Hoekman, Bernard. 1994. "Services and Intellectual Property Rights." In Susan Collins and Barry Bosworth, eds., *The New GATT, Implications for the United States,* Washington: Brookings, pp. 84-121.

Hoskins, Colin and Stuart McFadyen. 1992. *The importance of television co-productions and co-ventures and the motives of participants: the Canadian case.* Working paper, University of Alberta.

Jackson, John. 1994. "The World Trade Organization, Dispute Settlement, and Codes of Conduct." In Susan Collins and Barry Bosworth, eds., *The New GATT, Implications for the United States,* Washington: Brookings, pp. 63-83.

Keon, Jim. 1980. *A performing right for sound recordings: an analysis.* Ottawa: Minister of Supply and Services.

Keyes, A.A. 1993. "What is Canada's International Copyright Policy?" *Intellectual Property Journal.* pp. 299-319. Vol. 7. 3.

Keyes, A. A., and C. Brunet. 1977. *Copyright in Canada: proposals for a revision of the law.* Ottawa: Minister of Supply and Services.

Krasner, S.D., ed. 1983. *International Regimes.* Ithaca: Cornell University Press.

Kline, John. 1985. *International Codes and Multinational Business: Setting Guidelines for International Business Operations.* Westport CT: Quorum Books.

Kostecki, M. M. 1991. "Sharing intellectual property between the rich and the poor." *European Intellectual Property Review,* pp. 271-74. Vol. 13. 8.

Labour Canada. International Affairs. 1992. *Reply of the Government of Canada to the ILO Questionnaire in preparation for a tripartite meeting on conditions of employment and work of performers.* Ottawa.

Lardner, James. 1987. "Annals of Law: The Betamax Case. Part I." *The New Yorker.* April 6, pp. 45-71, and "Annals of Law: The Betamax Case. Part II." *The New Yorker.* April 13, pp. 60-81.

North American Free Trade Agreement between the Government of the United States of America, the Government of Canada and the Government of the United Mexican States. 1993. Unites States Government Printing Office, Washington, D.C.

OECD. 1985. *Declaration on international investment and multinational enterprises.* Paris: OECD.

———. 1992a. *Code of liberalization of capital movements.* Paris: OECD.

———. 1992b. *Code of liberalization of current invisible operations.* Paris: OECD.

Paul Audley and Associates. 1989. *Study of the revenues earned by Canadian productions: a study prepared for Telefilm Canada.* Toronto.

Plant, A. 1934. The Economic Aspects of Copyright in Books. *Economica*, n.s. 1, pp. 167-95.

Preston, Lee and Duane Windsor. 1992. *The Rules of the Game in the Global Economy.* Boston: Kluwer.

Report by the Think-Tank on the Audiovisual Policy in the European Union.. 1994. Luxembourg: Office of the Official Publications of the European Communities.

Sanderson, Paul. 1992. *A Guide to Musicians and the Law in Canada.* Scarborough: Carswell.

Schulte, Frank. 1991. "Immigration policy protest, a new U.S. visa law restricts Canadian musicians." *Canadian Musician*, October.

Smith, Douglas A. 1988. "Recent proposals for copyright revision: an evaluation." *Canadian Public Policy*, pp. 175-85. Vol. 14. 2.

Tackaberry, Paul. 1989. "Look what they done to my song, ma: the songwriter's moral right of integrity in Canada and the United States." *European Intellectual Property Review*, pp. 356-371. Vol. 11, 10

Telefilm Canada. 1987. *Nation to nation: a challenge for the future.* Montreal: Telefilm Canada.

———. 1989. *Coproductions, policies and procedures.* Montreal: Telefilm Canada.

Uruguay Round of Multilateral Trade Negotiations, General Agreement on Tariffs and Trade, Final Act. Marrakesh, 15 April 1994. Office of the United States Trade Representative: Washington, D.C.

Wildman, Stephen and S.E.Siwek. 1988. *International trade in films and television programs.* Cambridge, Mass.: Ballinger Publishing.

Wolfhard, Eric. 1991. "International trade in intellectual property: the emerging GATT regime." *University of Toronto Faculty of Law Review*, pp. 106-51. Vol. 49. 1.

12

The Cultural Industries Policy Apparatus

Kevin Dowler

One of the dominant themes in the discussion of cultural policy in Canada has been the apparent absence of a rationale for government planning in this area. Accordingly, at the beginning of his study of cultural regulation in Canada, Steven Globerman (1983: xxiii) argues that "the most important weakness of cultural policy making in Canada is to focus on operational considerations, that is, how to increase cultural production in Canada, rather than on the more fundamental issue of whether and why there is too little cultural output produced in Canada and by Canadians." In fact, the question of whether there is too little cultural output in Canada was decided long ago. Since the Massey Commission report in 1951, if not earlier, the problem of increasing cultural output has been a central issue of government policy, particularly at the federal level. The point of policy has been precisely the "operational considerations" aimed at increasing cultural production for its own sake. To achieve this goal government has constructed an elaborate apparatus to stimulate the growth of cultural production.

Globerman may have a point, however, when he suggests that the theme of *why* cultural output remains problematic has not received much attention. Little attention has been given to the historical conditions that led government to venture into the realm of culture. Globerman (1983: 3) claims that "the mapping out of a mandate, or at least the identification of a set of basic guiding principles, has been a perpetually neglected aspect of the cultural policy debate in Canada." Indeed, the development of policy in the Canadian cultural sphere has often been seen as a history of ineptitude and incoherence (cf. Dorland [1991]). Nevertheless, even if on the surface Canadian cultural policy may lack a certain coherence, this does not mean that it also suffers from an absence of an underlying rationality, even if that remains hidden from its authors. It may lack, from Globerman's economistic perspective, a certain logic, but that simply suggests that a mandate for Canadian culture must be found elsewhere. I will argue that it is to be found in the quest for national security.

Discussing what he calls the "national insecurity state" in an essay on Canadian security intelligence, Wesley Wark (1992: 162) writes that by the beginning of World War II in Canada "an insecure internal frontier opened up, geographically located in the west, metaphysically located in the racial tension between Canadians of British origin and the new Central European immigrants." The tension Wark describes can be understood not only in terms of the potential for internal subversion at that time (in the form of a Nazi cadre or Communist fifth column, for instance) but also in terms of the continuing threat posed by the importation, through immigration, of other cultures into the Canadian nation. This applies not only to the supposed threat represented by Central European immigrants, but equally well to concerns about the incursion of American culture into, and its colonization of, Canada.

What is most interesting about Wark's comment is the distinction he makes between an actual material space and this "metaphysical" space. This second space, although symbolic, is, nevertheless, no less real than the physical space within which it emerges; it is (as Wark implies) as much a site of struggle and policing as the actual borders of the nation. The Canadian state, in the struggle to form itself as a nation, was obliged to operate on both of these fronts; that is, to secure the actual physical and geographical frontiers, and to secure the internal, "metaphysical" frontier of culture. In the first stage of national development, the construction of a communications and transportation system became necessary to assert sovereignty over space and ensure the security of the perimeters of the state. This strategy failed, and in fact created further dependency. A second front therefore was opened to counteract the unforeseen effects of the communications system: this second front was culture.

The development of a strategy of cultural independence suggests that what could not be had in the material realm — freedom from economic dependency — was to be repaired in the realm of the metaphysical. To defend what Wark calls the "national insecurity state," a system, similar to the communications apparatus, but devoted to the administration of Canadian culture, was constructed. In the absence of security in either the military or the economic realm, culture was to provide the bulwark of security against absolute dependency. I want to suggest therefore, with Wark's comments in mind, that the rationale for a Canadian cultural policy is to be found in the security interests of the state.

Government discourse, as reflected in a myriad of reports, often frames its mandate in terms of the construction of a Canadian identity.[1] Here, however, I want to view the cultural policy apparatus as a set of structures and procedures designed to bolster security, not to shape identity. From the perspective of security, identity is simply one of the desired outcomes of state security aims. The governmental administration of culture should be seen as a set of "tactics" (as Foucault calls them)[2] to enhance security and ensure the continual reproduction of the Canadian state. Beyond the question of brute space and the issues of sovereignty that space implies, appears the question of managing the population; that is, after space, the people, and hence culture. It is here that the cultural apparatus finds its rationality. Culture is, from this perspective, a regime, or a regimen, that functions as a form of security. Beyond the binding of space (which has been the central concern of communications scholarship in Canada) is a whole other problematic of statehood that can only be addressed through the analysis of the governmental interventions into Canadian culture from a security perspective.

In order to understand how the administering of cultural policy in Canada performs the function of a security apparatus, I want to address a series of issues. In this chapter, I will begin with a brief discussion of the problems of national security and the administration of space; look at the origins of the Canadian cultural apparatus and administration in light of the "tradition" of government ownership; consider government intervention into culture as a shift from sovereignty interests to security tactics to compensate for economic underdevelopment; and discuss the recent convergence of culture and economic policy and its implications for further research. My aim is to sketch out a set of ideas that have potential ramifications for the research contained in this volume, and for subsequent analysis of what has come to be called the cultural industries. In the end, I want to suggest that the basis of national development in culture, communications and industry has to be rethought.

The "Uniqueness" of the Canadian State

Government intervention in Canada is not, of course, limited to culture. As Harold Innis notes in *The Fur Trade* (1930: 406), "The relation of the government of Canada to general economic growth has been unique. The heavy expenditures on transport improvements, including railways and canals, have involved government grants, subsidies and guaranties to an exceptional degree."

Government involvement in the construction of the transportation infrastructure was an outcome of the failure of private interests to complete large-scale projects. "The weakness of private capital," as Robin Neill (1981: 149) notes, "has been the occasion of government involvement in canals and railways. Indeed, part of the economic significance of 1867 can be found in the need to centralize the railway debts of the colonies." According to Innis (1956: 68), this weakness goes back even further, to the mid-nineteenth century and the Act of Union, when an "energetic canal policy ... begun as a private enterprise" could not find adequate capital, which "necessitated purchase by the government." Eventually, as Innis points out elsewhere (1933: 19), "Confederation became an effective credit institution with the demands for long-term securities which accompanied the spread of industrialism especially as shown in transportation."

In the vacuum created by the failure of private interests, government intervened with various financial instruments to ensure completion of the transportation system. The newly formed federal government found itself taking an enlarged role in the economic affairs of its citizens. Indeed, according to Innis (1956: 229), "To build canals and improve the St. Lawrence system, and to build railways ... necessitated reorganization of the political structure" and, furthermore, resulted in economic "[d]ependence on the Canadian political structure."

Innis' early work thus reveals that the uniqueness of the Canadian state lies in extensive government intervention. In response to the inability or lack of interest of a capitalist or entrepreneurial class to construct the necessary transportation infrastructure by which to administer and develop the economy of the new state, the government intervened in a strategic move aimed at establishing sovereignty and enabling the practice of colonial expansionism. The weakness of an indigenous capitalist class established conditions wherein the government was compelled to act on behalf of that class, thus putting into place what we can call a "tradition" of government ownership, sponsorship, subsidy and intervention that, as Innis notes (1956: 68), "became an important factor in later developments." Innis (1933: 48) states emphatically that "Government ownership is the legitimate child of government support of private enterprise in the construction of railways in Canada. It is the result of a policy directed toward building a nation in the northern part of North America." It is particularly important here to emphasize the policy dimension brought out in this latter citation: it indicates that government intervention served not only economic goals, but was also directed towards security interests and the consolidation of the space of the state.

Ironically, however, the attempts to consolidate the Canadian state through space-binding technologies in the end only generated further dependency. The transportation system, constructed to enhance unity and ensure sovereignty over the frontiers, is unfortunately bidirectional: it aided not only exports of the staples upon which the economy was based, but also the import of manufactured goods. The two-way structure of the transportation system, though it may improve the profitability of exports, also lays the nation open to the influx of less-expensive foreign manufactured goods — goods made less expensive by the very system used to distribute them. Thus, the net effect of improvements is actually further dependence on foreign commodities.

This contradiction — government construction of a transportation system for security reasons that undermines that very goal — is the first instance of what Gordon Laxer (1985: 94) has called Canada's "aborted development," particularly as it concerns Canadian defence interests:

Instead of a strategic logic leading to the build-up of a Canadian-owned armaments and engineering sector, the strategic question in Canada was fought over territory. The CPR was rushed into construction because the American government had explicit designs to annex Western Canada ... Such is the logic of the strategic question.

As a common carrier, the railroad effectively undermined the reason for which it was built: in attempting to establish sovereignty and security through mere presence, it became the medium by which imports could inhibit the development of indigenous industrial capacity, and thereby erode its status as an instrument of national security.

What Innis describes as the uniqueness of the Canadian state is thus twofold: first, society's dependence on government intervention and ownership for economic development and security; and second, the net effect of this intervention, which undermines the very aims of economic and defence policy. It is the effective collapse of the first front, the undermining of security aims through the construction of a nationwide communications system, that leads to the opening of the second front: the front of culture.

Toward a Simulated Civil Society

The problem with a nation such as Canada, which comes into being through the space-binding effect of its communications system, is that it remains empty except for the structure of that system itself. It remains a spatial abstraction. Maurice Charland (1986: 197) argues that this is a central feature of the Canadian state: the nation is constructed through the rhetoric of "technological nationalism."

> This rhetoric of a technological nation, basing itself on a romantic interpretation of history, equates the construction of the CPR with the constitution of Canada and praises each with reference to the other. Canada is valorized as a nation because it is the product of technological achievement ...

As a consequence, technology "cannot but offer the empty experience of mediation" (p. 217). The space that communications technology brings into being marks the beginning of a recurrent crisis:

> This vision of a nation is bankrupt, however, because it provides no substance or commonality for the *polis* except communication itself. As a consequence, technological nationalism's (anglophone) Canada has no defence against the power of the American culture industry or, indeed, of the technological experience (1986: 198).

According to Charland, this has resulted in Canada becoming an "absent nation." It is absent to the extent that the empty shell of space created by communications technology is ultimately filled with foreign content — in other words, American mass culture.

The problem of absent nationhood may be defined as follows. Sovereignty presides over space as mere presence, in the form of the communications apparatus. The communications system solves the question of sovereignty by sheer existence in material space. However, it creates as its byproduct another empty space — the empty experience of mediation. This "metaphysical" frontier is the locus of identity. The conquest of brute material space — sovereignty in other words — although it is not actually empty, is nevertheless devoid of symbolic content. It is here, within the discourse of the production of Canadian security, that cultural policy emerges as the content.

The relation of space to culture can be seen in the 1951 report of the Royal Commission on National Development in the Arts, Letters and Sciences (the Massey report). In the chapter entitled "The Forces of Geography," the commission emphasized the vitality of Canadian life, rooted in diversity: "Canadian civilization is all the stronger for its sincere and unaffected regionalism" (1951: 12). This regional diversity, if healthy, is also paradoxically problematic: "the isolations of this vast country exert their price" (p.12). The price of isolation was disunity, and the problem was how to forge this diversity into a national culture.

The Massey commission's solution was to bring the regions into the mainstream of Canadian life through national cultural programs: "In a country such as ours where many people are remote from the national capital and from other large centres of population, it is of obvious importance to extend to them as far as may be possible the services of the national institutions in Ottawa" (p.12). Thus, the government would tie the nation together not only through a communications infrastructure, but with a cultural infrastructure as well. The provision of national cultural programs by centrally administered agencies and institutions would establish the coherence required for the development of a Canadian culture.

The problem was not, however, merely one of logistics. At issue was the government's involvement at all. At the time of the commission, there was a great deal of sensitivity about government roles in the production of culture, specifically fears of totalitarianism that recent experience had taught was the result of central government control (cf. Litt [1992: 103-105]). Culture, therefore, had to be seen as distinct from the activities of the state proper. These concerns had been raised as early as the discussions leading toward the foundation of the CBC in the 1920s (cf. Raboy [1990: 24, 29]).

At the same time — despite concerns over government control — demands were made upon the government to develop a cultural policy, and further, to set up an institution or institutions that would provide a direct subsidy for cultural production. It is here that the "weakness of private capital" marks the moment of recurrence of government intervention. Significantly, rather than setting up their own institutions in response to the underdevelopment of culture, private interests preferred to lobby the federal government to provide what was required. In the history of dependence on government, protest against existing conditions takes the form of a demand that government act. Similar to the circumstances of Confederation, where a central government was formed to act as a "credit instrument" (as Innis put it) to finance the construction of transportation and communication networks in the absence of private initiative, the "problem" of culture was likewise to be solved by government. The marked absence of a civil society, both as an economic agent and as the "mobile interface between government and governed" (Gordon, 1991: 34) established the conditions for government investment in the production of culture. If culture was to be Canadian, the government would have to build it.

However, this could not be undertaken directly, because of the fear of government interference. The solution was, and remains, the creation of a structure of agencies that would administer culture on behalf of, and at a distance from, the federal government. In effect, these agencies, once created, would perform the function of an absent civil society. To the extent that they are held at a distance from both the civil service and the legislative branch — either through reporting procedures or through the use of the "arm's-length principle" — these agencies operate as the "mobile interface" between the government and Canadian citizens.

Over the years, a series of legislative acts have created the various agencies that are now responsible for the administration and maintenance of culture in Canada: the CBC, NFB, Telefilm Canada, and the Canada Council for the Arts are the primary instruments through which government implements cultural policy. At the same time, these agencies also act as the conduits through which cultural producers and communities can make their views and concerns known to government. The agencies thus act as the "mobile interface" by being simultaneously the instruments of government policy and lobbying agents for the cultural communities they serve. Therefore, in the absence of a genuine civil society that would construct (as Habermas [1989: 50-56] suggests) its own self-representation through cultural activity, the Canadian state has created a simulated civil society in the form of cultural agencies that are inserted between the formal structures of the state and its citizens.

In sum, the problematic of the sovereignty of the state, once thought to be solved through the construction of a communications and transportation apparatus, re-emerges at the level of culture. The solution to the crisis of what Charland called the "absent nation" produced through these space-binding technologies would be the inculcation of a Canadian culture through centrally administered programs delivered by federal agencies. From this perspective, culture functions not only as a "time-binding" mechanism, to use Innis' language, but also as a mechanism by which the space of the symbolic realm can be captured, to overcome the deficiencies engendered by dependency in the economic realm and the penetrative capacities of modern communications technologies. Culture thus functions as a security mechanism that compensates for dependency and works to secure the continued existence of the Canadian state.

From Sovereignty to Administrative Tactics

In his work on governmentality, Foucault describes the movement in modern governments from the conquest of territory to the development of an apparatus to administer those areas colonized. The object of sovereignty is territory: "the ensemble of objects of the prince's power ... are two things, on the one hand territory, and on the other its inhabitants. ... [S]overeignty is not exercised on things, but above all on territory and consequently on the subjects who inhabit it" (1991: 93). Foucault argues, however, that modern forms of government emerge with a different problematic — well-being (what Foucault refers to as the "proper distribution of things") — and therefore a different object: the welfare of the population. Arising from this transformation "from a regime dominated by structures of sovereignty to one ruled by techniques of government" is an ensemble of practices or "tactics" — what we might call policy — that is concerned not with space or territory, but with interventions to ensure the well-being of the populace; a society of government "which has as its target the population and as its essential mechanism the apparatuses of security" (Foucault, 1991: 102).

In Canada, the obsession with sovereignty and identity has obscured the analysis of forms of governmentality concerned with culture, of a set of tactics concerned with the security of the state through cultural regulation and administration. The entire problematic of culture emerges as an issue of security, once residual concerns over space subside (although they never vanish).[3] Policy here shifts from the direct concern for the maintenance of space to what, following Foucault, may be called the welfare of the population.

In one dimension, the administration of this welfare is undertaken (according to Foucault) by introducing the regimes of statistics, which become information bases for the practice of political economy with which modern government polices the state to ensure its well-being. What is important to note here is the introduction, through statistical methods, of the probable and the actuarial as the grounds for the maintenance of the population. Although this is understood by Foucault and others as the direct maintenance by the state of the population, through the control of birth-rates, public hygiene and the like, in Canada the probable also appears — not in relation to the economic welfare of the nation (which has been abandoned to various forms of dependency), but rather in relation to the presence or absence of culture, which has a direct bearing on the security of the state.

If we turn again to the Massey commission, we see how the probable enters the text in the form of dire consequences of governmental inaction. Inaction risks the probability of a slide into barbarism. This barbarism could come in two forms: the possibility of anarchy (as in Matthew Arnold's contrast of culture and anarchy);[4] or, the overwhelming of the Canadian state by American mass culture:

> a vast and disproportionate amount of material coming from a single alien source [the U.S.] may stifle rather than stimulate our own creative effort; and passively accepted without any standards of comparison, this may weaken critical faculties. We are now spending millions to maintain a national independence which would be nothing but an empty shell without a vigorous and distinctive cultural life (1951: 18).

The metaphor of an empty shell indicates the degree to which the commission understood implicitly that the defence of brute space is by itself insufficient. Culture would provide the bulwark to construct a strong nation with all its critical faculties intact, and to ward off the potentially harmful effects of creeping continentalism in the form of American mass culture.

It is here, with concerns over American culture on the airwaves and in the classroom, that the underlying logic of the cultural apparatus emerges: the security of the Canadian state. The function of culture would be to inculcate in Canadian citizens a sense of culture that would be both civilizing and — as a consequence — distinct from that of the United States. The Canadian state's formal entry into the production of culture marks the moment when government shifted from a preoccupation with sovereignty — that is, territoriality defined through the communications apparatus — to the tactics of governmentality: the use of culture as a disciplinary regime to ensure the development of a distinctive, and therefore defensible, character of the Canadian state.[5]

In Canada, culture is the nodal point at which policy and security interests converge. Clearly, in the terms set out by the Massey report, culture constituted a form of defence against both internal and external threats. Indeed, recent concerns over federal multicultural policies are yet another instance of the potential threat that culture represents to the internal order and security of the state. These concerns are, in turn, indicative of the "threats" that, as Wark has noted, have preoccupied the security intelligence apparatus in Canada since Confederation.

It is in recognizing the function of culture as a mechanism of security that we find culture's underlying rationality. In Foucault's schema, the modern state devolves its responsibility for security onto the private sector. Apart from insuring the "proper distribution of things" through various forms of intervention, the state leaves the market to run in a self-regulating fashion. The state simply provides insurance (cf. Gordon [1991: 40-41]). Once such things as basic social rights and health are secured, private institutions are freed to negotiate with labour and to develop contracts that work to ensure public order.[6] Culture here functions as part of the insurance that guarantees the civilizing regime required to ensure that citizens have inculcated civilized values and mores. Normally, this task would be left to private interests; like the transfer of power over production processes into the hands of civil society, responsibility for and powers over cultural production would also pass into private hands. Habermas (1989: 52) has suggested that in fact the "bourgeois public sphere" of eighteenth-century Europe arrogated to itself this power as a form of critical self-representation within which private forms of culture emerged.

In Canada, the absence or weakness of private interests and an underdeveloped civil society has virtually compelled the state to take up a direct role in most, if not all areas of the social. The predominance of government regulation suggests that, in Canada, the conditions for the transformation described by Foucault, that is, the devolution of certain powers onto the private sector, have been absent, and that therefore Canada developed in a different direction, that is, through the unique condition of government ownership.

Culture, however, potentially marks the moment when the Canadian state performs on its own behalf the transformation from preoccupation with issues of sovereignty toward a form of governmentality. The tactic employed to accomplish this is the creation of the conditions of self-regulation through the establishment of an apparatus that simulates civil society in the form of semi-autonomous cultural agencies. As a security apparatus, the agencies operate as forms of both discipline and surveillance that function to fend off the imminent collapse of the state. The central problematic of liberal governance — *omnium et singularum*, the simultaneous ordering of the individual and the whole — is to be solved through the regimen of culture. Each is to have a cultural identity through the process of *Bildung* or self-formation, organized by pedagogical strategies delivered through centralized national programs, and collectively, a Canadian culture, by virtue of the uniformity provided by cultural agencies offering programs of a nationwide scope.

The uniform national identity obtained through the cultural apparatus is then turned towards the maintenance of national security. As the Massey report points out,

If we as a nation are concerned with the problem of defence, what, we may ask ourselves, are we defending? We are defending civilisation, our share of it, our contribution to it. The things with which our inquiry deals are the elements which give civilisation its character and meaning. It would be paradoxical to defend something which we are unwilling to strengthen and enrich, and which we even allow to decline (1951: 274).

It would indeed be paradoxical to defend an empty space. Consequently, a culture must be constructed to meet the political objective of policing the actual borders, as well as what Wark refers to as the "metaphysical" frontier of the state, against both external and internal threats to national security.

Bernard Ostry places culture squarely within the context of defence interests: "Perhaps only the armed forces have understood from the start the importance of developing a sense of identity and the connection of culture with morale and community relations" (1978:5). The willingness of the Department of National Defence to develop "a conscious, consistent and imaginative cultural policy and provid[e] the funds to make it work," suggests that for some time it alone understood the crucial relation between security, culture and national interests (1978:5).

Ambivalence towards the role of culture is symptomatic of the ambivalent attitude in general of the Canadian state toward its own security interests. Laxer describes the unwillingness to create import substitutions — in the defence industries in particular — as a case of "aborted development." The attention given to communications and transportation at the expense of internal development is, Laxer emphasizes, an indication of the degree to which space has tended to preoccupy national policy at the expense of other forms of development and security. The attempt to shift the focus onto culture as a security apparatus may be read as an effort to counteract the dependency that has been encouraged by fiscal and industrial policies of the past and present. It is the recent attention given to the cultural industries that has come to make up for this deficit.

Industry and Culture

Reflecting on the Massey report in 1952, Innis (1952: 20) wrote that "By attempting constructive efforts to explore the cultural possibilities of various media and to develop them along lines free from commercialism, Canadians might make a contribution to the cultural life of the United States." It is perhaps fortunate that Innis did not live long enough to see his hopes dashed. Unlike the scenario envisioned by Innis, culture, rather than being peripheral to the economy (while remaining, of course, symbolically central), has come to be seen as the very core of Canadian economic activity, especially as the resource-based industries, the traditional epicentre of Canada's economy, wither away. As part of the process of strengthening the industrial base, decreasing dependency and increasing security, the industrialization of culture has become a significant economic strategy and policy objective of the state.

As Woodrow et. al. noted, by the late 1970s this transformation was already evident in the ministries directly concerned with the administration of culture:

The department [of communication] is coming to be perceived more as a science-based unit promoting an increasingly important aspect of Canada's overall industrial strategy and less as a culture-oriented unit responsible for managing the instruments whereby Canadian identity is shaped (1980: 65).

It is not, however, the substitution of an industrial strategy for a cultural mandate that has occurred, but rather a blending of these two areas into a combined strategy. Since the mid-seventies, there has been an increasing convergence of industrial, economic and cultural policy. Arguably, this began in the early seventies, with various programs introduced by the federal government, such as Opportunities for Youth and the Local Initiatives Program, that were designed as economic and employment stimuli and, at the same time, mandated as part of cultural initiatives such as the national unity program. With the creation of the Canadian Film Development Corporation in 1968, the federal government formally combined cultural activity with industrial strategy in one agency.

With the tenure of Francis Fox as minister of communications in the late 1970s, as André Fortier has noted, the expression "cultural industries" made its appearance in government discourse (Canada Council 1987: 11). It also marks the moment that the possibility of cultural innovation free from the pressures of the marketplace, a hope embodied in both the Massey report's recommendations and in Innis' reflections on its report, collapsed on desire of the government to see culture pay for itself, and as the resource economy withered away, to see culture as a new staple for export markets. As Ted Magder (1993: 195) has remarked, by 1980 "it was clear that the emphasis would be placed squarely on the development of Canada's cultural industries, as much for economic as cultural concerns."

Despite distinctions made when discussing cultural or industrial sectors, all of the institutions (both private and public) concerned with either cultural or industrial mandates are nevertheless united at the level of economic arrangements in relation to the Canadian state. These two areas — industry and culture — if conceptually distinct, share various forms of public-sector subsidy and administration by agencies and regulatory bodies. From this perspective, both industry and culture are identical in that they have developed historically under the more or less direct supervision of the public sector.

Culture, however, has become more than simply a counter-strategy to economic dependence. We must attend to the transformation of culture from a purely defence-oriented security apparatus into a basis for economic self-sufficiency. Once culture becomes an economic component, and industry and culture converge, a distinction appears between "pure" culture and industrially organized forms of cultural production. As culture is increasingly viewed through the optic of economy, its former status as the locus of the construction of identity must be renegotiated. As "pure" culture, the creation of creative and interpretive products was stimulated for the purposes of security in the absence of economic independence. Culture has now also become the means to achieve economic independence; its original function as the signature of Canadian distinctiveness is put to further use within the economic realm.

Rethinking Communications and Culture

To the extent that government support remains crucial for cultural production in general, we are faced with something of a paradox. To explore the "cultural possibilities" as Innis put it — or the economic possibilities — of communication media, requires, in the absence of the institutions of civil society and a strong internal market, extensive state involvement. Arguably, then, the innovative possibilities ascribed to Canadian cultural practices at the margin can only occur as the product of the consolidation of a relation organized by the state. Thus, dependency is reconstituted at another level: freeing cultural activities from market considerations results in reliance on the state. Returning culture to the economy likewise requires government assistance. This dependency however, as we have seen, is consistent with the history of Canada itself, and constitutes what Innis referred to as Canada's unique circumstances of development.

"Policy makers and government officials," writes Ted Magder, "make frequent reference to Canada's envious communications infrastructure as a source, sometimes *the* source, of nation building. Sovereignty, in this view, is a function of the cultural linkages afforded by communications technology" (1993: 237). However, as he goes on to say, quoting Robert Babe, it is possible, given the penetration of the communications system, that "Canada as a nation persists despite, not because of communication media." Arguably, it persists due to the resistance produced through cultural policy. This begs the question of whether it is appropriate to consider culture primarily within a communications perspective. The problem is, to put it simply, that the communications approach emphasizes communications at the expense of a consideration of culture. No doubt, communications research has examined the cultural effects of a national broadcasting infrastructure. Strategically, however, to define the analysis of cultural policy within the context of communications is to restrict it unduly. Although communication plays a key role in the formation of nation, it is inappropriate, both historically and in terms of current research, to identify the development of culture with the history of communications in Canada. Complicit with this is the term "cultural industries" itself.

I suppose it would do no harm here to remind ourselves of the origin of the term "cultural industries." Originally coined by Frankfurt School members Max Horkheimer and Theodor Adorno, the term was not plural, but singular — culture industry — which was meant to convey both its monolithic and oxymoronic status (Horkheimer and Adorno: 1986). In other words, it was formulated specifically to underline the contradiction between the idea of culture and industrial production. That recent usage has become commonplace and normative is an indication of distance between current research and the critical theory of the Frankfurt School.

In policy analysis, the problematics of industry and culture have to be separated again — if not pitted against each other, then at least understood as sites of friction and contestation, if we are to begin to grasp the historical development of cultural policy in Canada. In the past, it might have been claimed that it was relatively easy to distinguish between cultural policy and practices and industrial and economic policy. These two areas appeared, until recently at least, as discrete sectors of policy engagement. Indeed, a history of the cultural policy apparatus centred on the issue of security, as suggested here, might have been pursued with a disregard for the specifics of economic policy. This, however, is no longer possible.

To put it succinctly, we have to consider culture and industry not as an identity but in terms of their shifting relationship to each other, particularly where it concerns the analysis of cultural policy. What this entails, in brief, is the development of a historical and contemporary understanding of the relations between industrial policy and what one might call an "arts" policy. Cultural policy has been split into two: areas of culture implicated within economic strategies, the "cultural industries" proper, and "pure" culture — art. The negotiation between those two domains for scarce resources is crucial to understanding the development of cultural policy, particularly in recent times. In other words, the relationship between what the

Appelbaum-Hebert report called "industrial" and "non-industrial" cultural practices has to be taken into account (Canada, 1982: 33).

Although a sector-by-sector analysis can be valuable, as demonstrated by this volume, the genesis of the cultural policy apparatus and its logic cannot be derived in this manner. What I have suggested here is that the analysis of policy must begin with the question of security and governmentality. Much work remains to be done. A number of areas broached in this essay require further examination; among others, perhaps the most in need of explication is the relationship between culture and defence. Ostry's claim in particular, that the Department of National Defence was the first federal institution to develop a cultural program, warrants further investigation. In addition, the increasingly complex and intimate relation between economic strategies and cultural policy merits attention. Along with these two areas, considerable research is still to be done with regard to the interrelationship between defence and communications, especially signals intelligence, which remains as yet unexamined in communications scholarship. This latter topic might be especially enlightening in regard to the links between defence and culture.

A fuller understanding of the complexity of historical and current undertakings in these areas can only emerge by linking the studies presented in this volume with a thorough and extensive examination of policy discourses and instruments created to administer those undertakings. As indicated through the various domains touched on in this discussion, a much wider scope is required to examine the relationships between policy, industry and national development. Although hackneyed as an expression at this juncture, an "interdisciplinary approach" is more urgent than ever within communications scholarship.

Notes

1. As a recent report (Groupe Secor, 1994: 81) notes, government intervention in film and video is based "primarily on objectives relating to policy and cultural identity."
2. "[W]ith government it is a question not of imposing law on men, but of disposing things: that is to say, of employing tactics rather than laws ... to arrange things in such a way that, through a certain number of means, such and such ends may be achieved" (Foucault, 1991: 95).
3. One could provide any number of examples of persisting sovereign concerns, from the continuing problem of national interests in the far north to native land claims, and so on.

4. As Paul Litt (1992: 100) writes of Massey, "The members of the culture lobby were indebted to Arnold for more than just inspiring quotations; their views echoed his on a number of fundamental points."

5. As Marc Raboy (1990: 25) points out, the educational component of culture was central to the function of the CBC, formed some years before the Massey commission.

6. "This can be illustrated by the development ... of a hybrid space of government in which public law is coupled with forms of 'private' power and authority ... [T]he central state declares the determination of the specific regulatory and disciplinary requirements of different production processes to be beyond its legislative competence. The power and responsibility for determining the disciplinary order necessary for production is therefore best left to individual employers. The resultant system of employer tutelage might be described as a kind of private government order, legally sanctioned by the state ..." (Burchell, 1991: 141).

References

Burchell, Graham. 1991. "Peculiar Interests: Civil Society and Governing 'the System of Natural Liberty.'" In *The Foucault Effect: Studies in Governmentality*. Graham Burchell et al. (eds.). Chicago: University of Chicago.

Canada Council Policy Secretariat. 1987. Transcription of "Debate on Culture and Regionalism," June 18, 1987. Canada Council File 400-399: Arts and Regionalism-General.

Canada. Federal Cultural Policy Review Committee. 1982. *Report*. Ottawa: Minister of Supply and Services.

———. Royal Commission on National Development in the Arts, Letters, and Sciences. 1951. *Report*. Ottawa: King's Printer.

Charland, Maurice. 1986. "Technological Nationalism." *Canadian Journal of Political and Social Theory* X: 1-2.

Dorland, Michael. 1991. "The Discursive Economy of the Emergence of the Canadian Feature Film: Discourses of Dependency and Governmentalization of a Displaced National Cinema, 1957–1968." Ph.D. diss., Concordia University.

Foucault, Michel. 1991. "Governmentality." In *The Foucault Effect: Studies in Governmentality*. Graham Burchell et al. (eds.). Chicago: University of Chicago.

Globerman, Steven. 1983. *Cultural Regulation in Canada*. Montreal: Institute for Research in Public Policy.

Gordon, Colin. 1991. "Governmental Rationality: An Introduction." In *The Foucault Effect: Studies in Governmentality*. Graham Burchell et al. (eds.). Chicago: University of Chicago.

Groupe Secor. 1994. *Canadian Government Intervention in the Film and Video Industry*. Ottawa: Heritage Canada.

Habermas, Jürgen. 1989. *The Structural Transformation of the Public Sphere*. Thomas Burger (trans.). Cambridge, Mass.: M.I.T.

Horkheimer, Max and Theodor Adorno. 1986. *Dialectic of Enlightenment*. John Cumming (trans.). New York: Continuum.

Innis, Harold. 1930. *The Fur Trade in Canada: An Introduction to Canadian Economic History*. New Haven: Yale University.

———. 1933. *Problems of Staple Production in Canada.* Toronto: Ryerson.

———. 1952. *Changing Concepts of Time.* Toronto: University of Toronto.

———. 1956. *Essays in Canadian Economic History.* Toronto: University of Toronto.

Laxer, Gordon. 1985. "The Political Economy of Aborted Development: The Canadian Case." In Robert J. Brym (ed.). *The Structure of the Canadian Capitalist Class.* Toronto: Garamond.

Litt, Paul. 1992. *The Muses, the Masses, and the Massey Commission.* Toronto: University of Toronto.

Magder, Ted. 1993. *Canada's Hollywood: The Canadian State and Feature Films.* Toronto: University of Toronto.

Neill, Robin. 1981. "Imperialism and the Staple Theory of Development." In William Melody et al. (eds.). *Culture, Communication and Dependency: The Tradition of H.A. Innis.* Norwood, NJ: Ablex.

Ostry, Bernard. 1978. *The Cultural Connection: An Essay on Culture and Government Policy in Canada.* Toronto: McClelland and Stewart.

Raboy, Paul. 1990. *Missed Opportunities: The Story of Canada's Broadcasting Policy.* Montreal: McGill-Queen's.

Wark, Wesley. 1992. "Security Intelligence in Canada 1864–1945: The History of a National Insecurity State." In Keith Nelson and B.J.C. McKercher (eds.). *Go Spy the Land: Military Intelligence in History.* Westport, CT.: Praeger.

Woodrow, R. Brian, Kenneth Woodside, Henry Wiseman and John B. Black. 1980. *Conflict Over Communications Policy: A Study of Federal-Provincial Relations and Public Policy.* Montreal: C.D. Howe Institute.

13

Cultural Industries and the Canadian Experience: Reflections on the Emergence of a Field

Michael Dorland

Canada has had a relatively long experience with cultural industries. It was, in the early years of the twentieth century, one of the first modern states to recognize that the state itself could play a significant role in the production of motion-picture images to promote immigration and industrial development (see Backhouse [1974], also Hill [1977]). It was the first North American state to establish a national broadcasting system, modelled on the British Broadcasting Corporation's approach to public service broadcasting. During the years of the Second World War, the National Film Board of Canada grew into one of the major film propaganda factories serving the Allied war effort, its newsreels appearing on thousands of theatre screens across North America (Morris, 1986). The development of Canadian television in the 1950s, particularly in the French language, remains a triumph of technical innovation on a continental scale, as well as an extraordinarily creative use of limited dramatic resources for nation building (see Deutsch [1961], Laurence [1982], Miller [1987], Rutherford [1990]). Canada would, in the 1970s, extend its television-signal delivery infrastructure to become one of the most heavily cabled countries in the world (Babe, 1975). Whether one talks about film animation, community radio, educational television, telecommunications development, northern broadcasting, the development of new communications technologies or computer software, the role played by Canadian institutions and firms has been pioneering and consistently innovative, earning a well-deserved and worldwide reputation for technical excellence and high-quality standards (Graham, 1989).

At the same time, however, Canadian public life and policy have been bedevilled by an intense preoccupation, spanning most of the twentieth century, over how "expressive technologies" (Lanham, 1993: ix) intersect with national development and public policies in communication. For all its technical achievements, Canada remains a fragile communicative entity, plagued by recurring problems of national identity, both internal and external; internally, subject to chronic doubts, lengthily articulated, as to its fundamental viability as a political body; externally, repeatedly battered and buffeted by the storm winds blowing through the international political economy, whether in exchange rates, in trade flows, or in received wisdom, not the least of such storms being produced by the shifting currents of Canada's perpetually problematic economic, cultural and political relations with its principal continental neighbour. Nowhere have the problems appeared more seemingly self-evident than in the realm of cultural industries policy, as attested by the now-classic litany of statistics that document Canada's cultural domination by the media output of the United States: that country occupies some 97 per cent of Canada's theatrical film screens, over 90 per cent of the offerings of television drama on Canadian TV, some 76 per cent of the books sold in Canada, control of some 89 per cent of earnings in sound recording and so on (see data in Canada [1987: 11]). Indeed, until only recently, the term *Canadianization* was, in the vocabulary of international media analysts, a synonym for the dire fate that awaited other nations if they were to prove as unprotective of their cultural industries as Canada.

It has long been a largely unquestioned assumption of Canadian policy makers that such a cohabitation could only produce harmful cultural consequences among the citizenry, who thus had to be protected from the worst of its cultural effects by border controls and tariffs, censorship of the mails, censorship of the movies, regulation of the airwaves and an associated panoply of administrative and legal measures affecting everything from content to ownership. Foreign observers may perhaps be forgiven for harbouring similar assumptions about the overall impact of the United States upon Canada's cultural industries.

Paradoxically, and there is no shortage of paradoxes at play here, as a number of analyses, both national and international, have already made clear (see Gwyn [1985], Collins [1990], Tomlinson [1991], de la Garde, Gilsdorf and Wechselmann [1993]), assumptions about the injurious cultural effects of media imperialism may have served to conceal far more interesting and pertinent developments in the analysis of cultural industries and cultural industries policy. It is to a re-examination of these assumptions that this book seeks to address itself. As broadcasting policy historian Marc Raboy has put it, if the principal policy issue in Canada has been historically how to deal with American cultural domination and its damaging effects, "it may be time to consider whether that emphasis does not obscure more than it reveals about the real nature of Canadian media" (Raboy, 1990: 339).

Mapping Canada's Cultural Industries: The Nationalist Model

The standard Canadian text, published well over a decade ago and based on data collected in the late 1970s, is Paul Audley's influential *Canada's Cultural Industries* (1983). It accurately reflects the evolution of the field that the present volume, originally conceived of as a revision of Audley's pioneering study, is a work of multiple authorship and, accordingly, of a plurality of analytical perspectives. Not only, in the intervening years, has the number of Canadian cultural industries changed from the initial enumeration established by Audley, but so too have the questions that frame the analysis of cultural industries. If Audley's 1983 study represented the zenith of one particular analytical model, a nationalist model, one of the current difficulties is that it is far from evident that any one model is adequate to the complexity of its object. The contradictions of the term *cultural industries* show that what is at stake is the reconciliation of two possibly antithetical domains; one that is designated by the loose term *culture*, and the other by the equally variegated notion *industry*.

Audley's 1983 study put Canadian cultural industries on the map of international scholarship (McAnany, 1987: 1-30). Before that, the analysis of Canada's cultural industries had been almost entirely a preoccupation internal to the Canadian cultural policy apparatus (such as the CRTC and the Secretary of State, later the Department of Communication, today the Department of Canadian Heritage), the state agencies involved in the production and subsidization of film and television (such as the Canadian Broadcasting Corporation, the National Film Board and the Canadian Film Development Corporation, today Telefilm Canada) and the professional associations, trade unions and other professional lobby groups. Only rarely (with the one exception of the study of film) would a voice be heard from the Anglo-Canadian academic world expressing interest in the analysis of the cultural industries in Canada, but these isolated interventions were often only a step towards larger concerns in economic or political analysis (see e.g., Porter [1965], Clement [1975]), or so quirkily individualistic as to be unable to command more sustained interest (Smythe, 1981).

Audley's 1983 study, with its quantitative rigour that set a new standard of excellence, its even-handed relentlessness in mapping out, in one cultural industry after the other, the same recurring pattern of an industrial organization structured by the import of non-Canadian cultural materials, and its calm recommendations for practical public policy, was the first book to take the analysis of cultural industries in Canada seriously. This was both the study's great strength as well as its great weakness, for in squarely foregrounding the "deep structures" of Canada's cultural dependency and their influence, in turn, on the development of Canadian cultural industries, Audley did not consider how that pattern of development might have warped the policies themselves. Instead, Audley made two assumptions that, in retrospect, were premature. Firstly, he assumed that the development of the cultural industries would differ sensibly from the American or industrial model; that is, the outcome would be clearly more cultural than industrial; and, secondly, that this outcome was in the interests of public policy; that is, that agents, the state notably, were prepared to bring it to fruition.

In the historical context within which Audley wrote, the fit between such assumptions and the activities of policy makers was less dissonant than it would become subsequently. The period from the mid-1960s to the late 1970s were heady years for Canadian cultural nationalism, which established the principal legislative and institutional framework within which Canada's cultural industries would be regulated; indeed, these years saw the takeoff of a number of cultural industries as well as the principal policy measures enabling that development (state-subsidized capital pools and modifications to income-tax legislation) (see Lacroix and Lévesque [1988]). These are also years of increasing conflict between the federal government and the government of Quebec over the strategies and tactics of cultural development; and, furthermore, years in which the com-modification of Canadian cultural production as an increasingly in-dustrial or distinctly economic form of activity proceeded apace in unprecedented ways. In other words, at the very moment when Audley's path-breaking analysis of the principal Canadian cultural industries found its way into print, the increasing tensions between culture and industry brought about by the nationalist model of policy making, of which Audley's book remains perhaps the most distin-guished codification, would unravel at three points: in the increasing gap between a nationalist-culturalist policy discourse and its indus-trial creations; in the increasing reliance upon industrial or economic policy measures; and as a result, in the increasing commodification of Canadian cultural production, with its emphasis on profitability. It is also within this precise conjuncture that the term *cultural indus-tries* became current in policy discourse itself.

Cultural Industries Policy Origins

The term was brought into the discourse of Canadian policy when Michael McCabe, today head of the Canadian Association of Broadcasters, became executive director of the Canadian Film Development Corporation in the late 1970s. Although he would hold the position at the CFDC for only two years, the McCabe years were the heyday of the Capital Cost Allowance (income-tax shelter) boom in Canadian feature film production financing, which one analyst has described as "a monument to irresponsible policy making [that] comes as close to being a pure taxpayer 'rip-off' as one is ever likely to find" (Globerman, 1983: 77). Of more lasting significance than the high-rolling McCabe's pursuit of marketing strategies, production values and commercialization, an en-trepreneurial cadre of feature film producers and the internationali-zation of Canadian feature film production, was the reconceptualization of the very nature of Canada's involvement in cultural development (see Stiles [1980-81: 438-40]). At last, a name could be given to a phenomenon in which Canadians, whether as film-makers or broad-casters, as producers or as bureaucratic regulators, had already de-veloped some practical experience, but had never adequately articulated. In identifying the object of policy as the development of cultural industries (see especially Canada, DOC AR 1980–81, 1981: 7), policy makers not only named more accurately what previously had been an object of confusion, but also cut through many of the contradictory impetuses that had until then prevented a more coherent formation of policy.

Terminological Confusions

As a number of commentators have pointed out (Thomas, 1960, Fortner, 1986, Raboy, 1990), a good portion of the dilemmas in Canadian communication and cultural policy is terminological, most notably in the confusion of the terms *public* and *state*, which have traditionally been seen as interchangeable. This has served to obscure, as Raboy has made clear, the extent to which the broadcasting system has been a state broadcasting system, and not a public broadcaster (Raboy, 1990: xii). Re-emphasizing this distinction illuminates why the incorporation of the privately owned elements of the broadcasting system has historically been so problematic, and why, furthermore, Canadian-content programming would consistently arouse the passions it has, at least until the late 1980s (Peers, 1969, 1979). As a state broadcasting system — in other words, as an instrument of nationalist "political" development concerned with the management of scarcity (whether spectrum, channel or resource) — the Canadian version has embodied compromises between institutional contradictions (between nation and state, between state and public, between public and private). A similar, but slightly less complicated set of circumstances, has prevailed in the development of film production. But these at least, the Canadian Government Motion Picture Bureau (1917), and its institutional successor, the National Film Board of Canada (1939), were clearly state agencies, operating with relatively unproblematic mandates to produce documentary films for national propaganda purposes. Matters became more complex, however, when other film genres (the feature film, for example) or other technologies of delivery (such as television) came into the picture. Considering that the NFB already produced visual images, why should it not have primary institutional responsibility for television's development in Canada? In other words, what would happen, given not only the technological possibility of an increase in either production genres or communication media, but even more importantly of a shift in the fundamental principle of regulation? What were the regulatory implications of a shift from medium scarcity to an abundance of media?

Here matters became even more delicate. In the 1920s, Canadian independent movie theatres had, in the major urban centres, fallen under the control of the vertically integrated corporate chains elaborated in the United States (first in film and then in broadcasting). This chain ownership soon expanded worldwide, with Canada as the closest "foreign" market (Jarvie, 1992). In the movie theatres, Canadian state agencies in film produced documentary newsreel shorts that preceded the U.S.-produced feature films. In broadcasting, Canada produced news, some drama, some music, some variety programming, as well as coverage of special events and sports reporting. The rest of the programming originated in the United States. (In the French language in Canada, the premium was always on the production of indigenous content since there was no other readily available source of supply to draw upon.) The Canadian state agencies in film and broadcasting production in English accommodated themselves to the predominant North American media political economy, supplying in effect the *niche* programming necessary to satisfy some Canadian political imperatives the American media could not. In this way, the NFB, during the years of the Second World War, became integrated into the North American structure of theatrical ownership and programming, just as, with the advent of Canadian television, the CBC would eventually, every fall, join with CBS, NBC and ABC in the annual trek to Hollywood to purchase programming for the upcoming broadcast year (ex-CBC producer James Taylor, now at the Université de Montréal, personal communication). For Canadian state policy, there were remarkably few problems in an arrangement that appeared to suit all the parties concerned.

Problems of Canadian Cultural Development: From Scarcity to Abundance

The Second World War saw massive technological transformations and produced new forms of corporate organization, new generations of highly skilled technicians and new realms of social activity in which states would intervene in unprecedented scale and scope. The postwar period also witnessed new demands by new actors for state action in areas where the state had not traditionally played a significant role. In the Canadian context, one new domain of intervention was designated by the loose term of culture (Canada, 1951; Tippett, 1990; Litt 1992). Without retelling the 1950s institutional interventions in high culture or in the realm of post-secondary education (see Ostry [1978], Axelrod [1982], Cummings and Katz [1987]), it should be observed that the institutional development of Canada's mass media saw crisis after crisis, beginning with the post-Gouzenko national security evisceration of the National Film Board and its eventual expulsion from Ottawa in 1956 to Montreal (see Vronneau [1979]; Whitaker and Marcuse [1994: chs. 10 and 11]). These events occurred within the interinstitutional struggle between the NFB and the CBC for control of the new medium of television, a defeat for the NFB that was in turn followed by the institutional severing of the CBC from the regulation of broadcasting and the redrafting of the Broadcast Act in 1958 by the Diefenbaker Conservatives. On the other hand, it was also the Conservatives who implemented the rare recourse to screen quotas that would be Canadian content regulation in television. A tumultuous period that culminated in the Radio-Canada producers' strike of 1960, which cemented divisions within the broadcasting system along linguistic lines, the decade and a half from the mid-1940s to the early 1960s was a period of institutional upheaval for Canada's state-owned cultural industries (Peers, 1969, 1979, Raboy, 1990). Behind the upheaval was the policy problem of how to incorporate into the state sector the privately owned cultural industries. These private cultural industries were making their presence felt, particularly in broadcasting policy. So much so that, as one analyst put it, the universe of public policy in broadcasting changed completely in the course of the 1950s (Fortner, 1986: 32) as the discourse shifted away from a focus on scarcity (whether of spectrum or content) to the problems of programming and media abundance. Conversely, if it was becoming increasingly evident that the private cultural industries were able to command sufficient policy clout as to have the Broadcasting Act rewritten, to oust the CBC from the regulation of broadcasting and to develop second (i.e., privately owned) television networks (CTV and TVA in 1961), it was equally evident that the responses of the state sector rang hollow when confronted by ever more vocal charges that it constituted unfair competition, that it inefficiently monopolized substantial production resources and that the private sector constituted a competitive industrial model with a potentially global capacity, a development that would be in the national interest to encourage, if not subsidize.

Rhetorics of Canadian Broadcasting

However appealing such arguments were, they remained nevertheless open to criticism because the discourse on Canadian (state) broadcasting was still couched in national security language. The policy origins of Canadian broadcasting, in Graham Spry's clever slogan of the early 1930s, had been posed as a stark choice: "The State or the United States." In this light, Canadian broadcasting represented the symbolic transposition of the imperatives of national security into the cultural domain. Thus, the constant emphasis was on cultural fortification and edification, defence against cultural contamination, especially the contaminations of commercial or mass culture, with its advertising and "lowest-common-denominator" programming and so on. That such a rhetorical construction was, in fundamental respects, largely untrue, and daily betrayed by the media practices of the very state institutions established to embody the cultural defence of Canada did not, however, make it any less effective as rhetoric. Year after year, both the legislation regulating Canadian broadcasting and the various royal commissions and inquiries since Aird (1928) elaborated the rhetorical mythologies of Canadian broadcasting (see Bird [1988]). By conflating cultural development with the defence of territorial security, an approach to culture had been institutionalized that was top-heavy with political considerations; indeed, that privileged politics over any alternative form of discourse; in other words, that made media programming a test of political loyalty (see Raboy [1990: 8-10]). Given such a discursive framework, the potential economic challenge posed by the development of private Canadian cultural industries was always open to rhetorical attack as a covert conduit not only for American media interests, but also for "American" forms of programming. What such a rhetoric could conveniently disregard was, for one, the extent to which the Canadian state institutions had accommodated themselves to the North American marketplace; secondly, that the modus vivendi established between the Canadian state institutions and the dominant American media interests had created, within Canada, an institutional bottleneck that restrained the future growth of private cultural industries; and thirdly that Canadian state institutions, because of interinstitutional rivalries, had never been able adequately to supply Canadian programming. It was precisely the need for more programming that, in the late 1950s, was becoming central. Given the voracious programming demands of a new technology such as television, not only was the need for supply increasing exponentially in light of the extension of the broadcasting day, but it was also increasing qualitatively because of a proliferation of new genres, particularly television series (see Ballio [1990], Rutherford [1990]).

Thus, it was not coincidental that the issue of Canadian-content programming became a policy preoccupation in the late 1950s. Given the Canadian context, with its particular politicization of broadcasting, the problems of new production forms — here, film and feature film production in particular, now moved increasingly toward the centre of the policy agenda. As would, in tandem, the problems of other cultural industries, such as magazine and book publishing, since, in fundamental respects, they were all of a piece: how, in the Canadian context, to facilitate the commodification of cultural production and make Canadian production more saleable? (see Canada [1961], [1970], Ontario [1973])

Paradoxical Byproducts

One of the paradoxical initial byproducts of Canadian television, then, was the unintentional creation of a film industry. Not only were the state institutions such as the CBC and the NFB obliged to co-operate with each other in order, however inadequately, to rationalize the production of Canadian programming, the ever-growing flow of television production demanded a seeming infinity of filler, of short films and animation that before long generated a secondary level of production infrastructure that absorbed the excess capacity of the primary production infrastructure — the in-house production capability of the state-sector. The increasing demand for Canadian television programming, initially of the CBC, and subsequently with the creation of second, private networks (1961), also attracted the interest of American firms, which developed both a generic and a transnational approach to supply in the form of series production. The CBC at the beginning of the 1950s was the sole Canadian TV producer; by the end of the decade there would be two more sources of programming supply, one in Canadian private production and the other in the transnational spillover of American television production companies. Significantly, the latter two both spoke a similar language that combined a discourse of popular forms of entertainment with the categories of economic efficiency (growth) and consumer sovereignty (choice); both represented privately owned (capitalistic) forms of the economic organization of cultural production; and, most alarmingly for the state sector, the transcontinental private sector was exploring mergers and equivalent forms of resource pooling to ensure continuities in the future supply of programming. But in what sense would that programming be Canadian?

The difficulty was that it would never be clear exactly what was meant by Canadian programming, as the initial efforts by the Board of Broadcast Governors in the late 1950s to establish criteria for the evaluation of Canadian content were to show (Stewart and Hull, 1994). Part of the difficulties stemmed from making political criteria the standard of measurement for what was arguably a different domain of activity, either cultural or economic. Even on its own terms, the notion of Canadian content implied relations between differential domains of social activity that were by no means self-evident: was "Canadianness" solely an effect of political affiliation, a byproduct of citizenship? In this sense, only Canadian citizens could produce Canadian content. But what about certain events, such as, say, the coronation or marriages of members of the British royal family, or sports events such as the World Series, or entertainment events such as the Oscars, that were of public interest to large numbers of Canadian citizens? Was coverage of these to count as Canadian content since Canadian citizens watched them? If so, then citizenship alone could not be a sufficient criterion since these events were Canadian not on political grounds, but on the basis of some other, broader principle of association, say, of culture or economics.

Clearly, the question of Canadian content posed a whole range of problems about the state's legal authority to demand such a thing as Canadian content from the activities, either leisure or business, of its citizens. How much, in fact, could the federal state actually intervene in international trade flows when it was bound, by international agreements such as the General Agreement on Tariffs and Trade, for instance, to specific policies of non-interference?

The Achievements of Canadian Cultural Nationalism

Most of these questions would be resolved in the course of the 1960s and 1970s, at least sufficiently to ensure that the ownership of the channels of communication had to be majoritarily in Canadian hands. The resolution of these questions (such as what is Canadian content and who enforces it?), required the various legal, institutional, administrative, economic and cultural measures that have since constituted the regulatory context within which the Canadian cultural industries have grown to relative maturity. Establishing this moderately formidable apparatus of laws, regulations and agencies was the extraordinary achievement of the heyday of Canadian cultural nationalism. For what was successfully achieved in those years, enabled by the rhetoric of cultural nationalism, was a relatively smooth transition from the pre-1960s universe of the regulation of media scarcity to the post-1960s management of media abundance. The 1950s development of the Canadian private cultural industries (in radio and television, in film, in book and magazine publishing, initially) had posed two principal problems — one of form and the other of content — that the regulatory apparatus could not respond to without tearing itself apart through its own contradictions. The principal one in broadcasting was that it constituted one entity, the so-called single system, that somehow reconciled two contradictory, constitutive logics, the one private, the other state. Given the development of private cultural industries, from where was their further growth to derive, and on the basis of what principle of growth? To the extent that the principle of growth within capitalist economies is that of private accumulation, that growth would only be possible either at the expense of the state-owned sector or by the increased dissemination of American private production — unless, of course, both courses could jointly be negotiated. The notion of Canadian content offered a way out of the dilemma, to the extent this was understood to mean 1) that Canadian content was equivalent to Canadian private production and, thus, 2) that the resources of the state-owned sector henceforth existed primarily to develop private production. In this light, from the mid-sixties on, the object of state policy was also to be understood primarily as the development of Canadian *private* cultural industries, producing cultural commodities for the purpose of profitable exchange in the potentially global marketplace of cultural production. On that basis could the Canadian state rationalize interventions in support of the development of new forms of Canadian industry (the cultural industries as infant industries). But, if the form of growth was henceforth to be private, the content of growth was also private (i.e., ownable by private parties and as such exchangeable as commodities). As Marshall McLuhan (1964) never tired of repeating, communication technologies were content-driven; what drove the development of media from one to another was the need for content. In this sense, the Canadian radio-television broadcasting system had developed as a paradox: formally Canadian, but at the level of content, primarily American in programming; its second tier, Canadian private television, also developed by carrying American programming; its third tier, the further extension of the Canadian broadcasting system by cable, was as well made possible by carrying American programming. But if all of these "import substitution" increases in technology and/or production had made possible the spinoff of new Canadian cultural industries, these came at a price: the onus increasingly rested upon them to make it in the marketplace as content-producers in their own right or, sooner or later, face extinction. The only question was when that day of reckoning would come. How, then, was Canadian content to become commodified? The answer would require some 25 years of hesitant experimentation to work out.

From Culture Industry to Cultural Industries

How did culture transform itself into commodities? How did one go about "industrializing" culture? The Ottawa bureaucrats who gave the term cultural industries currency in Canadian policy discourse most likely did not know its conceptual origins, in a then-obscure book written in the 1940s by two German refugee intellectuals who had taught at Columbia University before their postwar return to the University of Frankfurt. In their jointly written *Dialectic of Enlightenment* (1947), Max Horkheimer and T. W. Adorno included a chapter analysing the American film and television industry from the perspective of what they ironically and oxymoronically termed "the culture industry." For Horkheimer and Adorno, the culture industry represented the unprecedented extension into the realm of leisure of the rhythms, pace, simplifications and illusions of the industrial, assembly-line-based model of work. In Horkheimer and Adorno's view, among the "mass deceptions" effected by the culture industry was the illusion that there continued to be a distinction between work and non-work (leisure), when precisely what mattered was that the culture industry, by means of the concept of entertainment, since it combined elements of both work and leisure, had abolished that distinction — as well as that between life and art, original and copy, real and fake, authentic and inauthentic (1982: 120-167).

Adorno and Horkheimer's analysis of the culture industry languished, largely unread, until the 1970s when it was rediscovered by Marxist analysts of contemporary mass-media culture, initially in Germany (Enzensberger, 1971) and then in France (Piemme 1975, Huet et al., 1978, Gutierrez Vega, 1978, UNESCO, 1980). In its rediscovered form, the concept of the culture industry did seem to identify key dimensions of the puzzling fusion of cultural forms with capitalist modes of organization. At the same time, since it was clear that the cultural industries did not constitute an ideological monolith, as Adorno and Horkheimer had claimed, the arguably empirical differences between the capitalist organization of theatre, publishing, film or television production, say, meant that instead of one culture industry there were in fact a plurality of cultural industries. This pluralistic approach to the analysis of cultural industries thus generated new research approaches and topics for empirical investigation, particularly for Marxist economists and sociologists interested in the field of culture. It was this predominantly morphological approach to the analysis of cultural production that found its way from France into Canadian university sociology departments in the mid-1970s, and subsequently into policy discourses.

Living with Post-nationalism

The study of Canada's cultural industries in morphological terms has consisted in identifying the principal structural determinants that have shaped these industries. The cultural nationalist context within which Canadian cultural industries research began to develop posed the question: at what point did the intellectual activities of research and analysis become the more explicitly political ones of the management of change? In the Canadian context, the gap between the two was lesser than greater. As Globerman has insightfully observed: "The most important weakness of cultural policy making in Canada is its focus on operational considerations, that is, how to increase cultural production in Canada, rather than on the more fundamental issue of whether and why there is too little cultural output produced in Canada and by Canadians" (1983: xxiii). With a policy-making culture unreflectively oriented towards operationalization, that is to say, in which research has been primarily a response to political or policy demands, there is considerable risk of confusing the findings of analysis and the imperatives of policy implementation, but even more, of truncating the analysis, with unrealistic policies as a result. The morphological approach to Canada's cultural industries entailed the identification of the structural constraints that affected these industries, but how many such structures were there? This was tantamount to asking what the major structures of social action are. Arguably, the economic domain should be of major importance, so what are the pertinent economic dimensions? At the crudest level, what datum is to count as significant? Who is to do the counting, and according to what method? Assuming that the major economic structures constraining Canada's cultural industries could be adequately identified, are these the same for all cultural industries, or are there significant differences from one cultural industry to another? (Audley in 1983, for instance, concluded that on the whole the differences were minor [1983: 320-322]). But is an economic analysis of the cultural industries sufficient, especially when, however much they might be industries, they are also industries of a very particular kind?

How, then, does culture figure in the analysis? How is culture to be distinguished from ideology? And what implications does such a distinction raise for the study of cultural industries? And, finally, what of the state? What, for that matter, is to be understood by the state in the Canadian context? What kind of ideological, economic and/or cultural constraints impinge upon state formation? The study of cultural industries not only entailed (initially) new domains of policy activity, it also simultaneously entailed the creation of an intellectual field of inquiry in which fundamental questions of the ends and means of social organization were posed and debated, but not necessarily answered. Canadian academic analysts of cultural industries have begun to awaken from the nationalist dreams that have largely informed cultural industries research in the Canadian context (see Flaherty and Manning [1993]). This is not to say that academic analysts have become anti-nationalist (as many of the essays here evidence to the contrary), but rather that nationalism is no longer the principal analytical framework through which to think about the problems of Canada's cultural industries. Call it post-nationalism if you will, but particularly so if this be understood in the sense that some of the specificities of the Canadian context can (at last) be taken for granted so as to be able to see past them rather than making of them the foreground of analysis. A post-nationalist perspective means, most notably, to be able to grasp the extent to which Canadian cultural industries policy has been successful in counter-balancing by a range of structural policy measures the historical fact of the limited existence of a domestic market for Canadian cultural production, as the chapters in this book demonstrate. Canadian cultural industries policies have not been just a sorry litany of failures and false starts, as was often claimed to be the case, for example, in the domain of film policy in the 1970s (Gathercole, 1984). On the contrary, a certain kind of domestic Canadian market has been developed, not by means of the nationalization of the movie theatres initially assumed necessary in the 1960s and 1970s but instead by means of the domestic communication channel that was under Canadian control, the national broadcasting system. In many respects, nationalistic assumptions have blinded Canadian analysts to the far more paradoxical and interesting, because contradictory, set of circumstances that actually have come to prevail in this country; circumstances it behooves us as students, analysts and decision makers to understand better than has so far been the case — in a word, post-nationalism.

This means, then, that it is possible to postulate certain conclusions about the Canadian experience in cultural industries that have not been sufficiently clearly presented before. Firstly, that there is a historical coherence to Canadian cultural industries development. Secondly, that this development has been in relative terms a successful one. Thirdly, that a domestic market with its own distinctive characteristics has been more or less successfully established. Fourthly, that such a development has been possible because of the fundamental unanimity of the actors as regards the objects of policy. Fifthly, as a result, the domestic market need no longer continue to be the primary preoccupation either of actors or of policies. Sixthly, that the ambiguities inherent in the notion of Canadian content have to be confronted, as Canadian cultural industries will in future have increasingly non-Canadian audiences (for a recent reflection of the policy implications, see Sirois and Forget [1995: 39-57]). The importance of functioning in increasingly transnational contexts in particular is demonstrated here by the chapters that Attallah (narrowcasting) and Acheson and Maule (international audiovisual regimes) contribute to the collection. Indeed, it is the very successes of cultural industries policy, for instance in the domain of corporate Canada's new communication technologies, that gives Babe's chapter its polemical bite in understanding the contemporary convergence (and divergence) of broadcasting, cable and telecommunications.

It is these successes, furthermore, that in turn enable the contributors to this volume to engage in more critical scrutiny of the cultural industries that have either traditionally been the most protected by nationalist perspectives, such as broadcasting (see Filion's chapter on radio, as well as Raboy's on public broadcasting and Jeffrey's on private broadcasting), or conversely the least so, as in the case of the newspaper industry (whose cultural dimensions Chris Dornan brings to the fore in his chapter). A critical perspective is also what makes it possible for Kevin Dowler, in his chapter on the cultural policy apparatus, to raise some probing questions concerning the long-term agendas of the state institutions that have regulated the fields of cultural intervention in this country. As Dowler, informed by Harold Innis as well as Michel Foucault, suggests, bringing to the analysis of cultural industries policy a historical perspective can lead to surprising new paths for future inquiries. At least, that is the wager this book makes.

References

Adorno, T.W. and Max Horkheimer. 1982. (1982). *Dialectic of Enlightenment*. John Cumming (trans.). New York: Continuum.

Audley, Paul. 1983. *Canada's Cultural Industries: Broadcasting, Publishing, Records and Film*. Toronto: James Lorimer & Company.

Axelrod, Paul. 1982. *Scholars and Dollars*. Toronto: University of Toronto Press.

Babe, Robert E. 1975. *Cable Television and Telecommunications in Canada: An Economic Analysis*. East Lansing, Mich.: Michigan State University Press.

Backhouse, Charles. 1974. *The Canadian Government Motion Picture Bureau 1917–1941*. Ottawa: Canadian Film Institute.

Ballio, Tino (ed.). 1990. *Hollywood in the Age of Television*. Boston: Unwin Hyman.

Bird, Roger (ed.). 1988. *Documents of Canadian Broadcasting*. Ottawa: Carleton University Press.

Canada. Department of Communications. 1987. *Vital Links: Canadian Cultural Industries*. Ottawa: Minister of Supply and Services.

———. *Annual Reports*, 1977–78, 1978–79, 1979–80, 1980–81, Ottawa: Minister of Supply and Services.

———. Groupe Secor. 1994. *Canadian Government Intervention in the Film and Video Industry*. Final Report, October 19.

———. Royal Commission on National Development in the Arts, Letters and Sciences (Massey-Lévesque). 1951. *Report*. Ottawa: King's Printer.

———. Royal Commission on Publications. 1961. *Report*. Ottawa: Queen's Printer.

———. *Special Senate Committee on Mass Media*. 1970. Report. Ottawa: Queen's Printer.

Clement, Wallace. 1975. *The Canadian Corporate Elite: An Analysis of Economic Power. Toronto: McClelland & Stewart*.

Collins, Richard. 1990. *Culture, Communication and National Identity: The Case of Canadian Television. Toronto: University of Toronto Press*.

Cummings, Milton C. and Richard C. Katz. (eds.). 1987. *The Patron State. New York: Oxford University Press*.

de la Garde, Roger, William Gilsdorf and Ilya Wechselmann. (eds.). 1993. *Small Nations, Big Neighbour: Denmark and Quebec/Canada Compare Notes on American Popular Culture*. London: John Libby.

Deutsch, Karl. 1961. *Nationalism and Social Communication: An Inquiry into the Foundations of Nationality. Cambridge, MA: MIT Press*.

Dorland, Michael, M. St-Laurent and G. Tremblay. 1994. "Téléfilm Canada et la production audiovisuelle indépendante: la longue errance d'une politique gouvernementale." Communication, 14: 2, automne, pp. 101-36

———. forthcoming. "Changing Theorizations of Cultural Production in Canada and Quebec: A Review of Some Recent Literature on the Cultural Industries." *Journal of Canadian Studies*.

Enzensberer, Hans Magnus. 1974. *Consciousness Industry: On Literature, Politics and the Media. New York: Seabury*.

Flaherty, David H. and Frank E. Manning. (eds.). 1993. *The Beaver Bites Back? American Popular Culture in Canada*. Kingston and Montreal: McGill-Queen's University Press.

Fortner, Robert S. 1986. "The System of Relevances and the Politics of Language in Canadian Public Policy Formulation: The Case of Broadcasting" *Canadian Journal of Communication,* 12: 3-4, pp. 19-35.

Gathercole, Sandra. 1984. "The Best Film Policy This Country Never Had." In Seth Feldman (ed.). *Take Two: A Tribute to Film in Canada.* Toronto: Irwin, pp. 17-36.

Globerman, Steven. 1983. *Cultural Regulation in Canada.* Montreal: Institute for Research on Public Policy.

Graham, Gerald C. 1989. *Canadian Film Technology, 1896–1986.* Newark: University of Delaware Press.

Gutierrez Vega, Hugo. 1978. "The Culture Industry." Research document no. 77, UNESCO Commission for the Study of Communication Problems.

Gwyn, Richard. 1985. *The 49th Paradox: Canada in North America.* Toronto: McClelland & Stewart.

Hill, O. Mary. 1977. *Canada's Salesman to the World: The Department of Trade and Commerce, 1852–1939.* Kingston and Montreal: McGill-Queen's University Press.

Huet, A., J. Ion, A. Lefebvre, R. Peron, and B. Mige. 1978. *Capitalisme et industries culturelles.* Grenoble: PUG.

Jarvie, Ian. 1992. *Hollywood's Overseas Campaign: The North Atlantic Movie Trade, 1920–1950.* Cambridge, UK: Cambridge University Press.

Jay, Martin. 1973. *The Dialectical Imagination: A History of the Frankfurt School and the Institute of Social Research, 1923–1950.* Boston: Little Brown.

Lacroix, Jean-Guy and Benoit Lévesque. 1988. "Les Libéraux et la culture: De l'unité nationale à la marchandisation de la culture, 1963–1984." In Dorval Brunelle and Yves Bélanger (eds.)., *L'ère des Libéraux: Le pouvoir libéral de 1963 à 1984.* Québec: Presses de l'Université du Québec, pp. 406-42.

Lanham, Richard A. 1993. *The Electronic Word: Democracy, Technology and the Arts.* Chicago: University of Chicago Press.

Laurence, Gérard. 1982. "Les débuts des affaires publiques à la télévision québécoise." *Revue d'histoire de l'Amérique française.* 36: 2, Septembre, pp. 215-39.

Litt, Paul. 1992. *The Muses, the Masses and the Massey-Commission.* Toronto: University of Toronto Press.

Magder, Ted. 1993. *Canada's Hollywood: The Canadian State and Feature Films.* Toronto: University of Toronto Press.

McAnany, Emile G. 1987. "Cultural Industries in International Perspective: Convergence or Conflict?" In Brenda Devlin and Melvin J. Voigt (eds.). *Progress in Communication Sciences.* v. VII, Norwood, NJ: Ablex, pp. 1-30.

McLuhan, Marshall. 1964. *Understanding Media: The Extensions of Man.* New York: McGraw-Hill.

Miller, Mary Jane. 1987. *Turn Up the Contrast: CBC Drama Since 1952.* Vancouver: UBC Press.

Morris, Peter. 1986. "Backwards to the Future: John Grierson's Film Policy for Canada." In Gene Walz (ed.). *Flashback: People and Institutions in Canadian Film History.* Montreal: Mediatexte.

Ontario. Royal Commission on Book Publishing. 1973. *Report.* Toronto: Queen's Printer.

Ostry, Bernard. 1978. *The Cultural Connection: An Essay on Culture and Government Policy in Canada.* Toronto: McClelland & Stewart.

Peers, Frank W. 1969. *The Politics of Canadian Broadcasting, 1920–1951.* Toronto: University of Toronto Press.

———. 1979. *The Public Eye: Television and the Politics of Canadian Broadcasting 1952–1968.* Toronto: University of Toronto Press.

Piemme, J. M. 1975. *La propagande inavoue.* Paris: UGE.

Porter, John. 1965. *The Vertical Mosaic: An Analysis of Social Class and Power in Canada.* Toronto: University of Toronto Press.

Raboy, Marc. 1990. *Missed Opportunities: The Story of Canadian Broadcasting.* Kingston and Montreal: McGill-Queen's University Press.

———. 1995. *Accès inégal: le role des acteurs dans l'élaboration de la politique canadienne de la radiodiffusion.* Québec: PUQ.

Rutherford, Paul. 1990. *Primetime Canada, 1952–1967.* Toronto: University of Toronto Press.

Sirois, Charles and Claude E. Forget. 1995. *The Medium and the Muse: Culture, Telecommunications and the Information Highway.* Montreal: IRPP.

Smythe, Dallas. 1981. *Dependency Road: Communication, Capitalism, Consciousness & Canada.* Norwood, NJ: Ablex.

Stewart, Andrew and William H. N. Hull. 1994. *Canadian Television Policy and the Board of Broadcast Governors, 1958–1968.* Edmonton: University of Alberta Press.

Stiles, Mark. 1980–81. Interview with Michael McCabe. *Cinema Papers,* Dec./Jan., pp. 438-440.

Straw, Will. 1993. "The English Canadian Recording Industry Since 1970." In Tony Bennett et al. (eds.). *Rock and Popular Music: Politics, Policies, Institutions.* London: Routledge, 52-65.

Taras, David and Helen Holmes (eds.). 1992. *Seeing Ourselves: Media, Power & Policy in Canada.* Toronto: Harcourt.

Thomas, Alan M. 1960. "Audience, Market and Public: An Evaluation of Canadian Broadcasting." *Canadian Communication* 1:1, Summer, pp. 16-47.

Tippett, Maria. 1990. *Making Culture: English Canadian Institutions in the Arts Before the Massey Commission.* Toronto: University of Toronto Press.

Tomlinson, John. 1991. *Cultural Imperialism: A Critical Introduction.* London: Pinter.

UNESCO. 1982. *Cultural Industries: A Challenge for the Future of Culture.* Paris: UNESCO.

Vronneau, Pierre. 1979. *L'ONF, l'enfant martyr.* Montréal: Cinémathèque québécoise.

Whitaker, Reg and Gary Marcuse. 1994. *Cold War Canada: The Making of a National Insecurity State 1945–1957.* Toronto: University of Toronto Press.

Contributors

Keith Acheson has taught at Queen's University, the University of Toronto and Carleton University. Since the mid-1970s, his main research interest has been the economics of organization. He has published articles on central banking, government purchasing, the North American automotive industry and the airline industry. For the past five years, he has worked with Christopher Maule analyzing the broadcasting, cable and film industries.

Paul Attallah is the director of the Mass Communication Program in the School of Journalism and Communication, Carleton University, and an associate professor. He is the author of two textbooks on the philosophy of communication published by the Presses de l'Université du Québec. In 1995, he taught at the Queensland University of Technology in Brisbane, Australia, where he lectured on current problems in Canadian cultural and communication policy.

Robert E. Babe is a professor in the Department of Communication at the University of Ottawa. Since the mid-1970s, he has authored numerous studies in Canadian broadcasting, regulatory and telecommunications policy. His *Communication and the Transformation of Economics* is forthcoming from Westview.

Michael Dorland is an associate professor in the School of Journalism and Communication, Carleton University. In the early 1980s, he was an associate editor of *Cinema Canada* magazine and has published widely in the areas of film criticism and of Canadian film policy history. He has co-edited, with Pierre Véronneau and Seth Feldman, *Dialogue: Cinémas canadien et québécois* and has been an associated researcher with the Groupe de recherche sur les industries culturelles et l'informatisation sociale at the Université du Québec à Montréal.

Christopher Dornan is an associate professor and the acting director of the Mass Communication Program in the School of Journalism and Communication, Carleton University. He comments frequently on current developments in broadcasting, cultural policy and the communications industry on radio, television, and in the print media.

Kevin Dowler has taught in the School of Journalism and Communication at Carleton University. He has written on the development of American television criticism and researched the beginnings of Canadian video policy.

Lon Dubinsky teaches in the Fine Arts and Business Faculties of Concordia University, specializing in the area of cultural policy. He is a consultant in cultural policy to a wide range of foundations and philanthropical organizations.

Michel Filion is an archivist in the Government Archives Division, National Archives of Canada, responsible for the conservation of the archives of Canadian crown corporations such as the CBC and Canadian government cultural agencies. He has taught at the University of Ottawa and is the author of *Radiodiffusion et société distincte. Des origines de la radio à la Révolution tranquille au Québec.*

Liss Jeffrey is a senior research associate at the McLuhan Program in Culture and Technology at the University of Toronto. A former TV producer and broadcast policy journalist, she has been a consultant to academic, government and industry organizations. She recently co-curated "Watching TV" at the Royal Ontario Museum, as Acting Director of the MZTV Museum of Television in Toronto.

Rowland Lorimer is a professor in the Department of Communication and the director of the Canadian Centre for Studies in Publishing at Simon Fraser University. He is the co-author of *Mass Communication in Canada*, as well as the author of several major reports on the book publishing industry in Canada.

Ted Magder is an associate professor and the director of the Mass Communication Program at York University. He is the author of *Canada's Hollywood: The Canadian State and Feature Films*, as well as a number of articles in Canadian cultural policy.

Christopher J. Maule is a professor of economics and has been the director of the Norman Patterson School of International Affairs at Carleton University. He has researched Canada's cultural industries since the 1970s, and in 1994–95 was a Fulbright Fellow at Georgetown University.

Marc Raboy is a professor in the Department of Communication, Université de Montréal. His books include *Missed Opportunities: The Story of Canada's Broadcasting Policy*, *Les médias québécois*, as well as several edited collections. His current research focuses on the public policy implications of globalization.

Will Straw is an associate professor in the Graduate Program in Communications at McGill University, where he is currently the director of the Centre for Research on Canadian Cultural Industries and Institutions. He has published widely on many aspects of the popular music industries and is co-author, with Simon Frith, of the forthcoming *Cambridge Companion to Popular Music*.

Index

Index 375